rickstein's
Guide to
the food heroes
of Britain BBC

rickstein's
Guide to
the food heroes
of Britain BBC

Where to Buy the Best Produce
in Britain & Ireland

BBC
BOOKS

Chief Researcher: Christina Burnham

This book is published to accompany the television
series entitled *Rick Stein's Food Heroes: Another Helping*
The series was produced for BBC Television
by Denham Productions
Producer and Director: David Pritchard
Assistant Producer: Arezoo Farahzad
Executive Producer for the BBC: Andy Batten-Foster

First published in 2003 by BBC Books,
BBC Worldwide Limited
80 Wood Lane
London W12 0TT

ISBN 0 563 48742 9

Commissioning Editor: Vivien Bowler
Project Editor: Rachel Copus
Copy Editor: Deborah Savage
Book Art Director: Sarah Ponder
Designed by Ben Cracknell Studios
Illustrations by Ruth Murray
Production Controller: Kenneth McKay
Database Development: Mark Ginns
Map Coordinator: Stephen Wells

British Isles Maps © MAPS IN MINUTES™ 2001 ©
Crown Copyright, Ordnance Survey & Ordnance Survey
Northern Ireland 2001 Permit No. NI 1675 & ©
Government of Ireland, Ordnance Survey Ireland.

London Map © MAPS IN MINUTES™/AA 2001.
© Crown Copyright, Ordnance Survey 2001

Set in Helvetica Neue
Printed and bound in Great Britain by The Bath Press Ltd
Cover printed by The Bath Press Ltd

contents

introduction

I've long held the belief that to cook well you have to buy well. Often, when enthusing about my collection of seafood recipes, I've had a dismal sense of the sort of quality of fish that many people would be likely to find in an average supermarket, and how second-rate these dishes would then become. I wrote the *Seafood Lovers' Guide* a few years ago, partly to help people find the best fishmongers in the country. Out of that quest came my *Guide to the Food Heroes of Britain*. I reasoned that just as to enjoy my fish recipes you need to buy the best quality fish, so too with meat, poultry and game, fruit and vegetables, and eggs, butter, and cheese.

I never fail to get a thrill of certainty every time I buy produce from one of my food heroes and realize that it does taste better. The butter produced by Cream of Cumbria at Howberry Farm, outside Carlisle, has a sweet creaminess that makes spreading it on some crusty bread a special occasion. The meat from Lishmans of Ilkley makes you realize why great roast beef and Yorkshire pudding depends so much on a quality butcher, such as David Lishman, who looks for succulence, tenderness and flavour enhanced by the presence of fat, both on the surface and marbled throughout the flesh. The book concentrates on people like him and primary producers who have a commitment to quality and flavour and a determination to produce food properly, who care more about that than about selling high volumes. They have a feeling for the traditions and heritage of food, for animal welfare and good husbandry, for flavour and the pleasure of eating; everything, it seems, that modern farming has largely left behind.

It's all too easy to blame supermarkets for mediocrity in food. They are trying to target excellence in their own way with premium ranges such as Tesco's Finest and Sainsbury's Taste the Difference. Marks & Spencer too must be praised for a determination to opt for quality over price and a commitment to animal welfare, evidence of which can be found in their refusal to sell anything but free-range eggs, both fresh and in their cooked food. There are signs that all of the chains are starting to take the concept of buying locally seriously. Sainsbury's in Plymouth, for example, has given over its wet-fish counter to a local supplier, InterFish. Safeway have a system called Fresh from the West, where they supply eight stores in Devon and Cornwall from local fish markets, so that fish can be in store within 24 hours of being landed. Tesco has over 7000 locally obtained and sold items, though not all of these are food, while Waitrose has a clear policy of supporting small, local producers. They told me of a survey they carried out of 19 Cornish ice-creams, from which they discovered that only one was actually made using local milk, cream and eggs. Asda seem truly keen to use local produce, too, they buy from lots of local producers each of which supplies to only one or two stores. Somerfield have around 2000 local or regional suppliers, but they are making big efforts to increase this. Never-the-less they all lean heavily in the direction of large volume, simply because they need the quantity to supply all of their outlets, the result is that sometimes they don't give the same sort of advice about the local produce they are selling as you might get at a farm shop or farmers' market. This book's *raison d'être* is that small is beautiful.

Supermarkets offer a wide choice of foods at the best prices and are best used for buying every-day food. Variety is the spice of life and in this guide you will find vegetable growers who offer literally hundreds of varieties of vegetable throughout the season, varieties that are grown for their taste rather than their ability to survive weeks in cold rooms before being displayed. You will also find meat producers who rear a dazzling array of rare-breed pork, lamb and beef, with textures and flavours you are very unlikely to find in the supermarkets. There are delis brimming with foods from artisan producers, foods that will never find their way on to supermarket shelves because they are not made in large enough quantities.

The guide will enable you to find them and to enrich your life in the process but I had another reason for writing it – to do my bit to support small-scale producers. Sadly, most people think food should be ever cheaper, price is normally the governing factor in what consumers buy. The best food costs money to produce. Every week in this country, small farms go bust, often because the cost of producing the food is more than we are prepared to pay. In France, Italy and Spain, good food is a key part of life and people are happy to pay realistic prices for it. The UK lags behind, we spend the smallest proportion of our incomes on food compared to the populations of every other European country. On the continent producers of high-quality foods are revered; tradition and taste are afforded great respect. We need to have that respect here too.

Mass-produced food often exacts a high price on the environment, on rural economies, on the survival of traditional cultures and skills. Many of the producers featured here address these problems, painstakingly maintaining traditional methods, and passing them on through their families and staff, when a modern approach would almost certainly be more profitable. There are delis and farm shops that, when selling imported foods, choose to stock 'fair trade' produce – they want small-scale producers *abroad* to make a fair living from their skills too. Some producers go much further. Take the Camphill Communities, for example, where market gardens and bakeries are run to enable people with developmental disabilities to learn a trade and earn a living. These centres produce fantastic traditional breads and tasty organic vegetables, and have a far-reaching benefit for the community too. With so many of the producers there is a sense that food is not just fuel for the body, but a connection to the community and the outside world.

If you are going to buy and cook the best fresh produce yourself, it follows that when you eat out you will want to seek out those pubs and restaurants who follow a similar philosophy. Sadly there simply isn't room for me to include a list of recommended restaurants here. However, when looking for a place to eat, I would suggest that you look out for those restaurants that are members of The Campaign for Real Food. The organisation was formed in 1996 to encourage people to produce and eat home-made, fresh food made from ingredients supplied by local producers. It includes many pubs, cafés and restaurants among its members, all of which are listed on their website (www. thecarf.co.uk). If you fancy a meal out that comes with a real spirt of place, made from scratch with traditional skills, then give one of these establishments a try.

Buying and eating produce from local suppliers can offer so many benefits. Food will be fresher; it won't have travelled the length and breadth of the country, from packing plant to warehouse to shop shelves. Food miles – the hot environmental topic concerning the energy wasted as foods are trucked or flown around the world – are minimized. Rural economies, which have struggled for so long, are boosted – jobs are created or retained, the culture of traditional farms and smallholdings is maintained. Farmers' markets and farm shops can add a great sense of community to villages and towns; you can actually talk to the person who produced the food on your plate, find out more about it, and tell them what you think. Essentially, you are buying direct from specialists, with all their expertise and knowledge at your disposal. There are real opportunities now to get more involved in the production of what you eat, whether that be through farm shops and farmers' markets, a weekly vegetable box scheme delivered by the grower, or even by joining a community-supported agriculture scheme, where you pay a fee to a farm or group of farms, and then share in the entire harvest throughout the year. You'll often be surprised at the great value for money you get when you buy your food in this way, but equally, you'll be paying a fair price that enables the producers to make a decent living.

a note before you start

The entries for this guide have been accumulated from many different sources. I and my researchers approached institutions championing specialist producers, who told us about suppliers who are at the top of their game, have their feet firmly embedded in tradition, or, indeed, are particularly innovative in their field. These institutions are all listed at the back of the book. There are also producers who came to us highly recommended by friends and colleagues, and producers I have known for a long time, who supply to my restaurants, or to other restaurants around the country that require the very best ingredients. The directory is not exhaustive; to find every good small-scale producer in Britain and Ireland would be a lifetime's work, but I hope to have produced a workable guide the like of which has not been compiled since Henrietta Green's excellent *Food Lovers' Guide to Britain*, last published in the mid-nineties.

I hope too to impart a sense of excitement about the explosion in small-scale producers. I'd like to encourage you to support your farmers' markets, seek out producers in your own area, and find your own local food heritage. If anything can be said to describe the spirit that many of these producers and retailers embody, it is that they typify the ideals of the International Slow Food Movement. Slow Food aims to protect traditional foods against the deluge of industrial standardization; to ensure we don't forget how real food tastes. The entries within this directory have a great deal to contribute to this, and I hope you find them as inspiring as I do.

Many of the entries in my guide are busy, working farms. It is essential to phone before visiting, or your trip could be a disappointment. Equally, many of the producers we list only sell locally. We have mentioned if producers sell by mail order, but many don't, and that means you may have to travel, which is why the guide has been created in a format designed to slip into the door pocket of your car. Some of the producers we feature work on a small scale – it is worth phoning to find out if they have produce available before you make a trip. Seasons play a big part, too – producers can only sell you a food if it is in season. But what an added interest this book will become when you are travelling in different parts of the UK or Ireland.

how to use this book

I've divided my guidebook into nine chapters, each consisting of producers who supply a particular type of food, such as Bread, Dairy and Eggs, Meat, Poultry etc. Each one begins with a brief introduction, telling you a little about my criteria for choosing the entries and why I believe the suppliers I have selected are manufacturing produce of the highest quality. Within these chapters the producers are organised into regions (indicated on the top left-hand side of each entry) that fall along county boundaries. The regions are broken up as follows:

SOUTH WEST

Bristol and Bath, Cornwall, Devon, Dorset, Gloucestershire, Somerset, Wiltshire

SOUTH EAST

Bedfordshire, Berkshire, Buckinghamshire, East and West Sussex, Hampshire, Hertfordshire, Kent, London, Oxfordshire, Surrey

EAST ANGLIA

Cambridgeshire, Essex, Norfolk, Suffolk

MIDLANDS

Derbyshire, Hereford and Worcester, Leicestershire, Lincolnshire, Northamptonshire, Nottinghamshire, Shropshire, Staffordshire, Warwickshire, West Midlands (including Birmingham)

NORTH WEST

Cumbria, Cheshire, Greater Manchester, Lancashire, Merseyside

NORTH EAST

Cleveland, County Durham, Humberside, Northumberland, North, South and West Yorkshire, Tyne and Wear

NORTHERN IRELAND

REPUBLIC OF IRELAND

SCOTLAND

WALES

Once you've located the region relevant to you, the entries are organised alphabetically, by the nearest town or village (indicated on the top right-hand side of each entry).

super heroes and food-fact boxes

Also included within each chapter are boxed entries, which I've called my Super Heroes. These are the businesses or individual producers who I feel stand head and shoulders above the rest in terms of the work that they do and the quality of the food that they produce. As a consequence I have marked them out and, if you are visiting a specific region, I would put them at the top of your list of places to shop. I have also included some information boxes which look at specific issues faced by the industry in question, and which I hope will influence your choice of product when you shop in the future.

maps

The maps at the back of the book will give you an approximate location for all of the entries in the book. However, if a specific region is not familiar to you, you will need a good road atlas showing more detail than it's possible to include here. The maps will help to indicate which producers are situated in your area and, of course, if you are on holiday, whether there are any local producers that you can visit.

entries

Categorizing such a range of businesses is always going to be difficult. I have done my best to put each one in the section where it fits best. However, some of the producers that appear in the game section will also sell fantastic local meats and some producers in the fish section will stock local game. Equally, those in the delicatessens section might have a good in-store bakery, and some of the cheesemongers in the dairy section will have a great selection of deli goods. Each entry should be listed under its primary product or the product type for which it is best known, but don't be surprised if you find the best cheese you've ever tasted at a recommended fishmonger ... that's part of the fun of discovering fresh local food for yourself.

I have included full addresses and telephone numbers for each entry and a website address where applicable. E-mail addresses are only included where the supplier has no website. I've included a brief description of each supplier, but the following symbols should give an 'at a glance' guide to the facilities they offer:

farm shop: Entries that display this symbol have a dedicated farm shop where you can purchase their produce and sometimes that of other local producers. You may need to phone them directly for opening times.

farmers' markets: Farmers' markets are a great way to buy fresh, local produce when it's in season. This symbol indicates that the producer in question has stalls at their local market(s). Where possible, we have listed the relevant markets, but for more information phone the producer directly.

shop: Entries whose primary function is not that of a shop, but which have a shop on site (such as a cheese factory or a mill).

farm gate sales: Many of the producers featured in the guide may not have a recognized farm shop, but they are still happy to sell to individuals. I would recommend, that you phone ahead to check that someone will be available to help you.

delivery service: A local delivery service is offered.

mail order: A mail-order service is available.

box scheme: Box schemes vary greatly from producer to producer, but generally the supplier will offer either a weekly, monthly or one-off scheme whereby you can order either a specified selection of fresh, local goods or a surprise mixture, depending on what's in season.

associations and organizations – what do they stand for?

There are a number of associations and organizations throughout the UK and Ireland who are working hard to promote good quality, often organic, food and the various businesses that produce it. For clarity, I've included the logo for the most frequently occurring organizations next to the relevant suppliers and include a key, opposite, to show you what each stands for.

ARTISAN
BAKERS of NORTHERN IRELAND
Artisan Bakers of Northern Ireland: A small group of craft bakers situated within Northern Ireland endeavouring to uphold traditional methods of baking and traditional regional recipes.

Demeter: The association aims to help and support those wishing to put into practice the biodynamic method (see box on organic meat, page 316). With this objective in mind it keeps in close touch with biodynamic agriculture abroad and with various organizations concerned with a sustainable approach to soil, environment and health. Visit their website at www.anth.org.uk/biodynamic/demeter

Elite Guild of Butchers: A group of master butchers within Northern Ireland aiming to preserve traditional butchery skills and encouraging sourcing of local meats. Strict hygiene standards and an emphasis on personal service are also encouraged. For more information contact John Dowey at jrdowey@aol.com

Guild of Fine Food Retailers: The Guild of Fine Food Retailers is instrumental in the UK in encouraging small-scale producers of high-quality and fine foods and promoting specialist shops and delis that stock their produce. For more information visit their website at www.finefoodworld.co.uk

Guild of Q Butchers: The Guild of Q Butchers aims to tempt consumers back to buying from specialist butchers with the promise of properly hung, well-butchered meats, from named sources – often local farms – backed by rigorous hygiene standards. Visit their website at www.guildofqbutchers.co.uk

Irish Organic Farmers and Growers: An accreditation scheme for Irish organic producers, ensuring that the methods by which they produce food abide by the strict organic standards the association imposes. For more information visit their website at www.irishorganic.ie

Organic Farmers and Growers: An accreditation scheme for British organic producers, laying down a strict set of standards for food production (www.organicfarmers.uk.com).

Rare Breeds Survival Trust: The Rare Breeds Survival Trust (RBST) is a charity endeavouring to keep alive Britain's livestock heritage. The UK and Ireland have a magnificent selection of native breeds of farm animals, but many breeds are now at critically low levels of population and many more are on the vulnerable list. These don't suit modern farming methods and are not seen as commercially viable by conventional meat producers. Thankfully, however, since the RBST was founded in 1973 we have not lost a single breed. They insist that conserving these breeds is not romantic whimsy – 'rare breeds are an essential part of greener farming systems – helping the environment, and improving the quality of the food we eat'. Visit their website on www.rbst.org.uk.

Scottish Organic Producers Association: An accreditation scheme for Scottish organic producers, ensuring that the methods by which the foods are produced attain the exacting standards of UKROFS (the UK Register of Organic Food Standards). For more information visit their website on www.sopa.org.uk

Soil Association: Most people buying organic foods do so because they are concerned about chemical residues on and in food. The Soil Association has created a body of complex and far-reaching regulations that those growers who want to be accredited must abide by and the benefits range from the environmental and the cultural through to animal welfare and health. Visit their website on www.soilassociation.org.uk

Specialist Cheesemakers' Association and CAIS: The Specialist Cheesemakers Association was formed in 1989, in response to a threat by the Agriculture Minister to ban the sale of unpasteurized cheese. The SCA successfully managed to prevent this happening and is now firmly established as an institution championing the work of artisan and specialist cheesemakers around the country. The Association insists that it is 'vital that all members demonstrate their commitment to quality'. More information can be found on their website (www.specialistcheesemakers.co.uk). CAIS is the association for Irish farmhouse cheesemakers, endeavouring to maintain the cheese-making heritage of Ireland.

Wholesome Food Association: The costs of being accredited by the Soil Association are beyond some smaller-scale growers. The Wholesome Food Association represents these growers, giving customers a degree of assurance regarding the methods by which its members' produce has been grown or reared.

I asked the WFA about their ethical aims in food production, and they told me:

> *'The WFA is aimed mainly at the smallholder and small-scale farmer, as this group is the most disadvantaged by the current*

*political climate, which promotes the economies
of scale over the values of "small and local".'*

The basic principles members must abide by are:

*'Wholesome food is grown and processed using sustainable,
non-polluting methods as close as possible to those found in
nature.'* This includes growing without artificial pesticides,
herbicides or fertilizers, high animal welfare and animal feeds
free from antibiotics and genetically modified organisms.

*'Wholesome food is, wherever possible, traded and consumed
within a short distance of where it was grown.'*

*'Wholesome food is an integral part of life and community,
rather than merely a commodity for profit.'*

It is important to remember that WFA producers won't send food by mail
order across the country – they are passionate about keeping food local,
so try to find a producer in your area (www.wholesomefood.org).

CHAPTER 1

In this chapter, I have looked for craft and artisan bakeries, producing bread from scratch using time-honoured methods, with carefully sourced ingredients and a pride in their work. Sadly, these bakeries are an endangered species. Over recent years, the nation has been led to believe that bread is a cheap, basic food, worthy of little thought. Bakers who make a high-quality, tasty and nutritious product, without artificial additives and improvers, are being squeezed out of the market. Two technical 'advances' in production methods – the Chorleywood Process and the Milton Keynes Process (page 24) – are primarily responsible for the dominance of mass-produced, factory-made loaves on supermarket shelves and this dominance is bolstered by the additives put into such loaves, which create certain characteristics seen as desirable, and improve their shelf life.

bread

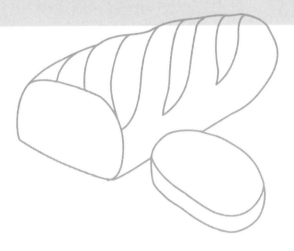

Not only are we losing the skills of traditional bread-baking – of making loaves slowly, to allow flavour and texture to develop – but we are also losing the regional heritage of bread and bakery goods. Local bakers will often bake regional specialities, such as Bedfordshire Clangers, Kent Huffkins cakes, or Cornish Hevva cake; if we lose those local bakers, the chances are that all that cultural diversity will be lost, too. Perhaps if we stopped thinking of bread as a cheap fuel and instead recognized the value of a loaf baked slowly, with proper time devoted to the development and fermentation of the dough, with local ingredients, using skills and knowledge passed down for generations, the tide would turn, and those dying baker's skills would once more be revered.

Leakers Bakery Ltd

29 East Street, Bridport, Dorset DT6 3JX   T: 01308 423296

Interesting breads are made at Leakers by baker Aidan Chapman, including cheese and herb spelt, Dorset apple and cider rye bread and lemon polenta. Many are organic; all are baked on the premises. Wheat- and yeast-free breads and cakes are also available daily.

Hobbs House   super hero

Office: Unit 6, Chipping Edge Estate, Hatters Lane, Chipping Sodbury, Bristol BS37 6AA Shops: 39 High Street, Chipping Sodbury, Bristol BS37 6BA AND 2 North Parade, Yate, Bristol BS37 4AN   T: 01454 317629 (OFFICE, FOR MAIL-ORDER ENQUIRIES); 01454 317525 (CHIPPING SODBURY); 01454 320890 (YATE)   W: www.hobbshousebakery.co.uk
🏠 shop ✉ mail order

An award-winning bakery using traditional techinques. Local ingredients are used when possible. See their Super Hero box, page 21, for more information. There is also a branch in Nailsworth, see page 20.

The Otterton Mill Bakery

Otterton Mill, Otterton, nr Budleigh Salterton, Devon EX9 7HG   T: 01395 568031 W: www.ottertonmill.com
🏠 shop

The old restored mill at Otterton uses traditional stones to grind local organic wheat. The flour is then made into an imaginative range of breads, including rye, spelt, tomato and herb bread, walnut bread and olive bread, all made by hand, without improvers or additives. Next door is a restaurant, with an outdoor terrace, providing a range of meals using only local Devon ingredients.

H M Pearce

Station Road, Kelly Bray, nr Callington, Cornwall PL17 8ER   T: 01579 383362

This is the home of one of the most famous Cornish saffron cakes. The recipe is from generations ago, the ingredients are chosen with incredible attention to detail, and the result is one of the best saffron cakes you'll ever taste.

Boulangerie de Paris

2 High Street, Chipping Campden, Gloucestershire GL55 6AT   T: 01386 849090
🍞 **farmers' markets**

A specialist French bakery, with a fantastic choice of artisan breads. None of the breads here happens quickly – dough fermentation times are rarely less than 16 hours, everything is made from scratch and baked in wood-fired ovens. The real specialities are the French varieties and the ryes and sourdoughs.

Seeds Bakery & Health Stores

22, Duke Street, Dartmouth, Devon TQ6 9TZ   T: 01803 833200

Hand-made breads and cakes made using organic ingredients: all the breads are 100% organic. Ingredients are chosen carefully; local free-range eggs are used, as is unhydrogenated fat. The shops (there is another branch in Totnes, see page 23) also stock local organic vegetables and milk.

Common Loaf Bakery

Stentwood Farm, Dunkeswell, nr Honiton, Devon EX14 4RW   T: 01823 681155
W: www.commonloaf.com
🍞 **farmers' markets**

The Common Loaf Bakery does not use wheat in its breads but only spelt, an old variety of grain. This is because the bakers here feel that wheat has been 'over-hybridized' and now contains too much gluten. All the breads are hand-made and come in a great selection of varieties, including sourdough, wholegrain with soaked seeds (easier to digest and more flavoursome), and Parmesan focaccia. Their bread is available from Bristol, Taunton, Honiton, Totnes, Tiverton and Exeter farmers' markets.

Hobbs House

super hero

4 George Street, Nailsworth, Gloucestershire GL6 0AG   T: 01453 839396
w: www.hobbshousebakery.co.uk

✉ **mail order**

See the Super Hero box, page 21, for more information. There are also
branches in Chipping Sodbury and Yate, near Bristol, see page 18.

The Authentic Bread Company

Strawberry Hill, Newent, Gloucestershire GL18 1LH   T: 01531 828181
w: www.authenticbread.co.uk

✉ **mail order**

Organic, traditionally baked bread in varieties including rye, walnut,
spelt and classic continental types. No flour improvers are used, the
dough is allowed to ferment naturally, twice, and Authentic Bread
states that 'taste rather than cost is paramount'. Call to find out
where your nearest stockist is, or buy mail order from Graig Farm
(see page 355).

Stein's Patisserie

1 Lanadwell Street, Padstow, Cornwall PL28 8AN   T: 01841 532700

There's no reason why I shouldn't include my bakery, since we make
good sourdough bread, pain levain, wholewheat with walnuts, white
tin loaves, foccacia and granary bread, all made with slowly
developed dough. We bake five different varieties of Cornish pasty
including steak, smoked haddock, and crab with saffron, which
naturally we think are rather good, and lots of pretty cakes and
pastries, which we sell in our small patisserie, right in the centre of
Padstow. The bread and pasties are also available at our deli on the
quayside below the Seafood School.

Portreath Bakery

3 The Square, Portreath, Cornwall TR16 4LA   T: 01209 842612

A bakery with a really imaginative range of breads and pasties,
made with locally produced ingredients wherever possible. Good

examples of saffron cake and Hevva cake are available and each morning the bakery has what they call a 'funny hour', in which they will make anything customers ask them to (within reason!).

Lydia's Cottage Industry

Southfields Piece, Carnkie, Redruth, Cornwall TR16 6SG   T: 01209 217352
🍴 **farmers' markets**

Old-fashioned methods and ingredients are the key to the breads, cakes and preserves from Lydia's Cottage Industry. Local ingredients are used as far as possible and there are gluten-free, wheat-free, sugar-free and dairy-free varieties to try. Available from St John's Hall market in Penzance and the Country Market in Truro and various other stockists.

super hero

THE WELLS FAMILY, owners of Hobbs House Bakery, Chipping Sodbury, Yate and Nailsworth (see pages 18 and 20)

Hobbs House Bakery has won many awards for its traditionally made breads. The mission statement of this family-run business is 'to produce honest bread with passion'; keen to retain traditional methods, they have even installed an old-fashioned wood-fired oven at their Nailsworth bakery and café. Packaging is kept to an absolute minimum for environmental reasons, organic breads are becoming an ever bigger part of their range (they've won Organic Food Awards for the last six years running) and local ingredients are sourced wherever possible.

Three generations of the Wells family are involved in the bakery and this, no doubt, is a key part of their desire to maintain a sense of community spirit in food production. Clive Wells told me that at Hobbs House, they 'mourn greatly the loss of the village bakery and corner shop, and are keen to support local village shops which are so vital to the community'. He went on to lament bread from large-scale bakeries, where products are made to a price rather than with quality as the primary concern. A loaf of Hobbs House sourdough or organic spelt bread shows clearly that this bakery aims to reverse that trend and more than adequately substantiates their slogan – 'discover real bread'.

super hero

TOBY AND LOUISE TOBIN-DOUGAN, of St Martin's Bakery, Higher Town, St Martin's, Isles of Scilly (see below).

Using mostly organic, mostly local produce, Toby and Louise of St Martin's Bakery make specialist continental-style breads and English loaves by hand, using old-fashioned methods. Croissants are made from scratch and quiches are available, filled with local salmon and grey mullet (caught and smoked by the couple themselves) or home-grown vegetables. The Cornish pasties they make contain home-grown potatoes and beef reared on the island. They are even trying their hands at cheesemaking. In a part of the world where 'food miles' could be a problem, Toby and Louise seem to have a talent for self-sufficiency – and the food they produce is all the fresher and tastier for it. And the couple are keen to share their skills – also on offer are baking courses in which customers can learn to bake traditional foods with local produce in the gorgeous setting of the Scilly Isles.

SOUTH WEST **SCILLY ISLES**

St Martin's Bakery **super hero**

Higher Town, St Martin's, Isles of Scilly TR25 0QL   T: 01720 423444
w: www.stmartinsbakery.co.uk

Continental-style breads and English loaves, all made using old-fashioned techniques. See the Super Hero box, above, for more information.

SOUTH WEST **SHAFTESBURY**

N R Stoate and Sons

Cann Mills, Shaftesbury, Dorset SP7 0BL   T: 01747 852475
⛩ **farm gate sales**

There has been a mill on this site since before the Domesday Book was written and the Stoate family are keen to retain the heritage of traditional milling in the watermill that now stands here. Using 19th-century French burr stones makes a soft flour, ideal for traditional bread-making. Using local wheat whenever possible, the range includes organic flours and is available to buy direct from the mill. Cann Mills is a member of the Traditional Corn Millers Guild.

Sunshine Health Shop

25 Church Street, Stroud, Gloucestershire GL5 1JL   T: 01453 763923
w: www.sunshinehealth.co.uk
✉ **mail order**

Sunshine Health Shop is supplied with great organic bread from its own bakery, with an interesting range that includes all the regular types as well as spelt, oat and sourdough breads and a unique recipe – 'Sunshine loaf' – a dense, nutty wholemeal bread made with English flour. The breads are all made without improvers – as Ray, the owner, says – 'a good thing doesn't need improving'.

Shipton Mill

Long Newnton, Tetbury, Gloucestershire GL8 8RP   T: 01666 505050
E: enquiries@shipton-mill.com
✉ **mail order**

Around 60 varieties of stoneground flour are produced at Shipton Mill, the majority of which are organic. There are some really unusual varieties that you are unlikely to find elsewhere, such as organic chestnut flour and an Egyptian pasta flour called *kamut*. Mail order is available (ask for Flour Direct when you call), and the staff are also happy to give advice on baking questions.

Seeds Bakery & Health Stores

35 High Street, Totnes, Devon TQ9 5NP   T: 01803 862526

For details see under the Dartmouth branch on page 19.

Carley's

34–36 St Austell Street, Truro, Cornwall TR1 1SE and also at The Parade, Truro TR1 1UJ
T: 01872 277686 (ST AUSTELL STREET); 01872 270091 (THE PARADE)   w: www.carleys.co.uk
🚚 **delivery service** 📦 **box scheme**

Carley's stocks all kinds of organic produce – locally grown vegetables, cheese and their own sauces and chutneys – but it is the bread that makes this shop really special. Made on the premises, there are all the basics, plus continental varieties and some made with spelt. They all have the slightly heavier feel and closer texture of proper home-made bread, and fantastic flavour.

SOUTH WEST   WIMBORNE

Long Crichel Bakery

Long Crichel, Wimborne, Dorset BH21 5SJ   T: 01258 830852   E: finebread@lineone.net

Very traditional methods are employed at this bakery, even down to the wood-fired oven that all the breads are baked in. An interesting range of both speciality breads and the more basic loaves, all organic. The dough is made for most of the breads at least 12 hours in advance, to allow proper development, and no additives are used at all.

food facts

MODERN BREAD

Lifestyles have changed a great deal in recent decades and we no longer shop for food on a daily basis. This means that our foods need to have a longer shelf life. We also want food to be cheap, and both these issues have caused most modern bread to be very different from traditional loaves. The baking industry has come up with two processes to enable bakers to produce longer lasting and cheaper bread. The first is the Chorleywood Process, introduced in the 1960s. As is so often the case with new food technologies, it is a way of cutting down the time it takes to make a product, so that more food can be made in less time, more cheaply. A traditional baker will allow his dough time to ferment and develop and it is during this time that the flavour unfolds and the flour becomes more digestible. Many artisan bakers will make dough the night before baking, leaving it overnight to develop. The result will be a loaf of satisfying texture and complex flavour. The Chorleywood method cuts this time to less than an hour, by agitating the dough at high speed, which mellows the gluten mechanically with the help of dough modifiers, such as ascorbic acid and potassium bromate. In this way, the bread can be made quickly, but it will lack some of the flavour and texture of a traditionally made loaf. We buy 70–80% of our bread from large commercial bakeries, so most of us are eating bread made using the Chorleywood Process.

The second process is the Milton Keynes Process, which produces 'bake off' breads. The dough is made in large bakeries and shipped to smaller bakeries, which then bake the dough as needed. This type of dough is made specifically for a long shelf life, and means that smaller bakeries need fewer fully trained bakers, as half the work is already done. Both these processes result in cheaper bread, but the casualty, as always, is flavour.

BREAD

The Old Farmhouse Bakery

Steventon, nr Abingdon, Oxfordshire OX13 6RP   T: 01235 831230

Katherine Bitmead specializes in old-fashioned, home-baked breads, using high-quality ingredients including locally milled flour. The breads, including the traditional cottage loaves, are all made by hand. To complement the range she also stocks a selection of farmhouse cheeses.

Bakers Basket

Woodway Farm, Bicester Road, Long Crendon, Aylesbury, Buckinghamshire HP18 9EP
T: 01844 202717
🍞 **farmers' markets**

Using local flour and baking from scratch, Ian Forster makes all manner of breads – from the basic white, brown and granary loaves, to rye bread, focaccias with pesto and black olives, and ciabatta. He even makes Danish pastries from scratch, too, and some of the breads are organic. Available only from farmers' markets around Oxfordshire – call for details, or see the Thames Valley Farmers Markets association website www.thamesvalleyfarmersmarket.co.uk

H P Jung

6 The Broadway, Beaconsfield, Buckinghamshire HP9 2PD   T: 01494 673070
w: www.hpjung.com

A bakery and café specializing in continental breads, using recipes the owner brought back from many years training on the Continent. Everything is hand made, and specialities include rye, corn and olive breads.

Infinity Foods Bakery

25 North Road, Brighton BN1 1YA   T: 01273 603563   w: www.infinityfoods.co.uk

A workers' co-operative of just four bakers, Infinity Foods produces breads from 100% organic ingredients. The interesting varieties include rye, sourdough, spelt, linseed, walnut and sunflower seed breads and focaccia.

Real Pâtisserie

43 Trafalgar Square, Brighton BN1 4ED   T: 01273 570719   W: www.realpatisserie.co.uk

farmers' markets

Very traditional French-style breads and cakes are sold here, with a great choice of four different kinds of croissant and really authentic pastries and brioches. Buy direct from the shop or from many Sussex farmers' markets.

The Pâtisserie

38 Station Road, Stoke D'Abernon, Cobham, Surrey KT11 3HZ   T: 01932 863926
W: www.thepatisserie.co.uk

Long proving times and the stone-soled oven at The Pâtisserie combine to make tasty, traditional breads. Some are organic, and some are salt-free. Continental types of bread are well represented and also rye and sourdough.

Marsh Mellow Bakery

11 High Street, Dymchurch, Kent TN29 0NH   T: 01303 873297

farmers' markets

Using wheat grown and milled in the south east, Marsh Mellow Bakery make imaginative breads, including their Devil's Breath chilli bread. The breads are all hand-made, with great attention to detail. Buy direct from the shop, or from Rye or Rolvenden farmers' markets.

Oscar's Bakery

3 Limes Place, Preston Street, Faversham, Kent ME13 8PQ   T: 01795 532218

farmers' markets

A husband-and-wife team run this artisan bakery, producing classic British breads and Irish batch and rye breads. Nothing is rushed – the doughs used are traditional sponge doughs – and the flour is grown and milled locally. The bread can also be found at Faversham and Cliftonville farmers' markets.

THE CELTIC BAKERS, London (see page 28)

The Celtic Bakers have thought of every way possible to make their bread as ethically as they can. Not only is it 'real' bread – properly fermented, with no artificial additives and baked thoroughly on the oven bottom, but every measure has been taken to ensure it is environmentally friendly; everything is organic, the staff are finding ways to decrease their use of fossil fuels and are introducing recycled wrapping. Even the chocolate in the chocolate brownies is from a fairly traded source. Food miles, and the support of British agriculture, are all addressed with these thoughtful methods. The range is impressive, too – all the regulars, plus spelt, pain levain (a traditional French loaf made with natural leaven rather than commercial yeast), rye and sourdough. There is a real sense of openness about the company – absolutely nothing is hidden from its customers. Sarah at The Celtic Bakers is adamant that this is the bakery's policy. 'We feel that the message about honesty about what goes in bread is really important – down to the sunflower oil we line tins with (which in theory we don't have to mention in the ingredients because it's a 'processing aid'). We choose to mention our processing aids because our customers might be allergic to them so they ought to know.' The website is a great education about the bread.

Find The Celtic Bakers at many London farmers' markets – call to find out where.

SOUTH EAST   **FOREST ROW**

Cyrnel Bakery

Lower Road, Forest Row, East Sussex RH18 5HE   T: 01342 822283
farmers' markets

Cyrnel Bakery produce a big choice of breads, many of which are organic. Local ingredients are used wherever possible, including locally milled flour and free-range eggs from a nearby farm. The bread is available direct from the shop, or from several Sussex farmers' markets – call for details.

FOOD HEROES OF BRITAIN

Baker & Spice

41 Denyer Street, London SW3 2LX and also at 75 Salusbury Road, Queens Park, London NW6 6NH   T: 020 7589 4734 (DENYER ST) 020 7604 3636 (SALUSBURY ROAD)
w: www.bakerandspice.com

Traditional British breads, baked without additives. A true artisan bakery.

Breads Etcetera

Unit 1 Charterhouse Works, Eltringham Street, London SW18 1TD   T: 07811 189545
w: www.breadsetcetera.com

Is this the smallest artisan bakery in London? The two members of staff at Breads Etcetera believe so. Rustic, hand-made loaves are produced here without commercial yeast, using organic flours. No artificial additives are used and time is of the essence – the dough is allowed plenty of time to develop before baking. Many London delis stock the bread – call to find your nearest.

The Celtic Bakers

42b Waterloo Road, Cricklewood, London NW2 7UH   T: 020 8452 4390
w: www.thecelticbakers.co.uk
🛒 farmers' markets

Bread baked at The Celtic Bakers is all organic and the techniques used are environmentally friendly. See the Super Hero box, page 27, for more information.

& Clarkes

122–124 Kensington Church Street, London W8 4BH   T: 020 7229 2190
w: www.sallyclarke.com

A great range of traditional British and continental breads, all baked without artificial colours, preservatives or improvers and also available from Carluccio's, Selfridges and Harvey Nichols.

De Gustibus

53 Blandford Street, London W1H 3AF and also at 53–55 Carter Lane, London EC4V 5AE and 4 Southwark Street, London SE1 0JE T: 020 7486 6608 (BLANDFORD ST); 020 7236 0056 (CARTER LANE); 020 7407 3625 (SOUTHWARK ST)

De Gustibus's bread is legendary. Their range of hand-made breads is incredible – recipes from America, Ireland, the continent, Eastern Europe and the Mediterranean have all been sought, and some of the more unusual breads include Old Milwaukee rye, honey and lavender, savoury potato bread, Portuguese cornbread and potato and yogurt bread. Imagination and skill blended perfectly.

The Lighthouse Bakery

64 Northcote Road, London SW11 6QL T: 020 7228 4537 w: www.lighthousebakery.co.uk

Classic British loaves and speciality continental breads rub shoulders at the Lighthouse Bakery, all made with traditional methods. Organic flour is used in many of the breads, but artificial additives and improvers never are.

Neal's Yard Bakery

6 Neal's Yard, Covent Garden, London WC2H 9DP T: 020 7836 5199
w: www.nealsyardbakery.co.uk

Organic breads are made by hand on site at Neal's Yard Bakery, which produces a wide variety of loaves, some of which are wheat free. There is also a café, with lots of home-made dishes, and sandwiches made with their own breads.

The Old Post Office Bakery Ltd

76 Landor Road, London SW9 9PH T: 020 7326 4408

All the breads made at the Old Post Office are accredited organic by the Soil Association. This bakery has been producing organic, hand-made, hand-kneaded breads for over 18 years, long before the organic movement was as well known as it is now. No improvers or additives are used and a particular speciality is the range of sourdough breads.

Poilâne

46 Elizabeth Street, London SW1W 9PA   T: 020 7808 4910

This French bakery is famous for its sourdough, baked on site in a wood and brick oven, an exact replica of a Roman oven. The shop is an off-shoot of the justly famous Parisienne bakery that has been an institution for those seeking the best bread in Paris since Pierre Poilâne opened it in 1932.

Origin Foods

Unit 5, Bell Farm Industrial Park, Nut Hampstead, Royston, Hertfordshire SG8 8ND
T: 01763 849993

farmers' markets

100% organic, hand-made breads, including sourdoughs and unusual varieties such as hazelnut and raisin, and rosemary. No additives or flour improvers are used and the bakers allow proper fermentation times, starting baking at midnight to have bread ready for the morning. Available from many local farmers' markets – call for details.

Sarre Windmill

Canterbury Road, Sarre, Kent CT7 0JU   T: 01843 847573
shop

The wheat milled at Sarre comes from fields nearby, grown specially for them. One of only a handful of working, commercial windmills in the UK, the old-fashioned stonegrinding method produces tasty flour – the stones don't get hot, which can affect the flavour adversely. There is also a bakery and café on site.

Slindon Bakery

Top Road, Slindon, West Sussex BN18 0RP   T: 01243 814369 OR 07741 053764
E: atc121@msn.com
farmers' markets

Traditional British breads such as the Sussex Kibble, milk and cottage loaves, and a Roman Army bread (made with spelt flour) are hand-made here with local ingredients and, always, English flour.

Available from many farmers' markets in Hampshire, Sussex and
Surrey – call for details.

Flour Power City

19 Vale Road, Tunbridge Wells, Kent TN1 1BS   T: 01892 547456
w: www.flourpowercity.com

Organic breads without additives, often using unusual grains, are
the order of the day here. Organic cakes are on offer too, and
everything is made by hand. Flour Power City is accedited by the
Organic Food Federation.

Artisan Bread

Units 16 & 17 John Wilson Business Park, Whitstable, Kent CT5 3QZ   T: 01227 771881
w: www.nature-cure.co.uk
✉ **mail order**

Artisan Bread mill their own grain for flour, often using unusual
varieties. No yeast or tap water is used (only spring water), and
minimal salt. Gluten-free breads are available. This is the UK's first
biodynamic bakery. Call or check out the website to find your
nearest stockist or order by mail.

The Winchester Bakery

51 Hatherley Road, Winchester, Hampshire SO22 6RR   T: 01962 861477
🚩 **farmers' markets**

Alison Reid makes proper bread – dense and heavy, a world away
from the pre-cut fluffy loaves many of us buy at supermarkets. She
makes around 16 different loaves, which include the basics, plus rye
bread, continental varieties and a sourdough using a 12-hour
fermentation period. Alison's bread is available from Winchester,
Basingstoke and Romsey farmers' markets.

The Mill Bakery

Harkers Lane, Swanton Morley, Dereham, Norfolk NR20 4PA T: 01362 637212
W: www.themillbakery.com

A craft bakery making traditional English breads, with an organic
range and some of the less well-known spelt and rye types. The Mill
is accredited by the Organic Food Federation and also makes a
speciality of Portuguese-style breads.

North Elmham Bakery

Eastgate Street, North Elmham, Dereham, Norfolk NR20 5HD T: 01362 668548
E: northelmhambakery@btinternet.com

North Elmham Bakery is run by Norman Ollie, a tireless campaigner
for 'real bread'. Everything here is made the old-fashioned way, with
no short cuts and no additives. The bread is available from other
outlets in Norfolk – call for details.

The Metfield Organic Bakery

The Stores, The Street, Metfield, Harleston, Norfolk IP20 0LB T: 01379 586798

Out of the 20 breads produced at the Metfield Organic Bakery, 18
are certified organic and all are patiently hand-made, without
additives. Some of the loaves are wheat-free and gluten-free; some
are made without yeast. Metfield Bakery bread can be found in
many healthfood stores around Norfolk and Suffolk; call to find your
nearest.

Fosters Mill

Swaffham Prior, Cambridgeshire CB5 0JZ T: 01638 741009 W: www.fostersmill.co.uk
✉ **mail order**

Fosters Mill is nine miles north east of Cambridge. A country mill
built in 1858 and restored to working order in 1991, it has two sets
of French burr stones, producing flours solely by wind power. The
mill is open to the public on the second Sunday of each month.
Flour can be ordered by telephone or purchased direct from local
shops (call to find out where). All flour is produced from organic

wheat – wholemeal, unbleached white, brown, semolina, rye and spelt. Wheat is sourced, where possible, from local farmers and through a local organic grain merchant. The milll also produces a range of breakfast cereals. Fosters Mill is a member of the Traditional Corn Millers Guild.

Tony's Bakery

1 Peel Street, Kidderminster, Worcestershire DY11 6UG   T: 01562 636463

Tony's use bread recipes going back 130 years and hand-make their bread without using any kinds of machines. The kitchens are open, so customers can see the bread being made.

True Loaf Bakery   super hero

Mount Pleasant Windmill, Kirton in Lindsey, North Lincolnshire DN21 4NH
T: 01652 640177   W: www.trueloafbakery.co.uk

Mervyn Austin bakes bread using his own flour made from English wheat. See the Super Hero box, below, for more information.

super hero

MERVIN AUSTIN, owner of True Loaf Bakery (see above)

Mervin Austin mills his own flour from English wheat, which marks him out right from the start. Canadian wheat has long been considered the best for breadmaking, because it can withstand the harsh commercial milling process better, allowing the starch to remain undamaged. Mervin comes at the process of milling from a different angle – instead of choosing wheat to fit the modern process, he has chosen old-fashioned methods, with traditional French burr stones and Derbyshire peak stones. This is a more gentle process, far less damaging to the wheat. The result is tasty, more digestible bread. His respect for tradition doesn't end there – the bread is baked in a wood-fired oven, which takes two weeks to reach temperature, and scrap wood is used as fuel wherever possible to limit the ecological impact. Both the flour and bread are available from the on site shop and café; try some of the traditional Lincolnshire Plum Loaf.

S C Price

7 Castle Street, Ludlow, Shropshire SY8 1AS   T: 01584 872815

Overnight fermenting is the method used at S C Price for their breads – made the old-fashioned way, the dough has time to develop flavour and texture before it reaches the oven. Among the regular types of bread you'll find some unusual loaves, such as the Turkestan-style bread.

Paul's

66–68 Snow Hill, Melton Mowbray, Leicestershire LE13 1PD   T: 01664 560572
w: www.soyfoods.co.uk

🗩 **farmers' markets** 🚚 **delivery service**

The staff at Paul's are not interested in fast food, and call their products 'slow bread' – everything is made by hand using traditional methods, with wheat from a local biodynamic farm, milled locally. Sourdoughs, spelt, rye and barley breads are the specialities, all made without any flour improvers. Find the breads at lots of local farmers' markets – call for details.

High Lane Oatcakes

597–599 High Lane, Burslem, Stoke-on-Trent, Staffordshire ST6 7EP   T: 01782 810180
w:www.highlaneoatcakes.co.uk

✉ **mail order**

One of the oldest established bakeries making traditional Staffordshire oatcakes, a speciality of this area. Like pancakes, but made with oatmeal, the oatcakes are a versatile food and can be used for sweet or savoury meals. High Lane are widely believed to make the best Staffordshire oakcakes, having developed their recipe over the years.

The Moody Baker Workers Cooperative

3 West View, Front Street, Alston, Cumbria CA9 3SF   T: 01434 382003

The Moody Baker sources its ingredients as locally as possible and uses organic flour and fair-trade products. Everything is hand-made and there is a constantly changing repertoire of breads, so there are always new products to try. A regional speciality available here is Miner's Pie – a pastry with a seven-eighths savoury filling and one-eighth sweet.

The Broughton Village Bakery

Princes Street, Broughton-in-Furness, Cumbria LA20 6HQ T: 01229 716284
🏠 **farmers' markets**

The bread at Broughton Village Bakery is made using mainly organic local ingredients – the free-range eggs used in the cakes are laid half a mile away and flour comes from The Watermill (see page 36 and the Super Hero box on page 37). The breads available range from the traditional to the imaginative: try basil and tomato bread, with fresh basil and fresh tomatoes, not the dried kind, or All-Day Breakfast bread, containing local bacon, eggs and cheese. The cinnamon rolls are even made with organic cinnamon. There is a café at the bakery, and the produce can also be found at Kendal, Orton and Ulverston farmers' markets. The bakery is not open every day, so call first.

Hazelmere Café and Bakery

1 & 2 Yewbarrow Terrace, Grange-over-Sands, Cumbria LA11 6ED T: 01539 532972
E: hazelmeregrange@yahoo.co.uk

A fantastic range of breads, cakes, deli goods, jams, chutneys, preserves and home-cooked meals, made predominantly with local ingredients, is available here. The breads – from basic white and brown loaves to focaccias and rye breads – is all hand-made without additives or improvers by craft bakers. Ian and Dorothy, the owners, recently won an award for their Cumberland Rum Nicky, a traditional pastry dessert made to a 250-year-old local recipe, from the times when Cumbria had strong trade links with the Caribbean. This really is a treasure-trove of local produce and there is also a café.

Staff of Life

2 Berrys Yard, 27 Finkle Street, Kendal, Cumbria LA9 4AB T: 01539 738606

Using flours from Little Salkeld (see page 36 and the Super Hero box on page 37), Simon Thomas makes a great range of Mediterranean breads and sourdoughs, including a damson sourdough. Overnight fermentation for the breads allows the flavour to develop fully and the rye breads take even longer – they are allowed three or four days to develop.

NORTH WEST   **PENRITH**

The Village Bakery

Melmerby, Penrith, Cumbria CA10 1HE   T: 01768 881811   w: www.village-bakery.com
✉ **mail order**

This is one of the country's biggest organic bakeries, with a great choice of bread varieties, including some for those with wheat or yeast intolerances and there is a restaurant at the bakery, too. Village Bakery breads are available in branches of Waitrose and Sainsbury.

NORTH WEST   **PENRITH**

The Watermill   super hero

Little Salkeld, Penrith, Cumbria CA10 1NN   T: 01768 881523   w: www.organicmill.co.uk
✉ **mail order**

A restored watermill milling the finest organic grains. See the Super Hero box, opposite, for more information.

NORTH EAST   **BARNSLEY**

Potts Bakers

Stanley Road, Stairfoot, Barnsley, South Yorkshire S70 3PG   T: 01226 249175
w: www.pottsbakers.co.uk
🛒 **farmers' markets**

A craft bakery, producing a wide assortment of breads, including focaccias, rye breads, sourdoughs and some organic varieties. The breads are made using the old-fashioned long-fermentation sponge process. All are available at the shop or from Wetherby, Wakefield, Holmfirth and Penistone farmers' markets.

NORTH EAST   **HEXHAM**

Jo's Home Baked Bread

33 Rye Terrace, Hexham, Northumberland NE46 3DX   T: 01434 608456
E: joburrill@btopenworld.com
🛒 **farmers' markets** 🚚 **delivery service**

Jo Burrill started baking because she couldn't find bread locally that she liked and now she sells her imaginative, home-baked breads through farmers' markets and a local delivery (by bicycle!) service. Using organic ingredients as far as possible, she bakes sourdoughs with long fermentation times, taking three or four days to be ready, as well as regular white, wholewheat and granary breads, spelt bread, and her own speciality, Hadrian's Wall Roman Loaf.

super hero

ANA AND NICK JONES, owners of The Watermill, Little Salkeld (see opposite)

Ana and Nick Jones restored the watermill at Little Salkeld in 1975, and have been milling the finest organic and biodynamic British grains ever since. They have a passion for local food and would like to be able to buy Cumbrian wheat but say 'there are no organic or biodynamic farms growing wheat in Cumbria at the moment so we get practically all our wheat from two farms – one in Kent and one in Leicestershire. I want to tell our customers about the wheat – who grows it, the different varieties, where it comes from, why we favour the biodynamic system'. The real secret of the quality of the flour lies in the original French stones used to grind the wheat; the process of traditional stonegrinding allows the wheatgerm oils to be distributed throughout the flour, giving the characteristic nutty taste.

Ana feels that many people are put off making their own bread, believing it to be a difficult and complicated process. 'I wish more people knew how quick, easy and satisfying it is to make bread by hand, especially if the flour has been ground the traditional way. I run a range of breadmaking, baking and vegetarian cooking workshops at the mill and people are always amazed at what fun it is and how easy too.' She is more than willing to offer help and advice to customers embarking on their first home-made loaves. 'I feel that "small is beautiful" when it comes to business, and put lots of care and commitment into the process, the product, and into getting to know and help our customers to get the best from our special flours'.

The wide range of flours, including spelt, wheat, rye, barley, high-protein blends, and all kinds of oat products, are available by mail order or from the mill, and there is a tea room on site, with at least four or five different types of bread available.

Thomson's Bakery

385 Stamfordham Road, Westerhope, Newcastle upon Tyne NE5 5HA
T: 0191 286 9375   w: www.geordiebakers.co.uk

Thomson's bake some very unusual breads – brown ale bread (using
the native brew) is a favourite, Spanish orange bread, soda breads
and their own-recipe ciabatta are all popular. All the breads are
made by hand and giving training to employees in traditional skills is
integral to the policy of this bakery.

Reeth Bakery

Silver Street, Reeth, Richmond, North Yorkshire DL11 6SP   T: 01748 884735
w: www.reethbakery.co.uk
✉ **mail order**

Reeth Bakery uses flour from Little Salkeld in Cumbria (see page 36
and the Super Hero box on page 37) and lots of other local organic
produce, such as free-range eggs, milk and butter. The breads are
traditionally made by hand, without additives or improvers.

Davills Pâtisserie

24 West Gate, Ripon, North Yorkshire HG4 2BQ   T: 01765 603544

The name Davills Pâtisserie could make you think you were going to
find all manner of continental confectionery in this bakery but Davills
is far better than that – it is a traditional artisan bakery, offering
proper craft breads, all made by hand with locally milled British flour.

Hunter's

34 Main Street, Ballykelly, Co. Londonderry BT49 9HS   T: 028 7776 6228

For details see under the Limavady branch on page 42.

Café Paul Rankin (Roscoff Bakery)

12–14 Arthur Street, Belfast BT1 4GD and also at 27–29 Fountain Street, Belfast BT1 5EA and Castle Court Shopping Centre BT1 1DD   T: 028 9031 0108 (ARTHUR STREET); 028 9031 5090 (FOUNTAIN STREET); 028 9024 8411 (CASTLE COURT)

The Paul Rankin cafés are also outlets for the Roscoff Bakery, a traditional artisanal Irish bakery. Everything is hand-made, and alongside the continental-style breads are native Irish varieties, such as soda and wheaten breads.

Kirk's Home Bakery

138 Sandy Row, Belfast BT12 5EY   T: 028 9023 1869

One of a small group of artisan bakers in Northern Ireland, Kirk's specialize in classic Irish breads – wheaten farls, soda bread, Belfast baps and treacle farls are all made with the best ingredients.

super hero

ROBERT DITTY, owner of Ditty's Home Bakery, Castledawson and Magherafelt (see pages 41 and 42)

Robert Ditty has a passion for keeping alive the traditions of Northern Irish baking. His two shops are filled with the heritage of his country – wheaten breads, soda breads, potato breads – all baked to the perfection that 30 years' experience allows. Ditty's is not a backward-looking establishment, though; Robert is always striving to bring new things to Irish taste buds, and he and a gang of equally enthusiastic Irish bakers often get together, swapping ideas and offering constructive criticism to ensure that artisan baking in Ireland remains part of modern culture. Instead of professional rivalry and secrets, this small guild of bakers (Artisan Bakers of Northern Ireland) is refreshingly eager to share knowledge in an effort to heighten the public's awareness of craft baking. Robert runs baking workshops at his premises, which attract amateur bakers from miles away, all keen to learn the secrets of traditional Irish baking. These workshops are so popular that they are usually booked up a year in advance.

food facts

THE IMPORTANCE OF THE RIGHT FLOUR

I can remember trying to bake some baguettes from a Juila Child recipe in the late 1970s and realizing that the only way I could hope for a good result was to try to get unbleached flour from France. Today the range of flours available is much more impressive. The bakers in this guide go to enormous lengths to locate the best flour, realizing that it makes a huge difference to the end result.

Many insist that Canadian hard wheat makes the best flour for bread. The hardness of the wheat is governed by the protein content: the higher it is, the stronger the flour. A stonger flour leads to a more elastic gluten structure in the dough, which traps more air and produces a lighter loaf. There are some millers in the UK, however, who grind traditional soft British wheats, such as spelt (an ancient grain), with great success, and mention the special nuances of flavour that local grain gives to bread – spelt imbues the bread with a pleasing nutty flavour, for instance. The Watermill at Little Salkeld in Cumbria (page 36) is a good example. Here, old British flours made from native grains are being revived, such as maslin flour (a mixture of soft wheat and rye), which was widely used in the Middle Ages but had been forgotten about until recently.

How flour is milled makes a difference to flavour, too. The modern way, using high-speed, steel rollers to crush the grain, is said by many to denature flour by excluding all the bran and wheat germ. The speed also produces a lot of heat, which can compromise the taste by damaging enzymes in the flour. The traditional way, using huge stones, doesn't produce heat and allows a little natural imperfection in the finished flour.

NORTHERN IRELAND	BELFAST

The Upper Crumb

878 Crumlin Road, Belfast BT14 8AE   T: 028 9071 2984

Traditional methods are used at The Upper Crumb to make great examples of native Irish breads, and the same level of skill is used to make some of the most mouth-watering pâtisserie you'll find in Northern Ireland.

Ditty's Home Bakery

44 Main Street, Castledawson BT45 8AB T: 028 7946 8243 OR 028 7963 3944
w: www.dittysbakery.com

Robert Ditty bakes traditional Irish breads including soda and potato
breads. See the Super Hero box, page 39, for more information.
There is also a branch in Magherafelt (see page 42).

Kitty's of Coleraine

3 Church Lane, Coleraine, Co. Londonderry BT52 1AG T: 028 7034 2347

A branch of Hunter's of Limavady, see page 42.

Leslie's Home Bakery

10 Church Street, Enniskillen, Co. Fermanagh BT74 7EJ
T: 028 6632 4902

The fruit loaf at Leslie's has a big and loyal following in Enniskillen, but
the specialist breads also rate highly, with sunflower- and pumpkin-
seed breads and malt and grain breads topping the list. Largely made
by hand, with skills Northern Ireland is in danger of losing, the
produce here proudly continues the heritage of baking in Ireland.

Camphill Organic Farm Shop & Bakery

8 Shore Road, Holywood, Co. Down BT18 9HX
T: 028 9042 3203

From entirely Soil-Association-accredited organic ingredients, Rob
Van Duin makes some unusual types of bread – sourdough, rye
bread, and bread from the old-fashioned spelt grain. Classic Irish
wheaten breads are available too.

The Cookie Jar

The Square, Kilkeel, Co. Down BT34 4AA T: 028 4176 3946

For details see under the Newcastle branch, overleaf.

Hunter's

5–9 Market Street, Limavady, Co. Londonderry BT49 0AB   T: 028 7772 2411

All the classic Northern Irish breads can be found here – wheaten, soda, and so on – all made by hand to old recipes. There is also plenty of new produce to try – continental-style breads and cakes, such as blueberry and cinnamon. There is another branch in Ballykelly as well as Kitty's in Coleraine (see pages 38 and 41).

The Country Kitchen Home Bakery

57–59 Sloan Street, Lisburn, Co Down BT27 5AG   T: 028 9267 1730
E: countrykitchen@bakery5759.fsnet.co.uk

A 4–5 year apprenticeship is required before you can call yourself a baker at the Country Kitchen, testament to the level of skill required to produce the breads and cakes. Great breads and really imaginative cakes are made here.

Ditty's Home Bakery

33 Rainey Street, Magherafelt, Co. Londonderry BT45 5DA   T: 028 7963 3944

A branch of Ditty's Home Bakery of Castledawson (see page 41). See also the Super Hero box on page 39.

The Cookie Jar

121 Main Street, Newcastle, Co. Down BT33 0AE   T: 028 4372 2427

Although called the Cookie Jar, the real speciality of this bakery is the bread, particularly the wheaten bread, made to an old recipe by craftsmen bakers.

The Corn Dolly Home Bakery

12 Marcus Square, Newry, Co. Down BT34 1AE   T: 028 3026 0524

Another great Irish artisan bakery, a member of Robert Ditty's group (see his Super Hero entry on page 39). While the Corn Dolly specializes in classic Irish breads, like batch bread and soda farls, they are also trying their hands at continental breads, and the ciabattas and focaccias, made with the same attention to detail as the Irish breads, are going down a storm. There is also a branch in Warrenpoint (see below).

The Carlton Bakery

39 High Street, Omagh, Co. Tyrone BT78 1BA   T: 028 8224 7046

A craft baker, painstakingly making bread in the time-honoured fashion. Wheaten bread, pancakes and scones are the specialities and there is also a restaurant on the premises.

The Corn Dolly Home Bakery

28 Church Street, Warrenpoint, Co. Down BT34 3HN   T: 028 4175 3596

A sister shop to Corn Dolly Home Bakery in Newry (see above).

The Stoneoven

Kingshill, Arklow, Co. Wicklow   T: 0402 39418

From this tiny bakery come some rare finds – pumpernickel, pure rye breads, organic spelt bread, 100% sourdoughs, and even 'grey bread' from the baker's native Cologne in Germany. All are made by hand with the kind of attention to detail you just don't get in big industrial bakeries.

Baking House

Harlockstown, Ashbourne, Co. Meath   T: 01 835 9010

This bakery has a great commitment to operating in an environmentally friendly fashion, with every aspect of production – including the wrappings used – considered. There is an amazing range of breads, all of which are vegan, organic and sugar-free, available from several local outlets – call to find your nearest.

food facts

ADDITIVES IN BREAD AND FLOUR

Most of us think of bread as a fairly unadulterated food; simply made from a few basic ingredients. So it should be, but many of the loaves available have been made quickly, to a price, with a longer shelf life in mind. This inevitably means that they need a range of additives. Flour improver is the first – often this additive is used to increase the volume of the bread, to get a bigger loaf, and to make the bread softer. Enzymes can be used to speed the baking process. Emulsifiers are sometimes used so that the dough can withstand the industrial treatment it will receive in the large-scale bakeries. Preservatives, mould-inhibitors and crumb softeners will be required to extend shelf life. A good local baker has no need for artificial additives – he will bake the bread from scratch in the morning, and it will be sold to customers who understand that the bread is designed to be eaten that day, or the next.

Millers in this country are forced to put additives into their flour – a preparation of artificial chalk and iron – and this goes for organic millers, too. This law is a somewhat anachronistic attempt to ensure that the population does not suffer from rickets or other diseases related to poor diet. Many organic millers are very unhappy with this regulation – they maintain that there is no need for these additives, and that they are absolutely contrary to what organic produce is all about. The Traditional Corn Millers Guild is at the forefront of the protest, and represents many millers who are upholding the skills, traditions and heritage of the milling industry in Britain. Some of the mills we feature in this guide are members. For more information, contact Fosters Mill (01638 741009).

REPUBLIC OF IRELAND	BANTRY

Organico

Glengarriff Road, Bantry, Co. Cork   T: 027 51391

A mainly organic shop with a strong commitment to buying local or fair-trade produce. There is plenty of good food to choose from here, with organic fruit and vegetables, groceries and even locally made vegetarian sushi, but a big attraction is the bakery on the premises. The baker, Rachel Dare, uses organic ingredients to produce hand-made loaves, the specialities being the classic soda bread and an HRT Cake, for women of a certain age!

Barron's Bakery

The Square, Cappoquin, Co. Waterford   T: 058 54045

Reputed to be the oldest bakery in Ireland, Barron's still use an old stone oven to bake their hand-made breads. Traditional breads such as soda bread and barm brack are the staples here. No mechanization is used at Barron's – as Esther Barron says, 'Bread-making is beyond science.' There is a teashop at the bakery, too.

Arbutus Bread

Rathdene, Montenotte, Cork   T: 021 450 1113   E: arbutus@iol.ie
🥖 farmers' markets

Fantastic hand-made breads, using long proving times and a range of French and Irish stoneground flours. West Cork brown soda bread, red wine and walnut bread, ryes, sourdoughs and continental varieties are all made, and are available from On The Pigs Back (see their entry on page 341), or from Midleton, Bantry, Kenmare, Clonakilty and Macroom farmers' markets.

The Bakery

Pudding Row, Temple Bar, Dublin 8   T: 016 729882

The kitchens at The Bakery are open plan and customers can watch the breads and cakes being made – no pre-mixed products or short cuts here, just the skills of trained bakers proudly on display. There are all the great Irish breads, with the soda and wheaten breads made the old-fashioned way, with buttermilk, not yeast, not to mention foccacias, rye breads, croissants, Danish pastries and pains au chocolat – all made by hand.

Goya's

Kirwan's Lane, Galway   T: 091 567010   W: www.goyas.ie

All the breads and pastries here are made by hand and with the best ingredients. The sweet pastries are what Goya's are renowned for, but they also a do good range of Irish breads.

super hero

JIM AND CRAIG MCPHIES, owners of McPhies Bakery, Glasgow (see opposite)

McPhies, a family-run bakery, is wholeheartedly resisting pressure to change from the traditional methods by which their bread is produced. Using wheat from Scottish millers, McPhies produce hand-made breads with very little mechanization. While this inevitably leads to long hours for the bakers, they have no intention of making life easier for themselves by turning to a modern, time-saving mode of baking. Jim McPhies and his son, Craig, are adamant that the skills of the craftsman baker will not be submerged in the tide of modernization. At a time when craft baking skills are becoming more and more marginalized, the McPhies family is determined that its bakery will be staffed only by those with a commitment to real baking and a thorough training in the discipline. Young bakers joining the company can expect a full schooling in the ways of a traditional bakery; an apprenticeship to become a baker at McPhies lasts three years, testament to the level of skill that is the backbone of this company.

SCOTLAND **ABERDEEN**

Newton Dee Bakery

Newton Dee Village, North Deeside Road, Bieldside, nr Aberdeen AB15 9DX
T: 01224 868243 OR 01224 868701   W: www.newtondee.org.uk

Part of the Camphill Trust centre for adults with learning disabilities, Newton Dee Bakery produces some unusual breads using organic flour and grains. Everything is hand-made using time-honoured methods – nothing is rushed, with many breads receiving an overnight fermentation to allow the flavour to develop. Sourdoughs and rye breads are a speciality and Clara, the baker, makes a Spanish farmhouse-style bread, using her grandparents' recipe.

SCOTLAND **CRIEFF**

Campbell's Bakery

59 King Street, Crieff, Perthshire PH7 3HB   T: 01764 652114
W: www.campbellsbakery.com
farmers' markets

Campbell's Bakery are busy encouraging Perthshire residents to try some unusual varieties of bread – sourdoughs are the speciality here, including honey and walnut and pumpkin-seed varieties. Everything is hand-made, using long fermentation times – the sourdoughs take around six days. All the regular types of bread are available here, too, but it is with their less-well-known varieties that Campbells really shine. Also available at Perth farmers' market.

SCOTLAND   EDINBURGH

Au Gourmand

1 Brandon Terrace, Edinburgh EH3 5EA   T: 0131 624 4666

Classic French breads made by hand on the Au Gourmand premises include baguettes, sourdoughs, walnut, olive and almond breads. The bakery is part of a café and deli where a respect for the traditions of French food is to the fore.

SCOTLAND   EDINBURGH

The Engine Shed Bakery

19 St Leonard's Lane, Edinburgh EH8 9SD and at 123 Bruntsfield Place, Edinburgh EH10 4EQ   T: 0131 662 0040 (ST LEONARD'S LANE); 0131 229 6494 (BRUNTSFIELD PLACE) E: engineshed@aol.com

All the breads made at the Engine Shed, a training centre for people with disabilities which has a small craft bakery, are organic, made with biodynamic flour. All the usual kinds of bread are available and also some more unusual loaves – rye sourdough, with 100% rye, grain molasses bread, herb bread, and oatbread. The breads are available from the shop at Bruntsfield Place. The Engine Shed is accredited by the Organic Food Federation.

SCOTLAND   GLASGOW

McPhies   super hero

1527 Shettleston Road, Glasgow G32 9AS   T: 0141 778 4732

Jim and Craig McPhies are craftsman bakers using traditional technqiues. See the Super Hero box, opposite, for more information.

SCOTLAND   GLASGOW

Star Continental Bakery

158 Fore Street, Glasgow G14 0AE   T: 0141 959 7307

Continental breads such as focaccia, ciabatta and panini rub shoulders with Russian rye and sourdoughs at this speciality bakery.

There is no machinery involved – everything is made by hand and baked in old stone ovens. Star Continental is really a wholesaler but, if you phone, their friendly staff will tell you where to find the bread or – if you are lucky – they might sell you some from the door.

SCOTLAND	INVERURIE

J G Ross

Elphinstone Road, Inverurie, Grampian AB51 3UR   T: 01467 620764

'Butteries' are a very popular north-east Scottish breakfast food similar to a croissant, and were developed for fishermen to take on the boats, as they last longer than bread. The bakers at J G Ross still make them by hand – they say that you just don't get as good a buttery if it is machine made. Though they make all kinds of breads, it is for their butteries that they are best known.

SCOTLAND	PITTENWEEM

Adamson's Bakery

12 Routine Row, Pittenweem, KY10 2LG   T: 01333 311336

Adamson's is famous for its oatcakes, made in the best Scottish tradition. So good are they that you will find them in Iain Mellis's cheese shops and Neal's Yard Dairy in London (see their separate entries in the dairy section, pages 91, 92, 93 and 66).

SCOTLAND	TOBERMORY

The Island Bakery

Main Street, Tobermory, Isle of Mull PA75 6PU   T: 01688 302225
w: www.islandbakery.co.uk
✉ **mail order**

Hand-crafted loaves, with great attention to detail, including rye, soda and pumpkin breads, appear here alongside regular kinds of loaves. The choice is constantly changing to keep customers interested. The Island Bakery has a second string to its bow, in the guise of Island Bakery Organics (01688 302997), producing hand-made, award-winning biscuits from organic ingredients. Made in small batches, with generous lashings of butter and chocolate, the biscuits are the kind you would like to make at home but know you'll never get round to. These are available from the bakery or from many outlets around the UK, including Harvey Nichols and Selfridges, and by mail order from Real Food Direct (www.realfooddirect.co.uk or call 0118 946 4706).

super hero

MICHAEL HALL, owner of Y Felin Mill, St Dogmaels (see page 51)

At last count, Y Felin was one of only a handful of working watermills in Wales and it has been around a very long time – since the 12th century. It has been completely renovated and visitors can see the original mechanisms at work – milling stones made of rock from France and Derbyshire. Michael Hall, the miller, is passionate about the flour he mills, and wherever possible, he uses Welsh grain. Although the mill itself is very traditional, Michael is distinctly forward-thinking in terms of the flour he produces; alongside organic wholemeal, he mills wholemeal mixed with seeds and herbs and even a garlic and chive flour. Organic spelt flour, 100% rye, gluten-free flour and even a mix for Irish soda bread is available – there really is everything a home baker could want here. The on-site tearoom sells bread made with all the varieties of flour. With so few traditional mills still working, Michael feels that his mill 'is an endangered species and needs tender loving care'. The survival of such vital parts of our food heritage depends on dedicated people like Michael.

WALES   **BRIDGEND**

Lewis Fine Foods

Unit 2, Village Farm Industrial Estate, Pyle, Bridgend CF33 6BJ T: 01656 749441

For details, see under the Porthcawl branch on page 51

WALES   **CARDIFF**

Allen's Bakery

Rear of 11 Arran Place, Roath, Cardiff CF24 3SA T: 02920 481219
E: johnbakerboy@aol.com

Hand-made bread, some organic, from traditional British varieties to focaccias, ciabattas and sourdoughs. A good range of flavoured breads is also available – walnut, garlic, onion and rosemary – and customers can watch the bread being made from the counter.

Popty'r Dref

Upper Smithfield Street, Dolgellau, Gwynedd LL40 1ET   T: 01341 422507

A craft bakery, using locally milled unbleached flours to produce classic breads. Everything is made by hand, including the famous bara brith.

Pantri Nolwenn

35 Barham Road, Trecwn, Haverfordwest, Pembrokeshire SA62 5XX   T: 01348 840840
w: www.pantrinolwenn.co.uk

🚩 **farmers' markets**

Using organic ingredients, Pantri Nolwenn make artisan (hearth-style) breads for which, in keeping with the tradition of the craft, spelt is the grain of choice. Other rustic grains include oat, rye and barley, so people with wheat intolerances are well catered for. All of the leavened breads use an 18-hour fermentation period and no commercial yeast is used. There are wholemeal and brown, fruit and nut loaves, the ever popular olive bread and other savouries, rye breads and many more. Spreads for the breads are also featured, such as hummus and baba ghanoush, all unpasteurized. There is also a mouthwatering choice of cookies and cakes, including a cognac fruit cake with 60% fruit and 24% French cognac! All available from Haverfordwest and Fishguard farmers' markets and some local outlets.

Wigmore's Bakery

9 St Mary's Street, Monmouth NP25 3DB   T: 01600 712083

🚩 **farmers' markets**

Using local ingredients as much as possible and employing an old-fashioned overnight resting period for the dough, Wigmore's make a good range of breads. All the regulars can be found (whites, browns and wholemeals), as well as sourdoughs, a Stilton and walnut bread and a classic bara brith cake. Find the produce at the bakery itself or at Usk farmers' market.

The Golden Crust Bakery

Lamphey, Pembroke, Pembrokeshire SA71 5NR   T: 01646 672102

BREAD

Ian White at The Golden Crust is proud of the bread he bakes. He uses the best-quality flour he can, saying, 'quality of bread depends on quality of flour', and bakes using a traditional fermentation cycle, leaving the dough to develop for varying periods to create different styles of bread. The third generation of bakers in his family, he is still using original family recipes.

Lewis Fine Foods

8 Well Street, Porthcawl, Bridgend CF36 3BE   T: 01656 783300

Hand-made speciality breads, including focaccia, brioches, rye bread, walnut bread, basic white and wholemeal bread, and speciality Welsh cakes. Some of the produce is organic.

Y Felin   super hero

St Dogmaels, Pembrokeshire SA43 3DY   T: 01239 613999   w:www.yfelin.com
🖳 farmers' markets 🏬 shop

A working water mill making its own flour and with a shop and café on site. See the Super Hero box, page 49, for more information.

CHAPTER 2

The majority of cheese bought in this country is in the form of rectangular blocks which come from industrial-scale dairies. Here, automated processes producing large quantities of cheese very cheaply have superseded the traditional art of cheesemaking. In recent years, however, there has been a small but growing renaissance of farmhouse, or artisan cheesemakers; producers using old-fashioned methods, making individual 'truckles' or wheels of cheese instead of bigger blocks and choosing their ingredients with the utmost care. Many cheesemakers insist that cows grazing the richest pasture produce the finest, tastiest milk. Many of the artisan cheesemakers we feature use the milk of their own single herd of animals, and they feel this gives the cheese a distinctiveness. The larger quantities of milk required for larger-scale cheesemaking are likely to be from mixed herds spread over a wide area. The choice of a specific breed of cow or sheep can result in a defined regional feel to some farmhouse cheeses; Ayrshire cows in Scotland, or Jerseys further south. Llanboidy Cheesemakers (see the entry on page 99) use the milk of their own rare-breed Red Poll cows – they are believed to be the only cheesemakers in Europe to use milk from this breed. Time is of the essence, too – the traditional cheesemaker will never hurry the process and will give his or her cheese the right length of time to mature; I have also included some

dairy and eggs

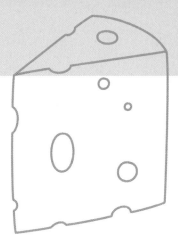

cheesemongers here who have their own maturing rooms, such is their dedication to keeping the cheese in perfect condition.

While large-scale commercially produced cheese is a consistent product, artisan cheeses change with the seasons, according to the pasture the animals are grazing and the weather. Industrial dairies tailor the milk they use to fit their processes; craftsmen cheesemakers are less rigid and will adjust the process to suit the milk they have, often making minute adjustments according to different seasonal conditions. Some cheesemakers only use summer milk, when the cows are grazing on fresh grass; they say the silage the cows eat over the winter has a detrimental effect on the flavour of the milk. Instead of producing cheese using a mechanized process, small dairies offer a hand-made product, in which the cheesemaker uses his or her skill and intuition to time every process to produce the best result. These variants result in a lack of uniformity; cheese bought from an artisan cheesemaker one month may have a slightly different taste or texture the next. In an age of standardization, these inconsistencies could be seen as imperfections but, really, we should see it as a link with our natural heritage. This section is not just about cheese, however, there are also producers of milk, cream and yoghurt, eggs and ice cream, all doing things very differently to the big commercial producers of these foods.

Bath Soft Cheese Company

Park Farm, Kelston, Bath BA1 9AG   T: 01225 331601   W: www.bathsoftcheese.co.uk
✉ **mail order**

In conversion to organic status, Park Farm have won both gold and silver medals at the British Cheese Awards. The soft cheese is made to an 1801 recipe, using the pasteurized cows' milk of the farm's own herd. Available by mail order and from shops and delis.

The Fine Cheese Co.

29–31 Walcot Street, Bath BA1 5BN   T: 01225 483407   W: www.finecheese.co.uk
✉ **mail order**

The product list of the Fine Cheese Company reads like the British Cheese Awards winners' list. Plenty of British artisan cheeses, and a good selection of continentals, too. There is another branch in Cheltenham (see opposite).

Paxton & Whitfield

1 John Street, Bath BA1 2JL   T: 01225 466403   W: www.paxtonandwhitfield.co.uk

A cheesemonger with a 200-year-history and a great selection of artisan cheeses – plenty of British cheeses are represented. There are other branches in London and Stratford-upon-Avon (see pages 67 and 75).

Forge Farm

Tregreenwell, nr St Teath, Bodmin, Cornwall PL30 3JJ   T: 01840 212348
🛒 **farmers' markets**

Eggs are the speciality here – hen, duck, goose, quail, and even ostrich – all free-range and available from all the Cornish farmers' markets – call to find out your nearest one.

Lower Bodiniel Farm

Bodmin, Cornwall PL31 2PF   T: 01208 74136   E: rosemarybryantx@hotmail.co.uk
✉ **farm gate sales**

Really tasty organic free-range eggs from birds raised in small flocks. Available from the farm gate or from Carley's in Truro (see page 23).

The Fine Cheese Co.

5 Regent Street, Cheltenham, Gloucestershire GL50 1HE   T: 01242 255022
w: www.finecheese.co.uk
🛒 **shop** ✉ **mail order**

For details see under the Bath branch, opposite.

Cerney Cheese

Chapel Farm, North Cerney, Cirencester, Gloucestershire GL7 7DE   T: 01285 831312
✉ **farmers' markets**

A recent winner of the Supreme Champion medal at the British Cheese Awards, Cerney Cheese produces goats' cheese in two varieties – a mild, black-ash-covered pyramid and a stronger rind variety, rind-washed in grape brandy and wrapped in vine leaves. Available from Stroud, Cheltenham, Cirencester, Stow-on-the-Wold and Bourton-on-the-Water farmers' markets, and also Fortnum & Mason in London and Paxton & Whitfield (see pages 54, 67 and 75).

Woolsery Cheese

The Old Dairy, Up Sydling, Dorchester, Dorset DT2 9PQ   T: 01300 341991
✉ **farmers' markets**

Woolsery Cheese is a consistent award-winner at the British Cheese Awards. The cheeses are made with goats' and cows' milk, all from local farms; a feta-style goats' cheese, a full-fat hard, a semi-soft and a soft goats' cheese are joined by a Cheddar-style and a semi-hard cows' milk cheese. Available from many local farmers' markets; call for details.

Cornish Farmhouse Cheeses

Menallack Farm, Treverva, nr Falmouth, Cornwall TR10 9BP   T: 01326 340333
w: www.cornishfarmhousecheeses.com

⬇ **farm shop**

Menallack Farm produces a varied range of their own cheeses, using local cows', goats' and ewes' milk, and buffalo milk from Devon. All unpasteurized, 16 varieties are produced in all, in small batches, and customers at the farm shop can watch the process by visiting the cheese room and participate in talks, tours and group tastings.

   Not content to just stock their own cheese, the Minson family also fill their farm shop with almost every other Cornish farmhouse cheese currently being made.

Little Bosoha

Trenear, Helston, Cornwall TR13 0HG   T: 01326 572409

✉ **farm gate sales**

Free-range eggs from a small flock with acres of fertilizer-free pasture to range on. The yolks are a deep golden yellow, great for baking.

food facts

THE PASTEURIZATION DEBATE

Whether or not to pasteurize the milk used for cheesemaking is a hotly debated topic. Many cheesemakers say that pasteurizing milk kills not only the 'bad' bacteria that can cause food poisoning but also the 'good' bacteria responsible for flavour. For the last decade or so there has been a great deal of pressure on cheesemakers to pasteurize all cheeses and many producers have felt forced to begin pasteurization. Others are happy to pasteurize, feeling that it is a small price to pay for peace of mind against the slightest risk of contamination, in spite of the fact that unpasteurized cheeses are almost never the cause of food poisoning. In this chapter I've included cheesemakers who produce both pasteurized and unpasteurized cheeses, all of fantastic quality — it's up to you to taste and decide which you prefer.

Pengoon Farm

Nancegollan, Helston, Cornwall TR13 0BH   T: 01326 561219

✦ **farm shop**

From a herd of just a half-dozen Jersey cows, Mr and Mrs East make traditional clotted cream and farmhouse butter, and untreated milk and free-range eggs are also available, direct from the farm.

Blissful Buffalo

Belland Farm, Tetcott, Holsworthy, Devon EX22 6RG   T: 01409 271406 OR 01409 271253   W: www.blissfulbuffalo.fsnet.co.uk

▨ **farmers' markets**

Mozzarella and a selection of hard cheeses made from the farm's own herd of water buffalo. The milk from these animals is higher in calcium and lower in cholesterol than cows' milk. Blissful Buffalo cheeses are available from lots of Devon farmers markets, including Cullompton, Crediton, Holsworthy, Exmouth, Tavistock and Honiton.

Middle Campscott Farm

Lee, Ilfracombe, Devon EX34 8LS   T: 01271 864621   W: www.middlecampscott.co.uk

▨ **farm gate sales** ✉ **mail order**

A range of four hand-made cheeses, using unpasteurized milk from the farm's own flocks of goats and sheep. Middle Campscott Farm cheeses have won four British Cheese Award medals and one at the World Cheese Awards. Available from Ilfracombe and Barnstaple Pannier markets.

West Hill Farm

West Down, Ilfracombe, North Devon EX34 8NF   T: 01271 815477 W: www.westhillfarm.org

▨ **farm gate sales**

West Hill Farm offers a rare chance to get your hands on milk that has not undergone homogenization, the process that breaks up the fat globules in the milk so that the fat is evenly distributed throughout. Why would you want unhomogenized milk? Sue

DAIRY AND EGGS

Batstone of West Hill Farm says that 'homogenization is a very fierce process', it changes the structure of the milk and hence its flavour. Health concerns have been raised with homogenized milk – some people believe that it renders the fat globules small enough to pass directly into the bloodstream.

The milk from West Hill has old-fashioned flavour and texture. Also available are organic clotted cream and a cream Sue has developed herself – she calls it 'crusty cream' – which is like clotted cream, but has been air dried, not cooked, so it has a fresher flavour.

SOUTH WEST	LOSTWITHIEL

Trewithen Farm Foods

Greymare Farm, Lostwithiel, Cornwall PL22 0LW T: 01208 872214
w: www.cornishfarmdairy.co.uk
✉ **farm gate sales** ✉ **mail order**

Trewithen Farm make clotted cream the traditional way – the milk used comes from the farm's own herd of cows, which are, in turn, fed on home-grown feed. Farmhouse butter and buttermilk are also available, along with crème fraîche and yoghurts.

SOUTH WEST	NEWQUAY

Cornish Country Larder

The Creamery, Trevarrian, Newquay, Cornwall TR8 4AH T: 01637 860331
w: www.ccl-ltd.co.uk

Interesting cheeses made from local Cornish milk, including an organic Brie, are available from supermarkets and good delis, and the company also supplies to the trade.

SOUTH WEST	OKEHAMPTON

Curworthy Cheese

Stockbeare Farm, Jacobstowe, Okehampton, Devon EX20 3PZ T: 01837 810587
✉ **farm gate sales**

Rachel Stevens makes her own-recipe cheese, lying somewhere between a Gouda and a Cheddar, from the pasteurized milk of her own cows. She sells the cheese at different stages of maturity, from three to six months. The latter – though well matured, she points out – is not a 'gum stinger': in other words, not so strong that it will take the roof of your mouth off! Available direct from the dairy, or from specialist cheese shops.

Ashmore Farmhouse Cheese

Lime Tree Cottage, Ashmore, Salisbury, Wiltshire SP5 5AQ. T: 01747 812337

farm gate sales **mail order**

Pat and David Doble make an unpasteurized cows' milk cheese to their own Cheddar-style recipe. Made by hand in small batches, the cheese won a silver medal at the 2002 British Cheese Awards. Available by mail order or direct from the dairy.

Lyburn Farmhouse Cheesemakers

Lyburn Farm, Landford, Salisbury, Wilts SP5 2DN T: 01794 390451
w: www.lyburncheese.co.uk

farm shop **farmers' markets**

The Smale family make pasteurized cheeses from the milk of their own cows and were successful at the 2002 British Cheese Awards, winning a silver medal for their Lyburn Garlic and Nettle. At the farm shop on site, visitors can watch the cheesemaking process, and seasonal organic vegetables are also on offer.

Alham Wood Cheeses

Higher Alham Farm, West Cranmore, Shepton Mallett, Somerset BA4 6DD
T: 01749 880221 w: www.buffalo-cheese.co.uk

farm shop **farmers' markets**

Organic unpasteurized buffalo milk is the basis of Frances Wood's cheese. The main variety is Junas, based on an old mountain recipe and a bit like pecorino; a fresh cheese, good for salads, is also available. There is a viewing area at the dairy so that visitors can watch the cheesemaking, and the farm shop also offers buffalo meat and related products, all from the farm's own herd.

Elms Dairy

Friars Oven Farm, West Compton, Shepton Mallet, Somerset BA4 4PD T: 01749 890371

farm gate sales **delivery service**

Friars Oven Farm has particularly herb-rich pasture and the goats that graze it produce tasty milk as a result. Easier to digest than cows' milk, the goats' milk is available unpasteurized, alongside goats' cream, which is less sweet than cows' cream, and absolutely pure white. ewes' milk and yoghurts complete the range.

| SOUTH WEST | SHEPTON MALLET |

H W Clothier

Westcombe Farm, Evercreech, nr Shepton Mallet, Somerset BA4 6ER   T: 01749 831300
farm shop

Richard Calver at Westcombe Farm makes an unpasteurized, traditional Somerset Cheddar with the milk from his own cows. Maturing for a minimum of 11 months, and often for over 18 months, the cheese is a very full flavoured, traditionally cloth-bound, mature Cheddar. Westcombe Farm is part of a 'Slow Food Presidium' – an endorsement from Slow Food International of the farm's commitment to the ethics of artisan cheesemaking. At the farm there is a viewing window, where visitors can see the cheese being made, which they can then buy from the on-site farm shop.

| SOUTH WEST | SHEPTON MALLET |

R A Duckett

Westcombe Farm, Evercreech, nr Shepton Mallet, Somerset BA4 6ER   T: 01749 831300
farm gate sales

Chris Duckett makes just one variety of cheese – a Caerphilly – but he is the third generation of his family to make it and has just been rewarded with a gold medal for it at the prestigious Nantwich Cheese Show. He shares facilities with the Cheddar-makers H W Clothier (see their entry, above), and both cheeses are made with milk from the herd at Westcombe Farm, ensuring full traceability.

| SOUTH WEST | STURMINSTER NEWTON |

Dorset Blue Cheese Company

Woodbridge Farm, Stock Gaylard, Sturminster Newton, Dorset DT10 2BD
T: 01963 23216   w: www.dorsetblue.com

Although Dorset Blue Vinny was a big part of West Country cheesemaking history, sadly, the art of making it had been lost until Mike Davies, after a prolonged period of trial and error, went into small-scale production of it a few years ago. It is now available in many good cheesemongers and delis.

Berkeley Farm Dairy

Swindon Road, Wroughton, Swindon, Wilts SN4 9AQ   T: 01793 812228
▱ farm gate sales

Organic farmhouse butter, milk and cream is made from the rich milk
of the farm's herd of Guernsey cows. There is an on-site servery for
visitors to buy from, but call first.

The House of Cheese

13 Church Street, Tetbury, Gloucestershire GL8 8JG   T: 01666 502865
w: www.houseofcheese.co.uk
✉ mail order

You will find 120 different types of cheese at this cheesemonger's,
many of them from small British producers.

food facts

ARE ALL HENS THE SAME?

No, they're not and, if you're lucky, opening a box of eggs from a good egg
producer can be quite a surprise. Blue eggs, chocolate brown, pale green,
dazzling white – when an egg producer keeps different breeds of hen, the
resulting eggs can be an explosion of colour. Not only does this make the box
of eggs such an aesthetic pleasure, it also means that some of the more
unusual or traditional breeds are being kept alive, sustaining the biodiversity in
farm breeds of this country. The Rare Breeds Survival Trust recognizes that
several poultry breeds are in danger of disappearing, including the Derbyshire
Redcap and the Scots Grey. The more small-scale producers move away from
high-egg-producing cross breeds and hybrids and start rearing these
endangered breeds, the more likely it is the breeds will survive. It would be
such a shame if eggs went the way of so many foodstuffs – governed by
uniformity and price. The only way to prevent that is to search out local
producers for whom the quality of their eggs, and the quality of life for their
hens, is paramount.

DAIRY AND EGGS

FOOD HEROES OF BRITAIN

Sharpham Creamery

Sharpham Partnership, Sharpham House, Ashprington, Totnes, Devon TQ9 7UT
T: 01803 732203   w: www.sharpham.com

🥄 **farm shop**

Sharpham Farm has its own herd of Jersey cows. The owners were
told many years ago that the milk would be no good for making
cheese – too creamy, fat globules too big, advisers said. Twenty-one
years on, the Jersey milk cheese at Sharpham is going strong. The
three types available at the on-site shop are a Brie-style, a triple-
cream, and a harder, natural-rind variety.

Barwick Farm

Tregony, Truro, Cornwall TR2 5SG   T: 01872 530208

🛒 **farmers' markets**   🚚 **delivery service**

Nick Michell is a traditional butter-maker, a great rarity now. See the
Super Hero box, opposite, for more information.

Ben's Hens

Little Callestock Farm, Zelah, Truro, Cornwall TR4 9HB   T: 01872 540445

📫 **farm gate sales**

Organic free-range eggs from a flock of fewer than 50 birds are
available direct from the farm. The Down family also have
accommodation available, where guests can enjoy other organic
produce from the farm.

Trevaylor

Killiow, Kea, Truro, Cornwall TR3 6AG   T: 01872 864949

📫 **farm gate sales**

Organic free-range eggs from small flocks are available from the
farm gate.

super hero

NICK MICHELL, of Barwick Farm, Truro (see opposite)

Traditional butter-makers are a rare breed these days, and getting rarer. This makes it all the more welcome to find Nick Michell at Barwick Farm, a man with very firm ideas about the food industry. The first thing he'll tell you is that you'll never find his products in a supermarket – he believes in selling locally. The butter and clotted cream he makes are further revelation – the butter a pronounced golden yellow colour, coming as it does from the milk of the farm's own herd of Jersey cows, a breed famed for butter-making. The clotted cream is made traditionally and is that perfect balance of firm crust and smooth cream. Both products owe their quality to the unhurried nature of their production and Nick and his wife Barbara's firm belief in doing things traditionally (the only way they've ever known) – watching Nick make the butter by hand is therapeutic and he clearly finds the process both creative and satisfying. Having been almost ruined by the artificially low price being paid by wholesalers for milk, the Michells, now they have diversified, find their products in great demand and they like the fact that they sell direct to their customers, building relationships with regulars and getting feedback about the produce. A great bonus is that all the products – milk, cream, salted, unsalted and garlic butter and curd cheese – are organic. Find the Michells at Truro Saturday farmers' market and Tuesday produce market and at Wadebridge and Veryan WI markets. They also do a delivery round in St Agnes – call for details.

SOUTH WEST   WINCANTON

Keens Cheddar (S H & G H Keen)

Moorhayes Farm, Verrington Lane, Wincanton, Somerset BA9 8JR T: 01963 32286
E: keenscheddar@hotmail.com

📭 **farm gate sales**

The Keen family are part of the 'Slow Food Presidium' for Cheddar cheese (see H W Clothier's entry, page 60), awarded for their commitment to traditional Cheddar-making. The Cheddar is unpasteurized, from milk provided by their own cows. The traditional cloth-bound cheese is matured on the farm for 12 months, and is available direct (call first) or from Waitrose.

J A & E Montgomery Ltd

Manor Farm, Woolston Rd, North Cadbury, Yeovil, Somerset BA22 7DW
T: 01963 440243

Montgomery's Cheddar is something of a legend, having scooped many medals at the British Cheese Awards. Made with the unpasteurized milk of the farm's own cows, the cheese is made using traditional methods and could be described as fruity and spicy. The family also make a raclette-style cheese from Jersey milk, believed to be the only one of its kind made in the UK. The cheeses can be found at lots of good cheesemongers or, if you are in the vicinity, the village shop two doors down from Montgomery's dairy.

The Cheese Kitchen

108 Castle Road, Bedford MK40 3QR   T: 01234 217325

Jennifer Grumbridge, having trained at Neal's Yard, knows her cheese and is always on the lookout for new artisan cheeses. She specializes in British cheeses, having around 70 different varieties at any one time, simply because she likes them – and what better reason is there?

Rumbolds Farm Dairy

Rumbolds Farm, Plaistow, Billingshurst, West Sussex RH14 0PZ   T: 01403 871404
🛒 **farmers' markets** ⊨ **farm gate sales**

Alison Gibbs has a herd of Guernsey cows that produces rich, creamy milk. She then makes cream, butter, yoghurt and cheese, all of which are available direct from the farm and through local outlets. Local game is also on offer, shot on the farm by Alison's husband, Andrew.

Meadow Cottage Farm

Churt Road, Headley, Borden, Hampshire GU35 8SS   T: 01428 712155
⊨ **farm gate sales**

Farm-gate sales of organic unhomogenized, unpasteurized milk, cream and award-winning ice cream, from the farm's own herd of Jersey cows.

Lower Basing Farm

Cowden, Kent TN8 7JU   T: 01342 850251

🥄 **farm shop**

Disappointed in the cheese offered by her local supermarket, Maureen Browning decided to have a go at making her own. Alongside her Caerphilly type, an unusual goats' milk cottage cheese is also available. Call to find out where to buy.

Crockham Hill Cheeses

Hurst Farm, Dairy Lane, Crockham Hill, Kent TN8 6RA   T: 01732 866516

Most Wensleydale is made using cows' milk but originally it would have been made with ewes' milk, which produces a creamier, less crumbly cheese. This unpasteurized ewes' milk Wensleydale, from a recipe dating from the 1920s, is available from many local outlets (call for details), or from Neal's Yard in London (see page 66).

Twineham Grange Farms Ltd

Bob Lane, Twineham, Haywards Heath, Sussex RH17 5NH   T: 01444 881394
w: www.tgfonline.com

✉ **mail order**

Cheesemakers trained by an Italian master-cheesemaker make English vegetarian alternatives to Parmesan and ricotta, using milk from local dairy herds at Twineham Grange. Available by mail order and Vegetarian Society accredited.

Nut Knowle Farm

World's End, Gun Hill, Horam, East Sussex TN21 0LA   T: 01825 872214
w: www.nutknowlefarm.com

🛒 **farmers' markets** ⊞ **farm gate sales**

The Jenners of Nut Knowle Farm believe they were the first in the UK to milk their own goats for commercial cheesemaking, and now they have a good range of cheeses, many with similarities to Camembert. All hand-made, the cheeses are allowed to mature well before being sold – mainly at local farmers' markets, where the Jenners are happy to tell customers how to cook with the cheese. Call to find out which markets they attend or to place an order.

SOUTH EAST HORSHAM

The Horsham Cheese Shop

20 Carfax, Horsham, West Sussex RH12 1EB T: 01403 254272 W: www.horshamcheeseshop.co.uk

mail order

Lots of artisan cheeses, with a pleasing selection of Sussex produce.

SOUTH EAST LEWES

Golden Cross Cheese Company

Greenacres Farm, Whitesmith, Lewes, East Sussex BN8 6JA T: 01825 872380

farm gate sales

Greenacres Farm produces a mould-ripened, lightly charcoaled ewes' milk cheese, which recently won first prize at the Nantwich Cheese Show. Using the milk from one flock of sheep, the cheese is made by hand in small batches. Buy direct from the farm – call first.

SOUTH EAST LONDON

La Fromagerie

30 Highbury Park, London N5 2AA and also at 2–4 Moxon Street, London W1U 4EW
T: 020 7359 7440 (HIGHBURY PARK); 020 7935 0341 (MOXON STREET)
W: www.lafromagerie.co.uk

delivery service

An Aladdin's cave of artisan produce, with some unusual cheeses from the UK and the continent. There is a café at the Moxon Street shop. La Fromagerie is a member of the *Guilde des Fromagers*.

SOUTH EAST LONDON

Neal's Yard Dairy

17 Shorts Gardens, London WC2H 9UP and also at 6 Park Street, Borough Market, London SE1 9AB T: 020 7240 5700 (SHORTS GARDENS) 020 7645 3554 (PARK STREET)
E: mailorder@nealsyarddairy.co.uk

mail order

A cheesemonger selling British and Irish cheeses that are selected direct from the farms, matured in cellars beneath the shop and sold when they are as near to their peak as possible.

Paxton & Whitfield

93 Jermyn Street, London SW1Y 6JE   T: 020 7930 0259
W: www.paxtonandwhitfield.co.uk

For details see under the Bath branch on page 54. There is also a branch in Stratford-upon-Avon (see page 75).

Happyday Holdings

Burford Road, Minster Lovell, Oxfordshire OX29 0RZ   T: 01993 772204
≅ **farm gate sales**

Free-range goose and ducks' eggs from corn-fed birds are available freshly laid each day, from the stall at the edge of this smallholding. In July and August, customers will also find unsprayed damsons, greengages, plums and the very unusual danzeines – a cross between plums and damsons.

Old Plaw Hatch Farm

Sharpthorne, West Sussex, RH19 4JL   T: 01342 810210
E: oldplawhatchfarm@hotmail.com
➜ **farm shop**

The farm shop stocks cream and yoghurt, as well as the farm's own organic Cheddar-type cheese, made from local unpasteurized milk. Visitors can watch the cheese being made. Home-grown and local biodynamic vegetables are also stocked, as well as biodynamic meat.

Hunts Hill Barn

Moon's Green, Wittersham, nr Tenterden, Kent TN30 7PR   T: 01797 270327
≅ **farmers' markets** ≅ **farm gate sales**

The organic orchard at Hunts Hill Barn produces 28 different varieties of apple, some of which are used to make single-variety juices. The orchards are also home to hens, geese and quail, which range freely, enjoying a diet of fallen apples and insects alongside their regular feed. The eggs and juice are available either direct from the farm or from Rye farmers' market and Tenterden Farmers' Fayre.

Tenterden Cheesemakers

Forstall Farm, Tenterden, Kent TN30 7DF T: 01580 765111 W:
www.tenterdencheese.co.uk

📬 **farm gate sales** ✉ **mail order**

Unpasteurized farmhouse cheese made using milk from the farm's
own prize-winning herd of pedigree Guernsey cows. Three different
cheeses are made – a semi-hard, a range of fresh soft cheese
(including the silver medal winner, Belle's Garlic) and a mozzarella
type. The Whitehead family who farm at Forstall won Young Farmers
of the Year in 2003.

super hero

MARTIN HUDSPITH, of The Chicken Rescue Centre, Wattisham (see page 69)

Most people know that the life of a battery hen is not a happy one and many
people, when they learn the facts about battery eggs, change their shopping
habits and buy free-range eggs. Martin Hudspith has gone much, much further.
He was so appalled by the practices within intensive egg factories that he set
up The Chicken Rescue Centre. Here, he takes on abused and neglected
battery hens and teaches them how to be chickens again. Most have been
debeaked and have never seen the light of day, so he has to teach them how
to feed by themselves and how to range outside, how to dust bathe, how to
scratch and peck. The birds almost always come to him in a truly dreadful
condition, having been discarded for no longer laying eggs in financially viable
quantities. The results of a little TLC are amazing – he currently has around
250 happy hens, all laying eggs contentedly. If the hens want to lay an egg
they do, but if they don't then they are not forced to with artificial lights or
medicated feeds. The chickens get let out at dawn, then they come back to
roost at night – they have the freedom of being in the Suffolk countryside
where they have free access to the grass, grubs, bugs, seeds and anything
else they can find as well as their normal feed. The Chicken Rescue Centre
is a non-profit making animal sanctuary – publicly funded with over 98% of
running costs coming from the sale of the free-range eggs. And Martin has
no doubts that these revived hens produce very tasty eggs – 'I believe in the
philosophy that a happy hen produces the best eggs and my own tight rule
of quality beats quantity means that if you can find any eggs that are better
anywhere then … I'll be surprised.' The eggs are available direct from
the farm.

Sussex High Weald Dairy

Putlands Farm, Duddleswell, Uckfield, East Sussex TN22 3BJ   T: 01825 712647
W: www.sussexhighwealddairy.co.uk
🖐 **farm shop** 📧 **mail order**

From the organic milk of the farm's herd, Sussex High Weald Dairy make a range of cheeses, including a semi-hard and a cream cheese. Ewes' milk cheeses are also made here, including a halloumi-style and a feta-style cheese. Available direct from the dairy, or by mail order.

EAST ANGLIA   DISS

Domini Quality Foods

Village Farm, Market Weston, Diss, Norfolk IP22 2NZ   T: 01359 221333
E: jcapon@dominifoods.fsnet.co.uk
🛒 **farmers' markets** 📪 **farm gate sales**

Buy untreated, organic milk, cream, and sweet, hand-patted butter from the small Domini herd of Jersey cows, directly from the farm or from Wyken farmers' market at Stanton each week.

EAST ANGLIA   SAXMUNDHAM

Suffolk Meadow Ice Cream

Rendham Hall, Rendham, Saxmundham, Suffolk IP17 2AW   T: 01728 663440
🛒 **farmers' markets**

Hand-made farmhouse ice cream, made with the milk of the farm's own award-winning dairy herd. There is a big choice of flavours, including the more unusual chilli and chocolate, mascarpone and mocha. Suffolk Meadow ice creams are available from local farm shops or at Easton, Woodbridge and Felixstowe farmers' markets.

EAST ANGLIA   WATTISHAM

The Chicken Rescue Centre   super hero

Roosters Range, Bildeston Lane, Wattisham, Suffolk IP7 7JT   T: 01449 741626 OR
07752 147937   W: www.chickenrescue.org.uk
📪 **farm gate sales**

A non-profit-making animal sanctuary that gives former battery hens a natural way of life and is rewarded by excellent-quality eggs whose sale largely supports its running costs. See the Super Hero box, page 68, for more information.

DAIRY AND EGGS

FOOD HEROES OF BRITAIN

Mrs Temple's Cheese

New Farm, Wells-next-the-Sea, Norfolk NR23 1NE   T: 01328 710376
E: mrstemplescheese@farmersweekly.net

🛒 **farmers' markets**

Catherine Temple was taught to make cheese and butter by her
mother and grandmother and still uses the same methods to make
by hand her three varieties of cows' milk cheese. The milk comes
from the family's own herd and the cheeses are available from
Aylsham, Dereham, Wymondham and Fakenham farmers' markets.

Fred W. Reade & Sons

Ulceby Grange, Alford, Lincolnshire, LN13 0HE   T: 01507 466987
E: tlj@lincolnshirepoacher.freeserve.co.uk

🛒 **farmers' markets**

Reade & Sons are famous for their Lincolnshire Poacher cheese, a
tangy Cheddar-style cheese that is a previous winner of Supreme
Champion at the British Cheese Awards. Made from the unpasteurized milk of the farm's own cows, the cheese is available from many
markets in the area, including Nottingham, Derby, Spalding and
Boston. In all, Reade & Sons attend around 28 farmers' markets per
month in the East Midlands area. Call for details.

food facts

UNTREATED MILK

The milk most of us buy will be pasteurized and homogenized. The
pasteurizing kills all bacteria, including some responsible for flavour, and
homogenization breaks up the fat globules to distribute them evenly
throughout the milk. This is quite a harsh process and many dairy farmers
firmly believe it affects the taste of the milk – and not for the better. By its
very nature, standardization eliminates character. Sometimes, it's good to
taste milk in its natural form and we list some producers who sell untreated
milk and cream, turning back the clock to offer dairy produce as it tasted
generations ago.

Keys Hill Poultry Farm

Sandy Lane, Wildmoor, Bromsgrove, Worcestershire B61 0RB T: 0121 453 3370

✉ **farm gate sales**

Free-range hens' eggs, laid on the morning of purchase, are available from the farm gate.

Ram Hall Dairy Sheep

Ram Hall Farm, Baulk Lane, Berkswell, Nr. Coventry, West Midlands CV7 7BD
T: 01676 532203 W: www.ram-hall.co.uk

A hard ewes' milk cheese, similar to a Caerphilly but matured for much longer, and two soft, mould-ripened cheeses are made at Ram Hall Farm. The unpasteurized milk from the farm's own flock of sheep is used and Ram Hall have won British Cheese Awards for the last seven years running. Call to find out about outlets.

Neal's Yard Creamery

Caeperthy, Arthurs Stone Lane, Dorstone, Herefordshire HR3 6AX T: 01981 500395

Charlie Westhead makes a range of small, hand-made soft cheeses from locally produced cows' and goats' milk, as well as Greek-style yoghurts and crème fraîche. The methods used are very labour-intensive – everything is done by hand because there are no machines at this dairy. All the cheeses are unpasteurized. Available from specialist cheese shops, including Neal's Yard Dairy in London, page 66; (Charlie's dairy is the production arm of this shop) and the Fine Cheese Co. in Bath and Cheltenham (pages 54 and 55).

Bridge Farm Organic Foods

Bridge Farm, Snitterby Carr, Gainsborough, Lincolnshire DN21 4UU T: 01673 818272

🛒 **farmers' markets** ✉ **farm gate sales**

Bridge Farm is run with a high regard for conservation and produces organic goats' milk and cheeses from the farm's own goats, free-range eggs and organic vegetables in season. Open days are occasionally held, to allow visitors to see how the farm works. Buy the produce direct from the farm shop, or from Lincoln and Brigg farmers' markets.

Shepherd's

9 High Town, Hay-on-Wye, Herefordshire HR3 5AE   T: 01497 821898

The ice cream served at Shepherd's ice-cream parlour is made with ewes' milk, from the milk of one local herd – great for ice-cream lovers with an intolerance to cows' milk. Up to 40 flavours are made, some using local fruit – the flavours are original and inventive.

Birdwood Farmhouse Cheesemakers

Birdwood, Huntley, Gloucestershire GL19 3EJ   T: 01452 750248

🖼 **farmers' markets**

A one-woman cheesemaking enterprise, with an interesting choice of cheeses including a Double Gloucester, a Scottish Dunlop style and her own recipe Forester. All the milk used is cows' milk, from the farm's own herd. Available from Stroud, Cirencester, Cheltenham, Tewkesbury and Stow-on-the-Wold farmers' markets.

September Organic Dairy

Newhouse Farm, Almeley, Nr Kington, Herefordshire HR3 6LJ   T: 01544 327561
W: www.september-organic.co.uk

🍴 **farm shop**   ✉ **mail order**

September Dairy makes 14 different varieties of ice cream, all with the organic milk, cream and eggs produced on the farm, supplemented with local and fair-trade ingredients. Unusual flavours are the order of the day – blackberry-and-apple crumble, brown bread, tayberry and elderflower cream, to name just a few. Ingredients are sourced as locally as possible and the farm is run with a commitment to environmentally sound practices.

Monkland Cheese Dairy

The Pleck, Monkland, Leominster, Herefordshire HR6 9DB   T: 01568 720307
W: www.mousetrapcheese.co.uk

🛖 **shop**

A few years ago, Monkland Dairy resurrected an old local cheese, Little Hereford, using a 1918 recipe. Unpasteurized, the cheese is brine-bathed for 24 hours and then left to mature for four months. Available direct from the dairy or from Monkland's three shops in Ludlow, Hereford and Leominster, where other British artisan cheeses are stocked.

super hero

CLARE DRAPER, of The Chicken Came First, Newport (see page 74)

The free-range hens that Clare Draper keeps are lucky birds. Their welfare is Clare's over-riding concern: they have a great deal of space to peck and scratch, as hens should; they're not cooped up in tiny cages and force-fed high-protein foods – they are fed hot organic porridge with apple and sultanas for breakfast in the winter, and they are not slaughtered when their egg production begins to decline as they age (as happens in most commercial egg production). The birds are an unusual mix of breeds, including Brown Leghorns, Gold Legbars and the exotically named Lavender Araucana, which lays blue eggs.

Clare's customers are also rewarded well for her unusual approach to food production: 'When people open a box of these eggs, they marvel at the rich chocolate brown, snowy white and jewel-like blue shells. Cracking an egg, they are often astonished by the rich, intense colour of the yolk and when they eat it, they discover how 'real' eggs are supposed to taste.' She says that the quality of the eggs is all down to the natural, GM- and chemical-free diet (the eggs are organic), and the fact that the hens live as they naturally would – 'the philosophy of good food going hand-in-hand with animal welfare is terrifically important to me'.

Clare runs a local delivery round distributing the eggs, but customers are welcomed on to the smallholding and can even feed the hens, collect the eggs, or if they are really keen, help weave willow field shelters for the birds. Such is the interest locally that Clare produces a newsletter to tell people what's going on with the birds. She has a very simple mission with her food production: 'If I can stop one consumer buying a battery egg, then I shall be a happy woman.' Call Clare if you'd like to get on to her delivery round or buy the eggs direct from the farm.

The Cheese Society

1 St Martins Lane, Lincoln LN2 1HY   T: 01522 511003
w: www.thecheesesociety.co.uk
🏠 **shop** ✉ **mail order**

Lots of British cheese, including produce from some of Britain's most famous artisan cheesemakers – Mrs Kirkham's Lancashire, Dorset Blue Vinny, and Stinking Bishop. As well as selling cheese by mail order, The Cheese Society has a shop and café at its Lincoln base.

The Chicken Came First

Lynton Mead, Outwoods, Newport, Shropshire TF10 9EB   T: 01952 691418
E: clareword@btconnect.com
🏠 **farm gate sales** 🚚 **delivery service**

Free-range, organic eggs from Clare Draper look and taste wonderful. See the Super Hero box, page 73, for more information.

Colston Bassett Dairy

Harby Lane, Colston Bassett, Nottingham NG12 3FN   T: 01949 81322
w: www.colstonbassettdairy.com
✉ **mail order**

Colston Basset Dairy is possibly one of the best-known traditional Stilton-makers in the UK and a member of the Stilton Cheesemakers Association.

Cropwell Bishop Creamery

Nottingham Road, Cropwell Bishop, Nottingham NG12 3BQ   T: 0115 989 2350
w: www.cropwellbishopstilton.com
✉ **mail order**

The producers of award-winning Cropwell Bishop blue Stilton and blue Shropshire cheeses are also members of the Stilton Cheesemakers Association.

Paxton & Whitfield

13 Wood Street, Stratford-upon-Avon, Warwickshire CV37 6JF   T: 01789 415544
w: www.paxtonandwhitfield.co.uk

One of three outlets: the others are in Bath and London (pages 54 and 67).

Appleby's of Hawkstone

Broadhay, Prees, Whitchurch, Shropshire SY13 2BJ   T: 01948 840387
w: www.applebysofhawkstone.co.uk

The Appleby family are the last cheesemakers to be producing a cloth-bound, unpasteurized, mature Cheshire cheese. The milk comes from their own cows, and the cheese is made entirely by hand. Available from many cheesemonger's – Iain Mellis in Scotland and Neal's Yard in London (see pages 91, 92, 93 and 66).

super hero

PHILIP ROGERS, OF LIGHTWOOD CHEESE, Worcester (see page 76)

Philip Rogers makes seven different types of cheese, all with the unpasteurized milk from the farm's own herd, which is looked after by his father. Almost every variety he makes has been honoured with a British Cheese Awards medal. He's up at around 4 am every morning, to get the cheeses started, using very old regional recipes – Elgar Mature, a cloth-matured hard cheese, is from a 19th-century family recipe and the recipe for Severn Sisters, a semi-soft cheese, dates back to 1780. Such is Philip's passion for cheesemaking that not only does he have a viewing room, where visitors can watch the cheese being made, but he also holds open days for local children to come and have a go themselves. This has proved so popular that he is planning a new education centre to house a full-time children's cheesemaking area. The cheese is available at the dairy itself or from several local farmers' markets – Cheltenham, Stratford, Worcester, Tewkesbury and Teme Valley.

Ansteys of Worcester

Broomhall Farm, Worcester WR5 2NT   T: 01905 820232   w: www.ansteys.com

shop **mail order**

Ansteys were the first cheesemakers to create a Worcester territorial cheese, which they named Old Worcester White, and have since followed this with Double Worcester cheese and a Worcestershire Sauce cheese. All are hand-made with local milk, in the traditional truckle form, and are hard, cloth-bound cheeses. Available mail order, or from their shop at St Peters Garden Centre (call for details).

Lightwood Cheese

Lower Lightwood Farm, Cotheridge, Worcester WR6 5LT   T: 01905 333468
w: www.lightwoodcheese.co.uk

farm shop **farmers' markets** **mail order**

Seven types of unpasteurized cheese are made from the farm's own herd. See the Super Hero box, page 75, for more information.

Mar Goats

St Michaels Farm, Great Witley, Worcester WR6 6JB   T: 01299 896608
w: www.margoats.co.uk

farm shop **farmers' markets**

The cheese at Mar Goats scooped numerous awards at the 2002 British Cheese Awards, including a gold, a silver and a bronze. The cheese is made with the unpasteurized milk of the farm's own goats – the goats feed on pesticide-free, clover-rich pasture and this produces particularly sweet milk. Mar Goats' cheeses are available from the farm shop and local farmers' markets.

Cream of Cumbria

Howberry Farm, Blackford, Carlisle, Cumbria CA6 4EN   T: 01228 675558
E: tomsusan@forrester32.fsnet.co.uk

farmers' markets

Rich yellow farmhouse butter, hand patted and made with the milk from a local cow herd is very different from the butter you find in supermarkets and is available from all the Cumbrian farmers' markets – call for details.

NORTH WEST   **CARLISLE**

Thornby Moor Dairy

Crofton Hall, Thursby, Carlisle, Cumbria CA5 6QB T: 01697 345555

✉ **farm gate sales** ✉ **mail order**

Goats' and cows' milk are the basis of the cheeses at Thornby Moor, all unpasteurized. There is a Cumberland farmhouse cheese, a traditional hard, cloth-bound cheese and a semi-soft, using both cows'and goats' milk.

NORTH WEST   **CHESTER**

The Cheese Shop

116 Northgate Street, Chester, Cheshire CH1 2HT T: 01244 346240
w: www.chestercheeseshop.com

British cheese specialists, stocking over 150 different UK cheeses, with a good selection of organic varieties.

NORTH WEST   **KENDAL**

The Cheese Shop

Unit D17 & 18, Kendal Market Hall, Westmoreland Shopping Centre, Kendal, Cumbria LA9 4LR T: 07791 559486 E: thecheeseshop@btopenworld.com

Of the great selection of cheeses on display here about half are British, from small dairies making artisan cheeses, including local varieties. Many are unpasteurized. There are also some good continental cheeses available, including Spanish Manchego and cave-aged Emmenthal. To complement the cheeses there are some interesting olives and charcuterie.

NORTH WEST   **KNUTSFORD**

Abbey Leys Farm

Peacock Lane, High Leigh, nr. Knutsford, Cheshire, WA16 6NS T: 01925 753465
w: www.abbeyleys.co.uk

⬥ **farm shop**

Organic eggs from traditional-breed free-range hens (Speckledy and Hebden Blacks) and from Khaki Campbell ducks.

FOOD HEROES OF BRITAIN

Staffordshire Cheese Company

Glenmore House, 55 Rose Bank, Leek, Staffordshire ST13 6AG   T: 01538 399733
E: jknox1066@aol.com

farmers' markets   **mail order**

A busy man, John Knox makes 14 varieties of cheese, using both goats' and cows' milk from local farms. Made using old methods, such as muslin wrapping and wax dipping, and old recipes (one dates back to 1860), these are very traditional cheeses. Available by mail order, at local farmers' markets and local farm shops, butcher's and garden centres in the Midlands – call for details.

H S Bourne

The Bank, Malpas, Cheshire SY14 7AL   T: 01948 770214
w: www.hsbourne.co.uk

farmers' markets   **mail order**

Cheesemaking has been in the Bourne family for around 200 years and they are still using the old-fashioned methods and traditional Cheshire recipes to make their artisan products. Available from Nantwich, Knutsford, Liverpool, Wrexham and Northop farmers' markets, and Borough Market in London.

Ravens Oak Dairy

Burland Farm, Wrexham Road, Burland, Nantwich, Cheshire CW5 8ND
T: 01270 524624   w: www.ravensoakdairy.co.uk

farmers' markets   **mail order**

From their organic farm, Michael and Sandra Allwood hand-make a range of award-winning organic cheeses. The cheese is made with their own cows' milk and also locally produced ewes', goats' and buffaloes' milk. Although all the cheeses are pasteurized, the pasteurization method used is very gentle and many people have claimed the cheeses taste unpasteurized. They are available from Borough Market in London, farmers' markets in the north west and West Midlands, and Neal's Yard in London (see page 66).

Staffordshire Organic Cheese

New House Farm, Acton, Newcastle-under-Lyme, Staffordshire ST5 4EE

T: 01782 680366

⬤ farm shop

From the unpasteurized organic cows' milk of a nearby farm, the Deavilles make a Cheddar-type cheese, in plain and flavoured varieties. The most popular flavour is the unusual wild garlic. Also available is a hard cheese made with ewes' milk. The farm shop is open on Fridays and on other days by appointment.

Cotherstone Cheese Company

Quarry House Farm, Marwood, Barnard Castle, County Durham DL12 9QL

T: 01833 650351

✉ farm gate sales

Made to an old Dales recipe that has been handed down from generation to generation, the cheese made here is reminiscent of Wensleydale. Made with cows' milk from a local farm, this cheese will never be found in supermarkets, but is available direct from the farm or from specialist farm shops.

The Swaledale Cheese Co.

Mercury Road, Gallowfields Trading Estate, Richmond, North Yorkshire DL10 4TQ

T: 01748 824932 W: www.swaledalecheese.co.uk

⬤ farmers' markets ✉ mail order

The Swaledale Cheese Co. produces 13 varieties of Swaledale cheese, using local cows' milk and also goats' and ewes' milk. Traditionally hand-made and brine-soaked to an old farmhouse recipe, the plain varieties are supplemented by some flavoured varieties, including two flavoured with local ale and mead. There is a farm shop and viewing room planned for the end of 2003. Available by mail order, or from farmers' markets in Yorkshire – the website lists them.

Northumberland Cheese Company

Make Me Rich Farm, Blagdon, Seaton Burn, Northumberland NE13 6BZ
T: 01670 789798   W: www.northumberland-cheese.co.uk

📬 **farm gate sales**   ✉ **mail order**

A range of cheeses, using local cows', goats' and ewes' milk are made here. One, the Chevington, is made to an old Northumberland recipe using rich Jersey milk – this cheese was popular over 100 years ago and then disappeared, but Mark Robertson has resurrected it. There is a coffee shop at the dairy and visitors can taste and buy the cheeses.

Wheelbirks Farm

Stocksfield, Northumberland NE43 7HY   T: 01661 842613
E: wheelbirks@farmersweekly.net

🛒 **farmers' markets**   📬 **farm gate sales**

Unpasteurized milk and cream, and pasteurized ice cream are all made with milk from Wheelbirks Farm's pedigree Jersey herd. The

food facts

FREE-RANGE EGGS

Why would you bother to buy free-range eggs direct from the farm, when they are available in the supermarket? During the filming of *Food Heroes* we tested fried eggs on 15 members of staff from a hotel near Carlisle. They each tried a supermarket free-range egg, an organic free-range egg from a local farm, and a battery-farmed egg. The results were decisive, five voted for the free-range eggs, ten for the organic eggs, and none for the battery eggs.

To use the term free range a producer must allow a mimimum space per hen, but the flocks can be enormous and there is no legislation regarding the quality of their feed. Our egg producers keep their hens in small flocks, which means that the birds live less stressful lives. The hen houses will be moved regularly to fresh pastures, and their diet will be varied and will not consist of high-protein feed, which increases egg production but can also taint the eggs with a fishy flavour. Happy, healthier hens produce better, tastier eggs, so why not find a local egg producer and discover the difference yourself?

double cream is simply separated from the milk, with no additives or processing, and local fruit is used in the ice cream. Available direct from the farm, or from Hexham farmers' market.

NORTH EAST **WOOLER**

Doddington Dairy

North Doddington Farm, Wooler, Northumberland NE71 6AN   T: 01668 283010
w: www.doddingtondairy.co.uk

This dairy farm produces a range of three cheeses and also ice cream using the milk from their own cows. Doddington cheese is a British territorial, lying somewhere between a Cheddar and a Leicester, Berwick Edge is a Gouda-style cheese and Cuddy's Cave is a natural-rinded cheese. The ice cream is free from artificial additives and the list of flavours is both long and imaginative. Available from many outlets, including Neal's Yard in London (cheese only, see page 66); see their website for full details, or phone.

NORTHERN IRELAND **BALLYMENA**

Causeway Cheese Company

Unit 1, Loughgiel Millennium Centre, Lough Road, Loughgiel, Ballymena, Co. Antrim
BT44 9JN   T: 028 2764 1241
🚐 **farmers' markets**

This is the only traditional farmhouse cheesemaker in Northern Ireland (unless you know differently). The most popular cheese made here is the Drumkeel – similar to Wensleydale. Available plain or with flavourings such as local seaweed. Find the cheese at Belfast's St Georges Market.

REPUBLIC OF IRELAND **ADAMSTOWN**

Carrigbyrne Farmhouse Cheese

Carrigbyrne Farmhouse, Adamstown, Co. Wexford   T: 054 40560   w: www.carrigbyrne.com
🚙 **farm gate sales**

Carrigbyrne is a Camembert-style cheese made with pasteurized milk from the farm's own herd of cows. Available from the farm gate (please phone first), or from Sheridans (see page 85, 86 and the Super Hero box on page 88), Caviston's (see page 195), or good specialist cheese shops. Carrigbyrne is a member of CAIS.

FOOD HEROES OF BRITAIN

Durrus Farmhouse Cheese

Coomkeen, Durrus, Bantry, Co. Cork   T: 027 61100   w: www.durruscheese.com

farm gate sales

One of the last remaining raw-milk cheeses in Cork, Durrus is a semi-soft cheese, very creamy with a hint of herbs and grass. Available direct from the farm (between 10am–1pm weekdays, please call first) or from Neal's Yard in London (see page 66), Iain Mellis in Scotland (see page 91, 92 and 93), Sheridans in Ireland (see pages 85, 86 and the Super Hero box on page 88) and many small independent cheese shops. The producer is a member of CAIS and Slow Food.

Milleens Cheese

Milleens, Eyeries, Beara, Co. Cork   T: 027 74079   E: milleens@eircom.net

farm gate sales

A single herd from a neighbour's farm provides the milk for Milleens cheese; grazing on herb- and-clover rich pasture, the cows produce sweet, rich milk. Winning Supreme Champion at the British Cheese Awards in 1997, CAIS members Norman and Veronica Steele make one type of cheese, a soft, rind-washed variety, which is recognized as a cheese in its own category. Available direct from the dairy.

Corleggy Cheese

Corleggy, Belturbet, Co. Cavan   T: 049 952 2930

farmers' markets

Silke Cropp, a CAIS member, is proudly upholding the tradition of raw-milk cheeses in Ireland and makes a good range of cheeses, using cows', goats' and ewes' milk. She sources her milk carefully, collecting it herself from nearby farms. The range includes some soft and some hard cheeses, all available from Temple Bar market in Dublin, Leopardstown and Dun Loaghaire farmers' markets, and markets around Wicklow.

Croghan Goat Farm

Ballynadrishogue, Blackwater, Enniscorthy, Co. Wexford   T: 053 27331

farm gate sales

One of the few remaining unpasteurized goats' milk cheeses in Ireland is made on this farm, which is a member of CAIS. There is a fresh cheese, in small logs, or the most popular, the French-style Mine Gabhar cheese. A pressed variety is also made. Available from the farm gate or call to find out about other outlets.

Cheese Etc

Beside The Bridge, Carrick-on-Shannon, Co. Leitrim   T: 078 22121

farmers' markets

Lots of artisan Irish cheeses are sold here, with some British and European varieties. Find Cheese Etc also at Belfast farmers' market and Lisburn Speciality Food Market.

Ardsallagh Goats' Products

Woodstock, Carrigtwohill, Co. Cork   T: 021 488 2336

farmers' markets

The Murphy family have cross-bred Saanen and Anglo-Nubian goats to find a breed that produces rich and creamy milk, and with this they make both a soft '*à la louche*' cheese (a slow, method producing very smooth and velvety cheese), and a hard cheese, similar to Gouda but unpressed. The soft cheese comes plain, rolled in cracked black pepper, coated in wholegrain honey mustard, or rolled in chives, and the Gouda-style is available beech smoked. The cheeses are available matured to varying ages to suit everyone's palates. Find them at Midleton farmers' markets or good cheesemongers.

Glyde Farm Produce

Mansfieldstown, Castlebellingham, Co. Louth   T: 042 937 2343   E: glydefarm@eircom.net

farm gate sales

Peter Thomas will cheerfully show visitors around his dairy, where he makes Bellingham Blue, reputedly the only raw-milk blue cheese currently made in Ireland. Every part of the cheesemaking is performed by hand, as Peter feels that this way he has total control over the development of the cheese. Best eaten well matured, the cheese is sold at anything from nine months to three years old. Available direct from the dairy, or from Sheridans (see pages 85 and 86, and the Super Hero box on page 88) and Superquinn stores.

food facts

STORING CHEESE AT HOME

I asked the Specialist Cheesemakers Association for their advice on buying and storing cheese, and here is an abridged version of their advice.

- Buy cheese on the same day, or as near to the time you want to eat it as possible, and keep it cool, in a good larder or cool place, but preferably not the fridge.
- Hard cheeses are relatively tolerant of plastic or vacuum wrapping and fridges, but not the softer cheeses, as they ripen more quickly and tend to sweat in plastic. If soft, white, Brie-type cheeses are kept very cold they will tend to become soapy or even damp and slimy with condensation, so an interesting alternative to the fridge is to put the cheese into a Chinese bamboo steamer basket and hang it in a cool place.
- The ideal storage location is a cellar, pantry or larder, where the temperature is around 8–10°C. Realistically, however, for most people, especially in warm weather, a fridge is the only option, in which case, the carefully wrapped cheeses should be kept in plastic boxes.
- Cheese is a living product and needs to breathe. Clear plastic film can be used to protect the cut surfaces of cheese, but leave some of the rind exposed. Use clear plastic film sparingly on hard and blue cheeses and wrap softer ones in wax paper, foil or, if it's all you have, greaseproof paper.
- Draping a damp linen napkin or cheesecloth over cheese will keep it from drying out, but it only works if the cloth is kept constantly damp.
- Rounds of cheese should be cut in half and then into small wedges, rather than cutting a cheese as you would a cake. This reduces wastage significantly – triangular spaces are impossible to seal satisfactorily. Unsealed surfaces and hollow spaces provide an opportunity for dehydration or mould to damage the cheese and Bries can collapse completely.
- If you have stored cheese in the fridge, allow it to come up to room temperature for an hour or two before eating – it will taste better.

Cratloe Hills Sheep's Cheese

Brickhill, Cratloe, Co. Clare   T: 061 357185

Cratloe Hills won three awards at the last British Cheese Awards, including Best Irish Cheese. Using the milk of their own flock of sheep, Cratloe make two cheeses, a mild and a mature. A member of CAIS and run by a husband and wife team, this is a small-scale, craft dairy. The cheeses are available from Sheridans in Ireland (see below, page 86, and the Super Hero box on page 88), Iain Mellis in Scotland (see pages 91, 92 and 93), the Cheese Shop in Chester (see page 77) and some branches of Waitrose.

Glenilen Farm

Gurteeniher, Drimoleague, Co. Cork   T: 028 31179   W: www.glenilenfarm.com
🏪 **farmers' markets**

The herd of Friesian and Jersey cows at Glenilen Farm produces rich milk, which Alan and Valerie Kingston make into award-winning fromage frais, butter, fruit mousses, clotted cream, and cheesecakes, all hand-made. Available from Clonakilty, Skibbereen and Midleton farmers' markets. The farm is a member of Slow Food.

Sheridans Cheesemongers   `super hero`

11 South Anne Street, Dublin 2 T: 01 679 3143   E: cheeseshop@eircom.net

The staff at Sheridans have an extensive knowledge of all the cheeses they sell, making shopping there a real experience. See the Super Hero box, page 88, for more information. There is also a branch in Galway (see page 86).

Coturnix Quail

Droumdrastil, Dunmanway, Co. Cork   T: 087 206 5067

The quail eggs at Coturnix are laid by birds housed in roomy open-floored barns (quail don't survive well outside in Ireland!). The birds are fed a diet of grain and grass, and are born, reared, and lay on the farm, so that total traceability is ensured. Several local outlets stock the eggs – call to find your nearest.

J & L Grubb

Beechmount, Fethard, Co. Tipperary   T: 052 31151   W: www.cashelblue.com

The Grubbs, who are CAIS members, are probably the largest of the farmhouse cheesemakers in Ireland, and they make the legendary Cashel Blue. When they developed this cheese, there were no other cheesemakers in Ireland making blue cheese. The milk used is from the farm's own cows, and they now make Crozier Blue, using ewes' milk from their nephew's flock. This is still very much a hand-made, farmhouse cheese from a family farm, but it is widely available, and has even found its way into a few selected supermarket stores.

Sheridans Cheesemongers

14–16 Churchyard Street, Galway   T: 091 564829   E: cheeseshop@eircom.net

See the Super Hero box, page 88, for more information. There is also a branch in Dublin (see page 85).

Inagh Farmhouse Cheese

Inagh, Co. Clare   T: 065 683 6633   E: info@st-tola.ie
🛒 **farmers' markets** 📦 **farm gate sales**

St Tola goats' cheese is made mainly with the raw, organic milk from the farm's pedigree herd of Saanen and Toggenburg goats. It comes in a log, a crottin (both soft cheeses) and a hard cheese. Due to the herb-rich pastures the goats graze near the coast, the flavour of the cheese has a suggestion of the sea with an underlying hint of peat. Available from the farm, or at Ennis farmers' market. Inagh Farmhouse Cheese is a member of CAIS and Slow Food.

Ardrahan Cheese

Ardrahan, Kanturk, Co. Cork   T: 029 78099   E: ardrahancheese.tinet.ie

Specializing in a pasteurized, semi-soft cheese, Ardrahan Cheese uses milk from the farm's own cows. Using traditional cheesemaking methods, Mary Burns, a CAIS member, has won an award for Best Irish Cheese at the World Cheese Awards. Widely available from Sheridans (see pages 85, 86 and the Super Hero box on page 88),

Caviston's (see page 195) and Superquinn in Ireland, and Neal's Yard (see page 66), Fortnum & Mason and some branches of Waitrose.

Poulcoin Cheese

Poulcoin, Kilnaboy, Co. Clare   T: 086 894 3832

CAIS members Poulcoin Cheese make a cows' milk and a goats' milk cheese, with raw milk from their own animals. Both are hard cheeses, which have a grassy nature due to the herb-rich pasture the animals graze on – they are fed no concentrates. Available from small local shops around Co. Clare, or from Sheridans in Dublin (see pages 85, 86 and the Super Hero box on page 88) and Neal's Yard in London (see page 66).

Killorglin Farmhouse Cheese

Ardmoniel, Killorglin, Co. Kerry   T: 066 976 1402   w: www.kerryflavours.com
📩 **farm gate sales** ✉ **mail order**

Killorglin make a raw-milk Gouda-style cheese, matured for anywhere between two months and a year. It is available either plain or flavoured with cloves, garlic and cumin, both of which have a great, long flavour. Available from the farm gate, where visitors can watch the cheese being made, or by mail order.

Knockanore Farmhouse Cheese

Ballyneety, Knockanore, Co. Waterford   T: 024 97275   w: www.knockanorecheese.com
🥄 **farm shop**

CAIS members Knockanore Farmhouse Cheese was the proud recipient of a Gold Medal at the British Cheese Awards for their semi-hard, unpasteurized-milk cheese. Buy the cheese direct from the dairy, or from Sheridans (see pages 85, 86 and the Super Hero box on page 88).

super hero

SHERIDANS CHEESEMONGERS, Dublin and Galway (see pages 85 and 86)

Sheridans is very serious about cheese. When staff join the company, they are often sent off to spend a day with one of Ireland's artisan cheesemakers, where they'll find out how the cheese is made, and even have a go at it themselves. Sheridans buys direct from the producers, from Irish farmhouse cheesemakers to olive oil producers in Spain, building relationships, visiting and learning from the producers. Shopping at either of the two shops is a real experience – customers are guided around the products, tasting and examining everything from cheese to oils to vinegars. The staff can answer any questions regarding the provenance of the foods and you can be assured that the produce is offered for sale in peak condition – the cheeses are never released from the maturing rooms until they are at their best and the shops are humidity-controlled. This is food knowledge and experience as an art form.

REPUBLIC OF IRELAND	MACROOOM

Coolea Farmhouse Cheese

Coolea, Macroom, Co. Cork   T: 026 45204
farm gate sales

When the Willems family moved to Ireland from Holland many years ago, they couldn't find anything like the Gouda cheese they loved, and so Mrs Willem set about making it at home for the family. Her son took over making the cheese and now it is widely available, from Sheridans (see pages 85, 86 and the Super Hero box on page 88) and Superquinn branches in Ireland, Iain Mellis in Scotland (see pages 91, 92 and 93) and Neal's Yard in London (see page 66). From a hobby to Supreme Champion at the British Cheese Awards in 2000, these CAIS-member cheesemakers have come a long way.

REPUBLIC OF IRELAND	SCHULL

Gubbeen Cheese

Gubbeen House, Schull, Cork   T: 028 28231   w: www.gubbeen.com
farmers' markets

One of the most famous Irish artisan cheeses, hand-made with the milk of the cheesemaker's own mixed herd, which includes some rare, native Kerry cows. Gubbeen Cheese is a CAIS member.

The West Cork Natural Cheese Co.

Schull, Co. Cork   T: 028 28593   W: www.wcnc.ie

🥢 **farmers' markets** 🥢 **farm gate sales**

The West Cork Cheese Co. use the alpine 'alpage' way of making cheese, using only the summer milk from cows fed on fresh grass – when the cows are eating silage in the winter the milk can have a bitter flavour. The two cheeses they make – Desmond and Gabriel – are both 'thermophilic', heat-treated in the early stages of production, as Parmesan-style cheeses are. Both are hard and good for cooking – Desmond has a piquant flavour and Gabriel is long-flavoured and aromatic – and are available direct from the farm or from Bantry and Cork City farmers' markets or Temple Bar market in Dublin and Neal's Yard (see page 66) in London and Sheridans (see pages 85, 86 and the Super Hero box on page 88) in Ireland. The company is a CAIS member.

Cooleeney Farmhouse Cheese

Moyne, Thurles, Co. Tipperary   T: 0504 45112   W: www.cooleeney.com

CAIS members Cooleeney produce three different cheeses using the milk of their own cows, all similar to Camembert or Brie in style and a new goats' milk cheese, using the milk from a Waterford goat herd. The goats' milk cheese is similar to a mild, velvety Brie – it's not too 'goaty', with a hint of mushroom – and won 'Best New Cheese' at the 2002 British Cheese awards. Widely available from cheese shops around Ireland and the UK.

McDonald's Cheese Shop

Westfields, Balmoral Road, Rattray, Blairgowrie, Perthshire PH10 7HY   T: 01250 872493

Caroline Robertson and her husband John are passionate about cheese and stock over 100 varieties – from Scotland, Ireland, England and Wales as well as from further afield on the contintent – in their shop. There is a wealth of Scottish artisan produce here, including high-quality chocolate and even ice cream from Arran.

The Island Cheese Company

Home Farm, Brodick, Isle of Arran, KA27 8DD   T: 01770 302788

farm shop

The Island Cheese Company makes eight varieties of cheese from local cows' and goats' milk, including a traditional Scottish Crowdie cheese. At the shop you can watch the cheeses being made from the viewing room, buy the company's cheese and other Scottish and English farmhouse cheeses too.

H J Errington & Co.

Walston Braehead Farm, Carnwath, Lanarkshire ML11 8NF   T: 01899 810257

farm gate sales   **mail order**

Blue cheeses are the speciality here, made with unpasteurized ewes' and cows' milk. Ayrshire cows from a neighbour's farm and Humphrey Errington's own sheep provide the milk. Humphrey also makes a cheese called Maisie's Kebbuck, which is not blue, as a special dispensation for his mother-in-law, who doesn't like blue cheese!

The Hand Made Cheese Co.

Swinlees Farm, Dalry, Ayrshire KA24 5JZ   T: 01294 832479

farmers' markets

Hazel Forsyth is not happy being called an artisan cheesemaker – she protests that it conveys 'images of hippies'! However, given that she makes small batches of her cloth-bound, Cheddar-style cheese using traditional methods, with the unpasteurized milk from local Ayrshire cows, and, as the name suggests, by hand, then artisan is what she is. Hazel's cheese is available at all the Ayrshire farmers' markets, see www.ayrshirefarmersmarket.co.uk or call Hazel for more details.

Loch Arthur Creamery

Camphill Village Trust, Beeswing, Dumfries DG2 8JQ   T: 01387 760296

farm shop

Four types of cheese are made at the Loch Arthur Creamery, including a farmhouse cloth-bound, Cheddar type. All are made from unpasteurized organic milk, most of which comes from the farm's own herd. As Loch Arthur is a mixed farm, the farm shop also stocks organic and biodynamic meat, home-baked bread, and vegetables.

SCOTLAND   EDINBURGH

Iain Mellis (The Cheesemonger)

30a Victoria Street, Edinburgh EH1 2JW and also at 6 Bakers Place, Edinburgh EH3 6SY and 205 Bruntsfield Place, Edinburgh EH10 4DH T: 0131 226 6215 (VICTORIA ST); 0131 225 6566 (BAKERS PLACE); 0131 447 8889 (BRUNTSFIELD PLACE)
w: www.ijmellischeesemonger.com
✉ mail order

Iain Mellis ripens the cheese he sells in his own maturing rooms, the sign of a cheesemonger truly passionate about cheese. He sells a huge range, including lots of British farmhouse cheese varieties. There is also a branch in Glasgow and one in St Andrews (see pages 92 and 93).

super hero

PAM RODWAY, owner of Wester Lawrenceton Farm, Moray (see page 92)

Pam Rodway has been making cheese for over 30 years, and is passionate about keeping the heritage of Scottish cheese alive. From the unpasteurized organic milk of her own herd of Ayrshire cows, famous for the creamy quality of their milk, she makes Dunlop, a traditional Scottish 'sweet milk' cheese. Instead of striving for uniformity, Pam takes pleasure in the way the colour and flavour of the cheese can vary subtly according to the season or the pasture the cows are grazing. She is now researching a 'lost' Scottish variety, Highland cheese, which has not been made for generations, with a view to resurrecting this old, traditional variety. Finding a defined recipe for this cheese is proving tricky; it comes from a time when cheese was usually made within the home, not commercially, with the recipe handed down from mother to daughter. Producers with such a keen sense of local history are a rare and refreshing find. Pam's cheeses can be found at Elgin farmers' market or specialist Scottish cheesemongers.

super hero

KINTALINE FARM, Oban (see opposite)

Hens have a more complicated natural lifecycle than most people think and require resting periods and moulting periods in order to function properly. Most commercial egg producers take no account of this; birds are expected to lay continuously until they effectively wear out. At Kintaline Farm, things are different. The Black Rock hens are allowed to behave naturally, with acres of fresh pasture to roam on and with their natural cycles of laying and resting respected. This particular breed of hen has never been known to have salmonella in any UK flock and Kintaline's flocks produce magnificent eggs. They are not fed with high-protein feed, which can give the eggs a fishy flavour. The hens' eggs, as well as duck eggs and herbs, are available from the farm gate or Oban farmers' market.

SCOTLAND | FORRES

Wester Lawrenceton Farm

Forres, Moray IV36 2RH T: 01309 676566
farmers' markets   farm gate sales

Pam Rodway makes traditional Scottish cheeses from unpasteurized organic milk. See the Super Hero box, page 91, for more information.

SCOTLAND | GLASGOW

Iain Mellis (The Cheesemonger)

492 Great Western Road, Glasgow G12 8EW T: 0141 339 8998
W: www.ijmellischeesemonger.com
mail order

For details, see under the Edinburgh branches on page 91. There is also a branch in St Andrews (see opposite).

SCOTLAND | KILMARNOCK

Dunlop Dairy

West Clerkland Farm, Stewarton, Kilmarnock, Ayrshire KA3 5LP T: 01560 482494
farmers' markets   farm gate sales

Using ewes', goats' and cows' milk, Ann Dorward makes a range of pasteurized cheeses, including the very traditional cloth-bound

Dunlop – from an old recipe – which is like a soft Cheddar. All the milk comes from the dairy's own animals.

93

DAIRY AND EGGS

SCOTLAND   KIRKWALL

Grimbister Farm Cheese

Grimbister Farm, by Kirkwall, Orkney KW15 1TT T: 01856 761318
E: grimbister@orknet.co.uk

📧 **farm gate sales** ✉ **mail order**

Specializing in one type of cheese – a crumbly, unpasteurized variety – Hilda Seator uses the milk from her own herd of cows. Her cheese is available direct from the dairy, but call first.

SCOTLAND   NEWTON STEWART

Galloway Farmhouse Cheese

Millaries Farm, Sorbie, Newton Stewart, Dumfries and Galloway DG8 8AL
T: 01988 850224 W: www.ewetoyou.co.uk

⚓ **farm shop**

Galloway Farmhouse specializes in a Cheddar-style cheese, using raw ewes' milk and with a complex nutty flavour. It is available from the shop at the dairy, but call first.

SCOTLAND   OBAN

Kintaline Farm

super hero

Benderloch, Oban, Argyll, PA37 1QS T: 01631 720223 W: www.kintaline.co.uk AND
www.poultryscotland.co.uk

🏪 **farmers' markets** 📧 **farm gate sales**

Kintaline Farm's Black Rock hens produce magnificent large eggs. See the Super Hero box, opposite, for more information.

SCOTLAND   ST ANDREWS

Iain Mellis (The Cheesemonger)

149 South Street, St Andrews KY16 9UN T: 01334 471410
W: www.ijmellischeesemonger.com

✉ **mail order**

For details, see under the Edinburgh branches on page 91. There is also a branch in Glasgow (see opposite).

food facts

FARMHOUSE BUTTER

We have featured a few producers who make traditional, farmhouse, hand-patted butter; only a few, sadly, as there are so few left. How is the butter they make different from the butter most of us buy? Farmhouse butter is made on a much smaller scale, by hand, with all the care and attention that affords. But the real key is the milk. The butter-makers we feature use the milk from one herd – often their own – and they may have chosen Jersey or Guernsey cows, famed for their rich, creamy milk, although these are not the highest yielding breeds. You'll notice that farmhouse butter is usually an incredibly vibrant yellow, almost orange sometimes. This is due to the cows' diet of rich, verdant pasture, making a richer, creamier milk; many dairy farmers believe that using the milk from just one herd allows the characteristics of time and place – the season, and the pasture – to shine through in the end product.

SCOTLAND   STROMEFERRY

West Highland Dairy

Achmore, Stromeferry, Ross-shire IV53 8UW   T: 01599 577203
w: www.westhighlanddairy.co.uk
⟶ farm shop

Kathy Biss of the West Highland Dairy has been making cheese for over 40 years, and her expertise is much sought-after – she has been asked by numerous institutions to conduct lectures on the finer points of cheesemaking. Eleven different cheeses are made here, all with cows' milk, and two won medals at the 2002 British Cheese Awards. Crème fraîche is also available – so rich and thick that it won't fall out of the pot if you turn it upside-down. All produce is available from the small shop at the dairy.

SCOTLAND   TAIN

Highland Fine Cheeses Ltd

Blarliath Farm, Shore Road, Tain, Ross-shire IV19 1EB   T: 01862 892034
⟶ farm shop ✉ mail order

Among other varieties, the Highland Fine Cheese Company make the traditional Scottish Crowdie, a soft and rich cheese that is an important part of the heritage of cheesemaking in Scotland.

Isle of Mull Cheese

Sgriob-Ruadh Farm, Tobermory, Isle of Mull PA75 6QD   T: 01688 302235
E: mull.cheese@btinternet.com

farm gate sales

From the milk of the assortment of cows on the farm (Ayrshires,
Jerseys and Brown Swiss), Jeff Reade makes unpasteurized
Cheddar-type cheeses. Visitors are welcome and can watch the
cheese being made from the viewing room, and buy the produce
from the farm. Jeff was the recent winner of the BBC Radio 4 Best
Food Producer award.

Bower Farm Dairy

Grosmont, Abergavenny, Gwent NP7 8HS   T: 01981 240219
W: www.bowerfarm.freeserve.co.uk

farmers' markets   farm gate sales

From the milk of their own herd of Jersey cows, the Collinson family
make cream, clotted cream and yoghurt. Also available is free-range
Gloucester Old Spot pork, from pigs reared on the farm. Available at
select retail outlets in Wales.

Little Acorn Products

Mesen Fach Farm, Bethania Llanon, Ceredigion SY23 5NS   T: 01974 821348

farm gate sales

Using raw ewes' milk, Linda Cousins makes a hard, full-fat cheese
in two varieties – one flavoured with saffron and one with mead –
which are available from the farm.

Caws Cenarth

Fferm Glyneithinog, Llancwch, Boncath, Ceredigion SA37 0LH   T: 01239 710432
W: www.cawscenarth.co.uk

farm gate sales

Award-winning unpasteurized organic cheese from the milk of
the dairy's own cows. See the Super Hero box, page 96, for
more information.

Caffi Patio

super hero

Llangrannog, Cardigan Bay, Ceredigion SA44 6SL   T: 01239 654502
E: the.patiocafe@virgin.net

A café serving wonderful home-made food but especially renowned for its own Italian-style ice cream. See the Super Hero box, page 99, for more information.

Clover Jerseys

Cwrcoed Farm, Llangoedmor, Cardigan SA43 2LG,   T: 01239 621658

farmers' markets   farm gate sales   mail order

Traditional Welsh farmhouse butter, hand-made from the Jersey milk of the farm's own herd. The butter is available in unsalted, medium-salted or the traditionally Welsh very salty versions. Buy it mail order, from the farm gate or from Usk and Cardiff farmers' markets.

super hero

THELMA ADAMS, cheesemaker at Caws Cenarth dairy, Ceredigion (see page 95)

Thelma Adams, the cheesemaker at Caws Cenarth, runs her dairy very much with an open-door policy. 'From day one I was adamant that the farm would be open to visitors to enable them to meet us and our animals and to watch the cheese being made, for them to gain a better understanding of the role played by farmers in producing the nation's food. This is the stimulus that makes me, a 64-year-old pensioner, carry on, when perhaps it would be more normal to put my feet up!'

The cheese is made with unpasteurized organic milk from Thelma's own herd, which is run with an emphasis on welfare – the calves are fed on their mother's milk until fully weaned. The varieties include a traditional Caerphilly, a blue cheese, and a semi-soft cheese, and the list of awards, including a gold from the British Cheese Awards, is impressive. Cheesemaking runs in the family – Thelma still makes it entirely by hand, the way she was taught by her mother and grandmother – the only difference is that Thelma uses vegetarian rennet. All the cheeses are accredited by the Soil Association. Buy on site, or from specialist cheesemongers such as Paxton & Whitfield.

Nantybwla

College Road, Carmarthen, Carmarthenshire SA31 3QS   T: 01267 237905

🛒 **farmers' markets** 📫 **farm gate sales**

Nantybwla make a great range of cheeses, all with the unpasteurized milk of their own cows. There is a Caerphilly and a matured Caerphilly, and a range of cheeses with flavourings – garlic and leek, laverbread, cranberry, apricots or chives, and a smoked variety. The cheeses have won many awards at the British Cheese Awards, the Royal Welsh Show and the National Farmers' Union – far too many to list. Find the cheese at Cowbridge, Penarth, Brecon, Aberystwyth, Lampeter and Carmarthen farmers' markets, or buy it direct from the farm.

Pant Mawr Farmhouse Cheese

Pant Mawr Farm, Rosebush, Clynderwen, Pembrokeshire SA66 7QU   T: 01437 532627

📫 **farm gate sales** 📧 **mail order**

Pant Mawr Farm produces cheese from both cows' and goats' milk. The goats' cheese is a soft curd cheese, available plain or in olive oil. The cows' milk is used to make Caws Cerwyn, a fresh, young cheese that is also available oak smoked; it is this version that won Pant Mawr Farm a gold medal at the 2002 World Cheese Awards. A Brie-like cheese – Caws Preseli – and a pungent, mead-washed cheese – Caws Coch – complete the range.

Llangloffan Farmhouse Cheese

Llangloffan, Castle Morris, nr Fishguard, Pembrokeshire SA62 5ET   T: 01348 891241
w: www.welshcheese.co.uk

🥄 **farm shop**

The Downey family make a full-fat, unpasteurized cheese with the milk from their own cows, and visitors can watch the cheesemaking process in demonstrations every morning at the farm shop on site. Breads made in the farmhouse kitchen are also available – among the regular loaves and rolls, you'll find Italian-style breads and Bara Brith (traditional fruit bread). Also on site is a new restaurant, Tides, run by the Downey's daughter Emma, with lots of Pembrokeshire seafood and a menu based on local organic produce. The farm is accredited by the Organic Food Federation.

Caws Caerfai

Caerfai Farm, St David's, Haverfordwest, Pembrokeshire SA62 6QT   T: 01437 720548
w: www.caerfai.co.uk

⬇ **farm shop**

The farm shop at Caerfai Farm stocks some good local produce –
organic vegetables, eggs and beef – but it is the home-made
cheeses that are the real attraction. Unpasteurized organic milk from
the farm's own cows is used to make Caerphilly cheeses, both plain
and flavoured, and a Cheddar-type cheese. Call before visiting.

Penbryn Cheese

Ty-Hen Farm, Sarnau, Llandysul, Ceredigion SA44 6RD   T: 01239 810347
E: alison@penbryncheese.co.uk

✉ **farm gate sales**

Unpasteurized, hard, pressed, Gouda-style cheese, hand-made with
milk from the farm's own herd, which is fed on homegrown corn. It's
available direct from the farm, but call first, or from Neal's Yard (see
page 66) and other independent cheese shops.

Teifi Cheese

Glynhynod, Farm, Llandysul, Ceredigion SA44 5JY   T: 01239 851528

⬇ **farm shop**

Winners of the Supreme Champion award at the British Cheese
Awards, John and Patrice Savage make a range of cheeses, including
a Gouda-style one. The cheese is made with the unpasteurized milk
from the Savages' own Jersey cows. There is a farm shop on site, or
find the cheeses in specialist cheese shops around the country.

Drim Farm

Llawhaden, Narberth, Pembrokeshire SA67 8DN,   T: 01437 541295

⬇ **farm shop** 🛒 **farmers' markets**

Mr McNamara, the farmer at Drim Farm, is giving the West Country a
run for its money when it comes to cream teas. He makes clotted
cream from his own herd of Jersey cows, and it is so tasty that it has

super hero

CAFFI PATIO, Cardigan Bay (see page 96)

This café has some lovely foods – home-made seafood chowder, rich with fish from Cardigan Bay, home-made soups and pizzas – but the star of the show is the home-made Italian-style ice cream. The owners, Julie and Mervyn, visit Italy regularly to learn techniques and get inspiration and it shows in the very imaginative flavours they make. They use raw local milk and cream, and the ice cream is not deep frozen – it really is 'iced cream', so it is softer and fresher than commercial ice cream. Incredibly rich and creamy, the ice cream has no artificial additives and fresh fruit, not concentrate, is used to flavour it.

beaten more famous West Country cream-makers in competitions. Available from Haverfordwest farmers' market in the summer.

WALES TREGARON

Gorwydd Caerphilly

Gorwydd Farm, Llanddewi Brefi, Tregaron, Ceredigion SY25 6NY   T: 01570 493516
E: morgan@gorwydd.com
�= **farmers' markets**

True specialists, the Trethowan family at Gorwydd Farm produce just one cheese – a mature Caerphilly. Using local milk, the cheese is unpasteurized and hand-made. Available from Borough Market in London or from local Welsh farmers' markets – call to find out where.

WALES WHITLAND

Llanboidy Cheesemakers

Cilowern, Uchaf Login, Whitland, Carmarthenshire SA34 0TJ   T: 01994 448303
W: www.llanboidycheese.co.uk
✉ **mail order**

At Llanboidy Cheesemakers, the unpasteurized milk of rare-breed Red Poll cows is used to make a hard-pressed cheese – believed to be the only cheese in Europe made with this particular milk. The cheese is available plain or flavoured with laver bread, the Welsh seaweed. The cheesemakers have also recently developed an organic cheese, which won a gold medal at the British Cheese Awards.

This section is largely about delicatessens and specialist local food shops. I have focused on delis that endeavor to seek out and stock local, regional specialities: produce from British or Irish artisan producers. These are the stores that support small-scale producers and manufacturers and which offer unusual local foods that you are unlikely to find elsewhere. They may well sell some great-quality or hard-to-find imported produce – after all, good olive oils and balsamic vinegars are such an integral part of cooking these days, but are not produced on home turf. Alongside foreign delights, these shops will also provide a solid sense of local or regional flavour. In these times when it seems that food is becoming more and more standardized, indistinct and uniform, these shops proudly wave a flag for the obscure and the rare and are often an important part of the local community, where people can get a taste of traditional shopping, where the foods are tasted and discussed. Often staff will personally know many of the producers that they buy from and can give customers background information. I have also listed some farm shops here,

delicatessens and specialist food shops

because they have such a vast array of different types of food on offer that they did not fit comfortably into any of the other categories.

While so much of this book is about the home-produced treasures that the UK and Ireland abound in, it would be unrealistic to deny the pleasures that some good quality imported foods bring – after all, there are many things that this country is unable to produce, and I'm not suggesting we shouldn't have access to them. So, alongside the delis, where you'll find delicacies from around the world, often from artisan producers, I've also listed a few other fine retail emporia, such as chocolate shops that have raised chocolate to an art form – after all, we are a nation of chocoholics. I hope that you discover new edible pleasures within this section. The Guild of Fine Food Retailers is instrumental in this country in encouraging small-scale producers and promoting specialist shops and delis that stock their produce. The annual Great Taste Awards that the Guild runs is a celebration of the diversity and skill of small producers in the UK and Ireland, and I have listed many winners in this section.

Washing Pool Farm Shop

North Allington, Bridport, Dorset DT6 5HP   T: 01308 459549
w: www.washingpoolfarm.co.uk

⚓ **farm shop**

This farm shop is absolutely packed with produce from Dorset.
Food from over 50 local producers is represented here, from
chocolates to bread, meat and a great range of fresh fruit and
vegetables grown on the farm. There is also a coffee shop on site,
again using local produce.

Tamarisk Farm

West Bexington, Dorchester, Dorset DT2 9DF   T: 01308 897781 OR 01308 897784
w: www.tamariskfarm.co.uk

🛒 **farmers' markets** ✉ **farm gate sales** 📦 **box scheme**

Conservation is an issue at the heart of this Dorset organic farm –
proper crop rotation maintains the soil's natural fertility and the
species-rich permanent pasture is well looked after. The farm
produces organic lamb, hogget, mutton and beef, a good range of
vegetables in season (sold through the box scheme) and even flour
from home-grown grains, including a rye flour, and a wheat flour
made using an old variety of wheat, good for making a firm, nutty
loaf. All are available direct from the farm. Flour is also available
from Washing Pool Farm shop and Modbury Farm (see above and
page 274) and meat from West Dorset Organic Foods, see entry for
Becklands Farm, page 273).

Sageberry Cheese Delicatessen

21 Cheap Street, Frome, Somerset BA11 1BN   T: 01373 462543

The staff at Sageberry Cheese are always willing to search out
that elusive ingredient. A great selection of local cheeses, high-
quality chocolate and locally produced smoked meats are always
on display.

Lefktro UK Ltd

Somerville House, High Street, Hinton St George, Somerset TA17 8SE T: 01460 72931
w: www.getoily.com

✉ **mail order**

A great selection of extra-virgin olive oils from around the world, plus Mediterranean foods and kitchen accessories can be found at this shop.

Honeybuns

Naish Farm, Stony Lane, Holwell, Dorset DT9 5LJ T: 01963 23597
w: www.wemadeitourselves.com

Honeybuns produce exquisite, artisan cakes, by hand, with largely locally produced ingredients. If chocolate is required, they'll use Valrhona and the butter is traditional farmhouse – margarine is never used. The eggs are laid only two fields away – there is a distinct community feel to the business. As yet, Honeybuns have no retail outlet themselves (you can find the cakes at John Lewis cafés) but they are toying with the idea of a café on site and are happy for visitors to come along, with a day's notice.

Burts Potato Chips

The Parcel Shed, Station Yard, Kingsbridge, Devon TQ7 1ES T: 01548 852220
w: www.burtschips.com

Crisps with personality! Burts Potato Chips are made from potatoes from farms that the makers know – in fact, each bag is labelled with the field that the potatoes came from and which member of staff fried that particular batch. Burts really do take potato chips to a whole new level. Phone to find your nearest outlet.

Longborough Farm Shop

Longborough, Moreton-in-Marsh, Gloucestershire GL56 0QZ   T: 01451 830469
w: www.longboroughfarmshop.com

farm shop

The knowledgeable and helpful staff at the Longborough Farm Shop
will happily guide you through their incredible range of local produce
– rare-breed meats, game from nearby shoots, local cheeses, even
local crisps. In season, home-grown asparagus is available and in
summer there is the opportunity to pick your own fruit.

Stein's Seafood Deli

South Quay, Padstow, Cornwall PL28 8BY   T: 01841 533466   w: www.rickstein.com

mail order

Alongside great cheeses, home-made chutneys and jams, salads
and pâtés, hot home-made dishes are available to take away. With
an emphasis on local seafood, some of the favourites include stir-
fried salt-and-pepper squid, Goan fish curry, and Mediterranean
fish soup.

Enys Wartha

28 Market Jew Street, Penzance, Cornwall TR18 2HR   T: 01736 367375

A deli specializing in all things Cornish. Over two-thirds of the
produce stocked is home-produced by the owners, Michael and
Debbie Sculthorp-Wright. Specialities include free-range duck and
goose eggs, Cornish-recipe cakes, Cornish cheese and smoked
fish, and home-made pâtés and pies. There is a tearoom at the deli.

Riverford at Kitley

Yealmpton, nr Plymouth, Devon PL8 2LT   T: 01752 880925   w:www.riverford.co.uk

farm shop

A branch of the Riverford Farm Shop. See their main entry, page
106, for more information.

Emma B. Delicatessen

6 West Street, Somerton, Somerset TA11 7PS   T: 01458 273444

In the face of stiff competition from supermarkets, Emma has two plans – to try to source any foods her customers ask for and to make shopping fun, instead of a chore. The rich heritage of Somerset foods is well represented here, with over 90 varieties of cheese available at any one time.

Provender Delicatessen

3 Market Square, South Petherton, Somerset TA13 5BT   T: 01460 240681
w: www.provender.net

✉ **mail order**

The emphasis at Provender is on the produce of the West Country, so artisan cheeses, cider, air-dried ham and locally sourced smoked meat and fish are found here in profusion.

Hampton's Deli

1 Digbeth Street, Stow-on-the-Wold, Gloucestershire GL54 1BN   T: 01451 831733
w: www.hamptons-hampers.co.uk

A good selection of British cheeses, predominantly from small, less-well-known dairies, including the famous Stinking Bishop and the local single Gloucester. A range of French-style breads from a local bakery, home-baked raised pies and interesting oils and vinegars are all included. Tasting is encouraged.

Wellswood Village Pantry

11 Ilsham Road, Torquay, Devon TQ1 2JG   T: 01803 292315

A deli selling home-made, award-winning sausages made with local meats, locally baked bread and a great range of cheeses. The owner's policy on buying is 'if we can get it locally, we will'.

food facts

OLIVE OIL

The most prized type of olive oil is the result of the first cold pressing, known as extra-virgin oil. This can come in either filtered or unfiltered form; the unfiltered variety will have a slightly hazy look, while the filtered will be clear and bright. Many consider that the unfiltered oil has a purity of flavour lacking in the filtered oil. The most easily found olive oils come from Italy, Greece and Spain and the oils of each country tend to have common characteristics – Spanish oil is often fruity, with undertones of melon or even banana; Greek oils will have a more recognizable rich olive flavour, with a grassy taste, and Italian oils tend to be robust and peppery. Oils will change flavour to a degree when heated. Some purists believe that to heat fine extra-virgin oil is crass, and that it should only ever be consumed cold and raw. The olive oil industry seems to be mirroring the wine world; alongside the classic Mediterranean countries, great oils are now coming out of New World countries – Australia, the US (California), Chile and New Zealand. With lesser-known countries like Portugal and Tunisia also producing fine oils, there are so many to try.

SOUTH WEST   TOTNES

Riverford Farm Shop

Staverton, nr Totnes, Devon TQ9 6AF T: 01803 762523 W: www.riverford.co.uk
🌿 farm shop

Owned by the Watson family, the Riverford Farm Shop is a mecca for serious food lovers and aims to be 'the complete one-stop food shop'. The store sells a wide variety of products from bread to meat, to vegetables and dairy produce and even a selection of wines. The family aim to make their customers more aware of the source of their food and believe in stocking local organic produce where possible. Other products, such as olive oils and vinegars, which cannot be bought from local firms, are all acquired from fair-trade sources. There is a second shop in Yealmpton, near Plymouth, see page 104.

Porteath Bee Centre

nr Polzeath, Wadebridge, Cornwall PL27 6RA   T: 01208 863718
farm gate sales

Cornish honey available as clear, set or creamed; none of the types has been heat treated, as many commercial honeys are. Visitors are welcome on site, where there is a live bee exhibition.

Wells Stores at Peachcroft Farm

Twelveacre Drive, Abingdon, Oxfordshire OX14 2HP   T: 01235 535978

Wells Stores originally began as a cheese shop and still stocks an array of artisan British cheeses from small dairies. Alongside these are some great home-produced foods – free-range seasonal geese, fruit and vegetables (all produced on the farm), and even game that the owners shoot themselves. Bread from De Gustibus (see page 29), local apple juice and a host of deli items make this a treasure-trove.

Cake That

Unit 7, Bessemer Crescent, Rabans Lane Industrial Estate, Aylesbury, Buckinghamshire HP19 8TF   T: 01296 482730   W: www.cakethat.co.uk
mail order

Cake That won nine awards including 'Best Speciality from the South East' at the 2002 Great Taste Awards. Imagination is a key ingredient here – Chocolate Mash Potato, Chocolate Cherry Polenta and Chocolate Raspberry Cakes being just some of the delights on offer. The ingredients are fresh, often local and the cakes are created by a chef of 25 years experience. Visit the website to check out the range, ring to order your cake, and collect it when it has been baked.

Montezuma's Chocolate

15 Duke Street, Brighton BN1 1AH   T: 01273 324979   W: www.montezumas.co.uk
mail order

Montezuma's make wonderful hand-made chocolates. See the Super Hero box, page 108, for more information. There are also branches in Chichester (page 109) and Solihull (page 120).

FOOD HEROES OF BRITAIN

The Goods Shed

Station Road West, Canterbury, Kent CT2 8AN T: 01227 459153

farmers' markets

A six-day-a-week farmers' market, with local producers gathering to sell their food all under one roof. Meat – free-range and organic – cheeses, fish, beer, cider and bread are all on offer. There is an on-site bakery and a restaurant, where only foods from the stalls are used. The chef chooses his ingredients from the market each morning, and devises that day's menu accordingly. Closed Mondays.

super hero

SIMON AND HELEN PATTINSON, of Montezuma's Chocolate, Brighton, Chichester and Solihull (see pages 107, 109 and 120)

Although Montezuma's is a young company, having only been established in 2001, it has already received high-profile acclaim, including winning a Soil Association award. Though the chocolate is organic, this is not the only key to its success. Simon Pattinson and his wife Helen, both ex-lawyers, make it their mission to find the best raw materials with which to make their chocolates and they believe they have found them in the cocoa beans they buy from organic estates in the Dominican Republic. They then make everything by hand at their headquarters in Sussex, endlessly experimenting to find the best combinations of flavours and the percentages of cocoa solids that make the chocolates the perfect balance of sweetness and bitterness. Simon told me that there is a great deal of snobbery in the chocolate industry and that many people think that the higher the level of cocoa solids in a bar, the better the chocolate. Not so, he says. Too high a percentage and the chocolate is too bitter, making it necessary to add sweet fillings or sugar to alleviate this. The excess sugar then destroys the flavour of the chocolate. Simon has settled on 73% cocoa solids for his 'Very Dark' chocolate. After a great deal of testing and trying, he feels this is the balance that allows the chocolate taste to shine through without being overly bitter. And for the non-purist, he has added some wonderful flavourings – from chilli, cinnamon and cardamom to lime, apple and ground coffee. This is a food obsession at its best!

Montezuma's Chocolate

29 East Street, Chichester PO19 1HF   T: 01243 537385
w: www.montezumas.co.uk

✉ **mail order**

See the Super Hero box, opposite, for more information. There are branches in Brighton (page 107) and Solihull (page 120).

Trencherman and Turner

52 Grove Road, Little Chelsea, Eastbourne, East Sussex BN21 4UD   T: 01323 737535
w: www.loadedtable.com

Local cheeses, including 'Scrumpy Sussex', a variety made with local cider, Sussex 'Champagne', organic ham on the bone, bacon and free-range eggs from a local farm and unusual English wines – all great foods that you won't find in supermarkets – are available here.

The Food Halls

5–9 Packhorse Road, Gerrards Cross, Buckinghamshire SL9 7QA   T: 01753 893071
w: www.thefoodhalls.co.uk

This is the sister outlet of H P Jung, the baker (see page 25), but is also an alliance of several local companies – the great continental bread is here, but there is a charcuterie section, a butchery, a pâtisserie counter and even a Champagne bar. A foodie's delight.

The Silver Palate

3 Vaughan Road, Harpenden, Hertfordshire AL5 4HU   T: 01582 713722
w: www.hotolives.com

✉ **mail order**

Paul at The Silver Palate is a crusader for good food, and among the specialities at this large food emporium are Cypriot-style breads (including a halloumi bread), lots of fair-trade produce, artisan cheeses and their own-made Turkish delight. A huge olive selection is also on display.

FOOD HEROES OF BRITAIN

Roots Deli

33 Crendon Street, High Wycombe, Buckinghamshire HP13 6LJ   T: 01494 524243
w: www.rootsdeli.demon.co.uk

✉ **mail order**

Lots of British cheeses, olive oils to taste and a strong organic
section, too, make this deli well worth a visit.

Mrs Huddleston's

5 Dingle Dell, Leighton Buzzard, Bedfordshire LU7 3JL   T: 01525 381621
w: www.mrshuddleston.com

✉ **mail order**

Mrs Huddleston scooped two major awards at the 2002 Great Taste
Awards, including one for her English-wine jelly, made with New
Wave Wine (see page 150). She makes mulled-wine jelly, ginger-
wine jelly and a cider-and-sage jelly, all of which are great as
accompaniments to cold meats. Many of the ingredients Mrs
Huddleston uses are from local sources. Conserves, marmalades,
sauces and chutneys complete the range, and can be bought by
mail order, or from Fortnum & Mason in London or from some
branches of Waitrose. Mrs Huddleston's is a member of Slow Food.

The Chocolate Society

36 Elizabeth Street, London SW1W 9NZ   T: 0207 259 9222 OR 01423 322230
(MAIL ORDER)   W: www.chocolate.co.uk

✉ **mail order**

Hand-made truffles, Valrhona bars, and organic, single-bean bars
are available from The Chocolate Society's shop. There is a small
café selling chocolate brownies, ice cream and milkshakes – all
underpinned by the highest quality chocolate. See also the entry on
page 126.

El Rey Chocolate

123 Buspace Studios, Conlan Street, London W10 5AP   T: 020 7854 7770
W: www.elrey.co.uk

El Rey produce 'single-bean' chocolate, the chocolate equivalent of
vintage wine. Six different varieties are available from the darkest,
with a whopping 73.5% cocoa content, to white chocolate, which
still packs a good cocoa punch. Find El Rey at Waitrose and good
delis.

Forman & Field

30a Marshgate Lane, London E15 2NH   T: 020 8221 3939
W: www.formanandfield.com
✉ **mail order**

Forman and Field have brought together many traditional, small-
scale producers from around the country and are offering a selection
of high-quality foods with a luxurious feel. Some of the producers
are people we feature individually here, such as Seldom Seen Farm,
Richard Woodall and La Fromagerie (see pages 369, 327 and 66).
Forman and Field are offering a one-stop-shop for traditionally
produced foods.

Gourmet World

101 Lonsdale Road, London SW13 9DA   T: 020 8748 0125 W: www.gourmet-world.com
✉ **mail order**

Gourmet World seek out artisan producers around Europe, finding
the unusual and the small scale. Everything is high quality, produced
without artificial additives.

The Oil Merchant Ltd

47 Ashchurch Grove, London W12 9BU   T: 020 8740 1335
E: the_oil_merchant@compuserve.com
✉ **mail order**

The Oil Merchant is a specialist importer of single-estate olive oils
and oil-related products such as vinegars and salsas from small-

scale producers throughout Europe, Australia, New Zealand and South Africa. The Oil Merchant is a member of Slow Food.

| SOUTH EAST | LONDON |

Rococo Chocolates

321 Kings Road, London SW3 5EP T: 0207 352 5857 W: www.rococochocolates.com
✉ **mail order**

Among the hand-made chocolates – the pinnacle of luxury, made from chocolate with a very high cocoa content – you'll find organic 'artisan' bars of dark and milk chocolate. Rococo are keen to promote the planting of rare cocoa bean plants to conserve biodiversity, and their chocolate is fairly traded.

| SOUTH EAST | LONDON |

The Spice Shop

1 Blenheim Crescent, London W11 2EE T: 0207 221 4448
W: www.thespiceshop.co.uk
✉ **mail order**

The Spice Shop currently stocks around 2,500 different spices and blends. All the blends are mixed on the premises by Birgitt, the

super hero

THE HARDINGHAM FAMILY, of Alder Carr Farm, Needham Market
(see page 115)

This farm shop is committed to environmentally sensitive farming, leaving many areas wild and using biological pest control (introducing birds and insects to keep pests under control); as a result the farm is teeming with wildlife and is even a haven for the endangered otter. Alder Carr has an equally sensitive attitude to the foods sold in the shop. Home-grown fruits and vegetables are available and the farm shop is also brimming with locally produced and organic food. Their own fruit is used to make unique ice-cream, containing nothing but fruit, cream and sugar, with imaginative flavours such as rhubarb and ginger. Even the imported produce they stock is fairly traded – the family is keen to support small-scale farmers in other countries, too. Alder Carr even runs a farmers' market on site, with 25 stalls selling local foods including unpasteurized Jersey cream, free-range pork, game and organic meat, fruits, vegetables, juices and herbs.

owner, using the best-quality spices on the market. No salt, MSG, starch, wheat nuts or any artificial additives are used. Oils are also available, including the highly prized Argan oil from North Africa. This is a treasure-trove of the unusual.

Lymington Larder

7 St Thomas Street, Lymington, Hampshire SO41 9NA   T: 01590 676740
w: www.lymingtonlarder.co.uk

Charles Du Parc, the owner of this deli, sources most of his stock from the south of England, including almost all the cheeses he sells. The cheeses are mainly from small producers who make cheese using milk from their herds, and he has a good selection of ewes' and goats' milk cheeses – generally, Charles personally knows the producers that he buys from. Other foods available include meats and pâtés, and local free-range eggs.

The Grapevine Delicatessen

77 High Street, Odiham, Hampshire RG29 1LB   T: 01256 704466 (MAIL ORDER)
01256 701900 (DELI)   w: www.grapevine-gourmet.co.uk
✉ **mail order**

Foods from all over the continent and the Far East, but also specialities from closer to home, sourced from specialist growers and producers. Lots of home-made food, too.

County Delicacies

35–37 St Mary's Butts, Reading, Berkshire RG1 2LS   T: 0118 957 4653

A deli keen to support small local producers, sourcing mainly from southern England. Berkshire ham on the bone, local cheeses and some interesting speciality breads are the most popular products.

Angela's Delicatessen

The Square, Yarmouth, Isle of Wight PO41 0NS   T: 01983 761196

A deli with a really wide scope of produce, from British artisan cheeses to organic smoked salmon, free-range local chicken, local game and dry-cured bacon. The shop is even open at 7am on Sundays to provide freshly baked bread, croissants and pains au chocolat.

EAST ANGLIA CLEY-NEXT-THE-SEA

Picnic Fayre Delicatessen

The Old Forge, Cley-next-the-Sea, Norfolk NR25 7AP T: 01263 740587
w: www.picnicfayre.co.uk

There are some quirky items available at Picnic Fayre – lavender focaccia bread and perry vinegar to name just two. The accent is on East Anglian produce, with Norfolk free-range bacon and Norfolk fruit wines heading the list.

EAST ANGLIA COLCHESTER

The Dedham Gourmet

High Street, Dedham, Colchester, Essex CO7 6HA T: 01206 323623
w: www.dedham-gourmet.co.uk

Though they specialize in artisan British cheeses, of which there are 40 or 50 to choose from, there is still plenty of regional East Anglian fare here, with local jams, honeys and fruit juices all well represented.

EAST ANGLIA COLCHESTER

H Gunton

81–83 Crouch Street, Colchester, Essex CO3 3EZ T: 01206 572200
w: www.guntons.co.uk

A deli with a mind-boggling array of cheeses – over 100, with some hard-to-find varieties such as Single Gloucester. Alongside the British farmhouse cheeses, continental cheeses are well represented. There is also an interesting selection of cooked meats, such as home-cooked hams, ox tongue, kassler and cabanos, and tuna salami is available.

EAST ANGLIA COLCHESTER

The Vineyard Delicatessen

23–24 Eld Lane, Colchester, Essex CO1 1LS T: 01206 573363
w: www.vineyard-deli.co.uk

Iain Wicks is so passionate about food that he even makes much of the produce in his shop himself, including pesto, pickles and chutneys and home-cooked meats. All are hand-made in small batches and his red onion marmalade recently won a Great Taste Award. Overall, he reckons he stocks over 200 products from East Anglia, including wines, although he's also got some interesting foods from Italy, too.

EAST ANGLIA — ELY

La Hogue Farm Shop and Delicatessen

La Hogue Farm Foods, Chippenham, Ely, Cambridgeshire CB7 5PZ T: 01638 751128
W: www.lahogue.co.uk

farm shop

An enormous array of home-produced and local produce – fruit, vegetables and salads, free-range meats, farmhouse cheeses, and game (in season) shot on the farm. The farm kitchen produces some really good breads, cakes and pastries and ready meals, and the farm shop has an off-licence, selling wines and local ales.

EAST ANGLIA — IPSWICH

Alder Carr Farm

superhero

Needham Market, Ipswich, Suffolk IP6 8LX T: 01449 720820
W: www.aldercarrfarm.co.uk

farm shop **farmers' markets**

Committed to environmentally sensitive farming, Alder Carr Farm Shop sells a good selection of their own and locally produced products. See the Super Hero box, page 112, for more information.

EAST ANGLIA — IPSWICH

Fruits of Suffolk

Mill House, Stone Street, Crowfield, Ipswich, Suffolk IP6 9SZ T: 01449 760397

farmers' markets

Hand-made preserves and chutneys, using local ingredients, are made in small batches, which has a significant effect on the flavour – they are cooked for less time, and so remain tastier. Some unusual jams are available – greengage, damson and Victoria plum, along with apple chutney and spicy plum chutney. Old-fashioned lemon curd is also available, made from fresh lemons, pure butter and free-range eggs. Available from Woodbridge, Needham (Alder Carr), South Lopham and Tivetshall farmers' markets.

The Manningtree Delicatessen

21 The High Street, Manningtree, Essex CO11 1AG   T: 01206 395071

delivery service   **mail order**

Simon of The Manningtree Deli is passionate about good food, and is keen to stock local produce – he tends to know all his suppliers very well and has local wines, Suffolk bacon, and fresh fish from Lowestoft, with live lobsters to choose from. The choice of cheeses is impressive – around 120 different types, of which about three-quarters are British.

EAST ANGLIA   ROMFORD

Hoo Hing

Commercial Centre, Freshwater Road, Chadwell Heath, Romford, Essex RM8 1RX
T: 020 8548 3636   w: www.hoohing.com

mail order

As far as Eastern ingredients go, if it's not available at Hoo Hing, then it probably doesn't exist!

EAST ANGLIA   SAFFRON WALDEN

Chisnalls Delicatessen

3 Market Walk, Saffron Walden, Essex CB10 1JZ   T: 01799 528239

The shopping experience at Chisnalls is described as 'interactive' – lots of customer tastings, and advice and help from the staff. All the usual deli items here, with a really good choice of farmhouse cheeses.

EAST ANGLIA   SWAVESEY

Swayfen Herb Farm

Swayfen House, Rose and Crown Road, Swavesey, Cambridgeshire CB4 5RB
T: 01954 267111   w: www.swayfen.co.uk

mail order

Home-grown, unsprayed herbs form the basis for many of the products here. Extra-virgin olive oil, traditional vinegars and fresh herbs are combined for a flavourful range of condiments, dressings and salads. Swayfen Herb Farm was the proud recipient of three Great Taste Awards in 2002.

Didlington Manor

Didlington, nr Thetford, Norfolk IP26 5AT   T: 01842 878673

✉ **mail order**

Unpasteurized single-crop honey, from hives placed in some of the Royal Parks of London, where bees gather nectar from aboretums rich in unusual tree varieties.

Thorpeness Village Store

Peace Place, Thorpeness, Suffolk IP16 4PL   T: 01728 454464

🚚 **delivery service**

Thorpeness Village Store is run with a commitment to locally produced, high-quality food, and to maintaining a sense of community in the village. Among the produce the owner stocks are her own organically grown vegetables, local cheeses and bread baked in the village. She also does a free delivery round for those customers unable to get to the shop.

Tastebuds

The Street, Earl Soham, Woodbridge, Suffolk IP13 7RT   T: 01728 685557

The foods available at Tastebuds are entirely British in origin, from East Anglia wherever possible, and Lucie Walker, the owner, makes great 'takeaway' foods from local produce – Suffolk ham and hickory-cured pork from locally reared pigs, fish cakes made from fish caught at Lowestoft, and organic, locally grown fruits and vegetables. There's local game available, and even bottled beer from the brewery next door.

The Original Farmers Market Shop

3 Market Street, Bakewell, Derbyshire DE45 1HG   T: 01629 815814

🥄 **farm shop**

Many people love to shop at farmers' markets but find that the markets are not frequent enough. The Original Farmers Market Shop in Bakewell seeks to be a permanent farmers' market, with all the stock coming from small-scale producers within a 35-mile radius.

Rare-breed free-range pork, local game, home-baked breads and locally smoked meats and fish are all available – the range is huge.

The Granary

Hungerford, Craven Arms, Shropshire SY7 9HG   T: 01584 841027
w: www.corvedale.com

A great place to find the best produce from Shropshire, Herefordshire and Worcestershire, The Granary offers Neal's Yard Creamery, Lightwood and Anstey's cheeses (see pages 71 and 76 and the Super Hero box on page 75), Maynard's bacon, Corvedale lamb and chutneys, jams, beer and fruit gins. There is a tearoom on site.

Ceci Paolo

21 High Street, Ledbury, Herefordshire HR8 1DS   T: 01531 632976
w: www.cecipaolo.com

A deli for the adventurous home cook, the owner, Pat Harrison, aims to stock the best ingredients for serious cooks. Mediterranean, oriental and Australian delectables sit next to home-made dips and purées, regional cheeses and locally grown salads and herbs.

The Chocolate Gourmet

16 Castle Street, Ludlow, Shropshire SY8 1AT   T: 01584 879332   w: www.chocmail.co.uk
✉ **mail order**

Alongside all the delicious truffles and filled chocolates, The Chocolate Gourmet has a great range of couverture chocolate, with many single-origin, 'grand cru' bars from Valrhona, Michel Cluizel and El Rey. These are fantastic very-high-cocoa-content chocolates, made with the very best beans.

Deli on the Square

4 Church Street, Ludlow, Shropshire SY8 1AP   T: 01584 877353
w: www.justmustard.com

In the centre of Ludlow, the legendary 'foodie's' paradise, is this deli selling great local produce, including fresh foods such as free-range ham on the bone, organic smoked salmon and unpasteurized cheeses. A subsidiary company, Just Mustard, is part of the deli, allowing the owner, Tracey Colley, to indulge her love of mustard – a huge selection is available, from the well known to the esoteric.

MIDLANDS MARKET RASEN

Special Edition Continental Chocolate

Willingham Hall, Market Rasen, Lincolnshire LN8 3RH T: 01673 844073 OR
0800 316 0834 E: willingham.rasen@virgin.net
✉ **mail order**

Good-quality couverture chocolate can be found here, with dark chocolate at 70% cocoa solids and white chocolate with 30% cocoa solids. Special Edition are particulary interesting for their unusual hand-made chocolates; the double-cream truffles recently won a Great Taste Award and there are all kinds of unusual combinations to try, such as dark chocolate with chilli or cranberry and nutmeg. For those with nut allergies, this chocolate shop is paradise – nothing contains nuts. Available from the shop or by mail order.

MIDLANDS NOTTINGHAM

The Cheese Shop

6 Flying Horse Walk, Nottingham NG1 2HN T: 0115 941 9114

With a range of over 200 cheeses, The Cheese Shop specializes in British farmhouse cheese, mainly unpasteurized, with ewes'- and goats'-milk cheeses well represented. Lots of local deli goods can be found here, too, along with Italian specialities. Tasting of the cheeses and other foods is encouraged.

MIDLANDS NUNEATON

Kim's Cakes

39, Shanklin Drive, Weddington, Nuneaton, Warwickshire CV10 0BA T: 02476 351421
E: colin.a.bickley@btinternet.com
🛒 **farmers' markets** ✉ **farm gate sales**

A one-woman cottage industry, Kim bakes a staggering range of 38 different cakes and pickles, almost all organic. Using ingredients procured as locally as possible, with fruit she has picked herself, she also makes jams and chutneys. Everything is laboriously made by hand and when she arrives at her farmers' market stalls, the cakes and scones are so fresh that they are often still warm. Find Kim at Stratford, Leamington Spa, Warwick and Solihull farmers' markets, or call her to place an order.

Plantation Cottage Herbs

1 Plantation Cottage, Bricklehampton, Pershore, Worcestershire WR10 3HL
T: 01386 861507   w: www.plantation-cottage.com

farmers' markets

Locally grown apples and home-grown, pesticide-free herbs are the
foundations of the traditional 'drip-bag' process fruit jellies and herb
vinegars sold here. The vinegars start with a basis of local cider
vinegar, and the jellies range from the traditional mint or quince, to
the unusual jalapeño pepper. All made in small batches, and
available from lots of farmers' markets, including Worcester,
Stratford-upon-Avon and Mosley.

Meg Rivers

Blackwell Business Park, Blackwell, Shipston-on-Stour, Warwickshire CV36 4PE
T: 01608 682858   w: www.megrivers.com

mail order

Cakes like your grandmother used to make (if you were very lucky!).
Julian Day says their cakes are 'nothing grand or exotic' – but he
simply makes the best traditional cakes you have ever tasted,
through his attention to detail and the quality of his ingredients.
Favourites include ginger cake (with stem ginger) and festival cake –
a riot of fruits and nuts. All available mail order, or you can join the
Cake Club – an annual subscription fee gets you a monthly delicious
surprise through the post.

Montezuma's Chocolate   **super hero**

9 Poplar Arcade, Touchwood, Solihull B91 3HG   T: 0121 711 3720
w: www.montezumas.co.uk

mail order

Montezuma's make wonderful hand-made chocolates. See the
Super Hero box, page 108, for more information. There are
branches in Brighton (page 107) and Chichester (page 109).

Greenfields Farm Shop

Station Road, Donnington, Telford, Shropshire TF2 8JY T: 01952 677345

farm shop **box scheme**

A farm shop filled with local produce – home-produced fruit and vegetables, local cheese, local beef (hung for three weeks), cakes, dry-cured bacon and even wild boar.

Berrow Honey

The Berrow, Martley, Worcester WR6 6PQ T: 01886 821237
W: www.theberrow.co.uk/honey

farm shop **mail order**

Honey from the old native British Black bee, gathering nectar from wild flowers and heather. Available mail order, or from several local farmers' markets, including Teme Valley – call for details.

Granthams of Alderley Edge

68 Heyes Lane, Alderley Edge, Cheshire SK9 7LB T: 01625 583286
E: mrmikegrantham@aol.com

This traditional family grocer's has developed into a great deli. Alongside the fresh fruit and vegetables are local dry-cured bacon, 150 different kinds of cheese, home-cooked hams and locally reared chicken. Customers are welcome to taste many of the products.

Cartmel Sticky Toffee Pudding Co. Ltd

Cartmel Village Shop, The Square, Cartmel, Cumbria LA11 6QB T: 01539 536201
W: www.stickytoffeepudding.co.uk

shop **mail order**

The home of gooey, home-made comfort food! Available from the shop, by mail order or from Fortnum & Mason and some branches of Waitrose.

The Organic Pudding Co. Ltd

Cartmel, Grange-over-Sands, Cumbria LA11 7SS   T: 01539 536330
w: www.wildpuddings.com

✉ **mail order**

With a clutch of awards from Great Taste and the Soil Association,
the Organic Pudding Co. offers serious organic luxury – sticky
toffee, chocolate fudge, tangy lemon, summer fruits and bread-and-
butter puddings, all made with copious quantities of fruit and cream
but no additives or preservatives. There are also vegan and gluten-
free puddings. These delights are available from many independent
shops or by mail order. The Organic Pudding Co. is part of
Howbarrow Organic Farm (see page 234).

1657 Chocolate House   **super hero**

54 Branthwaite Brow, Kendal, Cumbria LA9 4TX   T: 01539 740702
w: www.thechocolatehouse.co.uk

This is not just a chocolate shop, but an entire chocolate experience
– 395 varieties are available, all hand made. See the Super Hero
box, below, for more information.

super hero

JOY MOORE, of 1657 Chocolate House, Kendal (above)

Joy, the owner of 1657 Chocolate House, is truly passionate about chocolate.
Her family owns a cocoa plantation in Trinidad and she has 144 trees there
herself. She is driven by the need to conserve the biodiversity of cocoa plants
and her chocolate shop in Kendal is both a shrine to and an information centre
for the history of chocolate. This is not just a chocolate shop, but an entire
chocolate experience in which to immerse oneself – 395 varieties of chocolate
are available, all hand-made with the most exceptional raw ingredients, and the
choice of boxes and wrappings is staggering. Upstairs is a café, where 32 types
of drinking chocolate are served, alongside chocolate cakes and gâteaux made
with the same care and attention that goes into the chocolates downstairs.

Low Sizergh Barn Farm Shop

Low Sizergh Farm, Sizergh, Kendal, Cumbria LA8 8AE   T: 01539 560426
w: www.low-sizergh-barn.co.uk

🥄 **farm shop**

Low Sizergh Farm is an organic, family-run dairy farm, with its own
farm shop and café. The focus is on local and regional foods, from
small-scale producers. There is a big range of British farmhouse
cheese, including an organic Lancashire made with the farm's own
milk, home-grown organic vegetables, local meat and game, home-
produced free-range eggs and traditional Cumbrian baking. The
staff know the stories behind the produce, as they personally know
many of the producers. The tearooms overlook the milking parlour,
so diners can see the cows being milked, and there is also a farm
trail. A one-stop-shop, with plenty more besides.

Country Fare

Dale Foot, Mallerstang, Kirkby Stephen, Cumbria CA17 4JT   T: 01768 372519
E: countryfareuk@aol.com

🍽 **farmers' markets**

Country Fare won two Great Taste Awards in 2002, most notably for
their pickled damsons – local damsons, pickled in vinegar, spices
and brown sugar, according to an old recipe. The small staff of
farmers' wives and daughters at Country Fare make a vast range of
cakes, from fruit cakes, gingerbread and parkin to flapjacks and tray
bakes – they simply make whatever they like to eat themselves.
There are even gluten-free cakes and some suitable for diabetics.
Find the produce at Kendal, Orton, Carlisle, Brough and Liverpool
farmers' markets.

Seasoned Pioneers

Unit 101 Summers Road, Brunswick Business Park, Liverpool L3 4BJ
T: 0800 068 2348   w: www.seasonedpioneers.co.uk

✉ **mail order**

Whatever kind of spice you need, Seasoned Pioneers will have it,
often in organic form. The house blends are revered by many food
writers for their authenticity.

deFINE Food and Wine

Chester Road, Sandiway, nr Northwich, Cheshire CW8 2NH   T: 01606 882101
E: office@definefoodandwine.com

'If it's good, and it's British, we'll stock it!' the owner of deFINE, Jon Campbell told me. The range of products, such as the British artisan cheeses, comes from sources as local as possible, with Jon demanding that the small producers he buys from exhibit 'good production practices'.

Wholesome Food Company

Dobbies Garden Centre, Blackpool Road, Clifton, nr Preston, Lancashire PR4 0XL
T: 01772 672027

Not just a deli, this is more like a large food hall. Simon Cunningham, the owner, stocks fully traceable meats, sourced from one local farm, cheeses from small dairies in the north-west, and smoked foods from not just one, but two local smokehouses.

Godfrey C Williams & Son

9–11 The Square, Corner House, Sandbach, Cheshire CW11 1AP   T: 01270 762817
E: godfreycwilliams@supanet.com

Mr Williams has been busy experimenting with a local cheesemaker, and between them they have come up with blue Cheshire, which is a rare find. Other goodies include home-cured bacon, locally baked bread and the coffee beans that are roasted on the premises. Provenance is a priority – Mr Williams states that 'we like to know the whole story behind a food before we stock it'.

The Hollies Farm Shop

Forest Road, Little Budworth, nr Tarporley, Cheshire CW6 9ES   T: 01829 760414
E: holliesfarmshop@aol.com
➍ **farm shop**

Twice a year, in March and October, the Cowap family hold a food festival at their farm shop, inviting their suppliers (often small-scale, regional producers) to come along and speak to the customers about the produce. The emphasis is on artisan producers, 'anything that's a little bit different', and customers are encouraged to taste the foods. Fruit and vegetables grown on the family farm are always available, freshly picked, and Edward Cowap says the joy of this is that with the changing seasons there is always something new being harvested.

NORTH WEST   ULVERSTON

Demel's Sri Lankan Chutneys

The Barn, Gawithfields, Arradfoot, Ulverston, Cumbria LA12 7SL   T: 01229 861012
w: www.demels.speciality-foods.com
✉ **mail order**

Chutneys and pickles made to old Sri Lankan recipes that have been handed down through the generations of this family.

food facts

CHOCOLATE

Fine chocolate is a very different food from the confectionery available in most corner shops. Chocolate should be a combination of both cocoa solids and cocoa butter extracted from the cocoa bean. Most well-known brands contain a remarkably low percentage of cocoa-solids – as little as 25% – and in some cases hardly qualify as chocolate at all, since the butter content is often mixed with other fats. Good quality chocolate should have at least a 50% cocoa-solid content, and much of the rest should be pure cocoa butter. The best-known cocoa bean types are Criollo, Forastero and Trinitario, which is a hybrid of the first two. The best, Criollo, comes from Central America, with the very finest believed to be grown in Venezuela and, like so many of the finest foodstuffs, it is in danger of dying out – it's expensive, relatively low yielding, and not particularly disease resistant. There are, however, chocolate shops that offer chocolate made from these magical beans; some even stock 'single-bean variety' chocolate – made from the highest quality beans, from one cocoa estate, not blended with cheaper beans. The resulting chocolate is a revelation, but beware – buying from the chocolate shops we've listed will ruin you for cheaper varieties forever.

The Chocolate Society

Clay Pit Lane, Roecliffe, nr Boroughbridge, North Yorkshire YO51 9LS   T: 01423 322230
w: www.chocolate.co.uk

✉ **mail order**

Hand-made truffles, Valrhona bars, and organic, single-bean bars.
This is the home of chocolate obsession! See also the London
branch, page 110.

Campbell Lindley's

49 Cold Bath Road, Harrogate, North Yorkshire HG2 0NL   T: 01423 564270
w: www.campbelllindleys.co.uk

Martin Lindley of Campbell Lindley's says that Harrogate citizens are
very loyal to Yorkshire produce, and so his shop is filled with foods
from small-scale, regional producers. Before opening the deli, he and
his partner spent three years researching the local produce available
and the fruit of their labours is now visible on the shelves of the shop.

The Rocky Valley Deli

19 Grove Promenade, Ilkley, West Yorkshire LS29 8AF   T: 01943 607681
w: www.rockyvalleydeli.co.uk

The aim of Sarah and Simon Lawson is to make shopping a happy
experience, rather than a chore, and the staff at Rocky Valley are all

super hero

JIM TYNAN, of The Kitchen and Food Hall, Portlaoise (page 130)

'Some people say we're nitpicking,' says Jim Tynan of The Kitchen. He's talking
about the attention to detail when it comes to stocking the shop – every
ingredient of every product is looked at and, if it falls short of the high standards
employed here, the product is rejected. Irish artisan products are what The
Kitchen is all about – cheese from small dairies, traditionally smoked salmon,
classic Irish soda breads – everything is hand-made. Jim's motto is simple:
quoting Oscar Wilde, he says, 'I have simple tastes – I only want the best.'

enthusiastic and knowledgeable about the produce on the shelves. Yorkshire and Cumbrian goods are well represented here, all coming from small-scale, passionate producers. Discussion and tasting is a big part of the experience of shopping at Rocky Valley.

Garth Cottage Nursery

Newby Wiske, Northallerton, North Yorkshire DL7 9ET T: 01609 777233
E: mail@garth-cottage.fsnet.co.uk
🖳 farmers' markets

Over 340 different culinary herbs are grown at Garth Cottage Nursery, with a staggering range of 46 varieties of mint alone (including the chocolate mint, great sprinkled on hot chocolate!). Paul and Chris Turner are constantly increasing their collection of herbs, searching abroad for new varieties. All the herbs are grown without any pesticides. Cold-infused herb oils, vinegars, marinades and salad dressings are also available. The nursery is not open to the public – the produce is available from farmers' markets and food events in the north; call for details.

The Garden House

Anvil Square, Reeth, nr Richmond, North Yorkshire DL11 6TE T: 01748 884188
W: www.gardenhousepottery.co.uk
🛒 shop ✉ mail order

Jane Davies specializes in traditional damson cheese, a regional speciality in North Yorkshire and Cumbria. Contrary to its name, this is not a dairy product but is more closely related to a preserve. Made with just damsons and sugar, it is a very intensely fruity, set conserve, and can be eaten as a dessert, or as a 'tracklement' with meat and game. An added bonus is that the damson cheese comes in a lovely pottery container, made by Jane's husband. Jane won the prestigious Small Producers Award in conjunction with Waitrose in 2002, for 'excellence and innovation in food production'.

Northumbrian Hamper

25b Main Street, Seahouses, Northumberland NE68 7RE T: 01665 720999
W: www.thenorthumbrianhamper.co.uk

This deli sells plenty of native Northumbrian produce but the real speciality is the kipper stotty – local kipper fillets in a soft bun.

The Chocolate Room

529 Lisburn Road, Belfast BT9 7GS   T: 028 9066 2110
W: www.thechocolateroom.com

People in Belfast who are serious about chocolate need to get themselves down to The Chocolate Room. Many of the chocolates are sourced direct from the makers, from Ireland, Belgium, France and England, and there are many brands that you will struggle to find elsewhere. With over 150 different types of chocolate and hot chocolate drinks made with the finest melted chocolate, not powder, this is heaven for chocoholics.

Feasts

39 Dublin Road, Belfast BT2 7HD   T: 028 9033 2787

Feasts has all the usual deli foods – oils, vinegars, charcuterie and chocolates – but it specializes in Irish farmhouse cheeses – all the classic, award-winning Irish cheeses and those from small, less-well-known dairies can be found here. Feasts is also the first establishment in Ireland to be making their own biscotti.

The Olive Tree Company

353 Ormeau Road, Belfast BT7 3GL   T: 028 9064 8898
W: www.olivetreecompany.com

The aim of the Olive Tree Company is to stock foods that you won't find anywhere else – there is a great choice of olives, an ever-growing selection of artisan cheeses, oils and vinegars and some local produce.

The Belfry Deli and Café

4–5 Church Lane, Coleraine, Co. Londonderry BT52 1AG   T: 028 7034 2906 OR
0800 3280212 (FREEPHONE)   E: paul@thebelfrydeli.fsnet.co.uk

Plenty of Irish produce graces the shelves of this deli, accompanied by English and continental delicacies. Dulse cheese, made a few miles away, dry-cured bacon and hams from Limerick, artisan Irish cheeses, and home-made wheaten, potato and soda breads are all popular.

McCambridges of Galway Ltd

38–39 Shop Street, Galway   T: 091 563470   W: www.mccambridges.com

McCambridges has great wines, own-baked breads and own-grown soft fruit in season, alongside all the other deli foods stocked, but a big attraction are the cheeses – over 100 at any one time, many of which are from small-scale Irish dairies.

Country Choice

25 Kenyon Street, Nenagh, Tipperary   T: 067 32596   W: www.countrychoice.ie

This is the sort of shop that gourmands dream about – packed full of fantastic artisan Irish produce, with farmhouse cheeses ripened in the maturing room on site and fresh produce from local farms and gardens. There is also plenty of continental deli fare to choose from, all of it out of the ordinary. The café at the back of the shop serves home-made local foods like beef and Guinness pie and bacon and cabbage, with great coffee, fruit crumbles, rich chocolate cakes or home-made scones and jam for dessert.

Farmer Direct

New Ross, Co. Wexford   T: 051 420816

Jimmy Ryan can tell you where everything comes from at Farmer Direct – he'll tell you exactly who grew, reared or made whatever product you care to point at. Local vegetables arrive fresh each day, as does the locally baked bread. Milk and butter, cheese, bacon and meat, eggs, ice cream and fruit juices all come from the best local producers.

Aines Chocolates

Oliver Plunkett Street, Oldcastle, Co. Meath   T: 049 854 2769
W: www.aineschocolates.com
✉ **mail order**

The starting point of Aines is the best couverture chocolate, often a blend of varieties to get just the right balance. Everything is hand-made and only natural ingredients are used – fresh butter and cream. This attention to detail has paid off – Aines Chocolates have won a gold Great Taste Award and a Good Housekeeping Award.

REPUBLIC OF IRELAND   PORTLAOISE

The Kitchen and Food Hall   super hero

Hynds Square, Portlaoise, Co. Laois   T: 0502 62061

Jim Tynan of The Kitchen and Food Hall prides himself on the high standards he sets for all the produce he stocks. See the Super Hero box, page 126, for more information.

REPUBLIC OF IRELAND   SLIGO

Tir na nOg

Grattan Street, Sligo   T: 071 62752

A treasure-trove of the best local produce, with fruit and vegetables, artisan cheeses, organic eggs and honey.

super hero

IAIN MCALLISTER, of Gourmet's Lair, Inverness (see page 132)

When I asked Iain at the Gourmet's Lair what the driving force behind his deli is, he replied, 'Above all, to provide a shopping experience that makes you drool and is great fun.' On his buying policy, he categorically states: 'If it's the best, or the most traditional, I want it.' So what will you find in the Gourmet's Lair? The first thing you'll notice is the cheese – a dizzying number of different kinds, 171 at the last count, and a great many of those are Scottish, from small artisan cheesemakers. There is a defined sense of luxury here – the best balsamics, oils, truffles, foie gras and caviar can be found, all presented without snobbery but with a sense of humour and fun. Iain laughs at what could be seen as an incongruous selection of products – 'Where else in the world would you find Charlie Barley's Stornoway Black Pudding sitting next to white winter truffles?' but says that is all part of the experience – 'our aim is to have as much fun as possible sourcing, learning the background to the foods, tasting and selling'. This approach means that customers will always find the unusual and the surprising at the Gourmet's Lair.

Isle of Colonsay Apiaries

Isle of Colonsay, Argyle PA61 7YR   T: 01951 200365   W: www.colonsay.org.uk

✉ **mail order**

Wildflower honey is difficult to produce in Britain – so much land here is taken up with commercial crops, such as rapeseed, and hedgerows and field margins have been eroded. Given a choice between wild flowers and commercial agricultural crops, a bee will head for the agricultural fields, as they generally contain more nectar. What makes Colonsay wildflower honey so unique is that the bees that make it have no choice – there are only flowers and herbs for them to collect from. While this means that they make less honey overall, it also means that the flavour of the honey they do produce has an unrivalled depth and complexity. It is completely different from honeys based on commercial crops and is available by mail order.

Plaisir du Chocolat

251–253 Canongate, Edinburgh EH8 8BQ and also at 270 Canongate, Edinburgh, EH8 8HA   T: 0131 556 9524 (NO. 251–253); 0131 556 0112 (NO. 270)
W: www.plaisirduchocolat.co.uk

✉ **mail order**

A shrine to the cocoa bean, Plaisir du Chocolat offers hand-made chocolates and the best couverture money can buy.

Valvona & Crolla

19 Elm Row, Edinburgh EH7 4AA   T: 0131 556 6066   W: www.valvonacrolla.com

✉ **mail order**

Valvona & Crolla are renowned throughout the country, not just in Edinburgh, for their astonishing array of continental produce, all offered with a distinctive Italian flair.

super hero

JENNY AND TEIFI DAVIES, of Llwynhelyg Farm Shop, Llandysul (see page 134)

Recently awarded the honour of Best Farm Shop in Wales by the National Farmers Union, Llwynhelyg is a celebration of the freshest and most interesting produce that West Wales offers. Jenny and Teifi Davies are tireless campaigners for Welsh producers, and encourage customers to see the benefits of spending their money with local businesses. They have seen the far-reaching repercussions of local businesses closing – affecting not just the owners of that business, but the whole local network of firms, and are keen to support small producers. This attitude makes for a shop brimming with locally grown fruit and vegetables, meat reared on nearby farms, Welsh farmhouse cheese, milk, cream and butter, home-made chutneys, jams, cakes, pies … the list goes on and on. There is nothing in the shop that Jenny hasn't tasted – she can tell you everything about what's on the shelves, and her enthusiasm is infectious.

SCOTLAND   FINDHORN BAY

Phoenix Community Stores

The Park, Findhorn Bay, Moray IV36 3TZ   T: 01309 690110
w: www.findhorn.org/store

This award-winning community-run shop has a great deli-style section alongside the books and local crafts it sells. An organic bakery on site provides fresh bread, made with local flour, and local cheeses, vegetables and honey are available, as is organic smoked salmon from the Western Isles.

SCOTLAND   INVERNESS

Gourmet's Lair

8 Union Street, Inverness IV1 1PL   T: 01463 225151   w: www.gourmetslair.co.uk

A delicatessen specializing in the unusual and surprising, Gourmet's Lair offers the luxurious, the original and the best; see the Super Hero box, page 130, for more information.

Wholesome Food Company

Dobbies Garden Centre, Lasswade, Midlothian EH18 1AZ T: 0131 663 9204

This food hall functions as a permanent farmers' market, showcasing meats, cheeses, vegetables and deli foods from local producers.

Gillies Fine Foods

Cromartie Buildings, Strathpeffer, Ross-shire IV14 9DG T: 01997 420042
w: www.gilliesfinefoods.co.uk

✉ **mail order**

All kinds of unusual condiments and the like – rowan jelly, lavender vinegar, cinnamon mustard, and Glenferlie, an own-recipe hot toddy, to name just a fraction of the range. Almost all the ingredients are either home-grown or locally produced and there is a purity about the flavours of the products that is in sharp contrast with much of the over-processed food available today. Available direct from the shop (although a move is planned for the end of 2003 – check out the website), or by mail order.

The Old Welsh Cellar

19 Pier Street, Aberystwyth, Ceredigion SY23 2LJ T: 01970 627121

Andy Tatch is proud of his range of chilli sauces: at three whole shelves, he believes his selection is the biggest in Wales. Some are so ferocious that he is still working his way up to trying them. Among the unusual imports he also has some good Welsh foods – three local honeys, Welsh cheeses and wines and local mead.

The Treehouse

14 Baker Street, Aberystwyth, Ceredigion SY23 2BJ T: 01970 615791
w: www.aber-treehouse.com

A great example of local produce staying local – Jane Burnham at The Treehouse grows organic fruit and vegetables, which she stocks in her organic shop, and uses in her organic restaurant. There is also lots of local produce stocked alongside her own, and Jane can happily and confidently tell customers the provenance of everything in the shop.

FOOD HEROES OF BRITAIN

Wendy Brandon Handmade Preserves

Felin Wen, Boncath, Pembrokeshire SA37 0JR   T: 01239 841568
W: www.wendybrandon.co.uk

🛒 **shop**   ✉ **mail order**

Although this is a very small company, the range of jams, jellies and
chutneys produced here currently stands at about 150 different
varieties. All are hand-made in small batches, and there is a happy
meeting of tradition and imagination – Victorian-sounding rose-petal
jelly and damson cheese are accompanied by Indian-inspired
chutneys and orange with molasses and rum marmalade. Fruit
vinegars and unusual jams (Warwickshire Drooper Yellow Plum jam!)
complete the range.

Popty Cara

Lawrenny, Pembrokeshire SA68 0PN   T: 01646 651690
W: www.poptycara.co.uk

🛒 **farmers' markets**

Popty Cara have won many Great Taste awards for their hand-made
cakes, including Bara Brith (traditional fruit bread) made to a 200-
year-old recipe. Local ingredients predominate, and all the cakes are
preservative free. Their own recipe black sticky ginger cake recently
won a silver medal at the Great Taste Awards.

Llwynhelyg Farm Shop   super hero

Sarnau, Llandysul, Ceredigion SA44 6QU   T: 01239 811079
E: llwynhelygfarm@aol.com

A truly outstanding farm shop, Llwynhelyg offers the freshest and
most interesting produce from West Wales; see the Super Hero box
page 132, for more information.

Blas Ar Fwyd

Heol yr Orsaf, Llanrwst, Conwy, North Wales LL26 0BT   т: 01492 640215
w: www.blasarfwyd.com

An award-winning Welsh deli with a real commitment to local and
Welsh produce. Blas Ar Fwyd holds the widest range of Welsh
cheeses and Welsh alcoholic drinks in the country, and much of the
fresh produce is home-made.

Foxy's Deli

7 Royal Buildings, Penarth, Vale of Glamorgan CF64 3ED   т: 02920 251666
E: foxysiany@aol.com

Having fulfilled a long-held dream to run a deli, Foxy is busy
gathering Welsh produce to fill the shelves; he strongly believes that
the quality of the local produce is excellent and has some interesting
Welsh cheeses and Glamorgan sausages available.

DELICATESSENS ...

CHAPTER

4

This book has a clear bias towards traditional foodstuffs, foods made with time and thoughtfulness, with respect for old recipes and old methods and with respect for our heritage. The focus will be the same in this section, and I've listed makers of cider and perry, real ale, pure juices pressed from the fruits of the producer's own orchards, vineyards fighting for the recognition of English and Welsh wines and even fruit wine and mead producers.

I recall reading a less than complimentary remark about English wine in an edition of Robert Parker's *Wine Buyer's Guide*. Robert Parker is by far and away the most influential wine writer in the world. He said that our country was too far north and too wet and windy to be taken seriously as a wine-growing nation. Quite humorous he was about it. Sitting, writing this, during an unbelievably hot summer and beginning to think that maybe our climate is changing, I wonder if he is right – particularly when you consider somewhere like the Nyetimber Vineyard in Sussex (see page 152). Their sparkling wine has beaten the best Champagnes in the world in blind tasting competitions. We have a very good sparkling wine in Cornwall, too, from Camel Valley Vineyard

drinks

(see page 138). I think their Camel Valley Brut shows that our climate suits sparkling wine very well indeed, because it needs good acidity.

As to our ability to make other excellent beverages there is no doubt. But you'll notice there is something significant missing – whisky. The range of producers making whisky is now so big that I felt this was a book in itself, so sadly, I will have to leave whisky for another day. However, I did find someone whose knowledge of whisky is positively encyclopaedic so, if you'd like to explore the world of this drink, I can think of no better hands to leave you in than Mr Wright of the Wright Wine Company (see page 161). Mr Wright currently holds over 500 Scottish malts alone in his shop, so perhaps you'll see why I felt there was not space in these pages to do justice to this particular topic!

The producers featured all have one thing in common: they are struggling against the tide of modern production, and cheap imitations. And yet, featured here are artisans making honest, unadulterated drinks, using methods that allow the flavours to achieve their true potential. These producers embody so much of the history of these isles, so search out and taste some liquid heritage.

Camel Valley Vineyard

Nanstallon, Bodmin, Cornwall PL30 5LG   T: 01208 77959   w: www.camelvalley.com
farm gate sales   **mail order**

Dry white wine specialists, with a Champagne-style brut called
Cornwall, which has recently been winning awards, Camel Valley
also make a red wine that has the distinction of aging well. Wines
are available direct from the vineyard, where tours can be arranged.

K G Consultants

The Bailiff's Cottage, The Green, Compton Dando, Bristol BS39 4LE   T: 01761 490624
farmers' markets

Keith Goverd has the biggest collection of single-variety apple juices
in the world, with over 100 to choose from. He seeks out rare
varieties, some of which don't even have a name, and presses the
fruit to make pure juice. He also makes pear and damson juice, and
cider, perry and damson vinegars. His ciders, juices and vinegars are
available from Bath, Bradford-on-Avon, Frome, Thornbury,
Warminster, Devizes and Westbury farmers' markets.

Haye Farm Scrumpy Cider

Haye Farm, St Veep, Lerryn, Lostwithiel, Cornwall PL22 0PB   T: 01208 872250
farm gate sales

Using only windfall apples from Haye Farm's own orchard, Rita
Vincent makes unpasteurized, barrel-fermented traditional cider.
Nothing is added to the apples and Rita says that many customers
are surprised how 'appley' the cider tastes. According to folklore,
cider has been made on this farm since the 1200s.

Somerset Cider Brandy Company

Pass Vale Farm, Burrow Hill, Kingsbury Episcopi, Martock, Somerset TA12 5BU
T: 01460 240782   w: www.ciderbrandy.co.uk
shop   **mail order**

Traditional cider-makers, the Somerset Cider Brandy Company
have diversified into cider brandy and now offer three-, five- and

ten-year-old versions of their distilled cider. The cider is made with vintage cider apples from the farm's own orchards and, once distilled, is aged in oak barrels. This is an artisan product in the best of Somerset cider-making traditions, using over 40 different varieties of apple. It's also an unusual product: although cider brandy has a history going back hundreds of years, the Somerset Cider Brandy Company were granted the first cider-distilling licence in recorded history.

SOUTH WEST   **NEWENT**

Three Choirs Vineyards

Newent, Gloucestershire GL18 1LS   T: 01531 890223   w: www.threechoirs.com

✉ **farm gate sales**

Three Choirs make wines made from a huge range of grape varieties, including a good selection of reds – 13 different wines at the time of writing. This is considered a leading vineyard for its experimentation with new grape varieties. Tastings and tours are offered and wines are available to buy.

super hero

AVALON VINEYARD (Pennard Organic Wines), Shepton Mallet (see page 140)

Many different kinds of drinks are made at the Avalon Vineyard, from grape wines and fruit wines to cider and mead. The traditional fruit wines include some unusual varieties – particularly the Folly wine, made with vine leaves. All the wines are organic and vegetarian and made using traditional methods – the cider is made using an ancient hand-turned press, in which the apples are made into a 'cheese' with straw, the old way of stacking the fruit to press it, and this has been adapted to use with the grapes. Hugh Tripp, the cider- and winemaker, feels strongly that these old-fashioned methods are vital for the quality of the drinks – 'they keep all their individuality of flavour intact'. Admitting that England is not the kindest environment for grape-growing, Hugh nonetheless turns the problems into positives: 'Grapes grown in this country may appear disadvantaged by our climate. Indeed they do struggle, but this very difficulty can to be turned to advantage by the fact that the long season and the slow ripening actually produces grapes of better quality for wine-making.'

FOOD HEROES OF BRITAIN

Tuckers Maltings

Teign Road, Newton Abbott, Devon TQ12 4AA T: 01626 334734
w: www.tuckersmaltings.com

🛒 **shop**

Tuckers Maltings hold a beer festival every year in April, celebrating real ales from around the country, and they also have a shop selling over 200 different types of beers from small breweries. This is also the home to Teignworthy Brewery, a microbrewery producing four beers made with local barley. All are unpasteurized cask or bottle-conditioned brews.

Plymouth Gin

60 Southside Street, Plymouth, Devon PL1 2LQ T: 01752 665292
w: www.plymouthgin.com

🛒 **shop**   ✉ **mail order**

Plymouth Gin is now believed to be the only traditionally made gin in the UK, in a dedicated distillery that was last modernized in 1855; the gin is still made by hand using Victorian methods. There is a specialist distiller, who spends three months of each year analysing and selecting the correct botanical ingredients to make the perfect balance of flavours and, as a result, the gin is much softer tasting than other gins. Sloe gin is also made, with wild sloes from Dartmoor, and damson gin is available. The distillery is open to the public, or you can buy mail order, or from many supermarkets.

Avalon Vineyard (Pennard Organic Wines)

The Drove, East Pennard, Shepton Mallet, Somerset BA4 6UA T: 01749 860393
w: www.pennardorganicwines.co.uk

🛒 **farmers' markets**   ✉ **mail order**

A wide variety of organic drinks is produced at Avalon, from wines to cider and mead. See the Super Hero box, page 139, for more information.

SOUTH WEST SHERBORNE

Benson's Fruit Juices

Stones Farm, Sherborne, Gloucestershire GL54 3DH T: 01451 844134
W: www.bensonsapplejuice.co.uk
farmers' markets **mail order**

Using entirely English fruit, Benson's makes some interesting combinations of juices – apple and rhubarb, plum and carrot, apple and cinnamon. The key to the flavour lies in the fact that the juices are left unfiltered and Benson's say this leaves all the flavour intact. Buy mail order, or the juices are available at many local and London farmers' markets – call to find out where.

SOUTH WEST SOUTH BRENT

Bramley and Gage

4 Long Meadow, South Brent, Devon TQ10 9YT T: 01364 73722
W: www.speciality-foods.com
mail order

Fruit liqueurs are made here using whole fruit from the West Country – damsons, greengages, blackberries and many more – simply pressed and preserved with alcohol and sugar. Sloe and damson gin are favourites and a recent addition to the range is a herb liqueur.

SOUTH WEST STREET

Hecks Farmhouse Cider

911 Middle Leigh, Street, Somerset BA16 0LB T: 01458 442367
farm shop

A staggering 20 varieties of cider are made at Hecks, all from single varieties of apple, and five varieties of perry. Made with the apples from the orchard on site, the cider is made the traditional West Country way. The farm shop (also on site) is open all week.

SOUTH WEST TEDBURN ST MARY

Grays Farm Cider

Halstow, Tedburn St Mary, Devon EX6 6AN T: 01647 61236
E: ben@graysdevoncider.co.uk
farm gate sales

The Gray family have been in continuous production of cider for over 300 years, from the same Devon farm. Made today just as it has always been made, the cider is a blend of apples from the Grays' own orchard, pressed and fermented naturally on the farm and is available direct from the farm, or from local farm shops.

Minchews Real Cyder and Perry

Rose Cottage, Aston Cross, Tewkesbury, Gloucestershire GL20 8HX   T: 07974 034331
w: www.minchews.co.uk

The list of awards that Minchews have won for their single-variety, traditionally made ciders and perries is incredibly long – the produce from this cider maker is very well respected in the industry. Find the cider and perry at Orchard Hive and Vine (page 157).

Sharpham Vineyard

Ashprington, Totnes, Devon TQ9 7UT   T: 01803 732203   w: www.sharpham.com
⬆ **farm shop**

Sharpham Vineyard is part of the Sharpham Estate, which also specializes in cheesemaking (see the separate entry, page 62). Classic grape varieties are used here, including Cabernet Sauvignon, and, unusually, Merlot. Sharpham have received the English Red Wine of the Year award four times now, and have attracted a lot of attention from wine experts. There are two trails at the vineyard, allowing customers to see the vines at close quarters, and also walk along the banks of the River Dart, which runs through the vineyard, making for a great day out, especially when accompanied by a tasting session (of both wine and cheese) back at the winery.

Hayles Fruit Farm

Winchcombe, Cheltenham, Gloucestershire GL54 5PB   T: 01242 602123
w: www.hayles-fruit-farm.co.uk
⬆ **farm shop**

Hayles Fruit Farm make pure juices from the fruit grown in their orchards – in all, there are 11 apple varieties, nine plum varieties, and two pear types. Soft fruit is also available and, unusually in this part of England, cob nuts. It's also possible to pick your own and there is a tearoom at the farm.

DRINKS

Biddenden Vineyards and Cider Works

Little Whatmans, Gribble Bridge Lane, Biddenden, Kent TN27 8DF   T: 01580 291726
W: www.biddendenvineyards.com

≋ farm gate sales   ✉ mail order

Not just wines, but also fresh pressed apple juice and classic Kent
cider (made using culinary apple varieties, not cider apples) are
made at Biddenden. The wines include single-variety oaked whites,
sparkling whites and a rosé made partly with Pinot Noir grapes. This
is believed to be the oldest commercial vineyard in Kent and
customers are welcome to take tours, either guided or self-guided,
and can taste and buy the wines, juice and cider on site.

Neals Place Farm

Neals Place Road, Canterbury, Kent CT2 8HX   T: 01227 765632
E: kenro@onetel.net.uk

≌ farmers' markets   ≋ farm gate sales

Ken Jordan of Neals Place Farm won the Best Bottled Cider title at
the CAMRA awards in 2002. Growing his own apples, he uses a
single variety (Cox's), and adds absolutely nothing – no sugar, no
water, no carbonates. A minimum of six months in the barrel
produces a very dry, tasty cider. Apple juices are also available – six
single varieties and some blends, including Cox's and ginger, and
Bramley and honey. All available direct from the farm or from
Epsom, Croydon, Egham and Wokingham farmers' markets.

Ridgeview Wine Estate

Fragbarrow Lane, Ditchling Common, Sussex BN6 8TP   T: 01444 258039
W: www.ridgeview.co.uk

≋ farm gate sales

Sparkling wine specialists, Ridgeview makes wines in the
Champagne style, using exactly the same methods as the
traditional Champagne houses, and from the three traditional
Champagne grape varieties. In blind tastings, Ridgeview has, on
numerous occasions, beaten classic Champagnes such as Veuve
Clicquot. Tastings, tours and sales of the wines are all available at
the vineyard.

FOOD HEROES OF BRITAIN

Denbies Wine Estate

London Road, Dorking, Surrey RH5 6AA   T: 01306 876616
w: www.denbiesvineyard.co.uk

✉ **farm gate sales** ✉ **mail order**

This is the largest of the English vineyards, making wine with 14 different grape varieties, including the famous Chardonnay (when grown in England, Chardonnay grapes produce a 'greener', aromatic wine, less heavy than those grown in warmer climates). This vineyard is really geared up for visitors, with tours, tastings, a cinema showing films about the winemaking and two restaurants, one with a viewing gallery over the vineyard. The wine can be bought from the vineyard, or by mail order.

Ringden Farm Apple Juice

London Road, Hurst Green, Etchingham, East Sussex TN19 7QY   T: 01580 879385
w: www.ringdenfarm.co.uk

🥄 **farm shop**

Traditional cloudy apple juice – just pressed, gently pasteurized, and bottled. All the apples used are from the farm's own orchards, where there are around 25 different apple varieties. There is a shop on site, where customers can see demonstrations of the juice being pressed. The juice has won many Great Taste Awards.

Suthwyk Ales

Offwell Farm, Southwick, Fareham, Hampshire PO17 6DX   T: 023 9232 5252
w: www.suthwykales.com

🥄 **farmers' markets**

CAMRA-recognized Martin Bazeley grows barley in two fields on his farm. The fields are named Skew and Bloomfields and the two types of beer he makes with the barley are named after the fields. Numerous local businesses are involved in the production of Skew Ale and Bloomfields Bitter, including a company that malts the barley by hand, the old-fashioned way. The beer is available by the bottle (bottle-conditioned) at several Hampshire farmers' markets (listed on the website), or by the pint at the Golden Lion in Southwick. Call Martin for more details of outlets.

JON LEIGHTON, of Valley Vineyard, Twyford, (see page 152)

Unusually for an English vineyard, Jon Leighton at Valley Vineyard produces a Pinot Noir red wine – unusual, because this is a grape that is generally unwilling to grow this far north. Jon told friends and acquaintances some years ago that he was going to win a top British wine award for a red wine, and they all laughed – it was considered impossible – and yet in 1998 he did just that. In fact, Valley Vineyard has probably won more awards over the years than any other British vineyard. Classic French grapes are the order of the day here, with still reds and whites, and sparkling whites; this vineyard is constantly pushing the boundaries to see what varieties can be grown in this country. Jon is proud that he produces English wine recognized for its high quality – he says it is time that the British stopped being 'besotted by the idea that anything from abroad is better than the British version'. There is an off licence on site that sells the wines, and customers can take a tour of the vineyard. The wines are also available by mail order.

SOUTH EAST   **FAVERSHAM**

Pawley Farm Traditional Kentish Cider

Painters Forstal, Faversham, Kent ME13 0EN   T: 01795 532043
farm gate sales

The Macey family have been cider-makers for over 200 years; the current representative, Derek Macey, has been doing it for 40 years. The ciders are made the traditional Kentish way, with culinary apples, not cider apples, and the cider is blended from any number of the eight varieties grown in the Maceys' orchard. The cider is matured for up to two years in oak casks, for a far fuller flavour than you would get with commercially produced ciders. The Maceys also make apple juice.

SOUTH EAST   **HARTFIELD**

Kent and Sussex Apple Juice and Cider Centre

Perryhill Orchard, Edenbridge Road, Hartfield, East Sussex TN7 4JJ   T: 01892 770595
farm shop

This is the hub for a group of farms producing traditional ciders and pressed apple juices in Sussex. Perryhill Orchard itself produces juices from eight varieties of apple, along with a clutch of single-variety ciders, and these and others can be tasted and bought at the farm shop on site at the orchard.

Gospel Green Cyder

Gospel Green Cottage, Haslemere, West Sussex GU27 3BH   T: 01428 654120
✉ **farm gate sales**   ✉ **mail order**

The Lane family take apples from their own orchards and from neighbouring farms and make cider by the Champagne method, which produces a very different drink from traditional ciders. It has been described as 'very French' in style – dry, with a distinct apple flavour.

food facts

CIDER AND PERRY

Traditional cider makers have a very simple list of ingredients: apples. No added sugar or yeast, no preservatives, no flavour enhancers. On a traditional cider farm, the apples are picked by hand (the old trees don't suit mechanized picking) and milled into pulp. Pressing takes place in a cider 'cheese' – a stack of cloth envelopes containing the pulp, layered with oat straw or wooden slatted boards, up to 20 layers high. The pressing of this stack to extract the juice can take two days, before the juice is put into oak barrels without pasteurization. Fermentation will then take place, using only the wild yeasts already present in the apple skins, and maturing in the barrel can last six months or more.

The vast majority of old and traditional cider orchards have been grubbed up and destroyed to make way for more economical crops. Many native varieties of cider apple have been made extremely difficult to find or, in some cases, have disappeared altogether. Perry pear varieties have suffered to an even greater degree. Perry making has declined enormously – it is more difficult than cider making, and is a poor candidate for a profit generating product. Perry pear trees do not bear fruit for at least 30 years after planting, so many people would consider them obsolete in these days of 'fast food'. The survival of many old varieties of apples and pears hangs in the balance, but some of the producers listed are helping to keep them alive, maintaining old orchards, and planting new ones, keeping this heritage alive.

Owlet Apple Juice

Owl House Fruit Farm, Lamberhurst, Kent TN3 8LY   T: 01892 890553
🍽 **farmers' markets**

Owl Farm produces award-winning unfiltered, cloudy fruit juices
from fruit grown on the farm and in neighbouring orchards. Some
single-variety apple juices are available, along with a few blends,
pear juice, and some flavoured with raspberries or blueberries.
Available from Tunbridge Wells farmers' market or from many farm
shops in the south east – call to find your nearest outlet.

Breaky Bottom Vineyard

Rodmell, Lewes, East Sussex BN7 3EX   T: 01273 476427
w: www.breakybottom.co.uk
✉ **mail order**

Peter Hall makes Loire-style wines, predominantly with the Seyval
Blanc grape. The still whites age well, maturing well in the bottle for
up to a decade, and are available lightly oaked or unoaked. A
classic Champagne-style sparkling white is also available. Breaky
Bottom has won a Gold Medal at the International Wine Challenge
and the wines are available direct from the vineyard, or mail order.

Middle Farm

West Firle, Lewes, East Sussex BN8 6LJ   T: 01323 811411
w: www.middlefarm.com
🥄 **farm shop**

Middle Farm is home to the National Collection of Cider and Perry –
and what a collection it is, with around 250 different ciders and
perries available to taste and buy. These are farm ciders – made
with just the fruit, and nothing else – from all over the country, many
from producers who make very small quantities, so you are unlikely
to find them anywhere else. Middle Farm produces its own drinks,
too, with apple juices pressed fresh each day, and cider made the
old-fashioned way. This is also a working farm, with a huge farm
shop stocking their own organic beef, cheese made with the farm's
Jersey milk, alongside a great range of British cheeses and lots of
fresh local produce.

Pitfield Brewery (The Beer Shop)

14 Pitfield Street, London N1 6EY   T: 020 7739 3701   w: www.pitfieldbeershop.co.uk

🛒 **shop** ✉ **mail order**

The Pitfield Beer Shop is both a microbrewery and a beer shop. They produce their own range of 14 traditional ales, based on old recipes (one, Imperial Stout, comes from a 1792 recipe), none of which are filtered or pasteurized and all of which are cask- or bottle-conditioned. The shop has an incredible range of beers from all over the world – around 600 different kinds – available by mail order. Pitfield's own beer is available on tap in numerous London pubs – call to find out where.

The Porterhouse

21–22 Maiden Lane, Covent Garden, London WC2E 7NA   T: 0207 836 9931
w: www.porterhousebrewco.com

This microbrewery is a branch of an Irish one. It makes six different beers, including a traditional red ale and an oyster stout. For details, see under the Dublin branch on page 163. There is another branch in Bray (see page 162).

Bearsted Vineyard

Bearsted, Maidstone, Kent   ME14 4NJ   T: 01622 736974
w: www.bearstedwines.co.uk

✉ **mail order**

The Gibson family produce eight different varieties of wine, including a red and a rosé. Mail order is available, but do visit if you are in the area – the Gibsons love to talk to customers and get their feedback.

Chegworth Valley Juices

Water Lane Farm, Chegworth, Harrietsham, Maidstone, Kent ME17 1DE
T: 01622 859272   w: www.applejuicedirect.com

🛒 **farmers' markets** ✉ **mail order**

The juices made at Chegworth Valley are recent winners at the Great Taste awards. Most of the fruit used – lots of varieties of apples, pears, and soft fruit – is grown on the farm, which has some organic land, with more planned. The apple juices are available as single varieties, blends, or mixed with strawberries, raspberries, blackberries and even rhubarb, and have no additives. All are available from many London farmers' markets – call for details.

SOUTH EAST	PETWORTH

Lurgashall Winery

Dial Green, Lurgashall, nr Petworth, West Sussex GU28 9HA T: 01428 707292
w: www.lurgashall.co.uk

shop   **mail order**

Lurgashall Winery specializes in English country fruit wines, based on old recipes, using old-fashioned ingredients such as rose petals and silver birch. Ingredients are sourced as locally as possible. Visitors can take a tour of the winery and visit the shop. Lurgashall is a member of the UK Vineyards Association.

SOUTH EAST	ROBERTSBRIDGE

Sedlescombe Organic Vineyard

Cripps Corner, nr Robertsbridge, East Sussex TN32 5SA T: 01580 830715 OR
0800 980 2884   w: www.englishorganicwine.co.uk AND www.rentavine.co.uk

shop   **mail order**

A staggering array of English drinks is made here. Amongst the choice are red and white wines using Bacchus and Pinot Noir grapes, including, unusually for England, a full-bodied red. Fruit wines are also produced – apple, cherry and plum, traditional still cider, pear juice and even blackberry liqueur. All are organic and vegan. You can even rent your own vine and benefit from the wine that it produces.

SOUTH EAST	ROTHERFIELD

Davenport Vineyards

Limney Farm, Castle Hill, Rotherfield, East Sussex TN6 3RR T: 01892 852380
w: www.davenportvineyards.co.uk

farm gate sales   **mail order**

Will Davenport is currently converting his vineyard to organic status and has not used artificial pesticides or fertilizers for over two years. He made this decision as he feels that growing organically produces the highest quality possible, and the wines – a dry white still variety and a Pinot Noir Champagne-style – are aromatic, fresh and clean-tasting. No yeast is added in the winemaking process, so fermentation is achieved with the wild yeasts in the grape skins and this lends greater complexity to the wine itself. Wines are available mail order or directly from the vineyard, but call first.

SOUTH EAST   SHOREHAM-BY-SEA

Gran Stead's Ginger Wine

43 Old Fort Road, Shoreham-by-Sea, West Sussex BN43 5RL   T: 01273 452644
w: www.gransteadsginger.co.uk

🛒 **farmers' markets** ✉ **mail order**

Made with a 150-year-old recipe, this ginger wine is made with pure ginger oil. A true cottage industry, Gran Stead's make wine in only five-gallon batches to ensure the balance of ingredients is perfect. The ginger wine is available mail order or from many farmers' markets – call for details.

SOUTH EAST   SOUTHAMPTON

Wickham Vineyard

Botley Road, Shedfield, Southampton SO32 2HL   T: 01329 834042
w: www.wickhamvineyard.co.uk

🛒 **shop**

Dry whites, including single varietals and a lightly oaked type, are the speciality here, and Wickham vineyard has the distinction of being served both in the House of Commons and on the Ark Royal. There is a small shop on site, tours of the vineyard can be taken, and now there is also a restaurant, which was named Les Routiers Restaurant of the Year.

SOUTH EAST   TENTERDEN

New Wave Wines

Small Hythe, Tenterden, Kent TN30 7NG   T: 01580 763033   w: www.newwavewines.com

Having scooped 24 of the 30 available English wine awards last year, New Wave is considered to be at the top of its game. Using unusual grape varieties has prompted the vineyard to call one of its ranges Curious Grape (the other range is called Chapel Down). The vineyard grows some of its own grapes and sources more from grape-growers around the country. Passionate about retaining the heritage of Kent as 'the garden of England', New Wave encourages farmers to develop vineyards. Tastings and tours are available at the vineyard and a pub at the edge of the vineyard, owned by New Wave and also called the Curious Grape, serves food made with local produce, and only English wines.

ENGLISH AND WELSH WINES

Like the wine of any other country, there are good Welsh and English wines and there are less than good ones. Many people have never tasted wine from the UK and those that have done may have been unfortunate enough to taste one in the latter category, enforcing a widely held belief that wine from this country is a very poor relation to the produce from French or Italian vineyards. There is a vital difference between English and Welsh wine and British wine. English and Welsh wine must adhere to strict regulations; the grapes must have been grown and the wine made in this country. Wine labelled as British is almost certainly made from cheap, imported concentrate; it will probably be cheap on the shop shelves and it will taste … cheap. When trying native wine, choose bottles that are labelled English or Welsh.

The majority of UK wines are whites; we are too far north to grow most black grape varieties, so only around 10% of the wines made here are red. The wines we produce offer a myriad of different taste experiences but a classic English wine will have a floral bouquet, a fresh taste and an acidic finish.

British vineyards have many hurdles to overcome when it comes to producing wine. As we are rarely blessed with long, hot and sunny summers, the growers have to harvest the grapes as late as possible, to maximize the sugar content, and this can be as late as November. This is fraught with peril – disease can strike, birds can destroy the crop, frost can ruin the grapes or wet weather can prevent picking. And yet these vineyards are producing world-class wines. In a recent blind tasting at *Wine* magazine, a sparkling white from Camel Valley vineyard in Cornwall outscored every French and Italian wine in the same category. It is high time we took wine made in this country more seriously. English Wine Producers, the body promoting the vineyards of England and Wales, is a treasure-trove of information and advice about buying native wines. Julia Trustram Eve, from English Wine Producers, gave us a great deal of advice in compiling our list of featured vineyards. Find out more on their website www.englishwineproducers.com

FOOD HEROES OF BRITAIN

Broughton Pastures Organic Fruit Wine

The Silk Mill, Brook Street, Tring, Herts HP23 5EF   T: 01442 823993
w: www.broughtonpastures.co.uk

✉ **mail order**

Broughton Pastures are the only organic fruit-wine specialists in the country and have twice won Soil Association organic awards for their drinks. Seven varieties are available, including blackberry, mead, and a *Méthode Champenoise* elderflower sparkling wine. All the wines are available by mail order.

Valley Vineyard

superhero

Stanlake Park, Twyford, Berkshire, RG10 0BN   T: 0118 934 0176
w: www.valleyvineyards.co.uk

🛒 **shop**   ✉ **mail order**

Award-winning wines including an unusual English Pinot Noir red wine. See the Super Hero box, page 145, for more information.

Nyetimber Vineyard

Gay Street, West Chiltington, West Sussex RH20 2HH   T: 01798 813989
w: www.nyetimber-vineyard.com

✉ **mail order**

The winner of many, many awards, Nyetimber Vineyard produces Champagne-style sparkling wines, only ever vintage, using the Chardonnay and Pinot grape varieties. Nyetimber was served at numerous royal events during the Golden Jubilee. Available by mail order (the vineyard is not open to the public), or from outlets such as Fortnum & Mason and Berry Bros in London.

St Peter's Brewery Co

St Peter's Hall, St Peter, South Elmham, nr Bungay, Suffolk NR35 1NQ
T: 01986 782322   w: www.stpetersbrewery.co.uk

✉ **mail order**

St Peter's Brewery is an intriguing combination of tradition and innovation, brewing 18 beers. These are a mixture of fruit beers (including grapefruit, elderberry, and lemon and ginger), old-fashioned porters and an unhopped beer, using nettles and junipers in place of hops, as beer was made hundreds of years ago. There is even an organic ale, which won the top prize at the Soil Association awards in 2002. Available by mail order, or from some Sainsbury and Waitrose branches.

Chilford Hall Vineyard

Linton, Cambridge CB1 6LE   T: 01223 895600   w: www.chilfordhall.co.uk
✉ **farm gate sales**

Simon Alper at Chilford Hall makes wines that range from 'fresh and bright' to 'full and rounded'. Some are made to go with specific foods (there is even advice on the website regarding which of the wines would suit Chinese and Vietnamese dishes) while others can be drunk very happily on their own. Their sparkling rosé has gained many accolades. All the wines can be tasted and bought at the vineyard.

food facts

REAL ALES

The definition of real ale is very simple – according to CAMRA (the Campaign for Real Ale), it is 'beer brewed from traditional ingredients, matured by secondary fermentation in the container from which it is dispensed and served without the use of extraneous carbon dioxide'. Real ale is effectively alive in the bottle or cask – still with active yeasts fermenting the liquid. It is not pasteurized, which kills off the live organisms, and so real ale can be compared to an unpasteurized artisan cheese. Britain is alive with a culture of small breweries making real ale in time-honoured fashion. These are people who are not interested in the uniform beers coming out of the large breweries; instead, they are making drinks, often in small quantities, that are imbued with a real sense of heritage and of place. We asked CAMRA which breweries were really exceptional – were winning awards, were really pushing the field of real ale forward, or that were particularly interesting in terms of the heritage of ale, and you'll find them here.

FOOD HEROES OF BRITAIN

The Old Chimneys Brewery

Church Road, Market Weston, Diss, Norfolk IP22 2NX   T: 01359 221013

Alan Thompson brews 19 different real ales, all either cask- or bottle-conditioned, and two ciders, from his Norfolk brewery. He happily admits to being obsessed with real ale and even stocks ales from other small local breweries and some from further afield, too, including a range of Belgian fruit beers. Available from the brewery on Friday afternoons and Saturday mornings.

Norfolk Fruit Growers Juice Co.

Tunstead Road, Hoveton, Norfolk NR12 8QN   T: 01603 783040
w: www.norfolkapplejuice.co.uk
✉ **mail order**

Award-winning cloudy fruit juices made with apples from a co-operative of Norfolk growers. Nothing is added to the juice except vitamin C, and there are five single-variety juices on offer. Each bottle of juice can be traced back to the orchard the fruit was grown in.

super hero

THE TALBOT AND THE TEME BREWERY, Worcester
(see page 158)

The Talbot is a unique establishment. It is the home of the Teme Brewery, which brews three 'real' beers all year (This, That and T'other), with some seasonal specialities at certain times of year. The owners of the Talbot, the Clift family, are not content just to brew their own beers – they also grow their own vegetables and herbs, make their own preserves, breads, black pudding and raised pies, and forage around the fields and hedgerows to gather 'wild food'. No processed food is bought into the pub and their menu reflects this – the dishes have a real regional feel, with their firm belief that 'food should have an identifiable character' clearly expressed. As if all this were not enough, they even have a local produce market at the pub once a month. The Talbot is an inspiration for those committed to buying local food.

Crones Cider

Fairview, Fersfield Road, Kenninghall, Norfolk NR16 2DP   T: 01379 687687
w: www.crones.co.uk

~ **farm gate sales**

Award-winning cider and juices (single-variety apple juices and
cherry juice) are made by Crones Cider. The cider is made with a
traditional stack press, from a mix of culinary and dessert apples, as
is customary in East Anglia. Both it and the fruit juices are available
direct from the premises (call first) or from many wholefood shops
and delis in the south east.

Woodforde's Norfolk Ales

Broadland Brewery, Woodbastwick, Norwich, Norfolk NR13 6SW   T: 01603 720353
w: www.woodfordes.co.uk

~ **shop** ~ **mail order**

Woodforde's are unique in having won the Supreme Champion Beer
at CAMRA's Great British Beer Festival twice for two different beers,
although this is only the tip of the iceberg when it comes to awards
won by this brewery. The heritage of real ale in Britain is alive and
well at this Norfolk brewery, which has CAMRA's philosophy of
educating the public in the merits of real ale at heart. The beers are
available at the three 'tied' pubs, which have Woodforde's beers on
tap (all in Norfolk): The Fur and Feather Inn, Woodbastwick, 01603
720003; The Billy Bluelight, 27 Hall Road, Norwich, 01603 623768;
and the Swan Inn, Ingham, 01692 581099.

Shawsgate Vineyard

Badingham Road, Framlingham, Woodbridge, Suffolk IP13 9HZ   T: 01728 724060
w: www.shawsgate.co.uk

~ **shop**

Shawsgate Vineyard makes 11 different varieties of wine, using
predominantly the Bacchus grape variety, which produces delicate,
aromatic wines with a similarity to those from the Alsace region.
There is also a dry, still cider and an apple dessert wine. Leasing is
also available – rent a row of vines, have your own wine made for
you and personalize your labels – you can check the progress of
your grapes throughout the season and learn all about grape-
growing and winemaking.

super hero

TOM OLIVER, owner of Oliver's Cider and Perry, Ocle Pychard (see opposite)

Tom Oliver makes a myriad of different ciders and perries, searching out rare and old varieties of fruit, and making unadulterated drinks, tasting as they would have done generations ago. I asked him about his work: 'Cider and perry starts and finishes for me with the fruit. Growing on trees, especially perry pear trees, that are frequently planted by orchardists and enthusiasts who take the "long view" on life. Trees of 50 to 300 years old, whose size and canopy can only develop over many generations. These older trees frequently defy commercial exploitation and consequently build up an ecosystem of varied habitats for all manner of wildlife and insects while providing a fruit that is ideally suited to the craft cider- and perry-maker. Fruit that is free of chemicals, lower in nitrogen, falling when ripe onto a thicker grass sward to minimize bruising and providing an environment that is good for the heart and soul to work in.' Even the names of the apple and pear varieties Tom uses have a sense of history and myth about them – Foxwhelp, Ten Commandments and Cider Lady's Finger and perry pear varieties such as Stinking Bishop, Merrylegs and Painted Lady.

At the last count, Tom was offering eight different types of perry alone, with accompanying advice regarding the foods they work well with. There are perry varieties that go with fish, lamb, game and desserts – it's a very versatile drink. Call Tom to find out where to buy his cider and perry.

MIDLANDS   ABBEY-DORE

Gwatkin Cider

Moorhampton Park Farm, Abbey-Dore, Herefordshire HR2 0AL   T: 01981 550258
farm shop

Award-winning cider from over a dozen old English apple varieties is made by Gwatkin's without added yeast or carbonates – nothing but fruit is used. All the apples are either from the farm's own orchard, or nearby local orchards. The farm also sells its own fresh meat.

MIDLANDS   LEDBURY

Jus

Glebe Farm, Aylton, Ledbury, Herefordshire HR8 2RQ   T: 01531 670121
farm gate sales **mail order**

Traditional unfiltered juices from around 35 different apple and pear varieties, some blended, some left as single varieties, are made here.

The fruit is from the family's orchard, or sometimes from other local orchards. The juices are available direct from the farm, but call first.

MIDLANDS   LEOMINSTER

Orchard Hive and Vine

4 High Street, Leominster, Herefordshire HR6 8LZ T: 01568 611232
w: www.orchard-hive-and-vine.co.uk
✉ **mail order**

Orchard Hive and Vine stocks a fantastic selection of juices, cider and perry from many artisan producers around the country. Bottled beers and wines, both local and overseas – from small-scale producers whose drinks are otherwise difficult to find – are also available.

MIDLANDS   MUCH MARCLE

Gregg's Pit Cider and Perry

Much Marcle, Herefordshire HR8 2NL T: 01531 660687 w: www.greggs-pit.co.uk

Using windfall fruit from his own and a neighbouring orchard (all grown without artificial fertilizers or pesticides), James Marsden makes single-variety and blended perries and ciders. These drinks have won many awards, having been overall champion on six occasions at the Big Apple Cider and Perry Trials; many people in the industry feel that Gregg's Pit traditionally made perry is simply one of the best in the country. Available from many local outlets including Ceci Paolo (page 118) and Orchard Hive and Vine (above) and James is currently applying for a licence to be able to sell direct from the premises.

MIDLANDS   OCLE PYCHARD

Oliver's Cider and Perry   super hero

Stanksbridge, Ocle Pychard, Herefordshire HR1 3RE T: 01432 820569
w: www.theolivers.org.uk

Tom Oliver makes a variety of ciders and perries. See the Super Hero box, opposite, for more information.

Avonbank

Pershore College of Horticulture, Avonbank, Pershore, Worcestershire WR10 3JP
T: 01386 551200

🛒 **shop**

Award-winning single-variety and blended perries and ciders, some
made using unusual varieties of apples and pears. Courses in cider
and perry making are run here.

Astley Vineyards

Astley, Stourport-on-Severn, Worcestershire DY13 0RU   T: 01299 822907

🛒 **shop**

Consistent award winners, Astley Vineyards make white wines
ranging from dry to medium dry and also a dessert wine. English
grape varieties are used; Jonty Daniels, the winemaker, believes that
'at their best, wines should reflect where they come from'. There is
a shop at the vineyard, where customers can taste and buy.

The Talbot at Knightwick   super hero

Knightwick, Worcester WR6 5PH   T: 01886 821235   w: www.the-talbot.co.uk

The Talbot is the home of the Teme brewery as well as being a pub
with an amazing commitment to producing home-made food and
serving a menu of local specialities made with local produce. See
the Super Hero box, page 154, for more information.

Strawberry Bank Liqueurs

Crosthwaite, Cumbria LA8 8HX   T: 015395 68812   w: www.damsongin.com

🛒 **farmers' markets**   ✉ **mail order**

Mike and Helen Walsh have their own damson orchard and, some
years ago, decided they wanted to make a drink that had a firm sense
of place. The result was damson beer, a double-fermented fruit beer,
which perfectly combines the fruit Cumbria is associated with and the
heritage of real ales in Britain. Next came damson gin, followed by
blackberry liqueur. All the drinks are available from Penrith, Carlisle,
Kendal, Ulverston or Orton farmers' markets, or by mail order.

PAUL THEAKSTON, of the Black Sheep Brewery Plc, Wellgarth
(see page 161)

The Black Sheep Brewery was founded by Paul Theakston, a fifth-generation member of the famous Theakston brewing family that has been resident in Masham for over 500 years. Paul was worried about the increasing levels of technology used in big brewing companies, and set up Black Sheep to get back to a simpler and more traditional way of producing cask-conditioned real ale. There is no modern technology used at Black Sheep, old-fashioned types of barley and hops are used, and some of the vessels used for the brewing are over 100 years old. Paul firmly believes that going back to basics in this way results in ales that have more body and flavour. Black Sheep ales are available from the cask in many pubs around the north east, and the bottled versions are available from supermarkets throughout the country.

NORTH WEST   KENDAL

Cowmire Hall Damson Gin

Cowmire Hall, Crosthwaite, Kendal, Cumbria LA8 8JJ T: 015395 68200
🛒 **farmers' markets**

Damson gin is an old English drink, associated strongly with the Lake District. Cumbria is rich in damson orchards and Cowmire Hall are helping to conserve this piece of English heritage, using damsons from their own orchards and from other local orchards. The gin is a hand-made product, using old-fashioned methods, and is available from Kendal and Orton farmers' markets, from various local outlets, including Low Sizergh Barn (page 123), and Fortnum & Mason in London.

NORTH WEST   SEDBURGH

Think Drink

PO Box 10, Sedbergh, Cumbria LA10 5GH T: 015396 25148
🛒 **farmers' markets**

John Sheard gathers old varieties of Cumbrian apples, mainly from orchards within the Countryside Stewardship Scheme, and simply presses them to make pure juice. He sells these juices at local farmers' markets, including Carlisle, Orton and Kendal, where he also sells a local real ale from a nearby microbrewery, Dent Brewery, who make a cask-conditioned, live beer using spring water from their own well.

Lanchester Fruit

Brockwell Farm, Lanchester, Co. Durham DH7 0TQ T: 01207 528805
E: lanchesterfruit@onyxnet.co.uk
🥄 **farm shop** 🛒 **farmers' markets**

Lanchester Fruit takes a wide variety of English apples and presses traditional juices – no additives, no blends (although some are flavoured with rhubarb, elderflower or redcurrant), no pasteurizing, and no filtering – just unadulterated juice. The farm also has plenty of soft fruit and asparagus to pick in season. There is a farm shop in the summer, and the juice is available at farm shops throughout the country. There is also a tea room.

Leventhorpe Vineyard

Bullerthorpe Lane, Woodlesford, Leeds, West Yorkshire LS26 8AF T: 0113 288 9088
🛒 **farm gate sales**

Leventhorpe is England's most northerly commercial vineyard, producing mainly light, dry whites using classic French grapes. The wines are available direct from the vineyard, which is a member of the UK Vineyards Association.

super hero

THE HILDEN BREWING CO., Lisburn (see page 162)

The Hilden Brewing Co. is a passionate campaigner for the return of real ale to Northern Ireland. The province is dominated by just two huge breweries, leaving little room for small independent breweries, and this has meant that, over the years, Northern Irish drinkers have lost their taste for real ale. To reverse this trend Hilden offers a great range of fantastic real ales, from stouts, to porters, to pale ales, all made traditionally without chemical additives. Visitors to the brewery can take a tour and taste the beer or settle down to a meal and a few pints in the restaurant on site.

Black Sheep Brewery plc

`super hero`

Wellgarth, Masham, Ripon, North Yorkshire HG4 4EN · T: 01765 689227
w: www.blacksheepbrewery.com

✉ **mail order**

Paul Theakston brews traditional cask-conditioned ale. See the Super Hero box, page 159, for more information.

The Wright Wine Company

The Old Smithy, Raikes Road, Skipton, North Yorkshire BD23 1NP · T: 01756 700886
w: www.wineandwhisky.co.uk

✉ **mail order**

The Wright Wine Company are specialists in both wine and whisky. With over 1000 wines, and around 500 Scottish malts alone, this shop has been described as 'encyclopaedic'. Filled with the rare and unusual, these are drinks that you will find difficult to get elsewhere, with whisky from New Zealand and Japan and spirits and wines from the smallest producers around the world. The range of Irish whiskies is growing apace, too. The staff are enthusiastic and keen to pass on their expertise.

York Beer and Wine Shop

28 Sandringham Street, Fishergate, York YO10 4BA · T: 01904 647136
w: www.yorkbeerandwineshop.co.uk

A legendary shop selling the rare, the unusual and the obscure in beers, wines, ciders and cheese. Plenty of bottle-conditioned real ales, traditional ciders and perries, and wines from small vineyards that you are unlikely ever to see on a supermarket shelf. The cheeses they stock come from smaller dairies and artisan cheesemakers.

The Vineyard Belfast Ltd

375–377 Ormeau Road, Belfast BT7 3GP · T: 028 9064 5774
w: www.vineyardbelfast.co.uk

Obscure and unusual alcoholic drinks are the speciality here, with over 200 different beers, 45 different vodkas, and liqueurs, wines and whiskies from little-known producers. Bottle-conditioned real ales, including ale from the Hilden Brewing Co. (see below and the Super Hero box, page 160) can be found here.

NORTHERN IRELAND   KILKEEL

Whitewater Brewery

40 Tullyframe Road, Kilkeel, Co. Down BT34 4RZ ⊤: 028 417 69449

One of only two microbreweries in the whole of Northern Ireland, the beers made here are real ales with a splash of imagination. The staples are a dark ale, and a session ale, with seasonal specials like the summer honey and ginger beer, and the winter beer with hedgerow fruits. Available from many pubs in Belfast (call for details), or from the brewery's own pub, the White Horse Inn, 47–51 Main Street, Saintfield, Co. Down, 028 9751 1143 or 028 9751 0417.

NORTHERN IRELAND   LISBURN

The Hilden Brewing Co.   super hero

Hilden House, Hilden, Lisburn, Co. Antrim BT27 4TY ⊤: 028 9266 3863

A brewery making a great range of traditionally made real ales and offering brewery tours, with a restaurant on site, Hilden is well worth a visit. See the Super Hero box, page 160, for more information.

REPUBLIC OF IRELAND   BRAY

The Porterhouse

Strand Road, Bray, Co. Wicklow ⊤: 01 286 0668 ⩗: www.porterhousebrewco.com

This Irish microbrewery make six different beers, including a traditional red ale and an oyster stout. For details, see under the Dublin branch, opposite. There is another branch in London, see page 148.

REPUBLIC OF IRELAND   CORK

The Franciscan Well

14 North Mall, Cork, Co. Cork ⊤: 021 439 3434

A centre for real ale in Ireland, the Franciscan Well brew pub holds two beer festivals each year, with one focussing on and celebrating microbreweries. The pub is also home to seven real ales, along with some seasonal specials, many of which have won awards for the brewery.

Messrs Maguire

1–2 Burgh Quay, Dublin 2   T: 01 670 5777

There is a growing number of brew pubs and microbreweries in
Ireland, mainly concentrated in Dublin and Cork. Ireland has been
dominated by big industrial breweries for many years, and it is good
to see some smaller breweries springing up and making real ales.
Messrs Maguire is one where the beers that they make are only
available in the pub itself, and the beers include a traditional Irish
red ale and a wheat beer, among others.

The Porterhouse

16–18 Parliament Street, Dublin 2   T: 01 672 8087   W: www.porterhousebrewco.com

This Irish microbrewery makes six different beers, including a
traditional red ale, but perhaps most interesting is its oyster stout.
Ireland has a great tradition of eating oysters with stout and this ale,
which has whole oysters added in the brewing process, combines
the two perfectly. This creates a slightly sweet flavour, with a very
smooth consistency. There are also branches in London and Bray
(see page 148 and opposite).

super hero

NIALL GARVEY of the Biddy Early Brewery, Inagh (see page 164)

When the Biddy Early Brewery was first established in 1995, Ireland had only
three breweries left, none of which were Irish owned and none making real ale.
Niall Garvey started Biddy Early in an attempt to revive the tradition of real
beer in Ireland, making, among other beers, Red Biddy, which is Ireland's only
herb beer. Red Biddy is made with bog myrtle, a wild herb growing in the hills
just next to the brewery, which was traditionally used instead of hops many
generations ago. The beer is then clarified with carrigeen moss, a local
seaweed: left unpasteurized and without preservatives, Red Biddy exemplifies
the company ethos of using natural and local ingredients. Biddy Early makes a
stout, a beer and a lager, with a few seasonal specials throughout the year; the
defining characteristic of them all is a commitment to the heritage of brewing
in Ireland.

super hero

THE COOPER FAMILY, of New Quay Honey Farm, Ceredigion, (see page 166)

The Cooper family at New Quay Honey Farm are very careful where they place their hives – dotted around the Pembrokeshire coast, the bees have access to heather, wild flowers and borage. The Coopers then take the honey and allow it to ferment at air temperature during the summer months, maturing the liquid in oak barrels for several months. This simple process results in honey wine, or mead, an ancient drink that has strong links with Wales – it has been made in Wales since at least AD 600. Making the mead in such an uncomplicated way allows the drink to retain 'a complex bouquet … the original flavour of the honey comes through'. It is so easy, in these times of labour-saving devices and 'added value' products to get carried away and lose the original nature of a foodstuff. New Quay Honey Farm demonstrates that, sometimes, the old ways are the best: 'if it ain't broke, don't fix it'.

REPUBLIC OF IRELAND   INAGH

The Biddy Early Brewery   super hero

Inagh, Ennis, Co. Clare   T: 065 683 6976   W: www.beb.ie

A brew pub with a deep commitment tor reviving the best of Ireland's beer-making traditions, Biddy Early brewery makes Ireland's only herb beer. See the Super Hero box, page 163, for more information.

REPUBLIC OF IRELAND   LUSK

Llewellyn's

Quickpenny Road, Lusk, Dublin   T: 01 8431 650 OR 087 284 3879
E: pureapple@eircom.net

farmers' markets

A rarity in Ireland – traditional farmhouse cider. David Llewellyn's cider is made with apples from his own orchard, which receive no insecticide sprays. He makes single-variety and blended ciders, all without additives. The ciders are fermented in the bottle, which gives a slight natural sparkle. Pure apple juices are also available. Find the drinks at Temple Bar Market in Dublin, and farmers' markets in Wicklow.

Beers Scotland Ltd

Manor Farm, Stirling FK9 5QA   T: 01786 446224   .w: www.beersscotland.co.uk
✉ mail order

Scotland has a thriving real ale and microbrewery industry and
CAMRA have bestowed many awards on some of the small
breweries of Scotland. Beers Scotland are passionate about these
real ales and offer many award-winners, including the 2002 winners
Dark Island and Red MacGregor from the Orkney Brewery, and
Bitter and Twisted from the Harviestoun Brewery. If the ale you are
after is not on the Beers Scotland website, call them – they'll do
their utmost to find it for you.

WALES   CARDIFF

Seidr Dai   super hero

Cardiff   T: 029 2075 8193   W: www.welshcider.co.uk

Fiona and Dave Matthews are busy trying to resurrect the Welsh
cider-making tradition. See the Super Hero box, page 166, for more
information.

WALES   CORWEN

The Natural Mead Company

Ty Brethyn Meadery, Maesmor Hall, Maerdy, Corwen, Conwy   T: 01490 460456
🖂 **farm gate sales**

Many people think that mead, as it is made from honey, must be a
very sweet drink. The Natural Mead Company are at pains to point
out that they fully ferment their mead for at least four months and
this results in an almost dry beverage – not at all sweet. As well as
the plain version there are varieties flavoured with traditional British
fruits – sloes, quince and blackberries. Available direct from
Maesmor Hall (call first), or from local delis.

super hero

FIONA AND DAVE MATTHEWS, of Seidr Dai, Cardiff (see page 165)

Cider-making has a long heritage in Wales, but the tradition all but died out around 40 years ago. Fiona and Dave Matthews are busy trying to resurrect it, finding and propagating old and rare Welsh apple trees from ancient orchards. While they make many single varietal ciders and perries, the Matthews also experiment with blends to find the best ways to use these rare varieties of fruit. A recent triumph was finding and using the incredibly rare Potato pear for perry. The ciders and perries have won numerous awards, and, while they are not available direct from the producers (the Matthews are not full-time cider-makers yet), they can be regularly found at the Boar's Head pub in Pontyclun, the Chapter Arts Centre in Cardiff and the Clytha Arms near Abergavenny.

WALES   **CRICKHOWELL**

Gellirhyd Farm

Llangenny, nr Crickhowell, Powys NP8 1HF   T: 01873 810466
w: www.gellirhydfarm.co.uk

farmers' markets

Colin and Daphne Gardiner produce around 40 different award-winning single-variety apple juices, made with organic apples grown on this farm in the Welsh hills. Most of the apple varieties are very unusual; in some cases, there is only one tree of a particular variety. Available from Usk farmers' market, or from local delis.

WALES   **NEW QUAY**

New Quay Honey Farm

Cross Inn, New Quay, Ceredigion SA44 6NN   T: 01545 560822
w: www.thehoneyfarm.co.uk

farm shop

The Cooper family at New Quay Honey Farm make honey wine, or mead, an ancient drink that has strong links with Wales. See the Super Hero box, page 164, for more information.

Bragdy Ceredigion Brewery

Unit 2, Wervil Grange Farm, Pentregat, Ceredigion SA44 6HW   T: 01545 561417 OR
01239 654888

✉ **mail order**

Bragdy is a real family business – Brian brews the beer, his wife
designs the (very artistic) labels and even their children are
occasionally roped in to help. The brewery grew out of Brian's
hobby of home-brewing, and now there are six beers, one of which
is organic, all of which are cask- or bottle-conditioned. The family
have always been strong advocates for 'real food', and now they
have turned to making real ale. Available by mail order direct from
the brewery, or find the beer on tap at the Ship Inn in Tresaith.

As an island nation, we are spoilt by the richness of seafood surrounding us just beyond our shores. The World Wildlife Fund says there are so many species local to our waters that we could happily eat a different type of fish every week of the year without eating the same type twice. How odd, then, that the fish we buy is dominated by only five types – cod, haddock, plaice, salmon and prawns – and most of these are from foreign seas. As has happened in almost every type of food supply, the specialists, the fishmongers, have been squeezed out and most of the produce offered to us is imported. This has caused some real problems. The wild stocks of those five popular types of fish are in a desperate state, our fishing industry is in decline and we are missing out on good-quality, locally caught fish, sold by people who really know their trade. For this section, I've tried to find fishmongers

fish

who understand the issues, who can offer you local produce and great variety and can answer all your questions.

Farmed fish, such as the ever-popular salmon, does help to ease the pressure on wild fish stocks, but brings its own problems: over-crowded cages, pollution, and escape of the farmed fish into the wild (where they can spread disease) being the key issues. Ultimately, farmed fish do not represent a perfect cure for over-fishing – farmed salmon and trout are fed fishmeal, made with smaller fish, which still depletes the oceans. We've listed some of the fish farms that are trying to tackle those issues and, in the process, are offering really good-quality fish. Fish is a contentious issue right now but, by extending the range you buy, trying new types and asking questions, you could help solve some of the problems and also find some very tasty fish on your plate.

Club Chef Direct

Lakeside, Bridgewater Road, Barrow Gurney, Bristol BS48 3SJ   T: 01275 475252
w: www.clubchefdirect.co.uk

✉ **mail order**

An amazing, ever-changing choice of fish. Look out for the
sustainably caught fish – line-caught mackerel, creel-caught
langoustines, hand-dived scallops and organically farmed salmon.

Barnacle Bill Direct

Harbour House, Unit 24, Northfields Industrial Estate, Northfields Lane, Brixham, Devon
T: 0800 970 5102   w: www.barnaclebilldirect.co.uk

✉ **mail order**

Barnacle Bill Direct source the majority of their fish from the day
boats landing at Brixham, and there is plenty of choice. At the top of
their list of priorities is sustainability – Barnacle Bill made the news
last year for suspending sales of sea bass when there was a
possibility that the pair of trawlers catching it were linked with
dolphin deaths, and this company won't hesitate to remove a
species of fish from its list if they think stocks are too low.

Browse Seafoods

The Old Market House, The Quay, Brixham, Devon TQ5 8AW   T: 01803 882484

The only remaining fresh fish shop in Brixham, Browse Seafoods are
crab specialists, and testament to the quality of their fish is the fact
that many good London restaurants buy their crustacea from
Browse. The shop is also filled with really fresh wet fish, all chosen
from the day boats landing at Brixham.

Bude Shellfish

5 The Seres, Lansdown Road, Bude, Cornwall EX23 8BH   T: 01288 354727

Bude Shellfish is run by Cliff, an ex-fisherman, who buys his fish
from Looe market, only ever from day boats. He selects the fish
each morning from the fishermen, never buying from boats that have
been out for more than a day.

TONY FREE, owner of Purely Organic, Warminster (see page 179)

One of the few trout farms in the UK that holds Soil Association organic accreditation, Purely Organic treats its rainbow trout very differently from most trout farms. The water the fish live in is exceptionally pure, having been underground for around 400 years, and it first passes through watercress beds, picking up tiny freshwater shrimps as it goes. These shrimps make up around 90% of the diet of the trout and they grow fit and healthy catching this live food. A big factor in their rearing is the space the fish have – they are stocked at one-third of the density of non-organic fish. Equally important is the lack of antibiotics in their diet. Tony Free, the owner of Purely Organic, told me that antibiotics can cause fish to take on 10–20% of their own weight in water. When they are cooked, this water evaporates and, if they have been reared in less than clean water, there can be an unpleasant earthy residue, affecting the flavour. Tony believes it is vital to respect the fish he rears and the environment he rears them in and says that the firm, well-flavoured fish he sells are worth this care and attention. There is a farm shop on site, where not only are the trout available, but also a wide range of local organic fruit and vegetables, local honey and all sorts of grocery items. The trout is also available from numerous local farmers' markets, or by mail order.

SOUTH WEST   CHRISTCHURCH

The Fish Stall

Mudeford Quay, Christchurch, Dorset BH23 4AB   T: 01425 275389

The fish on display at The Fish Stall is hand-picked from local day boats, with a good choice of fish from the less pressurized species. Hand-lined mackerel and wild sea bass are available in season. The Fish Stall is a member of the National Federation of Fishmongers.

SOUTH WEST   CURRY RIVEL

Brown and Forrest

The Smokery, Bowdens Farm, Hambridge, nr Curry Rivel, Somerset TA10 0BP
T: 01458 250875   w: www.smokedeel.co.uk

shop   **mail order**

Brown and Forrest smoke all kinds of foods – duck, trout, chicken, salmon, pork and even lamb – but it is for their smoked eels that they are really famous. The eels are caught in rivers in Wiltshire and Hampshire, and then smoked in old wood-fired smokers – no electricity or modern aids here. While oak is used for all the other produce, beech and apple wood is used for the eels, to impart a more delicate flavour. Available from the smokery shop, or by mail order and there is a restaurant on the premises.

SOUTH WEST   **DARTMOUTH**

The Dartmouth Smokehouse

Nelson Road, Dartmouth, Devon TQ6 9LA   T: 01803 833123
w: www.dartmouthsmokehouse.co.uk

🧺 **shop** ✉ **mail order**

A traditional smokehouse, producing a wide variety of gourmet smoked food using blends of wood smoke (oak, hickory, apple wood and alder) and herbs. Fresh fish and West Country meats are used to produce delicious cured and smoked food including: smoked Cornish chicken, hickory-roasted salmon, smoked eel fillets and smoked cherry tomatoes.

SOUTH WEST   **DARTMOUTH**

The Market Fish Shop

Victoria Road, Dartmouth, Devon TQ6 9SE   T: 01803 832782

Jenny Mackesey stocks fish from nearby Brixham, gently encouraging customers to try sustainably caught types of fish, such as the tasty red gurnard, John Dory and hand-dived scallops. All from day boats, the fish is fantastically fresh.

SOUTH WEST   **EAST LOOE**

Pengelly's

The Fish Market, The Quay, East Looe, Cornwall PL13 1DX   T: 01503 262246

These two fish shops are run by fifth-generation fishmongers. Angela, the owner, is the only woman buying direct from Looe market each morning, selecting only fish from day boats, and offering line-caught fish whenever she can get it. Conservation is a big issue for her – she only buys fish that has been caught sustainably. There is also a branch in Liskeard, see opposite.

The Duchy of Cornwall Oyster Farm

Port Navas, Falmouth, Cornwall TR11 5RJ   T: 01326 340210

⚜ **shop**

Both native and Pacific oysters are available here, along with mussels. If you are visiting, try to get there in the morning to buy the produce, as the staff are likely to be out in the boats fishing in the afternoons.

Falmouth Bay Oysters

The Docks, Falmouth, Cornwall TR11 4NR   T: 01326 316600
w: www.falmouthoysters.co.uk

✉ **mail order**

Wild native oysters are harvested by traditional sailing boats from October to March in the Marine Conservation area around Falmouth. Lobsters, crabs, cockles and all other shellfish are also available.

Fowey Fish

37 Fore Street, Fowey, Cornwall PL23 1AH   T: 01726 832422
w: www.foweyfish.com

✉ **mail order**

Fish only sourced from day boats landing at Looe or Fowey.

Pengelley's

2 The Arcade, Fore Street, Liskeard, Cornwall PL14 3JB   T: 01579 340777

For details, see under the East Looe branch, opposite.

Mevagissey Wet Fish

The West Quay, Mevagissey, Cornwall PL26 6QU   T: 01726 843839

Everything sold at this fish shop is from local waters, bought direct from the day boats landing each morning at Mevagissey.

super hero

NIGEL AND JUDE EKINS, of Cornish Cuisine, Penryn (see opposite)

Nigel and Jude Ekins are a father-and-son team who select some of the finest Cornish produce and smoke it traditionally using the draft method – the smoke is drawn gently across the food, ensuring the produce is not damaged by harsh high temperatures. The mackerel they use is caught locally by the ecologically sound method of hand-lining, and each fillet is hand-prepared for smoking. This old-fashioned method of smoking requires constant attention – smoked over a lengthy period of time, the kiln cannot be just left to its own devices because the temperature and smoke must remain consistent. This means that Nigel or Jude will often find themselves at the smokehouse at 2am, checking on the fish in the kiln.

A great range of local cheeses, often organic, also gets the smoking treatment, including a feta-style cheese – all ingredients are bought as close to home as possible. One of their smoked cheeses won the Supreme Award at the 2002 World Cheese Awards. The wood used can be apple, cherry or almond, which have a more delicate smoke than the oak usually used in smokeries, allowing the flavour of the fish, cheese or meat to shine through. Available mail order, or from the shop on site at the smokery.

SOUTH WEST   NAILSWORTH

William's Kitchen

3 Fountain Street, Nailsworth, Gloucestershire GL6 0BL   T: 01453 832240
w: www.williamskitchen.co.uk

Billed as 'the antidote to supermarkets', William's Kitchen offers a fish slab consisting of incredibly fresh fish from Cornwall, only from day boats. Fruits and vegetables, meats and deli foods are all of the best quality available.

SOUTH WEST   NEWLYN

The Pilchard Works/Cornish Fish Direct

Tolcarne, Newlyn, Cornwall TR18 5QH   T: 01736 332112
w: www.pilchardworks.co.uk AND www.cornishfish.co.uk
🛖 **shop** ✉ **mail order**

This is the only salt pilchard works in the UK, preserving and packing the fish in the traditional manner – layered in barrels with salt, and left for at least six weeks. An intensely flavoured food, salt pilchard can be used in any dishes that call for anchovies. At the pilchard works is a museum giving an insight into the history of this food. Fresh Cornish fish is also available by mail order.

Cornish Cuisine

super hero

The Smokehouse, Islington Wharf, Penryn, Cornwall TR10 8AT   T: 01326 376244
w: www.smokedsalmon-ltd.com

🚢 **shop**   ✉ **mail order**

Traditionally smoked fresh Cornish produce. Nigel and Jude Ekins offer a selection of find smoked foods including mackerel and cheese. See the Super Hero box, opposite, for more information.

Seabourne Fish

The Fish Shop, Unit T, Islington Wharf, Penryn, Cornwall TR10 8AT   T: 01326 378478
🚚 **delivery service**

David Seabourne goes to Newlyn market every morning to choose the fish he will stock in his shop, buying from day boats operating with good sustainable practices. Hand-lined mackerel, pollack and bass and hand-dived scallops are all on offer.

Ocean Harvest

53 The Ridgeway, Plympton, nr Plymouth, Devon PL7 2AW   T: 01752 331132
w: www.oceanharvest.co.uk

✉ **mail order**

Andy Trust gets up at the crack of dawn most days to visit Looe fish market, where he buys the freshest fish, only from day boats. He chooses the fish himself, so that he can be confident that he gets the best.

Frank Greenslade

Fish Market, New Quay Road, Poole, Dorset BH15 4AF   T: 01202 672199

Lots of fish from local waters are sold at this shop, mainly from day boats landing at Bournemouth. Local scallops, lobster and oysters are the stars.

Quayside Fish Centre

The Harbourside, Porthleven, Cornwall TR13 9JU T: 01326 562008
w: www.quaysidefish.co.uk

✉ **mail order**

A great place for fresh, sustainably caught fish – everything is local and from day boats, or line caught.

The Cornish Smoked Fish Company

Charlestown, St Austell, Cornwall PL25 3NY T: 01726 72356
w: www.cornishsmokedfish.co.uk

🏪 **shop** ✉ **mail order**

Smoked traditionally with oak, the Cornish Smoked Fish Company offer a dizzying choice of produce, from trout and salmon to prawns and mussels, and even eel. The majority of the fish is from Cornish waters.

Wing of St Mawes

4 Warren Road, Indian Queens, St Columb, Cornwall TR9 6TL T: 01726 861666
w: www.cornish-seafood.co.uk

✉ **mail order**

The fishmongers at Wing are all happy to offer advice and suggestions and will prepare the fish according to the customer's requirements. All the fish is from Cornish day boats and the aim is for it to be delivered to you the day after it was caught (or customers can collect direct from the premises).

Martin's Seafresh

St Columb Business Centre, Barn Lane, St Columb Major, Cornwall TR9 6BU
T: 0800 027 2066 w: www.martins-seafresh.co.uk

✉ **mail order**

Plenty of fresh Cornish fish from a fishmonger's run by an ex-fisherman. Lobsters, oysters and mussels are specialities at Martin's Seafresh. Mail order only. Martin's Seafresh is a member of the National Federation of Fishmongers.

Matthew Stevens & Son

Back Road East, St Ives, Cornwall TR26 1NW   T: 01736 799392
w: www.mstevensandson.com

✉ **mail order**

Wet fish and shellfish, landed at Newlyn, St Ives and Looe, mainly
from day boats are sold here. There is sometimes hand-lined
mackerel available, too.

Market Fish

Market Place, Sidmouth, Devon EX10 8AR   T: 01395 577342

Fish comes fresh each morning to Market Fish's stall from the day
boats landing at Brixham and Exmouth. During the summer, fish
comes straight off the boats landing at Sidmouth, bringing crabs
and lobsters and some hand-lined fish. Market Fish is a member of
the National Federation of Fishmongers.

super hero

FREIA AND NIGEL SAYER, of Fish at the Square, Brighton (page 180)

When I spoke to Freia Sayer, one half of the husband and wife team running Fish
at the Square in Brighton, they had a sign outside their shop with a list of fish
they refuse to sell. Fish at the Square is a rare fishmonger's indeed – it has put
the fisheries' crisis before profits and stocks only those types of fish that are not
under pressure from overfishing, a move inspired by increasing concern over the
sustainability of the fishing industry. Shopping here, you'll find gurnard, saithe,
pollack and a great range of local fish, all at the peak of freshness, but no
monkfish or cod. Although this could have been a very dangerous move
financially, they have found that their customers have supported them
wholeheartedly and are reaping the benefits by trying out a whole range of
different, delicious fish. Freia told me that their new policy was a 'leap of faith',
but that 'it's really exciting how it's changing the direction of our business'. While
Freia's husband, Nigel, sources the very best local fish, Freia is on hand to
advise customers on how to cook some of the less familiar types.

Donnington Trout Farm

Upper Swell, nr Stow-on-the-Wold, Gloucestershire GL54 1EP   T: 01451 830873
W: www.donningtontrout.co.uk

↙ **farm shop**

Brown trout and rainbow trout grown in pure spring-water ponds.

Phil Bowditch

7 Bath Place, Taunton, Somerset TA1 4ER   T: 01823 253500

✉ **mail order**

Phil Bowditch imports virtually no fish at all – the majority of what he
sells comes from the day boats landing at Brixham, or from his own
boat.

The Ticklemore Fish Shop

10 Ticklemore Street, Totnes, Devon TQ9 5EJ   T: 01803 867805

The owner of the Ticklemore Fish Shop goes to Brixham fish market
each morning, selecting fish from the day boats that land there.
While he is keen to stock local fish, he won't sell cod from local
waters, feeling that the stocks are too low. Instead, he offers
Icelandic cod, from the sustainable fisheries there.

Mere Fish Farm

Ivymead Mere, Warminster, Wiltshire BA12 6EN   T: 01747 860461
E: sales@merefishfarm.demon.co.uk

↙ **farm shop**   🚚 **delivery service**

Cold- or hot-smoked rainbow trout, using fish reared in pure spring
water. Local deliveries.

Purely Organic

FISH

Deverill Trout Farm, Longbridge Deverill, Warminster, Wiltshire BA12 7DZ
T: 01985 841093 w: www.purelyorganic.co.uk

farm shop **farmers' markets** **mail order**

Well-flavoured, firm trout, reared to exceptionally high standards by
Tony Free, are available from Purely Organic. See the Super Hero
box, page 171, for more information.

Severn and Wye Smokery

Chaxhill, Westbury-on-Severn, Gloucestershire GL14 1QW T: 01452 760190
w: www.severnandwye.co.uk

shop **mail order**

Traditionally smoked wild salmon and also organically farmed
salmon are available here. Smoked eel, trout and mackerel are also
on offer, as well as line-caught, fresh wild sea bass.

Bell's Fisheries

Rear of 1 High Street, Wimborne, Dorset BH21 5PS T: 07850 093096

Bell's Fisheries is a permanent fish stall rather than a shop, selling
day-caught fish landed mainly at Brixham. There is plenty of fish
from species less endangered than cod and Mr Bell will happily
advise on cooking. Bell's Fisheries is a member of the National
Federation of Fishmongers.

Hand Picked Shellfish Company

The Market, Festival Square, Festival Place, Basingstoke, Berkshire T: 07968 176485
w: www.handpickedshellfish.com

farmers' markets

A fishmonger's run by fishermen, everything sold here has been
caught by the staff. Alongside the hand-dived shellfish is a range of
unusual wet fish, with species less pressurized by overfishing, such
as gurnard. The fish is caught off Weymouth. Available from the food
hall at Festival Place Wednesday to Saturday and also at many
London farmers' markets.

Fish at the Square

super hero

2 St Georges Road, Brighton BN2 1EB   T: 01273 680808

Husband and wife team Freia and Nigel Sayer sell a whole range of local fish, none of which is under pressure from overfishing. See the Super Hero box, page 177, for more information.

The Fresh Food Company

The Orchard, 50 Wormholt Road, London W12 0LS   T: 020 8749 8778
w: www.freshfood.co.uk

✉ **mail order**

This pioneering company, established in 1989, select sustainably fished seafood from Cornwall and the south coast for nationwide home-delivery within 48 hours of the fish being landed at port. There is plenty of fish from inshore boats and, when available, fish from Marine Stewardship Council-approved fisheries, such as hand-lined mackerel, Thames herring and cockles from the Burry Inlet. Organic fruit, vegetables, meat and wild-harvested game are also on offer.

H Forman & Son

30a Marshgate Lane, London E15 2NH   T: 020 8221 3900   w: www.formanandfield.com

🏪 **shop**   ✉ **mail order**

Forman's is one of the oldest smokehouses in the country, smoking wild salmon to great critical acclaim.

Steve Hatt

88–90 Essex Road, Islington, London N1 8LU   T: 020 7226 3963

Steve Hatt is a committed campaigner for UK fishing rights and quality fish. The fish is always bought by Steve on quality, not price.

PHILLIP GUY, of the Whitstable Shellfish Company, Whitstable (see page 182)

Native oysters are difficult to find these days – they are notoriously tricky to farm, taking five years to grow to maturity, and are more vulnerable to disease than the more commonly farmed Pacific variety. Ask an oyster connoisseur which variety he'd rather eat and there will be no hesitation – he'll always say the native. When Phillip Guy of the Whitstable Shellfish Company describes the taste of the native oyster, it is not immediately obvious why they are held in such high regard: 'They have a mineral taste, not unlike rusty nails!' Phillip has his own boat, the Angelina, and harvests the oysters from the wild beds around Whitstable Bay. This is not as easy as it sounds; there used to be inshore beds of oysters, but these were almost wiped out by a fungus unwittingly spread when French and Dutch oysters were imported to help bolster the stock, and so Philip has to fish further out to sea, where the beds were not damaged. These oysters are in deeper water, in small pockets. Says Philip: 'Finding the small pockets of oysters is a task on its own, further off shore it is more exposed in the bad weather, so limiting the days available for fishing. A small boat will average about 200 oysters on a good 12-hour day.' Add to this the fact that native oysters are only available from September to April, and we are talking about a very special food. Given the less than consistent supplies of the natives, the Whitstable Shellfish Company also supply Pacific oysters, sent live from the west coast of Scotland. While Whitstable provides truly excellent native oysters, Pacific oysters are less happy growing there and Philip chooses to source his in Scotland, where the quality is outstanding. 'We have formed a very strong working partnership with some of the crofters in the Scottish Highlands who also cultivate Pacific oysters on the west coast. This high-quality Pacific oyster acts as an excellent all-year-round complement to the native. Our specialized sea-water holding tanks enable oysters from a remote area to reach otherwise unobtainable markets in prime condition and in turn allows the Whitstable Shellfish Company to sell a very high-quality Pacific oyster all year round.' This variety has a fresh, salty flavour with a hint of cucumber.

SOUTH EAST   OXFORD

Hayman's Fisheries

21–23 Covered Market, Avenue One, Market Street, Oxford OX1 3DU   T: 01865 242827
w: www.haymansfisheries.co.uk

The majority of the fish at Hayman's comes from British waters, with a really wide range available. Fish straight from the day boats landing at Looe and Grimsby, shellfish from clean Scottish waters and hand-dived scallops are all available.

SOUTH EAST	RYE

Botterell's

Seafarers, Harbour Road, Rye Harbour, Rye, East Sussex TN31 7TT   T: 01797 222875

farmers' markets

The Botterell Family buy their fish direct from day boats landing at Rye, and always have a big selection of whatever is in season. Flat fish are the staples here, with crabs and lobster, scallops and samphire available in season. Everything is super-fresh – the fish on the Botterell's stall is always less than 24 hours old. Find the produce at local farmers' markets, including Rolvenden, Rye and Battle.

SOUTH EAST	WHITSTABLE

Whitstable Shellfish Company   super hero

Westmead Road, Whitstable, Kent, CT5 1LW   T: 01227 282375
w: www.whitstable-shellfish.co.uk

mail order

Philip Guy harvests native oysters from Whitstable Bay. Only available from September until April, the oysters are a rare delicacy. See the Super Hero box, page 181, for more information.

EAST ANGLIA	BRANCASTER STAITHE

The Fish Shed

Brancaster Staithe, Norfolk PE31 8BY   T: 01485 210532

Fish from local day boats provides the mainstay of the produce at the Fish Shed and in season there are crabs and lobsters straight from the boats. Local game is also available in season.

EAST ANGLIA	COLCHESTER

Colchester Oyster Fishery Ltd

Pyefleet Quay, Mersea Island, Colchester, Essex CO5 8UN   T: 01206 384141
w: www.colchesteroysterfishery.com

shop   **mail order**

The native oysters on sale here are harvested from the famous fattening grounds around Mersea Island. The fishery also sells rock oysters, lobsters, clams and crabs, all at the height of freshness.

The Company Shed

129 Coast Road, West Mersea, Colchester, Essex CO5 8PA   T: 01206 382700

🛒 **shop**   ✉ **mail order**

Famous Colchester native oysters are available here between September and April, harvested locally by the Hawarth family, now in their sixth generation of oyster fishing.

Richard and Julie Davies

7 Garden Street, Cromer, Norfolk NR27 9HN   T: 01263 512727

Cromer is famous for its crabs, which are small and sweet, with a distinctive flavour. The crabs and lobsters at the Davies' shop are caught by the shop's own boat.

food facts

WHICH KINDS OF FISH SHOULD I BUY?

There is a long list of fish types that are less well known, but versatile and delicious. Pollack and saithe are both similar to cod, but their stocks are under much less pressure. Herring, while once endangered, is well on the way to recovery, but people have not yet got back into the habit of buying and cooking herring, even though it is incredibly tasty and very good for you. Megrim sole, mackerel, john dory, wolf fish, weaver, black bream, trigger fish, flounder, dabs, the list goes on and on — a good fishmonger will have up to 50 different types of fish to choose from. It is still important to buy cod and haddock every once in a while — there needs to be a market for them when the stocks recover or the fishing industry will never get back on its feet. At present, most of the cod and prawns we buy come from Iceland and Norway; these countries are relatively successful at maintaining the stocks of these fish within safe limits, so it makes sense to buy from them. Don't boycott fish because of over-fishing worries. It could force the price down due to lack of demand, ending in more of each species being caught to pay fishermens' bills. Go for other species, but we must eat fish. It's an essential part of our diet, as research into the fatty acid omega, found in fish oil, has proved.

food facts

DOES IT MATTER HOW THE FISH WAS CAUGHT?

In terms of sustaining the fisheries, yes, it does. The Marine Stewardship Council is busy encouraging fishermen to use sustainable methods to catch fish, and as a result, they accredit certain products from fisheries that have demonstrated that they are catching fish with the future of the stocks in mind – look out for them in supermarkets. Sustainable methods tend to include the old-fashioned ways – hand-lining, creeling, hand-diving for shellfish. These methods usually give better-quality fish – they cause the fish far less damage. Day boats, as opposed to the large factory freezer trawlers that go out for weeks at a time, can offer fresher fish – the fish is back in port the same day it was caught, and it is more sustainable, as the boats can only go so far out to sea, leaving large areas unfished, where stocks can recover. The thing to do is ask questions when you buy fish. You might not always get an answer, but the more people that ask, the more suppliers will want to be able to answer you. The best fishmongers are those that hand-pick fish from the markets or ports themselves every day. They know which boats they want to buy from and they have built up relationships with the fishermen; they will be able to tell you a lot more about the fish, and how and when it was caught.

For more information on the MSC and its accredited products, check out the website www.msc.org

---

EAST ANGLIA   HOLT

Cookies Crab Shop

The Green, Salthouse, Holt, Norfolk NR25 7AJ   T: 01263 740352   w: www.salthouse.org.uk

The crabs and lobsters at Cookies are all caught using the shop's own boats in local waters. Available to take home fresh, or you can eat them at Cookies' own restaurant.

EAST ANGLIA   HOLT

W J Weston

5A Westgate Street, Blakeney, Holt, Norfolk NR25 7NQ   T: 01263 741112

William Weston is a fisherman himself and his shop in Blakeney is filled with local delicacies such as lobster, crab, cockles and home-potted shrimps. His wife Dawn makes all kinds of deli-style foods with the fresh seafood – smoked salmon tortilla wraps, seafood quiches and fish pâtés.

Crowe Fishmongers

3 Provisional Market, Gentleman's Walk, Norwich, Norfolk NR2 1ND   T: 01603 767411

A vast selection of fish is on offer at Crowe's stall, usually around 40 varieties, with plenty coming from day boats landing at Lowestoft.

John's Fish Shop

5 East Street, Southwold, Suffolk IP18 6EH   T: 01502 724253
w: www.johns-fish-shop.co.uk

Owned and run by an ex-fisherman, John's is a fishmonger selling fish mainly from Southwold harbour and Lowestoft; John hand-picks the fish every morning.

Butley Orford Oysterage

Market Hill, Orford, Woodbridge, Suffolk IP12 2LH   T: 01394 450277

Most of the fish sold at Butley Orford are caught with the shop's own boats. Pacific oysters and wet fish are on offer, including cod, skate, and brill, and traditionally smoked fish. There is also a restaurant.

Loaves and Fishes

52 The Thoroughfare, Woodbridge, Suffolk IP12 1AL   T: 01394 385650

A real find for foodies, Loaves and Fishes stocks great local fresh fish and all manner of locally produced foods, even hard-to-find wet walnuts from local trees.

Stephenson's Fishmongers

205 Retail Market, Queen Victoria Road, Coventry CV1 3HT   T: 07974 140255
w: www.stephenson-fish.co.uk

Robert Stephenson has a firm policy when it comes to buying fish – he buys with sustainability in mind. This means he won't cater for the fashion in 'baby' fish – young fish that have not had a chance to reproduce. The fish is always British and always from day boats.

The Organic Smokehouse

Clunbury Hall, Clunbury, Craven Arms, Shropshire SY7 0HG   T: 01588 660206
w: www.organicsmokehouse.com

📣 **farmers' markets**   ✉ **mail order**

Organic salmon from the Shetlands and the Hebrides is dry-salted and air-dried before being smoked for at least 24 hours over naturally fallen Shropshire oak – a traditional method, performed in an unhurried manner. Smoked organic butter, Cheddar cheese, sea salt and ricotta cheese are also available.

Alfred Enderby

Fish Dock Road, Grimsby, Lincolnshire DN31 3NE   T: 01472 342984
w: www.alfredenderby.co.uk

✉ **mail order**

Famous for large undyed smoked haddock and cod fillets, Enderby's buys its fish fresh off the quayside every morning and smokes it the slow, traditional way overnight in 100-year-old brick smokehouses. Their sides of smoked salmon are from fish sourced direct from salmon farms in the Shetland Isles.

Grapevine

31 High Street, Kington, Herefordshire HR5 3BJ   T: 01544 231202

Organic fish is well represented here, with organic salmon from Orkney and organic trout from Wales. Welsh crabs and lobsters are also available, along with local organic fruit and vegetables.

Simply Organic Food Company Ltd

Horsley Road, Kingsthorpe Hollow, Northampton NN2 6LJ   T: 0870 7606001
w: www.simplyorganic.net

✉ **mail order**

Simply Organic has an enormous range of certified organic produce, from meat to vegetables, dairy and groceries. There is also a great choice in fresh and smoked fish, all of it sourced with a keen eye on the sustainability issues affecting the fishing industry. All manner of wet fish, only from day boats, is available, and seasonality plays a key role – 'closed seasons' to enable fish to re-stock are well observed by all the fishermen Simply Organic buy from. Fillets, steaks or whole fish can be ordered, and the fish is always incredibly fresh – it is sourced to order, so nothing ever sits around in the warehouse.

Hawkshead Trout Farm

The Boat House, Ridding Wood, Hawkshead, Ambleside, Cumbria LA22 0QF T: 01539 436541 w: www.organicfish.com

✉ **mail order**

Organic trout are reared in roomy conditions at Hawkshead, with much lower stocking densities than conventional fish farms. No chemicals or colourings are involved in their production. Organic salmon from Orkney is also available form the shop or via mail order.

Bessy Beck Trout Farm

Newbiggin-on-Lune, Kirkby Stephen, Cumbria CA17 4LY T: 01539 623303
E: bessybecktrout@aol.com

⬇ **farm shop** ✉ **mail order**

The trout at Bessy Beck, owned by Simon and Vera Norman-Ballantyne, are farmed non-intensively – the stocking densities are much lower than conventional fish farms and the fish are fed by hand. They are reared slowly, only reaching table size at around 18 months to two years, as opposed to conventionally farmed fish, killed at around a year old. This slow rearing gives the flesh a flakier texture, with more flavour. The fish are available fresh from the farm shop or traditionally hot-smoked by mail order.

Moore's Traditional Curers

Mill Road, Peel, Isle of Man, IM5 1TA T: 01624 812155 w: www.manxkippers.com

✉ **mail order**

The kippers at Moore's are smoked for 12 hours using the old-fashioned draft method, above burning oak chips. They are the last traditional Manx kipper curer on the Isle of Man. The fish is undyed. Bacon is also smoked slowly (for up to a week). Tours of the smokery are available and Moore's is a member of the Manx Producers Organisation.

Southport Potted Shrimps

66 Station Road, Banks Village, Southport, Lancashire PR9 8BB   T: 01704 229266
w: www.pottedshrimp.co.uk

✉ **mail order**

James Peet manufactures potted brown shrimps to his own specially devised recipe. He tried traditional recipes first, from the times before refrigeration, but felt that the old recipes overpowered the shrimp flavour with their need for preserving ingredients. James's recipe is simpler – shrimps, butter, and a light shake of ground mace, salt and pepper – the flavour of the shrimp shines through. Southport Potted Shrimps belongs to the Shellfish Association of Great Britain.

The Cheshire Smokehouse

Vost Farm, Morley Green, Wilmslow, Cheshire SK9 5NU   T: 01625 548499
w: www.cheshiresmokehouse.co.uk

🛒 **shop** ✉ **mail order**

The Ward family smoke all kinds of foods, from salmon and trout to bacon and ham and even nuts (the smoked cashews are fantastic). Old-fashioned methods are used – oak and beech chips, and an unhurried attitude. Fresh foods are also available – local fruit and veg and fresh bread made on the premises daily.

Robertson's Prime

Unit 1d Willowtree Industrial Estate, Alnwick, Northumberland NE66 2HA   T: 01665 604386

Most of the fish at Robertson's Prime comes from day boats landing at nearby Amble, and some is line-caught. Ian Robertson hand-picks the fish for the shop each day as it comes into the port. Local game in season is also offered.

Lindisfarne Oysters

West House, Ross Farm, Belford, Northumberland NE70 7EN   T: 01668 213870

✉ **farm gate sales**

There has been a long tradition of oyster beds around Lindisfarne but these declined some time in the 19th century. Chris Sutherland's father resurrected the beds a few years ago and now Chris and his wife Helen are continuing the tradition. The Pacific oysters they farm take three or four years to reach maturity before they are purified at the Sutherlands' own tanks at the farm. Available direct from the farm, from Swallow Fish in Seahouses (see their entry, page 190), and other local outlets – call for details.

NORTH EAST   CORBRIDGE

Ridley's Fish and Game

17 Watling Street, Corbridge, Northumberland NE45 5AH   T: 01434 632640

The fish at Ridley's is hand-chosen by the owner, David, from the local ports, direct from the fishermen. He only uses fish from day boats, ensuring freshness. Local game from nearby estates is also sold here – all bought direct from the shoots and prepared at the shop. There is also a branch in Hexham, see page 190.

food facts

FARMED FISH

Fish farming has lowered the price of salmon, making what was once a luxury food available to most of us. Sometimes, however, the salmon can be disappointing – an artificially bright pink, with a flabby texture and bland flavour. Many people point the finger of blame for this at the conditions in which the fish are reared. As salmon grew in popularity, farmers endeavoured to produce greater quantities at a lower price. As a result, more fish are crammed into smaller spaces, fed high-protein foods to accelerate growth, and this food is often full of antibiotics to prevent the spread of disease in such crowded conditions. With less than half a bathful of water each to swim in, it's hardly surprising that the fish are not firm and muscular like their wild equivalents. Some fish farms are much better than others – those sited out to sea, where the fish swim against powerful currents, which in turn clean away the waste the farm produces, and organic farms, which, by regulation, give the fish more space and don't feed antibiotics or growth promoters.

Shellfish farming is different – the pollution is minimal, the fish live virtually as they would were they wild and for those concerned about sustainability issues farmed shellfish are a good choice. We've found some great producers, including those who farm the prized native oyster, notoriously difficult to farm, but well worth the effort.

Bleikers Smokehouse

Unit 88 Glasshouses Mill, Glasshouses, Harrogate, North Yorkshire HG3 5QH   T: 01423 711411   w: www.bleikers.co.uk

✉ **mail order**

When it comes to smoking, at Bleikers they admit that nothing happens quickly. The salmon used are hand-fed fish from low-density farms in the Hebrides, and they are smoked very slowly in an old-fashioned smokery. Poultry, game, meat, cheese and vegetables are also smoked without using any colourings or artificial preservatives. Bleikers' produce has won a clutch of medals from the Great Taste awards. They supply mail order.

Ridley's Fish and Game

2 Battle Hill, Hexham, Northumberland NE46 1BB   T: 01434 603138

For details, see under the Corbridge branch on page 189.

Swallow Fish

2 South Street, Seahouses, Northumberland NE68 7RB   T: 01665 721052
w: www.swallowfish.co.uk

🛒 **shop**   ✉ **mail order**

The smokehouse at Swallow Fish dates from the 19th century, and the fish smoked in it are locally caught, undyed haddock and cod and wild salmon. Fresh local fish is also available. Everything is smoked slowly and gently for a traditional flavour. Swallow Fish is a member of the National Federation of Fishmongers.

Kilnsey Park

Kilnsey, nr Skipton, North Yorkshire BD23 5PS   T: 01756 752150
w: www.kilnseypark.co.uk

🌾 **farm shop**   📇 **farmers' markets**   ✉ **mail order**

Kilnsey Park is blessed with a natural spring in the grounds and it is in this clean water that trout are reared. Lower than average stocking densities allow the fish plenty of room to grow and the attention to detail extends to hand feeding. Buy the fish whole or made into a variety of dishes – chowder, pâtés, terrines or fishcakes – from the farm shop, by mail order, or from many local farmers' markets. There is also a restaurant.

NORTH EAST   STOCKSFIELD

Bywell Fish and Game Smokery

South Acomb Farm, Bywell, Stocksfield, Northumberland NE43 7AQ T: 01661 844084

🛒 **farmers' markets** ✉ **mail order**

Locally caught cod and haddock, and pheasant and venison are smoked over oak, prepared using traditional curing methods and recipes. All the produce is undyed and prepared by hand. Available by mail order, from Hexham and Morpeth farmers' markets.

NORTH EAST   TADCASTER

Organic Pantry

St Helen's Farm, Newton Kyme, Tadcaster, North Yorkshire LS24 9LY T: 01937 531693

🚚 **delivery service**

Amongst the array of organic produce here – local vegetables and dairy produce and organic meat from local farms – organic fish can be found. There is both smoked and roast organic salmon from Ireland and fresh organic trout.

NORTH EAST   WHITBY

Fortunes

22 Henrietta Street, Whitby, North Yorkshire YO22 4DW, T: 01947 601659

🏬 **shop**

Fortunes is a long-established traditional smokehouse, producing good old-fashioned kippers. The fish are hung over beech and oak shavings and smoked for at least 16–18 hours, resulting in a rich, strong flavour.

NORTH EAST   YORK

Cross of York

3&4 Newgate Market, York YO1 2LA T: 01904 627590

The majority of the fish here is landed at Scarborough or Whitby. Cross of York was a previous winner of the Best Fishmonger in Northern England award.

FOOD HEROES OF BRITAIN

Morton's

9 Bayview Road, Ballycastle BT54 6BP   T: 028 2076 2348

Morton's have their own fishing boats, so the fish comes straight off the boat and into the shop – no middlemen, no delay.

Walter Ewing

124 Shankhill Road, Belfast BT13 2BD   T: 028 9032 5534

Wet fish and shellfish from local waters, chosen from day boats. Walter Ewing is justly famous for the freshness of his fish.

The Northern Salmon Company

Glenarm, Co. Antrim BT44 0AA   T: 028 2884 1691   E: northernsalmon@btclick.com
✉ **mail order**

The Northern Salmon Company were one of the first to farm salmon organically. Close attention to water quality, feed and stocking densities results in fitter fish, and organic salmon, generally having firmer and paler flesh, are considered closer in eating quality to wild salmon. The Northern Salmon Company gently smokes the organically reared fish, which are available by mail order.

Cuan Sea Fisheries

Sketrick Island, Killinchy, Co. Down BT23 6QH   T: 028 9754 1461   w: www.cuanoysters.com
✉ **mail order**

Pacific and native oysters grown in the very clean waters of Strangford Lough, a designated Marine Nature Reserve.

The Connemara Smoke House

Bunowen Pier, Ballyconneely, Clifden, Co. Galway   T: 095 23739
w: www.smokehouse.ie

✉ **mail order**

The Connemara Smoke House has won a prestigious Bridgestone
Guide Award for its mouthwatering specialist products, namely,
smoked salmon, tuna and gravadlax. Only natural ingredients are
used – just fish, salt, sugar, honey, Irish whiskey and herbs – with no
colourings or artificial additives. This smokehouse specializes in wild
salmon, although organic salmon from Clare Island is also available.
Smoked line-caught Irish tuna is a product unique to this
smokehouse. All the fish is filleted by hand and traditionally dry-
cured, followed by a long drying and smoking period over
beechwood in an old-fashioned kiln that dates from 1946.
Connemara Smoke House is accredited by the Organic Trust.

Woodcock Smokery

Castletownshend, Skibbereen, Co. Cork   T: 028 36232

✉ **mail order**

Traditionally smoked wild salmon, haddock, mackerel and kippers.
The smoked wild salmon won a gold Great Taste award in 2002.

Belvelly Smokehouse

Cobh, Co. Cork   T: 021 481 1089

🛒 **farmers' markets** ✉ **mail order**

In his old timber smokehouse Frank Hederman smokes wild and
organic Irish salmon using the delicate smoke of beech wood. Using
organic sea salt, he first dry-cures the fish and then, using exactly
the right size of beech wood chips, slowly smokes the salmon – the
size of the wood chips is vital in creating the correct density. Hot-
smoked mackerel and eel are also available; check them out at
Midleton farmers' market.

super hero

MARTIN SHANAHAN, of the Kinsale Gourmet Store, Kinsale (see opposite)

Kinsale Gourmet Store is a fish-lover's paradise. The restaurant on site serves only fish, no meat, and the same high standard of fish is available to take away from their fish counter. Everything comes from the local day boats landing at Kinsale Harbour and the range available at any given time is governed by seasonality. Martin Shanahan is a perfect example of a retailer working well with his suppliers. He's not content to buy fish from a wholesaler – by far the easiest option. Instead, he buys direct from the local fishermen and has worked hard with them, encouraging them to use good practices to raise the quality of the fish they bring in. Both parties are now reaping the benefits – Martin gets the best fish around and the fishermen know they have a guaranteed outlet for their produce.

REPUBLIC OF IRELAND   CORK

K O'Connell Ltd Fish Emporium

Cork English Market, 13–20 Grand Parade Market, Cork City, Co. Cork
T: 021 427 6380   E: freshfish@eircom.net

The O'Connells select the fish for their stall themselves, buying only with freshness in mind. Everything on the stall is from Irish waters and can be bought whole, or they will fillet it while you watch.

REPUBLIC OF IRELAND   DUBLIN

Nicky's Plaice

Store F, West Pier, Howth, Dublin   T: 01 832 3557 OR 832 6195
W: www.nickysplaice.ie

Nicky and his son Martin have many, many years of experience as fishmongers, and buy their fish straight from the boats. They know which skippers bring in the best fish and that's who they buy from.

REPUBLIC OF IRELAND   DUNGARVAN

Helvick Seafood

Cross Bridge Street, Dungarvan, Co. Waterford   T: 058 43585

The fish at Helvick Seafood comes straight from the local boats every morning – day boats, so the fish is always very fresh. Lots of choice, including fresh prawns, and all the fish is local, never imported. Most are available either whole or filleted.

Caviston's Seafood

59 Glastule Road, Sandycove, Dun Loaghaire   T: 01 280 9120   w: www.cavistons.com

A shop renowned for the freshness of the fish on display, supplemented with a good choice of Irish artisan cheeses. There is also a restaurant.

McDonagh's Seafood House

22 Quay Street, Galway   T: 091 565001   w: www.mcdonaghs.net

This fishmonger's sells locally caught fish and the famous oysters from Clarinbridge. There is a seafood bar and a fish and chip bar.

Michael Kelly (Shellfish) Ltd

Aisling, Tyrone, Kilcolgan, Co. Galway   T: 091 796120   w: www.kellyoysters.com
✉ mail order

Legendary native oysters from the west coast of Ireland – believed by many to be the best-tasting oysters in the world – fished to order.

Kinsale Gourmet Store   super hero

Guardwell, Kinsale, Co. Cork   T: 021 477 4453

Martin Shanahan buys only the best quality fish from local day boats to sell at his shop and restaurant. See the Super Hero box, opposite, for more information.

Kinvara Smoked Salmon

Kinvara, Co. Galway   T: 091 637489   w: www.kinvarasmokedsalmon.com
✉ mail order

Kinvara is one of the few smokeries offering organic salmon. The fish are reared on farms 5 km off the west coast of Ireland and the strong sea currents there ensure the farms are clean and the fish are fit and healthy. The stocking density is around half of that in conventional salmon farms, so the fish have much more space to swim around. The smoking is conducted over traditional oak shavings for a classic flavour.

REPUBLIC OF IRELAND · LISDOONVARNA

Burren Smokehouse

Lisdoonvarna, Co. Clare   T: 065 707 4432   w: www.burrensmokehouse.ie
✉ mail order

Much more than a smokehouse, Burren also offer hand-made Irish chocolates, artisan cheeses, pâtés, jams and chutneys. They remain most famous for their smoked fish – eel, mackerel, trout, and the organic salmon for which they won a Great Taste award.

REPUBLIC OF IRELAND · TIMOLEAGUE

Ummera Smoked Products

Inchybridge, Timoleague, Co. Cork   T: 023 46644   w: www.ummera.com
✉ mail order

Wild salmon from the Cork coastline and organic farmed salmon from Clare Island are traditionally smoked using oak. The fish is delicately smoked, allowing the flavour of the fish to balance well with the smoke. Hot-smoked chicken and eel are also available and the smokery is accredited by the Organic Trust.

SCOTLAND · ABERDEEN

Ken Watmough

29 Thistle Street, Aberdeen AB10 1UY   T: 01224 640321

Ken buys his fish fresh each morning at Aberdeen Market; he knows the schedules of landings and which skippers he wants to buy from. A really wide choice is on offer here.

SCOTLAND · ACHILTIBUIE

Summer Isles Foods

Achiltibuie, Ross-shire IV26 2YR,   T: 01854 622353   w: www.summerislesfoods.com
✉ mail order

The fish at Summer Isles Foods is smoked using oak shavings, which gives a slower burn that results in a sweeter flavour. Organic salmon is available and it is marinated in an unusual blend of rum, molasses, juniper and garlic before smoking.

The Hand-Made Fish Company

Bigton, Shetland ZE2 9JF T: 01950 422214 w: www.handmadefish.co.uk
✉ **mail order**

David Parham is keen to sell only sustainably sourced fish and often has line-caught fish available. Organic salmon is also on offer. He also smokes fish using an unusual selection of woods: alongside the regular oak he smokes with beech, plum wood, peat and olive wood.

Isle of Skye Seafood

Broadford Industrial Estate, Broadford, Isle of Skye IV49 9AP T: 01471 822135
w: www.skye-seafood.co.uk
✉ **mail order**

Fresh langoustines and lobster from the clean waters around Skye, and also traditionally smoked fish.

food facts

HOW CAN YOU TELL IF FISH IS TRULY FRESH?

Follow these simple clues, and you'll be able to tell at a glance how fresh the fish is:

- Are the eyes bright? Cloudy or sunken eyes indicate a fish well past its prime.
- Are the scales shiny and healthy looking? Reject fish with rough, dry or dull scales.
- Does the flesh feel firm? Soft or flabby flesh denotes a stale fish.
- Does the fish smell fresh, with the scent of the sea? Only old fish smells fishy.
- Are the gills a lustrous pink or red, moist and a delight to the eye, not at all faded or brown?
- Is the skin shiny and vivid, with colours such as orange spots on plaice or the turquoise green and blue lines on a mackerel, bright and cheerful?
- Are the fins clearly defined, not scraggy and broken?

Loch Fyne Oysters Ltd

Clachan, Clairndow, Argyll PA26 8BL   T: 01499 600264   w: www.lochfyne.com

✉ **mail order**

Smoked salmon, haddock, eels and kippers, using fish from suppliers who operate sustainably, and organically if possible. Oysters come from the company's own beds, in the clean waters of Loch Fyne. Scottish beef, lamb and game are also available.

The Lobster Store

34 Shoregate, Crail, Fife KY10 3SU   T: 01333 450476

Fantastically fresh lobsters and crabs from local waters sold from a stall.

Keltic Seafayre

Unit 6, Strathpeffer Road Industrial Estate, Dingwall, Ross-shire IV15 9SP   T: 01349 864087   w: www.kelticseafayre.com

✉ **mail order**

Keltic Seafayre specializes in langoustine and scallops caught in the clean northern Scottish waters. The fish is caught very sustainably – the langoustines are creeled in the old-fashioned way and the scallops are hand-dived. Not only are these methods much kinder to the fish stocks and the marine environment, but they also produce much higher quality fish, which are not damaged by the fishing process and so are in pristine condition when landed.

Crannog

Town Pier, Fort William, Inverness-shire PH33 7PT   T: 01397 700072 (OR 01397 705589 FOR RESTAURANT)   w: www.crannog.net

✉ **mail order**

Conservation is a key issue for Crannog, and so the fish available is caught using sustainable methods. Hand-dived shellfish, including scallops, are available, simply because Crannog never sell dredged shellfish, due to the damaging effects this has on the seabed. There is plenty of wet fish on offer, caught in local waters by the shop's

own boat, all of it at the peak of freshness – langoustines are a
speciality. You can even take a boat trip to see the fishermen at
work and the fish farms, and there is also a restaurant.

SCOTLAND   GLASGOW

MacCallums of Troon

71 Holdsworth Street, Glasgow G3 8ED   T: 0141 204 4456

Lots of locally caught prime fish, hand-dived scallops and razor
clams, native oysters in season and, occasionally, line-caught
mackerel.

SCOTLAND   HELMSDALE

Cowie's of Helmsdale

Shore Street, Helmsdale, Sutherland KW8 6JZ   T: 01431 821329

This fishmonger's is run by Sandy Cowie, the father of Alexander
and Fiona who run the Helmsdale Smokehouse next door (see
separate entry, page 200). The fish sold here is at the pinnacle of
freshness – the Cowies meet the boats as they come in and choose
from the local fish that have just been caught – scallops, prawns,
haddock, whiting, herring and lemon sole are just a few of the
varieties on offer.

super hero

ANDY RACE FISH MERCHANTS, The Port of Mallaig (see page 201)

Andy Race has a great guiding principle when it comes to the fish he buys
from the local west-coast fishermen. He simply asks himself, 'Would I want to
eat this?' Only the fish that he answers 'yes' to get on to his counter. He
believes firmly that the local waters are the cleanest around Britain and that is
why most of the fish he stocks is caught locally.

Peat-smoking is a speciality of Andy's. The smoked salmon he offers is not
a product that he cares to rush – it is gently smoked for a full three days; way
beyond the length of time most fish-smokers give their salmon. This wait is not
in vain; many have marvelled at the depth of flavour and the firm, muscular
texture this lengthy smoking gives the fish, and Andy's salmon has recently
received a great deal of acclaim in the national press.

The Helmsdale Smokehouse

1 Shore Street, Helmsdale, Sutherland KW8 6JZ   T: 01431 821370

shop

A source of pride for the Cowie family at the Helmsdale
Smokehouse is their use of local raw ingredients. The salmon is
from Orkney, the pork and chicken are from a nearby farm and the
venison is from a local estate. Local mussels and cheese are also
smoked. Oak from old whisky barrels is used in the smoker,
imparting its own delicate flavour, and nothing is rushed – the
salmon takes three days to be ready.

The Orkney Salmon Company

Crowness Point, Kirkwall, Orkney KW15 1RG   T: 01856 876101

w: www.orkneysalmon.co.uk

The Orkney Salmon Company stock salmon from numerous farms
around Orkney but perhaps most interesting is the organic salmon
from a farm off the island of Westray. The large roomy cages the
salmon are reared in allow for far greater movement, and the flesh of
the salmon is firmer as a result.

Salar Smokehouse Ltd

Lochcarnon, South Uist, Outer Hebrides HS8 5PD   T: 01870 610324

w: www.salar.co.uk

mail order

Award-winning hot-smoked salmon that is succulent, with a firm,
flaky texture from fish farmed on the site.

Cockles

11 Argyll Street, Lochgilphead, Argyll PA31 8LZ   T: 01546 606292

E: elizabeth.cockhill@btinternet.com

Elizabeth Cockhill, a member of the National Federation of
Fishmongers, has all manner of local delicacies in her deli-cum-fish
shop, such as local and British farmhouse cheeses, locally baked
bread and bread-making flours – including the hard-to-find chestnut

flour – oils and vinegars and many different varieties of olives. The speciality, though, is the fresh fish, particularly the local langoustines, caught by her husband.

Andy Race Fish Merchants

super hero

The Harbour, Port of Mallaig, Inverness-shire PH41 4PX T: 01687 462626
w: www.andyrace.co.uk

🛒 **shop** ✉ **mail order**

Salmon smoked slowly over peat is Andy Race's speciality. See the Super Hero box, page 199, for more information.

Anchor Seafoods

The Pier, Portree, Isle of Skye IV51 9DE T: 01478 612414

Anchor Seafoods is a permanent fish stall, stocking only local fish from the clean west-coast waters. Langoustines are a speciality and scallops, haddock and Dublin Bay prawns are all popular. Local lobster is available in season. Everything comes from day boats. Open six days a week in summer, limited hours in winter.

Colfin Smokehouse

Portpatrick, Stranraer, Dumfries and Galloway DG9 9BN T: 01776 820622
w: www.colfinsmokehouse.co.uk

🛒 **shop** ✉ **mail order**

The Colfin Smokehouse takes classic Scottish foods (salmon from Shetland and Orkney, Ayrshire bacon and Galloway Cheddar) and smoke it over the wood from old whisky casks.

Inverawe Smokehouse

Taynuilt, Argyll PA35 1HU T: 01866 822446 w: www.smokedsalmon.co.uk

🛒 **shop** ✉ **mail order**

Undyed salmon and trout, smoked over oak for 48 hours in a traditional brick smokehouse are available from Inverawe Smokehouse.

Tobermory Fish Company

Baliscate, Tobermory, Mull PA75 6QA   T: 01688 302120   w: www.tobermoryfish.co.uk

✉ **mail order**

The Tobermory Fish Company specializes in produce from Mull. Although the emphasis is on smoked fish (local trout, salmon and mussels), hard-to-find wild, hand-dived scallops are also available.

Fish on the Quay

Aberaeron, Ceredigion SA46 0BU   T: 01545 570599

There is plenty of local shellfish available at Fish on the Quay, caught using the shop's own boat. All the wet fish is from day boats and there is sometimes line-caught local sea bass, line-caught sewin and cockles from the Burry Inlet.

Minola Smoked Products

Triley Mill, Abergavenny, Monmouthshire NP7 8DE   T: 01873 736900

w: www.minola-smokery.com

✉ **mail order**

Welsh whole and split oak logs are used to smoke a vast range of produce at Minola, in five traditional smokehouses – trout, scallops, mussels and Scottish salmon, game, chicken, lamb, beef, bacon, cheese, even butter and vegetables. You can visit the mill and make your own selection at the shop or buy by mail order.

Celtic Dawn

The Shellfish Bar, Upper House, Aberiddy, nr St Davids, Haverfordwest, Pembrokeshire SA62 5AS   T: 01348 837732

The Phillipses have their own boat, fishing off the Pembrokeshire coast for crabs and lobsters, which are available, very fresh, from their shellfish bar. Dressed crabs and hand-picked crab meat are also available.

FISH

New Quay Fresh Fish Shop

South John Street, New Quay, Ceredigion SA45 9NP   T: 01545 560800

New Quay Fish Shop is seasonal, opening from around Easter until the autumn. There is plenty of fish to choose from, but the really interesting fish is the hand-lined mackerel and the crabs and lobsters that the owner, Winston, catches from his own boat.

Coakley-Greene

Stall 41c, The Market, Oxford Street, Swansea SA1 3PF   T: 01792 653416

Lots of local fish from day boats fishing off the Welsh coast. The staff are enthusiastic and happy to advise on cooking.

Due to the wide variety of soil types and local climates in this country, the range of fruit and particularly vegetables that can be grown here is staggering and so it seems sad that, with such bounty available, we import so much; currently around 70% of the organic produce we buy has been grown abroad.

The list of fruit and vegetable producers in this book predominantly consists of organic growers, many of them accredited by the Soil Association or other organic bodies. Others, though not recognized by one of these bodies, grow to organic standards and others still keep their crop-spraying to the absolute bare minimum, using the safest pesticides they can find and then only when there is a real danger of losing an entire crop (some crops, such as apples, are notoriously difficult to grow without a little intervention). Why spray produce unless it is absolutely necessary? A great many people are concerned about the possible effects of pesticides on health and on the soil, and organic farming can be seen to have a whole range of benefits, hence the bias towards organic growers in these listings.

It is in the fruit and vegetable sector that buying locally is perhaps most pertinent. The problem of food miles – the distance that food travels between producer and consumer, particularly excessive for imported foods – is very

fruit and vegetables

easy to address for fruit and vegetables; there are few parts of the country where a reasonable range is not grown. The added benefit of buying from a local grower is that the produce will be very fresh – many of the growers listed here pick the vegetables on the day they are sold, and some even pick to order.

I'm not suggesting that we should never buy imported fruit and vegetables – with fruit, in particular, there are times of the year when the native fruit available is few and far between and life without bananas and oranges would be all the poorer. Finding a local farm shop, joining a box scheme or rummaging around your local farmers' market, however, can reveal a treasure-trove of the freshest, tastiest, most nutritious fruit and vegetables, grown close to where they are being sold by farmers whose key concern is quality, not price. Look out for the members of the Northern Greengrocers Association in Northern Ireland – this is a small group of greengrocers who are committed to buying local fruit and vegetables direct from local producers. The rural economy is boosted, food miles are reduced and, because the produce is never warehoused, it arrives on your plate at the peak of freshness. It is heartening to see retailers taking this approach.

Orswell Cottage Organic Garden

Stoke Rivers, Barnstaple, Devon EX32 7LW   T: 01598 710558
farm gate sales   **box scheme**

Sue Lugg grows organic vegetables, trying to grow a selection of varieties for each type of vegetable. She also rears free-range chickens, guineafowl and organic lamb. Sue operates a local box scheme and sells at Barnstaple Pannier Market. She is a member of the Henry Doubleday Research Association.

Gold Hill Organic Farm

Childe Okeford, nr Blandford Forum, Dorset DT11 8HB   T: 01258 861413
farm shop

The maxim by which Sara and Andrew Cross farm is 'anything you can grow in this country, we'll try to grow', and the selection of fruit and vegetables is impressive, including aubergines, mange tout, peppers and chillies. Organic beef from British White cattle is also available, from the weekend farm shop or from Castle Cary market.

Elwell Fruit Farm

Waytown, Bridport, Dorset DT6 5LF   T: 01308 488283
farmers' markets   **farm gate sales**

Elwell Fruit Farm grows five varieties of pear and around 20 varieties of apple, from the familiar to the very rare. Bottled apple juice is available, too. All the produce can be found at Bridport, Dorchester (Poundbury), Sherborne and Blandford Forum farmers' markets, or direct from the farm, but call first.

Arne Herbes

Limeburn Nurseries, Limeburn Hill, Chew Magna, Bristol BS40 8QW   T: 01275 333399
W: www.arneherbs.co.uk
farm shop   **farmers' markets**

Anthony Lyman-Dixon is said to be a walking encyclopaedia when it comes to herbs and the list of varieties he grows at Limeburn Nurseries is incredibly long. From the well known to the exotic, the herbs are all grown without pesticides and can be bought direct from the nursery or at Bristol and Glastonbury farmers' markets.

SOUTH WEST   BRISTOL

Jekka's Herb Farm

Rose Cottage, Shellards Lane, Alveston, Bristol BS35 3SY   T: 01454 418878
W: www.jekkasherbfarm.com
✉ **mail order**

Plant and seed herbs from this award-winning organic grower are available by mail order. Jekka also runs four open days a year, and workshops, so you can learn about growing your own herb garden.

SOUTH WEST   BUCKFASTLEIGH

Riverford Farm Organic Vegetables

Wash Barn, Buckfastleigh, Devon TQ11 0LD   T: 01803 762720   W:www.riverford.co.uk
📋 **box scheme**

Award-winning organic growers, scooping six awards at the 2001 Organic Food Awards. Riverford Farm Organic Vegetables is a sister company to the Riverford Farm Shop, see pages 104 and 106.

SOUTH WEST   CHELTENHAM

Slipstream Organics

34a Langdon Road, Leckhampton, Cheltenham, Gloucestershire GL53 7NZ   T: 01242 227273   W: www.slipstream-organics.co.uk
📋 **box scheme**

Slipstream Organics' double-award-winning organic box scheme delivers to Gloucester, Stroud, Cheltenham and outlying villages. There is plenty of choice, with six different box sizes available. The produce is sourced as locally as possible and freshness is key – the vegetables have often been picked less than 24 hours before delivery.

SOUTH WEST   CHIPPENHAM

V & P Collins

81–83 Devizes Road, Bromham, Chippenham, Wilts SN15 2DZ   T: 01380 850228 OR 01380 850186
🚏 **farmers' markets**

The Collins family produce a huge selection of vegetables on their 70 acres, from the usual basics like root vegetables and brassicas

to the more unusual, such as the pink fir apple potato and white
sprouting broccoli. Using an integrated management system, they
encourage beneficial insects to control pests. Find them at almost
all the Wiltshire farmers' markets: call for details.

SOUTH WEST   CHIPPENHAM

Westwood Farm

Rode Hill, Colerne, nr Chippenham, Wilts SN14 8AR   T: 01225 742854
🥄 **farm shop** 🍎 **farmers' markets**

Mrs Trotman and her husband grow a vast range of organic
vegetables and fruit, including apples, plums and strawberries; they
offer a great salad bag of oriental leaves. There is a farm shop on
site, open on Fridays from 2–7pm and the Trotmans attend Bath
farmers' market every Saturday, selling their produce to, as Mrs
Trotman calls them, 'refugees from the supermarket'.

SOUTH WEST   CIRENCESTER

The Organic Farm Shop

Abbey Home Farm, Burford Road, Cirencester, Gloucestershire GL7 5HF   T: 01285
640441 w: www.theorganicfarmshop.co.uk
🥄 **farm shop**

Award-winning organic farm shop, selling incredibly fresh, home-
produced vegetables and herbs (over 100 varieties throughout the
season). The farm is committed to strengthening the link between
consumer and producer and runs farm trailer rides. Free-range meat
and all kinds of groceries are also available.

SOUTH WEST   CREDITON

Linscombe Farm

Newbuildings, Sandford, Crediton, Devon EX17 4PS   T: 01363 84291
E: farmers@linscombe.fsnet.co.uk
🍎 **farmers' markets** 📦 **box scheme**

Helen Case and Phil Thomas produce an awesome range of
vegetables – around 300 varieties in season, which can include over
20 different types of potato. This ensures that their box scheme
customers (who need to live within a five-mile radius of Linscombe
Farm) never get bored with the same vegetables, and 'heritage'
varieties are preserved. Linscombe Farm was joint winner of the
Best Box Scheme award at the 2001 Soil Association awards and is
a member of the Henry Doubleday Research Association.

FRUIT AND VEGETABLES

ROD AND BEN'S FOOD FROM THE SOIL, Exeter (see page 210)

It is dizzying to look at the list of fruit and vegetable varieties that Rod and Ben grow on their 106-acre Devon farm – from aubergines to watercress, artichokes to sweetcorn and even, for a brief spell in September, melons – all organic. With the chance of chocolate-brown free-range eggs from the Maran hens and honey from the farm's own hives, a vegetable box from Rod and Ben's box scheme will always be full of surprises. What drives them to grow such a huge diversity of vegetable varieties? 'Our aim is to supply fresh home-grown vegetables for as much of the year as possible. Good quality, variety and value for money are our key principles. We try and source any bought-in produce locally and have established links with local growers in order to compensate for shortfalls in our own production.' If you're a customer of theirs, Rod and Ben aren't content to let you just take your fruit and veg and run – they want you to feel involved. They'd really like you to visit at least once a year to find out what's going on at the farm. 'We involve our customers in the box scheme through a regular newsletter, *Rod and Ben's Roundup*, and farm walks, strengthening the link between producer and consumer. Many of our customers have followed our story through organic conversion and feel a stronger association with the farm as a result, as well as having a better understanding of what is involved and the principles of organic farming.'

SOUTH WEST   DORCHESTER

Green Valley Foods at Longmeadow

Godmanstone, nr Dorchester, Dorset DT2 7AE   T: 01300 342164

farm shop **box scheme**

Home-produced organic vegetables and locally produced foods, with an emphasis on organic are available from Green Valley Foods. There is also a good range of wholefoods.

SOUTH WEST   DORCHESTER

Peppers By Post

Sea Spring Farm, West Bexington, Dorchester, Dorset DT2 9DD   T: 01308 897892
W: www.peppersbypost.biz

mail order

A fantastic range of peppers and chillies and even tomatillos are all available by mail order.

Higher Crop

Pynes, Bridford, nr Exeter, Devon EX6 7JA   T: 01647 252470

farm gate sales

Chris Towell has a fascination with old varieties of vegetables that
are no longer commercially grown. He has grown nine different
varieties of garlic and blue potatoes! Call him to arrange an order
which you can then collect from the farm.

Rod and Ben's Food From the Soil

Bickham Farm, Kenn, Exeter, Devon EX6 7XL   T: 01392 833833
W: www.rodandbens.com

mail order   **box scheme**

Rod and Ben grow a dazzling variety of organic fruit and vegetables
on their 106-acre farm. See the Super Hero box, page 209, for more
information.

West Bradley Orchards

West Bradley, nr Glastonbury, Somerset BA6 8LT   T: 01458 850227
E: westbradleyorchards@ukonline.co.uk

farm shop   **farmers' markets**

Lots of varieties of apple and pear are grown here, many that you
will have never heard of, since they are old varieties seldom grown
now. Pick your own in season, or buy the fruit ready-picked at the
farm shop or at Glastonbury farmers' market.

Holsworthy Organics

Ceridwen, Old Rectory Lane, Pyworthy, Holsworthy, Devon EX22 6SW   T: 01409 254450

box scheme

Despite being a small-scale producer, Holsworthy Organics, a duet
of organic growers, won the Best Box Scheme Award at the 2002
Soil Association Organic Food Awards. A year-round box scheme,
with produce that is almost all home-grown with occasional
supplements of produce from other local organic growers,
Holsworthy offer a great variety of fresh fruit and veg.

Pinhayes Park Organic

Pinhayes Park, South Milton, nr Kingsbridge, Devon TQ7 3JZ   T: 01548 560059

🛒 **farmers' markets** 📮 **farm gate sales**

Mark and Theresa Mordue grow all kinds of organic salads and vegetables, from the basic to the exotic, and organic beef comes from their own herd of native South Devon cattle. All available direct from the farm (call first), or from Totnes, Ivybridge and Kingsbridge farmers' markets between June and November only.

Merricks Organic Farm

Park Lane, Langport, Somerset TA10 0NF   T: 01458 252901
w: www.merricksorganicfarm.co.uk

🛒 **farm shop** 📦 **box scheme**

Throughout the season, around 150 different varieties of fruit and vegetable are grown at Merricks Farm – anything it's possible to grow in this country, they'll have a go at. Nothing is ever imported or brought in from elsewhere. Alongside the vegetables, there is rare-breed organic pork, free-range hens' eggs and free-range geese and turkeys at Christmas. The fruit and vegetables are available through the box scheme; the meat is available at the farm shop on site.

Boddingtons Berries

The Ashes, Tregony Hill, Mevagissey, Cornwall PL26 6RQ   T: 01726 842346
w: www.boddingtonsberries.co.uk

🛒 **farm shop**

Boddingtons are strawberry specialists and grow all sorts of varieties. The Boddington family believe that the sea breezes blowing over the fields allow the fruit to ripen more slowly, increasing the sugar content and making for a deliciously sweet strawberry. PYO is available.

Camphill Village Trust (Oaklands Park)

Newnham-on-Severn, Gloucestershire GL14 1EF   T: 01594 516344
E: cvtoaklandspark@hotmail.com

box scheme

A biodynamic box scheme, with fruit, vegetables, lamb and beef, all grown or reared at Oaklands Park.

Bosavern Farm

Bosavern, St Just, Penzance, Cornwall TR19 7RD   T: 01736 786739
E: joandguy@bosavern.fsnet.co.uk

farm shop

Everything sold at Bosavern farm shop is home-grown or home-reared and for the meat a local butcher and abattoir are used. Organic vegetables, grass-fed Hereford beef, free-range pork and eggs are all available.

Guernsey Organic Growers

La Marcherie, Ruette Rabey, St Martins, Guernsey GY4 6DU   T: 01481 237547
W: www.cwgsy.net/business/guernseyorganics

box scheme

An organic box scheme covering the island of Guernsey, with most of the contents of the weekly boxes being home-grown. Guernsey Organic Growers run the only mixed organic nursery on Guernsey.

Coleshill Organics

59 Coleshill, Swindon, Wilts SN6 7PT   T: 01793 861070

farm shop   **farmers' markets**   **box scheme**

Beautifully fresh, organic vegetables, delivered locally or buy them from Barnes farmers' market in London. Organic free-range eggs are also available.

Charlton Orchards

Charlton Road, Creech St Michael, Taunton, Somerset TA3 5PF   T: 01823 412959

⭷ **farm shop** 🛒 **farmers' markets**

Charlton Orchards yield 32 different varieties of apple, including one thought to date back to Roman times. Tours of the orchards are available, during which visitors can taste the fruit, which also includes pears, plums, damsons, quince and soft fruit.

Duchy Home Farm Organic Vegetables

Broadfield Farm, Tetbury, Gloucestershire GL8 8SE   T: 01666 504287

🛒 **farmers' markets** 📦 **box scheme**

An interesting selection of home-grown organic vegetables from the prestigious Duchy Estate. Find them at Tetbury, Cirencester and Stroud farmers' markets.

Bee Organic

Moothill Cross, Staverton, Totnes, Devon   T: 07817 467936

🛒 **farmers' markets**

Paul Hutchings likes to grow the less usual types of vegetable and has been known to grow up to 35 different types of tomato and ten kinds of chilli. He likes to grow 'heritage crops' – the varieties of fruit and vegetable that are in danger of dying out – and is also trying to establish nut trees on his land. Find Bee Organic produce every week at Buckfastleigh farmers' market.

Cusgarne Organics

Cusgarne Wollas, nr Truro, Cornwall TR4 8RL   T: 01872 865922

⭷ **farm shop** 📦 **box scheme**

An organic farm that runs a fantastic-value vegetable box scheme, comprising almost entirely home-grown produce, with a good selection of unusual varieties of vegetables. The produce is also available direct from the farm.

John Hurd's Organic Watercress

Stonewold, Hill Deverill, nr Warminster, Wilts BA12 7EF T: 01985 840260
w: www.organicwatercress.co.uk

farm shop

Traditionally bunched watercress, grown to maturity for a strong, peppery taste. Available direct from the farm or from Waitrose.

Pertwood Organics Co-operative

The Old Barn, Lords Hill, Lower Pertwood Farm, Longbridge Deverill, Warminster, Wilts
BA12 7DY T: 01985 840646   w: www.pertwood-organics.co.uk

farmers' markets   **box scheme**

Winners of the Soil Association's Box Scheme of the Year award, Pertwood Organics offer organic fruit and vegetables from a group of local growers, harvested the day before delivery for freshness.

The Bell and Birdtable

Runnington, Wellington, Somerset TA21 0QW T: 01823 663080
w: www.bellandbirdtable.com

farm gate sales

This tiny smallholding produces an amazing range of tomatoes – 49 varietes were grown here at the last count, none of which you'll ever see on supermarket shelves. The varieties are chosen for flavour; Anne McGrath, the grower, procures seeds from around the world to grow unusual varieties. She also rears rare-breed pork (Oxford Sandy & Blacks), which are slowly matured and range freely.

The Dorset Blueberry Company

352 Hampreston, Wimborne, Dorset BH21 7LX T: 01202 579342
w: www.dorset-blueberry.com

farmers' markets   **mail order**

The acidic, well-draining soil of Dorset is perfect for growing blueberries and the Dorset Blueberry Company have over 50 years of experience in growing them. Not only can you buy the fruit fresh direct from the farm or from the countless farmers' markets they attend (see their website), but you can also buy blueberry pies, sauce, juice and jam.

SOUTH EAST   ABINGDON

Millets Farm Centre

Kingston Road, Frilford, nr Abingdon, Oxfordshire OX13 5HB   T: 01865 392200
W: www.milletsfarmcentre.com

👅 **farm shop**

What started as a small PYO in an attempt at diversification in the 1970s has become a big farm centre with all sorts going on – a farm shop selling a good variety of home-grown apples, pears, plums and vegetables, fresh fish and local meats, a restaurant, and a 'maize maze'. The idea is for the farm to bridge the gap between town and country – kids can go on trailer rides and see the crops (even pick their own fruit) and see farm animals.

SOUTH EAST   AYLESBURY

The Sustainable Lifestyles Research Co-op Ltd

Pond Cottage East, Cuddington Road, Dinton, Aylesbury, Buckinghamshire HP18 0AD
T: 01296 747737   E: mike.george@euphony.net

👅 **farm shop**   🚚 **delivery service**

A co-operative of workers growing all kinds of fruit and vegetables using the permaculture method, a holistic form of agriculture. The speciality here is Victoria plums – there are 500 plum trees. Free-range chicken, eggs and lamb are available from the small on-site farm shop and the smallholding is run with an open policy – visitors are welcome. The co-operative is accredited by the Organic Food Federation.

SOUTH EAST   BASINGSTOKE

Laverstoke Park Produce

Home Farm, Laverstoke, Whitchurch, Hampshire RG28 7NT   T: 01256 890900

👅 **farm shop**   🛒 **box scheme**

Mike Fisher at Laverstoke Park provides a year-round organic box scheme in the Winchester and Basingstoke areas, producing the widest possible range of vegetables and fruit he can. Meat and free-range eggs are also available and almost everything in the boxes is home-grown.

Costrong Fruit Farm

Plaistow Road, Kirdford, Billingshurst, West Sussex RH14 0LA   T: 01403 820622
E: costrong2000@yahoo.co.uk

⬥ farm shop ⬛ farmers' markets

Over 40 varieties of apple and pear are available here, many of them
old British types. There is also a small apple and pear museum on
site. All the produce is available from the farm shop or Chichester
farmers' market.

Perry Court Farm Shop

Garlinge Green, Canterbury, Kent CT4 5RU   T: 01227 732001

⬥ farm shop ⬛ farmers' markets ⬛ box scheme

Lots of organic and biodynamic fruits and vegetables are available
here – over 50 varieties at the last count. This is a mixed farm, and
home-grown cereals are milled into flour on the farm and there is
also organic beef from a closed herd.

Sarsden Organics

Sarsden Estate Office, Sarsden, Chipping Norton, Oxfordshire OX7 6PW
T: 01608 659670   E: sarsdenorganics@btopenworld.com

⬛ farmers' markets ⬛ box scheme

Rachel Siegfried works within a classic two-acre Victorian walled
garden, growing a good range of vegetables, including some less
well-known heritage varieties. Unusual lettuces, herbs and salads are
a speciality. The produce is available through a box scheme but
customers can choose what their box contains – each week they are
sent an availability list from which to make their choices. The produce
is also available from Woodstock and Charlbury farmers' markets.

Kingfisher Farm Shop

Guildford Road, Abinger Hammer, Dorking, Surrey RH5 6QX   T: 01306 730703

⬥ farm shop

This farm shop specializes in fresh watercress, grown without
insecticides or fertilizers in natural spring water, and also stocks

organic local produce – goats' and ewes' milk cheese, yoghurt, chickens and cakes.

SOUTH EAST   GODSHILL

Godshill Organics

Yard Parlour, Newport Road, Godshill, Isle of Wight PO38 3LY T: 01983 840723
E: godshill.organics@virgin.net

🥕 **farm shop**   🏪 **farmers' markets**   📦 **box scheme**

There is a really extensive range of organic vegetables grown at Godshill Organics and everything in their box scheme and on their farmers' market stall is home-grown. Seasonality is important to Ruth, who runs the business – she strives to teach customers about the British seasons for food and will always tell you if she has had to buy something in.

super hero

SAMANTHA PETTER, of Allens Farm, Plaxtol (see page 221)

Allens is a traditional Kentish farm, growing cherries, damsons and cobnuts. Such is the scarcity of these crops – and of the traditional orchards that produce them because most have been grubbed up to make way for more commercial crops – that the farm has Countryside Stewardship status, to conserve the heritage of this area. So why do Samantha Petter and her family still grow these crops when, clearly, other crops would be far more profitable? 'Not for prestige or glamour, and certainly not for financial gain!' laughed Sam when I asked her, 'but because we feel a sense of responsibility towards preserving a unique but diminishing part of Kentish life, and because they taste fantastic….' Sam went on to tell me about the history behind the cobnut orchard she tends: 'Over 100 years ago, 2,700 Kentish Cobnut trees were planted in the Bourne Valley. This was at a time when nuts were prized as a delicious and nutritious crop … now the Kentish Cobnut is scarcely known, swamped by foreign imports. But our ancient, gnarled trees still stand, still bearing plentiful harvests … who could fail to be moved and impressed by the sense of history, by our great grandfathers' endeavours all those years ago? So we still continue to promote this wonderful fresh fruit, against all odds, to a small, but dedicated and passionate following.'

The cobnuts, cherries, plums, damsons and also home-reared lamb are all available direct from the farm, but call first before visiting.

Tendring Fruit Farm

Magham Down, Hailsham, East Sussex BN27 1QA T: 01323 841812 OR 01323
842116

farm shop

The farm shop at Tendring Fruit Farm offers so many different
varieties of apple and pear that Tony Eales, the grower, couldn't
remember exactly how many; he thought it was in the region of 27.
He also grows plums. Such is the range that there are varieties
cropping all the time, giving a year-round supply of fresh fruit.
While not organic, the fruit is grown with the absolute minimum
of spraying.

Home Cottage Farm

Bangors Road South, Iver, Buckinghamshire SL0 0BB T: 01753 653064
W: www.homecottagefarm.co.uk

farm shop

Fifteen varieties of apple, two of pear and four of plum are grown
here, along with summer and autumn raspberries and blackberries.
Buy from the farm shop or pick your own in season.

Boathouse Organic Farm Shop

The Orchards, Uckfield Road, Clayhill, Lewes, East Sussex BN8 5RX T: 01273 814188

farm shop

A farm shop boasting a huge range of home-grown organic
vegetables, organic beef, lamb and mutton, and local cheeses from
organic dairies.

Blackmoor Apple Shop

Blackmoor Estate, Liss, Hampshire GU33 6BS T: 01420 473782

farm shop

Twenty varieties of apple are grown at Blackmoor, with over 300
acres of orchard. Plums, quinces and strawberries are also grown
and all the produce is available, in season, from the farm shop.

Cool Chile Co.

PO Box 5702, London W11 2GS   T: 0870 902 1145   w: www.coolchile.co.uk
✉ **mail order**

Every kind of chilli you can imagine, along with some hard to find
Mexican ingredients.

Willows Farm Shop

Coursers Road, London Colney, Herts AL2 1BB   T: 01727 822444
w: www.willowsfarmvillage.com
⬇ **farm shop**

This is a farm shop with an extensive range of foods – a big deli
section, lots of fruit and vegetables that are all labelled with their
county of origin (all as local as possible), home-reared meat, game
shot on the farm and even flour from a local watermill.

Mrs Tees Wild Mushrooms

Gorse Meadow, Sway Road, Lymington, Hampshire SO41 8LR   T: 01590 673354
w: www.wildmushrooms.co.uk
✉ **mail order**

Fresh wild mushrooms from the New Forest, available mail order or
from Borough Market in London SE1.

Warborne Organic Farm

Boldre, Lymington, Hampshire SO41 5QD   T: 01590 688488
⬇ **farm shop** ▣ **box scheme**

Winner of the 2002 Best Mixed Producer award from the Soil
Association, Warborne Farm has an amazing range of vegetables
and fruit – around 300 varieties in season. Staunch believers in
eating locally and seasonally, the farmers at Warborne run a box
scheme within a 30-mile radius and have a Saturday farm shop.

super hero

ANDREW TANN, of Crapes Fruit Farm, Colchester (see page 224)

You could be forgiven for assuming that Andrew Tann is somewhat obsessed with apples – he grows around 150 different types, although in some cases there is only one tree of a particular variety. In a time when we think of apples only in terms of the three or four varieties available in supermarkets, most of which seem to have been imported, it is refreshing to find someone so dedicated to preserving the rich diversity of apple types that has been so overlooked. Apples are notoriously difficult to grow without pesticides and, while Crapes is not organic, the farm operates a system of 'sympathetic management' – no organophosphates, no preserving chemicals, no wax or other dressings to improve the appearance of the apple skins. Andrew Tann is pleased to report a recent renewed public interest in the more unusual varieties of apples – perhaps more of us are becoming concerned about the loss of such tasty fruits. Even though Crapes Fruit Farm has such an enormous range of apple varieties it is by no means exhaustive and Andrew says that there is a small but increasing band of fellow apple fans who enjoying seeking out the rare and unusual. If you are searching for a particular type that Andrew does not grow, he'll still be able to help you out – 'any enquiry is welcomed – if I cannot help, then it is usually possible to direct an avid apple hunter to another possible source'. The apples are available from the orchard direct, or by mail order, but only to individuals – Andrew does not wholesale.

SOUTH EAST	MAYFIELD

Herons Folly Garden

Fletching Street, Mayfield, East Sussex TN20 6TE   T: 07944 815357
🔃 **box scheme**

Patrick Treherne grows around 40 different fruit and vegetable varieties in season. The five-acre smallholding has been organic for 25 years and the produce is available through a box scheme – call for details.

Cross Lanes Fruit Farm

Mapledurham, Reading, Berkshire RG4 7UW T: 0118 972 3167
w: www.crosslanesfruitfarm.co.uk

➼ **farm shop** ✉ **mail order** ☑ **box scheme**

There are a staggering 60 varieties of fruit grown at Cross Lanes, including 46 varieties of apple. The Franklin family are keen to re-introduce the old and unusual varieties of fruit and choose the most flavourful varieties. At the farm shop, customers can taste the fruit before they buy. Available from the farm shop in season (late August to December), by mail order or at Reading, Henley, Beaconsfield, Maidenhead and Wallingford farmers' markets.

Simply Wild

Scragoak Farm, Brightling Road, Robertsbridge, East Sussex TN32 5EY
T: 01424 838420   E: enquiries@simplywildorganics.co.uk

➼ **farm shop** ☑ **box scheme**

A large range of organic vegetables, with several varieties of each type of vegetable on offer, in order to encourage species diversity. Home-reared organic meat, poultry and eggs are also available.

Allens Farm

Allens Lane, Plaxtol, nr Sevenoaks, Kent TN15 0QZ T: 01732 812215
w: www.allensfarm.co.uk

✉ **farm gate sales**

Allens Farm is a traditional Kentish farm growing cherries, damsons and cobnuts, available from the farm (phone first). See the Super Hero box, page 217, for more information.

Thrognall Farm

Bull Lane, Newington, Sittingbourne, Kent ME9 7SJ T: 01795 842220

☷ **farmers' markets**

Joan Atwood of Thrognall Farm is always on the lookout for interesting things to grow. Among the huge list of fruit and vegetables she offers at local farmers' markets are cherries, chillies, tomatillos and black cabbage. Although not registered organic, the produce is not sprayed with pesticides or herbicides and no artificial fertilizers are used. Call to find out which farmers' markets she attends.

SOUTH EAST   **SOUTHAMPTON**

Fruitwise

Winchester Street, Botley, Southampton, Hampshire SO30 2AA   T: 01489 796790
w: www.fruitwise.co.uk

🚐 **farmers' markets**

Dr and Mrs Hayes enthusiastically tend an orchard full of old English apple varieties (around 45 at the last count), varieties never seen in supermarkets. Vegetables are also grown in season, and home-made cider, and all the produce is available from local farmers' markets – call for details.

food facts

BIODIVERSITY

Thank goodness for the Henry Doubleday Research Association. They maintain a seed library conserving the huge number of varieties of fruit and vegetables that have been grown in this country. Thousands of plant varieties have been lost in this country since the 1970s alone. The main problem is that agribusiness, in its drive for bigger and bigger yields, has focussed on varieties that can achieve those high yields, and so the number of varieties grown commercially has progressively narrowed – it is thought that around 30 plant types now feed the majority of the world's population. Along comes the EU, with its reams of regulations, and decides that every variety that is to be marketed must be registered, classified, tested and trialled, shown to be 'sufficiently uniform and stable', with 'satisfactory value for cultivation and use'. This testing can take around two years and cost over £2000 – an unrealistic sum of money for a small-scale producer more interested in flavour and diversity than high yields and price points. Some of the growers listed in this section have no time for these rather imperious regulations and, if you are lucky, you might find an enlightened farmer growing blue potatoes, purple carrots, orange beetroot, or tomatoes the size of a fingernail. Not only will those vegetables be maintaining genetic diversity in this country, they'll be grown specifically because they are tasty; they'll also make a real talking point at dinner. Find out more on the Henry Doubleday website www.hdra.org.uk

SOUTH EAST WANTAGE

Brook Cottage Farm

Charney Bassett, Wantage, Oxfordshire OX12 0EN T: 01235 868492

farm gate sales **box scheme**

Brook Cottage Farm offers a year-round box scheme, with home-produced foods – vegetables and fruit and free-range organic eggs – and geese at Christmas. Their produce can be bought direct from the farm on Saturdays only.

SOUTH EAST WHEATLEY

Waterperry Gardens

Waterperry, nr Wheatley, Oxfordshire OX33 1JZ T: 01844 339226
W: www.waterperrygardens.co.uk

farm shop

Apples are the speciality here, with over 50 varieties being grown, many of them rare and unusual. There are also pears, raspberries and fresh herbs, and 16 single-variety apple juices. Everything sold is grown on the farm.

EAST ANGLIA CAMBRIDGE

Waterland Organics

Quaystone Cottage, The Hythe, Reach, Cambridge CB5 0JQ T: 01638 742178
W: www.waterlandorganics.co.uk

farmers' markets **box scheme**

A wonderful range of seasonal vegetables, available through a weekly box scheme or at Ely farmers' market. Everything is grown organically and the growers, Doreen and Paul Robinson, are committed to farming with minimal impact on the environment.

EAST ANGLIA CHELMSFORD

Lathcoats Farm

Beehive Lane, Galleywood, Chelmsford, Essex CM2 8LX T: 01245 353021
W: www.eapples.co.uk

farm shop

Lathcoats Farm operates an integrated farming system, which means that though they are not organic, a biological approach is taken – beneficial insects are encouraged to control pests and spraying is only undertaken when absolutely necessary. It's primarily a fruit farm; cherries and 40 varieties of apple are grown here, along with all kinds of soft fruits. The on-site farm shop stocks local produce – poultry, meat and dairy. You can even choose an apple tree and 'rent' it, which means you get all the apples from your tree at harvest time, and you can also pick your own.

EAST ANGLIA   CLACTON

Brooklynne Farm Shop

Chapel Road, Beaumont-cum-Moze, nr Clacton, Essex CO16 0AR   T: 01255 862184

🖐 **farm shop** 🛒 **farmers' markets**

A farm shop stocked with lots of home-grown produce – around three-quarters of the produce in the shop is grown on the farm. In season there is every vegetable you can imagine, some produce is organic, some conventionally grown. The shop is open every day except Monday or you can find Brooklynne produce at Long Melford and Dedham farmers' markets.

EAST ANGLIA   COLCHESTER

Clay Barn Orchard

Fingringhoe, Colchester, Essex CO5 7AR   T: 01206 735405

🛒 **farm gate sales** ✉ **mail order**

A rare quince orchard, offering the old-fashioned fruit by mail order. Quinces are notoriously vulnerable to bad weather and some years the harvest is very poor, so call for availability (season starts beginning of October).

EAST ANGLIA   COLCHESTER

Crapes Fruit Farm   super hero

Rectory Road, Aldham, Colchester, Essex CO6 3RR   T: 01206 212375
E: andrew.tann1@virgin.net

🛒 **farm gate sales** ✉ **mail order**

An apple orchard with over 150 varieties; see the Super Hero box, page 220, for more information.

Ashlyns Organic Farm Shop

Epping Road, North Weald, Epping, Essex CM16 6RZ T: 01992 225146 (SHOP) OR
01992 523038 (BOX SCHEME) W: www.ashlyns.co.uk

↧ **farm shop** ▨ **box scheme**

Ashlyns Farm produces over 30 different varieties of vegetables, and
free-range eggs from Black Rock hens, all organic. There is also a
small herd of Lincoln Red beef cattle. A driving aim behind the farm
is to create a stronger link between customers and the source of
their food, so open days are regularly held. Ashlyns Farm is
accredited by the Countryside Stewardship Scheme.

Clive Houlder, Mushroom Man

98 West Street, North Creake, Fakenham, Norfolk NR21 9LH T: 01328 738610
E: mushroomman@ntlworld.com

✉ **mail order**

Clive Houlder is expert at seeking out the wild mushrooms of East
Anglia.

Park Fruit Farm

Pork Lane, Great Holland, nr Frinton-on-Sea, Essex CO13 0ES T: 01255 674621
W: www.parkfruitfarm.co.uk

↧ **farm shop**

There is plenty of choice at Park Fruit Farm – 40 varieties of apple,
ten varieties of pear, with raspberries, wet walnuts, honey and
vegetables, all grown at the farm.

Gourmet Mushrooms

Morants Farm, Colchester Road, Great Bromley, Essex CO7 7TN T: 01206 231660
W: www.springfieldmushrooms.co.uk

🧺 **farmers' markets**

Over 20 different varieties of mushroom, all grown organically. are
available from Notting Hill, Leigh-on-Sea, Dedham, Alder Carr and
Woodbridge farmers' markets. Gourmet Mushrooms is accredited
by the Organic Food Federation.

Hollow Trees Farm Shop

Semer, Ipswich, Suffolk IP7 6HX   T: 01449 741247   W: www.hollowtrees.co.uk

🥄 **farm shop**

A recent winner of the National Farmers' Union Best Farm Shop award, Hollow Trees stocks home-grown fruit and vegetables, and home-reared meat, alongside produce from other small-scale producers, including beer, honey and cream.

Laurel Farm Herbs

Main Road, Kelsale, Suffolk, IP17 2RG   T: 01728 668223   W: www.laurelfarmherbs.co.uk

🥄 **shop**

Chris Seagon grows an astonishing range of herbs at Laurel Farm – including 45 different varieties of Thyme. They are all grown without heat, which means that the range is subject to seasonality. No pesticides are used, they are grown in peat-free compost, and Chris will even grow some of the more unusual herbs to order.

food facts

WHAT'S IN SEASON?

Ever bought strawberries in January and been disappointed when they tasted of almost nothing? Seasonality is a key aspect of getting the maximum flavour in food and that's especially true for fruit and vegetables. The growers we have featured all offer you great-tasting produce – but only when it is in season. Some may extend their growing seasons slightly or grow varieties not normally associated with these shores, such as peppers and aubergines, with the use of sheltering poly-tunnels (one grower in Wales can sometimes offer peaches!) but, in general, the seasons rule. This means flavoursome strawberries in the summer, not at Christmas – but crisp and sweet native apples in December. Local asparagus, peppery watercress and buttery new potatoes in the spring; richly flavoured blackberries, plums and courgettes in the autumn and sweet-tasting, comforting parsnips and leeks as the winter arrives all give a great sense of time and place. Accepting and understanding seasonality can re-awaken the sense of anticipation as a favourite food comes into season to be eaten at the peak of perfection.

Abbey Farm Organics

Flitcham, King's Lynn, Norfolk PE31 6BT   T: 01485 609094   E: flitcham@eidosnet.co.uk

farmers' markets **box scheme**

Offering a choice of set or 'à la carte' weekly boxes, Abbey Farm offers an ever-expanding range of organic vegetables. Delivered within 24 hours of harvest, the vegetables are at the peak of freshness. You can also find Abbey Farm vegetables at local farmers' markets – call for details – and King's Lynn Friday market.

Plumbe and Maufe

The Parsonage, Burnham Thorpe, King's Lynn, Norfolk PE31 8HW   T: 01328 738311
E: nina@creeke.demon.co.uk

farm shop

Over 30 varieties of unusual plums and gages are grown here, most of them no longer commercially grown. Available from the on-site farm shop, but please call first.

Barker Organics

The Walled Garden, Wolterton Hall, Wolterton, Norwich, Norfolk NR11 7LY
T: 01263 768966

box scheme

The Walled Garden at Wolterton dates back to the 18th century. Within it, David Barker grows between 30 and 40 different crops, from potatoes and carrots to aubergines and peppers, all biodynamically. Available through the box scheme David runs.

Stable Organics

The Stables, Gresham, Norwich, Norfolk NR11 8RW   T: 01263 577468

farm gate sales

Organic produce grown in an old walled garden – everything sold is grown on site and includes vegetables, soft and top fruit and salads. The aim is to provide 'a bit of everything'. The produce is picked to order, so it will be incredibly fresh! Available direct from the farm, but call first.

FOOD HEROES OF BRITAIN

Audley End Organic Kitchen Garden

Saffron Walden, Essex CB11 4JF   T: 01799 522842 OR 01799 522148

farm shop

The Henry Doubleday Research Association, for which Audley End
Organic Kitchen Garden is a display garden, is committed to both
organic gardening and maintaining the biodiversity of plant species
in the UK. At Audley End the walled garden produces many heritage
varieties of fruits and vegetables, all grown organically, and they are
available to buy from the shop on site.

High House Fruit Farm

Sudbourne, Woodbridge, Suffolk IP12 2BL   T: 01394 450263 OR 01394 450378
w: www.high-house.co.uk

farm shop

High House Fruit Farm has a wide choice of apples, from the well
known to the more unusual, along with loganberries, blackberries,
gooseberries, currants, asparagus, cherries and plums. Even
apricots are planned for the future! Single-variety apple juices are
also available. Only produce grown on the farm is available in the
farm shop. PYO is also on offer.

New Farm Organics

Soulby Lane, Wrangle, Boston, Lincolnshire PE22 9BT   T: 01205 870500
w: www.newfarmorganics.com

farm gate sales

Mrs Edwards grows a varied selection of organic fruits and
vegetables, available direct from the farm, usually harvested that
day for total freshness.

Trinity Farm

Awsworth Lane, Cossall, Notts NG16 2RZ   T: 0115 944 2545   w: www.trinityfarm.co.uk

farm shop   **box scheme**

Specializing in vegetable varieties you won't find in the supermarket,
Trinity Farm produces 30 types of lettuce and 12 types of tomato in

season, along with all manner of exciting fruit and vegetables. The farm shop stocks the home-grown vegetables picked on the day of sale and there is also a weekly box scheme. Organic fish is also available, as are pork and home-cured bacon and free-range eggs.

Ryton Organic Gardens

Ryton-on-Dunsmore, Coventry CV8 3LG   T: 02476 303517
w: www.hdra.org.uk/ryton.htm

shop   box scheme

The Henry Doubleday Research Association is committed to both organic gardening and maintaining the biodiversity of plant species in the UK. At Ryton there are acres of demonstration gardens, with a kitchen garden and an 'unusual vegetable' garden. You can buy the fabulous produce from the gardens in the shop, have a meal in the restaurant, visit the Vegetable Kingdom Museum and even sign up to the box scheme and get a weekly delivery.

super hero

THE STANIER FAMILY, of Dragon Orchard, Ledbury (see page 230)

English orchards, with their profusion of native apple, plum and pear varieties, are becoming more and more rare. They just don't pay – apples are cheaper from abroad – so many farmers simply cannot afford to keep their orchards; they need the land for more profitable crops. The Stanier family at Dragon Orchard faced a stark choice – stop growing apples altogether or find some way of making money from them. They came up with a novel idea – crop-sharing. For an annual fee, a family can become part of Dragon Orchard, visiting four times a year to see what is going on at the farm (and, depending on the season, this can include wassailing, blossom time, harvesting or cider-making). At the end of each season they will receive a share of the orchard's bounty – boxes of apples of numerous varieties, pears, bottled juice, cider and jams. It is a great way to explore the life cycle of a working orchard and you will be saving a traditional English orchard from being grubbed up and lost forever.

Hampton Farm Shop

Pershore Road, Evesham, Worcestershire WR11 6LT   T: 01386 41540
w: www.hamptonfarmshop.co.uk
⏬ farm shop

Seventeen varieties of plum are grown here, plus damsons. Ian
Lovall, the grower, is passionate about these fruits and grows many
rare and unusual varieties. The farm shop also stocks apples from a
nearby farm and locally grown vegetables.

Court Farm and Leisure

Tillington, Hereford HR4 8LG   T: 01432 760271   E: courtfarm@onetel.net.uk
⏬ farm shop

Soft fruit of every description is grown here, including blueberries,
raspberries, cherries and redcurrants and PYO is available.

Dragon Orchard   super hero

Dragon House, Putley, Ledbury, Herefordshire HR8 2RG   T: 01531 670071
w: www.dragonorchard.co.uk

A traditional English apple orchard that regained profitability by an
innovative crop-sharing scheme, in which families pay an annual fee
in exchange for visits and a share of the orchard's produce (see the
Super Hero box, page 229, for more information).

Hop Mania

Munsley Gate, Munsley, nr Ledbury, Herefordshire HR8 2SQ   T: 01531 670849
w: www.hopmania.com
⏬ farm shop ✉ mail order

Hop asparagus is the most expensive vegetable in the world, at
around £300 per kilo. It is available fresh for just two weeks in the
spring, although Hop Mania offer it pickled the rest of the year. Hop
asparagus is the tender first shoots of the hop plant and has been
eaten in this country for hundreds of years, although the popularity
of this vegetable in recent generations has declined. The leaves that
grow later in the year can be used in cooking, like vine leaves, to

wrap around other foods as is common in Greek and Turkish cuisine. The fresh hop asparagus and leaves are available direct from Hop Mania and the pickled version is available mail order.

MIDLANDS   LEDBURY

Pardoes

Priors Grove, Putley, Ledbury, Herefordshire HR8 2RE   T: 01531 670511

farm gate sales

Organic and biodynamic apples, pears and plums, in every colour and shape imaginable – 30 varieties of apple, four of pear and eight of plum, many of them rare.

MIDLANDS   MALVERN

Old Sandlin Fruit

Old Sandlin Farm, Leigh Sinton, nr Malvern, Worcestershire WR13 5DL   T: 01866 832244 OR 01866 833200

farmers' markets

A choice of apple varieties is offered here, with some of the rarer types available. There are also three kinds of pear and two of plum, with single-variety juices available, too. Strawberries and peas are also available in season. Find the produce at farmers' markets within Gloucestershire, Worcestershire and Herefordshire – call for details.

MIDLANDS   ROSS-ON-WYE

SoilMates

PO Box 67, Ross-on-Wye, Herefordshire HR9 5ZA   T: 01989 767444
w: www.soilmates.com

farm gate sales   **mail order**

A specialist chilli-grower; see the Super Hero box, page 232, for more information.

MIDLANDS   SHREWSBURY

Five Acres

Ford, nr Shrewsbury, Shropshire SY5 9LL   T: 01743 850832
w: www.organicapples.co.uk

farm gate sales

Ian Mason has over 100 different apple varieties in his orchards and around 15 varieties of plum. All are grown organically, with pests controlled by the 200 hens that range around the orchard, who also provide eggs. The fruit and eggs are available from the farm gate, but call first, or alternatively, buy the produce from Sue and Dave Clarke at Churncote Farm Shop (01743 850273).

MIDLANDS   SOLIHULL

Hopwood Organic Farm

Bickenhill Lane, Catherine de Barnes, Solihull, West Mids B92 0DE T: 0121 711 7787
w: www.hopwoodorganic.co.uk

🔻 **farm shop** 🔳 **box scheme**

Hopwood received the distinction of Highly Commended in the Producer of the Year category at the 2002 Soil Association Organic Food Awards. Their produce, which includes peppers, spinach and aubergines alongside the regular basic vegetables, is available from the farm shop on site, which also stocks other organic produce from nearby farms, or through the weekly box scheme.

super hero

RICHARD HUIJING, of SoilMates, Ross-on-Wye (see page 231)

Richard Huijing is a man obsessed by chillies – he must be, since he grows almost 300 varieties. He started growing them because he was disappointed by the lack of choice in supermarkets – it often comes down to just red or green, which is a poor representation of the variety that is actually available. Indeed, Richard grows brown chillies, white ones, purple ones … They come in a range of strengths, from the reasonably mild to the downright dangerous – for hard-core fans only! He has followed this with what he terms an 'heirloom' collection of tomatoes, currently running at about 160 varieties – 'all built around the criteria of exceptional taste, texture and intriguing appearance'. These two specializations are accompanied by other interesting fruit and vegetables that would be almost impossible to find elsewhere. While he sells to many professional chefs, he also offers the produce to 'adventurous cooks' direct from the smallholding or occasionally by mail order. Call for more information.

Walsgrove Farm

Egdon, Spetchley, Worcestershire WR7 4QL   T: 01905 345371   w: www.walsgrove.co.uk
farm shop

Over 60 varieties of apple and 18 of plum are available at Walsgrove
Farm. Conservation of heritage varieties is the driving force behind
this fruit farm, although varieties are also chosen with flavour in
mind. The farm is not organic but natural insect predators are used
to control pests as far as possible.

Fern Verrow Vegetables

Fern Verrow, St Margarets, Herefordshire HR2 0QF   T: 01981 510288
E: fernverrow@btopenworld.com
farmers' markets   **box scheme**

Fern Verrow operates a flexible local box scheme – customers can
choose what they'd like in the box instead of the more usual 'lucky
dip' arrangement. All the vegetables are biodynamically grown, with
a great selection of basics and some more unusual varieties. Rare-
breed pork and free-range eggs are also available.

Essington Fruit Farm

Bognop Road, Essington, Wolverhampton, Staffs WV11 2BA   T: 01902 735724
w: www.essingtonfarm.co.uk
farm shop

Soft fruit comes in every form imaginable at Essington – even
blueberries. The varieties grown are carefully selected for maximum
flavour and PYO is available, as well as a tearoom.

Field 2 Kitchen

Gailey Garden Centre, Watling Street, Gailey, Staffs ST19 5PP   T: 01902 798585
w: www.field2kitchen.co.uk
farm shop

Home-grown and local produce are picked fresh each day to go into
the farm shop here. There is a big choice of varieties, some of which
are organic.

FOOD HEROES OF BRITAIN

Howbarrow Organic Farm

Cartmel, Grange-over-Sands, Cumbria LA11 7SS   T: 01539 536330
w: www.howbarroworganic.demon.co.uk
farm shop   box scheme

Howbarrow Farm is part of the Soil Association's Open Farm
Network so it is open to visitors who would like to see how an
organic farm operates. The farm is run with great commitment to
sustainability and conservation – old stone walls are being repaired
and ancient hedgerows restored. There are plenty of organic
vegetables available from the farm shop, along with rare-breed meat
that has been reared slowly for maximum flavour. Howbarrow was
voted Organic Farm Shop of the Year in 2002. The Organic Pudding
Co. Ltd (see page 122) is part of Howbarrow Farm.

Eddisbury Fruit Farm

Yeld Lane, Kelsall, Cheshire CW6 0TE   T: 01829 759157   w: www.eddisbury.co.uk
farm shop   farmers' markets

Twenty-six varieties of apple grown here provide the basis for the
farm shop; they are made into pressed juices and, unusually this far
north, cider. Pears, soft fruit and vegetables complete the range.

super hero

GROWING WITH NATURE, Pilling (see opposite)

Growing With Nature is a co-operative of a handful of organic growers in
Lancashire, offering a really big range of vegetables throughout the season.
Most of the produce sold is home-grown and the company takes pride in its
ability to deliver everything incredibly fresh – for example, salad crops are
sent out within 24 hours of harvesting. Recipes and newsletters are included
in the weekly boxes. Growing With Nature's box scheme has been operating
for 12 years and was one of the first to be set up in Britain – a great example
of organic growers collaborating to provide a really good service.

Flodder Hall

Lythe, Kendal, Cumbria LA8 8DG   T: 01539 568261 OR 01539 552005
🥄 **farm shop**

The Lythe valley is famous for damsons and for three weeks of the
year, starting at the end of August, you can buy them from the
temporary farm shop at Flodder Hall.

Whitebeck Farm

Lythe Valley, nr Kendal, Cumbria LA8 8DB   T: 01539 568225
📨 **farm gate sales**

The damsons, for which the Lythe valley is so renowned, are grown
at Whitebeck Farm without fertilizers or pesticides. They are picked
to order for customers during their short season (end of August to
September).

Growing With Nature

Bradshaw Lane Nursery, Pilling, Lancashire PR3 6AX   T: 01253 790046
📦 **box scheme**

Growing With Nature is a co-operative of a handful of organic
growers in Lancashire, offering a really big range of vegetables
throughout the season. See the Super Hero box, opposite, for more
information.

Church Farm Organics

Church Farm, Church Lane, Thurstaston, Wirral CH61 0HW   T: 0151 648 7838
W: www.churchfarm.org.uk
🥄 **farm shop**

Church Farm Organics are past winners of the Best Farm Shop
award at the Soil Association Organic Food Awards and they offer a
fantastic range of organic fruit and vegetables, all home-grown.
Asparagus and strawberries are seasonal specialities.

Bluebell Organics

St Mary's Presbytery, Barnard Castle, County Durham DL12 9TT   T: 07759 8322234
E: katrina@bluebell30.fsbusiness.co.uk

🛒 **farmers' markets**   📦 **box scheme**

Bluebell Organics offer a good range of fresh fruit and vegetables, with many really unusual varieties. See the Super Hero box, opposite, for more information.

Eggleston Hall

Eggleston, Barnard Castle, Co. Durham DL12 0AG   T: 01833 650553
W: www.egglestonhall.co.uk

🛍 **shop**

Eggleston Hall has a five-acre old walled kitchen garden, producing organic vegetables and herbs. These can be bought at the shop on site, where you will also find some great local produce – lamb and venison, cheese, home-baked goods and gourmet ready-cooked meals. There is also a café.

North East Organic Growers Ltd

West Sleekburn Farm, Bomarsund, Bedlington, Northumberland NE22 7AD
T: 01670 821070   W: www.neog.co.uk

📦 **box scheme**

A workers' co-operative, growing and sourcing organically grown fruits and vegetables, as locally as possible. There is a big range of vegetable varieties, from the basic to the unusual, such as chard, sugar snap peas and kohlrabi. This is sold via a weekly box scheme, delivering between Durham and Alnwick.

Barmston Organics

Elm Tree Farm, Barmston, Driffield, East Yorkshire YO25 8PQ   T: 01262 468128

🛒 **farmers' markets**   📦 **box scheme**

The Hunt family grow their own wheat, have it milled at a local watermill and then sell the flour through their box scheme – and it has proved very popular with their customers. The box scheme also

contains great vegetables and lamb, reared on home-grown feed.
Find the produce at Driffield farmers' market, too.

NORTH EAST   EBCHESTER

The Herb Patch

Brockwell House, Newlands, Ebchester, Co. Durham DH8 9JA T: 01207 562099
w: www.herbpatch.fsnet.co.uk

⬇ **farm shop** 🛒 **farmers' markets**

Over 100 varieties of home-grown herbs, grown without chemicals
in peat-free compost. The farm shop also stocks plenty of local
produce, from Northumberland cheese to organic vegetables, and
the herbs can also be found at Hexham, Barnard Castle and Whitley
Bay farmers' markets.

super hero

BLUEBELL ORGANICS, of Barnard Castle (see opposite)

Bluebell Organics offer many delights. Yes, you'll find great Soil Association
accredited organic potatoes, carrots, cabbages and all the basics. But you'll
also find fruit and vegetables you may well have never seen before –
tomatillos (related to the cape gooseberry), stripy beetroot, exotic Chinese
vegetables – all in a riot of colour and shape. No, it's not an experiment in GM
foods; Katrina Palmer, the grower, likes to search out unusual, old and native
seeds of varieties no longer commercially grown and in danger of dying out
because they don't suit intensive growing methods. She has found that
customers at her farmers' market stalls in Richmond and Brough are happy
and willing to try the less well-known varieties of vegetables she grows 'as
long as I explain what it is and how to cook it!' and are amazed at the diversity
of flavours and textures. Also on offer are home-made soups, utilizing some of
the unusual ingredients; marrow and garlic, or pumpkin and chilli are two
examples. Katrina's aims are far more simple, however, than all this may
suggest – 'the thinking behind Bluebell Organics is quite simply to provide
people with good, healthy, fresh food'.

    She also runs a box scheme; call for details.

Garden Cottage

Swillington House Farm, Coach Road, Swillington, nr Leeds, West Yorkshire LS26 8QA
T: 0113 286 9129 OR 07974 826876

🏪 **farmers' markets** 🚜 **farm gate sales** 📦 **box scheme**

Jo Cartwright specializes in unusual kinds of vegetables – she says there are plenty of people around growing cabbages so she tries to go for more interesting varieties. The vegetables are harvested on the day of sale from the old walled garden that Jo farms; free-range eggs and rare-breed pork, all home-produced, are also available. Buy the produce direct from the farm (phone first), from Leeds, Wakefield or Otley farmers' markets or join the box scheme Jo runs.

Brickyard Farm Shop

Badsworth, nr Pontefract, West Yorkshire WF9 1AX   T: 01977 617327
E: brickyardorganics@yahoo.co.uk

🛒 **farm shop** 📦 **box scheme**

Over 40 different varieties of organic fruit and vegetables are grown here, all picked fresh every day.

super hero

GOOSEMOOR ORGANICS, of Wetherby (see opposite)

It would be difficult to find a box scheme run on more environmentally sound principles than those at Goosemoor Organics. Absolutely every aspect of their business has been considered. Despite taking back its packaging from customers, the company only produces one bag of rubbish every week. LPG vans (better ecologically than petrol) are used for deliveries, the electricity supply is from sustainable hydro-electrics, and local businesses are used (and paid on time) to ensure small producers are not under financial strain and can focus on organic growing. There is even a two-acre nature reserve on Goosemoor's land. But what about the vegetables? Goosemoor Organics grow an interesting selection of squashes and some unusual chilli peppers, salad leaves and potatoes, including the pink fir apple, great for salads but usually hard to find. A good range of other fresh vegetables from nearby organic farms supplements their own produce.

FRUIT AND VEGETABLES

E Oldroyd and Sons Ltd

Ashfield House, Main Street, Carlton, Wakefield, West Yorkshire WF3 3RW
T: 0113 282 2245   E: katrina@bluebell30.fsbusiness.co.uk
farm gate sales

Traditional 'Champagne' rhubarb from the famous 'Wakefield triangle' rhubarb-producing area.

Goosemoor Organics

Warfield Lane, Cowthorpe, Wetherby, West Yorkshire LS22 5EU   T: 01423 358887
W: www.goosemoor.info
box scheme

Goosemoor Organics have given thought to the environmental impact of every aspect of their business, from packaging to power-use, and their organic produce is available in a box scheme. See the Super Hero box, opposite, for more information.

Four Seasons

38–40 Gilnahirk Road, Belfast BT5 7DG   T: 028 9079 2701

If you're looking for super-fresh, locally grown fruit and veg, then Four Seasons can provide it. Buying direct from the growers, food miles are minimal, the local economy benefits, and there is very little time-lag between the grower harvesting and the customers eating the produce. Four Seasons belong to the Northern Greengrocers Association.

Michel's Fresh Fruit & Veg

435 Ormeau Road, Belfast BT7 3DW   T: 028 9064 2804   E: mjgroggin01@hotmail.com

A big selection of locally grown produce in season, bought direct from the growers. The fruit and vegetables offered at Michel's have not been warehoused, as they generally are at supermarkets, which means they arrive on your plate much fresher. There are seven varieties of potato to choose from and even fresh herbs. Michel's belong to the Northern Greengrocers Association.

Organic Doorstep

125 Strabane Road, Castlederg, Co. Tyrone BT81 7JD   T: 028 8167 9989
w: www.organicdoorstep.net

box scheme

This box scheme delivers within the Belfast area and almost everything in the boxes is grown in Northern Ireland. Organic Doorstep operates a flexible scheme, delivering home-grown vegetables and home-produced milk and yoghurt, along with bread and eggs. You choose what you want in the box and deliveries can be made two or three times a week. Everything is organic.

Sperrin's Organic Wholefoods

24 Gorse Road, Claudy, Co. Londonderry BT47 4HY   T: 028 7133 8462
w: www.sperrinsorganic.com

box scheme

None of the produce in the weekly boxes sent out by Sperrin's is imported – everything is home-grown, from the essential basics like potatoes, carrots and onions to the unusual fennel and Jerusalem artichokes through to fresh strawberries and raspberries in the summer. Great value and totally fresh – the produce is often harvested only a few hours before delivery.

Helen's Bay Organic Farm

Coastguard Avenue, Helen's Bay, Co. Down   T: 028 9185 3122

box scheme

Organic and biodynamic vegetables fill the boxes for local delivery at Helen's Bay Farm, all home-grown or sourced as locally as possible, with a little imported fruit when necessary. Locally baked organic bread and local organic eggs are also on offer.

Kelly's

116 Long Stone Street, Lisburn, Co. Antrim BT28 1TR   T: 028 9266 3371

As a member of the Northern Greengrocers Association, Kelly's are committed to buying direct from the local growers, ensuring that the produce is as fresh as possible and hasn't travelled halfway across the world before it lands in your shopping bag.

NORTHERN IRELAND   NEWTOWNARDS

Home Grown

66b East Street, Newtownards, Co. Down BT23 7DD   T: 028 9181 8318

Margaret Whyte comes from a farming background and she knows a good vegetable when she sees one. She buys the fresh produce for her shop direct from the growers around Northern Ireland – many are within two or three miles of the shop. You really can't get fresher than this – they are on the shelves in the shop less than 24 hours after harvesting. Home Grown belongs to the Northern Greengrocers Association.

super hero

THOMAS BECHT, of Donegal Organic Farm Produce, Glenties (see page 243)

Thomas Becht, the farmer at Donegal Organic, is a mine of information about organic and biodynamic farming; he can tell you all kinds of facts and history regarding chemical-free farming and easily convinces you that it all makes a great deal of sense. Donegal Organic Farm Produce is run on biodynamic principles and so it is a mixed farm, offering everything from fruit and vegetables, milk and dairy products, to meat and poultry, all grown and reared without pesticides or commercial fertilizers. Asked how this mode of farming affects the flavour of the food, Thomas felt that all the produce, from the meat to the vegetables, benefited from being allowed to grow at its own pace – not forced with artificial stimulants – and that the flavour is more intense as a result. Given also that he selects breeds and varieties specifically for flavour, the produce has a head start already. Passionate about good-quality food and equally passionate about sustainable production, Thomas takes a holistic approach to farming – not only are homeopathic remedies used for the livestock, they are also used for the soil, to maintain natural fertility. Donegal is famed for the good quality of its soil and Thomas Becht intends to keep it that way. The produce is available from the farm shop on site or is delivered locally through a weekly box scheme.

Brooklodge Nursery

The Old Monastery, Ballyglunin, Co. Galway   T: 093 41456

≢ farm gate sales   ⊠ box scheme

Brooklodge Nursery grows a wide range of fruit, herbs and vegetables, only selling what they themselves grow – they never buy produce in. Available through a weekly box scheme or direct from the farm.

Caroline's Home Grown Veg

Parkmore, Templemartin, Bandon, Co. Cork   T: 021 7330178

≣ farmers' markets

A great range of chemical-free vegetables, from salads to field vegetables, aubergines and courgettes. Free-range eggs are also available. Find Caroline at the Cornmarket Street market in Cork on Saturdays or Macroom farmers' market on Tuesdays.

Peppermint Farm & Garden

Toughraheen, Bantry, Co. Cork   T: 028 31869   W: www.peppermintfarm.com

≢ farm gate sales   ⊠ mail order

Around 100 different varieties of organic herbs, sold as growing potted herbs, are available mail order or direct from the farm. Peppermint Farm is accredited by the Organic Trust.

The Apple Farm

Moorstown, Cahir, Co. Tipperary   T: 052 41459   W: www.theapplefarm.com

↓ farm shop

While not actually certified, this fruit farm is run on principles pretty close to organic. There are ten varieties of apple to choose from here and single-variety juices too. The farm even makes jams and jellies with the fruit.

The Garden

English Market, Cork   T: 021 4272368

During the summer and autumn this market stall is packed with
dewy-fresh organic vegetables and fruit sourced direct from organic
growers around Cork. The winter and spring seasons call for
imported produce but this is still organic.

Donegal Organic Farm Produce   `super hero`

Doorian, Glenties, Co. Donegal   T: 075 51286   w: www.esatclear.ie/~tbecht
➤ **farm shop** ➤ **box scheme**

Donegal Organic Farm Produce is a mixed farm run on biodynamic
lines to produce organic fruit and vegetables, milk, dairy products,
meat and poultry. See the Super Hero box, page 241, for more
information.

Marc Michel

Tinna Park, Kilpedder, Co. Wicklow   T: 01 2011 882
➤ **farm shop**

Open on Thursdays, Fridays and Saturdays, this farm shop sells
wonderfully fresh, home-grown, organic vegetables. Marc Michel is
accredited by the Organic Trust.

Ballinroan

Kiltegan, Co. Wicklow   T: 0508 73278
➤ **farm shop** ➤ **box scheme**

Penny and Udo Lange grow 'anything you can grow on a mountain
top in Wicklow'. This includes all kinds of basics, and some more
unusual items, such as pak choi and sugarloaf lettuce. All the
vegetables are biodynamically grown and are available through the
box scheme that the Langes run. They also rear biodynamic lamb,
from a hotch-potch of breeds, and occasionally run open days so
that you can see how they do things. As well as the box scheme
and farm shop they also sell at local markets.

Briarneuk Nursery

Braidwood, Carluke, Lanarkshire ML8 5NG   T: 01555 860279

farmers' markets

Briarneuk Nursery specializes in tomatoes, with several different
sorts grown here, from cherry tomatoes and cocktail tomatoes to
full-size varieties. They arrive at the farmers' market having been
picked only the day before – they are fresher and picked when more
ripe than most of the tomatoes you'll find at supermarkets. Their
flavour remains sweet, as they are never put into cold stores.

Raasay Walled Garden

Isle of Raasay, Ross-shire IV40 8PB   T: 01478 660345

farm gate sales

A small walled garden but a big range of organic vegetables, fruit
and herbs. Call to find out what's in season, and to arrange to visit.

Pillars of Hercules Organic Farm

Falkland, Fife KY15 7AD   T: 01337 857749   w: www.pillars.co.uk

farm shop

Bruce Bennett of Pillars of Hercules aims to offer his customers a
one-stop shop, with great local fresh produce – from fruit and
vegetables, dairy produce and bread, to meat, all accredited to Soil
Association standards. There is also a café.

Glendale Salads

19 Upper Fasach, Glendale, Isle of Skye IV55 8WP   T: 01470 511349

box scheme

Really unusual salad leaves and herbs are grown at Glendale –
40 different varieties throughout the season, every kind of shape,
colour and flavour imaginable.

Huntly Herbs

Whitestones of Tillathrowie, Gartly, Huntly, Aberdeenshire AB54 4SB   T: 01466 720247
E: huntlyherbs@hotmail.com

farmers' markets   farm gate sales

About 150 different varieties of herbs are grown here, although some are seasonal and not always available. Organic vegetables are also available, picked only hours before sale, including specialist potatoes, such as the unusual pink fir apple.

Croft Organics

Skellarts Croft, Daviot, Inverurie, Aberdeenshire AB51 0JL   T: 01467 681717
w: www.croft-organics.co.uk

farm shop   box scheme

Croft Organics grow both basic fruit and vegetables and the more unusual – such as blueberries. Fresh herbs and free-range eggs are also available. A recipe sheet is supplied with the vegetable boxes, just in case you're not sure how to cook the more unusual items.

Lenshaw Organics

Upper Lenshaw Farm, Rothienorman, Inverurie, Aberdeenshire AB51 8XU
T: 01464 871243

farm shop   box scheme

The box scheme operated from Upper Lenshaw Farm is 100% organic and 100% home-produced. There is also free-range and organic Gloucester Old Spot pork and organic beef, both reared on the farm.

Earthshare Ltd

65 Society Street, Nairn IV12 4NL   T: 01667 452879   E: earthshare@macunlimited.net

box scheme

Earthshare is a Community Supported Agriculture scheme established in 1994, growing vegetables and soft fruit for up to 200 local families. People commit to the scheme for a year at a time and in return they receive their share of all that is harvested in the form of a weekly box. The boxes include all kinds of seasonal vegetables: root crops like carrots, parsnips, beetroot and kohlrabi in the winter, and courgettes, beans, tomatoes and Chinese greens in the summer. All produce is grown by organic methods. Subscribers are encouraged to become involved at the farm and receive a discount off the cost of their box if they commit to carry out three workshifts per year. Call Pam Bochel for more details.

SCOTLAND · STONEHAVEN

Burnarrachie

Bridge of Muchalls, Stonehaven, Kincardineshire AB39 3RU T: 01569 730195
⌂ **farm gate sales** ✉ **box scheme**

Long before organics or biodynamics were as well known as they are now, John and Maggie Fraser were growing winter vegetables. A huge range is available, far too many to list, and they are always picked to order. Call with your order first and it will be ready when you arrive.

WALES · ABERGAVENNY

Ty Mawr Organics

Greathouse Farm, Penpergwm, Abergavenny, Monmouthshire NP7 9UY
T: 01873 840247 E: pwjabevan@aol.com
⌂ **farmers' markets** ⌂ **farm gate sales**

Organic vegetables, cut fresh to order at the farm gate, or from Abergavenny, Brecon, Cowbridge or Penarth farmers' markets.

WALES · ABERYSTWYTH

Nantclyd Farm Produce

Nantclyd Farm, Llanilar, Aberystwyth, Ceredigion SY23 4SL T: 01974 241543
⌂ **farm gate sales**

Nantclyd Farm won the top award in the 2002 Soil Association Organic Food Awards for their strawberries, judged in a blind tasting by a panel of experts. The farm also has Poll Dorset lamb, which lamb in autumn, and free-range eggs, all certified by the Soil Association. All the produce is available from the farm direct or from local shops, including the Tree House in Aberystwyth (see page 133).

Porthamel Organic Farm

Porthamel, Llanedwen, Llanfair PG, Anglesey LL61 6PJ T: 01248 430355
E: porthamelfarm@virgin.net

⊨ farm gate sales

Porthamel Farm is a Soil Association demonstration farm, which often holds open days for members of the public to see how an organic farm is run. Seasonal vegetables are the mainstay here, with some fruit, and organic, free-range hens' eggs. Call before visiting or to arrange to place an order for collection.

Savages

21c High Street, Bethesda, Gwynedd, LL57 3AF T: 01248 605191
w: www.astorr.freeserve.co.uk/savageshome.htm

⊫ box scheme

Sandra Storr grows some interesting fruit and vegetables on her mountainside smallholding – the basics, along with pak choi, mizuna, pears, blueberries and raspberries – and operates a box scheme to local residents, giving them the benefit of super-fresh, local produce. She also has a shop that stocks all the fruit and vegetables and has a great selection of preserves (made with her own produce) and lots of local produce. She only buys from producers who grow without chemicals.

The Fruit Garden

Groesfaen Road, Peterston-super-Ely, Cardiff, South Glamorgan CF5 6NE
T: 01446 760358

↓ farm shop ⊨ farmers' markets

Specialist soft fruit growers, offering 18 varieties of strawberry, who are continually experimenting with varieties to achieve the best flavour. They also make their fruit into ice cream. PYO is on offer.

Glyn Fach Farm

Pontygates, Llanelli, Carmarthenshire SA15 5TG   T: 01269 861290
w: www.glynfachfarm.co.uk
✉ **farm gate sales**

This smallholding offers a wonderful range of fresh produce,
including free-range eggs, which can be bought direct from the farm
gate; call to arrange order and see the Super Hero box, opposite,
for more information.

Carrob Growers

Llangunville, Llanrothal, Monmouth NP25 5QL   T: 01600 714529
✉ **farm gate sales** 🛒 **farmers' markets**

Carrob Growers produce berries you may have never heard of –
such as sunberries and jostaberries. Unusual fruit is the norm here,
and there is a great range available in season, picked to order to
collect from the farm gate and also at Usk farmers' market.

Berryhill Fruit Farm

Coedkernew, Newport, Gwent NP1 9UD   T: 01633 680938
🛒 **farm shop**

Twelve varieties of apple, many of them rare, with pears, plums,
gooseberries, some unusual berries, raspberries and vegetables, all
home-grown. The farm shop also stocks local free-range eggs,
jams, chutneys and pickles.

Cwm Harry Land Trust

Lower Cwm Harry, Tregynon, Newtown, Powys SY16 3ES   T: 01686 650231
w: www.cwmharrylandtrust.org.uk

Cwm Harry Land Trust is a Community Supported Agriculture
Scheme. Similar to a vegetable box scheme, local growers produce
vegetables without chemicals and then offer a share of the harvest to
local consumers. Paying a subscription fee means that you get
regular deliveries of fresh vegetables and in a good year your share
of the harvest can be considerable. It's a great way to feel part of the

community, to reduce food miles and to be more involved with the production of the food you eat. Call to find out how to join.

WALES   PWLLHELI

Llangybi Organics

Mur Crusto, Llangybi, Pwllheli, Gwynedd LL53 6LX   T: 01766 819109
w: www.llangybi-organics.co.uk

box scheme

A small-scale box scheme but with an enormous range of produce – last season, around 50 different varieties of fruit and vegetables were grown, including apples and plums from the orchard on the farm. Call to find out if you can become part of the box scheme.

WALES   ST DAVIDS

Spring Meadow Farm

Caerfarchell, St Davids, Pembrokeshire SA62 6XG   T: 01437 721800

farm shop   farmers' markets

Spring Meadow Farm produces a fantastic range of vegetables – up to 60 different crops throughout the season. There are all the everyday favourites and then some of the more unusual varieties – fennel, celeriac, pattypan, yellow courgettes and sugar snap peas. Available from the farm shop on site (May 1st to Christmas) or from Fishguard and Haverfordwest farmers' markets.

super hero

JEFF AND JEAN PEACE, of Glyn Fach Farm, Llanelli (see opposite)

Members of the Wholesome Food Association, Jeff and Jean Peace are truly adventurous small-scale growers. Jean admitted to me that they'll have a go at growing anything, even having had some success with peaches, lemons and oranges – with the only artificial encouragement being a polytunnel. The range of fruit and vegetables offered from this smallholding is staggering – far too many to list – and is supplemented with free-range hens' and ducks' eggs, all sold from the farm gate (the Peaces firmly believe in keeping 'food miles' to a minimum). With so much produce growing in her own garden, Jean Peace cannot even remember the last time she visited a supermarket! The Peaces have a committed and loyal following of customers enjoying the ultimate freshness of produce picked on the day it is sold – call Jeff or Jean if you'd like to join them.

Game meats are beginning to grow in popularity, having once suffered from a poor image – they used to be thought of as either very expensive, for special occasions only, or as a food of inconsistent quality, bought from slightly shady characters. Some people associate game with meat that has been hung for so long that it has an incredibly strong flavour and a very potent aroma. These days, however, you can buy really fresh, good-quality game at reasonable prices, from suppliers who adhere to strict regulations. The meat is versatile and can be used for both traditional dishes and modern recipes and ways of cooking. Some of the suppliers I feature are members of the National Game Dealers Association (NGDA) or the Guild of Q Butchers, both of whom have stringent codes of practice.

The merits of wild game as opposed to farmed, especially with venison, is always a hotly contested topic. Farmed game offers an assurance of consistency and there is some superb venison and wild boar available now, from animals that have been reared on high-quality, home-produced feed and slaughtered at just the right age to produce tender and tasty meat. Equally, there are many who swear that wild venison is preferable – they say the texture is better, that it reacts better to traditional hanging and has a more authentic flavour. Wild

game

venison often has a stronger, 'gamier' taste, while farmed will often be milder, with a less robust texture.

The key to buying game is to know what to look for, to be aware of the shooting seasons and to buy from suppliers who can tell you exactly where their stock came from. The good news is that many gamekeepers on shooting estates (where most of the game you'll find in the shops will have come from) are raising standards constantly. The NGDA says that two-thirds of gamekeepers in this country have specially designed game larders and a third have chillers, to keep the meat in perfect condition before it is collected by the game dealer. Many have had professional training in food hygiene and this number is rising all the time. More and more members of the Guild of Q Butchers are becoming licensed game dealers, so they are able to give you more information about the provenance of the game and how to store and cook it. Most of the suppliers listed in this section source the game they sell direct from shoots – they have a higher level of quality control and usually receive the game before it has been processed. This makes it far easier to see how old the bird or animal is and if it has been damaged by poor shooting, and allows them to choose the best. If you've always been nervous about trying game at home, now is a great time to give it a go.

Framptons of Bridport

Market House, East Street, Bridport, Dorset DT6 3LF and also at, 9e Westbay, Westbay,
Bridport, Dorset DT6 4EW   T: 01308 422995 (EAST STREET) 01308 423124 (WESTBAY)
w: www.framptonsofbridport.co.uk

The game at this butcher's comes from local shoots around Dorset
and can include wild duck, pigeon, hare, snipe or teal as well as the
more usual pheasant and venison. Local organic pork and poultry
are specialities.

Somerset Organics

Gilcombe Farm Shop, Gilcombe Farm, Bruton, Somerset, BA10 0QE   T: 01749 813710
w: www.somersetorganics.co.uk
farm shop **farmers' markets** **mail order**

Somerset Organics produce and sell organic beef, pork, lamb and
chicken on their 300-acre farm as well as stocking all local game,
including rabbbit, hare, venison and wild boar. They also produce
the highest quality ready-meals, pies, pasties and soups from the
farm kitchen.

Deer Force 10

Mardlewood House, Higher Combe, Buckfastleigh, Devon TQ11 0JD   T: 01364 644420
farm gate sales

One of the very few producers of certified organic venison, Deer
Force 10 allow their deer to live as naturally as possible, with low
stocking rates giving them plenty of space to roam, with access to
woodland. The deer are shot on site, virtually eliminating stress, and
are then hung for a week to ten days. The venison is available direct
from the farm (by appointment only) or from Riverford Farm Shop
(see pages 104 and 106).

L & C Game

Court Farm, Buckland Newton, Dorset DT2 7BT   T: 01300 345271
E: adrianspicer@fsmail.net

↓ **farm shop**   🏠 **farmers' markets**   🚚 **delivery service**

Local game from small Dorset shoots and various different kinds of wild venison. The venison is hung to order and butchered on site and home-made sausages are available. There is a farm shop on Saturdays.

Moorland Larder

113 East Street, South Molton, Devon EX36 3BD   T: 01769 573554
W: www.moorlandlarder.co.uk

✉ **mail order**

Wild and farmed venison, wild boar and game birds are all sourced locally. Graham Wright, the owner, is very experienced in selecting the highest quality game.

Palmers of Tavistock

50 Brook Street, Tavistock, Devon PL19 0BJ,   T: 01822 612000
W: www.palmers-tavistock.com

✉ **mail order**

Devon is rich in wild game and Palmers make the most of it, offering plenty of choice in season. Locally sourced beef, pork and lamb is also available.

Gary Dutton Butchers

25 Molesworth Street, Wadebridge, Cornwall PL27 7DH   T: 01208 812866

Lots of local game is offered at Dutton's in season. Collected fresh from local shoots, there is pheasant, partridge, duck, woodcock and teal, and wild venison. All arrive at the shop unprepared so that Gary can gauge the condition easily. He'll even prepare and dress game that customers bring in themselves.

Barrow Boar

Fosters Farm, South Barrow, Yeovil, Somerset BA22 7LN   T: 01963 440315
w: www.barrowboar.co.uk

✉ **mail order**

Barrow Boar rears free-range wild boar and creates an interesting range of foods from them, including salami and prosciutto. Even the liver is available for making an unusual pâté. The farm also produces Hebridean lamb and Aberdeen Angus beef, and all kinds of game from local estates is available.

Manydown Farmshop

Scrapps Hill Farm, Worting Road, Basingstoke, Hampshire RG23 8PU   T: 01256 460068

👜 **farm shop**

In season there is a fantastic range of game available at this farm shop – pheasant, partridge and hare to name a few, all shot on the farm's own land. The shop also stocks home-reared, free-range chicken, Aberdeen Angus beef and Large Black pork.

Manor Farm Game

96 Berkeley Avenue, Chesham, Buckinghamshire HP5 2RS   T: 07778 706179
w: www.manorfarmgame.co.uk

🛒 **farmers' markets** 🚚 **delivery service** ✉ **mail order**

Game specialists, offering a big selection of game, including venison, sourced from Manor Farm's own shoot as well as other local shoots and estates. The game is available in the feather, oven-ready, jointed into breast, steak and stewing packs or processed into a wide range of sausages, burgers and pies.

George Arthur Ltd

70 Guildford Road, Lightwater, Surrey GU18 5SD   T: 01276 472191
w: www.georgearthur.com

Dry-cured bacon and free-range pork from Norfolk are two of the specialities at this butcher's shop and a full range of local game is also available in season.

Randalls Butchers

113 Wandsworth Bridge Road, Fulham, London SW6 2TE   T: 020 7736 3426

Randalls offers some seriously good organic meat and also some hand-picked game from shoots not far outside London.

Hamblings

2 Moneyhill Parade, Rickmansworth, Herts WD3 2BQ   T: 01923 772557
w: www.hamblingsbutchers.co.uk

Hamblings is a combination of butcher's and delicatessen, with a range of free-range meats always available, and local pheasant, partridge and venison.

Ashbee & Son

100 High Street, Rye, East Sussex TN31 7JN   T: 01797 223303
w: www.ashbeeandson.sageweb.co.uk

Local pheasant, grouse, duck, pigeon and rabbit are among the specialities at this traditional butcher's shop.

Dundale Farm

Dundale Road, Tunbridge Wells, Kent TN3 9AQ   T: 01892 822175
farmers' markets **farm gate sales**

The fresh game at Dundale Farm comes either from their own land or, in the case of the partridges, from a neighbour's farm. Pheasant, partridge, mallard and wild venison are all available in season.

Castleman's Farm

Green Common Lane, Woburn Common, Buckinghamshire HP10 0LH   T: 07900 886459
farmers' markets **farm gate sales**

The Rayner family run their own shoot at Castleman's Farm, using pheasants and partridges that they have reared themselves. Other game shot on their land is also available – wild venison, duck and rabbit. Free-range poultry, including chickens and guineafowl, and turkeys and geese at Christmas, are also on offer, along with unpasteurized milk and cream from the farm's Guernsey herd. Available direct from the farm (call first) or from Marlow and Beaconsfield farmers' markets.

EAST ANGLIA   BECCLES

Brampton Wild Boar

Blue Tile Farm, Lock's Road, Brampton, Beccles, Suffolk NR34 8DX   T: 01502 575246
🛒 **farmers' markets** ✉ **mail order**

The wild boar reared at Blue Tile Farm are pure-bred animals, from a stock brought over from the Polish/German border, and they have even been DNA-tested to verify their purity. Reared outdoors, the boar are fed a diet without artificial additives or GM foods and reared slowly to 12 months of age before slaughter. Steaks and roasting joints are available, along with parma-style ham, pancetta and a hot-smoked haunch that is glazed with the farm's own damson jam. Find all the produce at Hatfield, St Albans, Waltham Abbey and Halesworth farmers' markets or buy it mail order, by arrangement.

EAST ANGLIA   NORWICH

Harvey's Pure Meat

63 Grove Road, Norwich, Norfolk NR1 3RL   T: 01603 621908   w: www.puremeat.org.uk

---

Alongside all the local organic meats, Harvey's also offer plenty of fresh local game, all from Norfolk. The game comes from nearby shoots, collected personally from the gamekeepers. All varieties of venison are available – red, fallow, roe and muntjack – and all are prepared and hung on the premises. Partridge, pheasant, woodcock and some wild fowl are also available. Harvey's are accredited by the Organic Food Federation.

EAST ANGLIA   PETERBOROUGH

Brown's of Peterborough

3 Cumbergate, Peterborough, Cambridgeshire PE1 1YR   T: 01733 562104
w: www.browns-finefoods.co.uk
✉ **mail order**

Most of the game at Brown's is locally sourced and includes pheasant, venison, rabbit and wild boar.

GAME

Saxmundham Butchers

8 High Street, Saxmundham, Suffolk IP17 1DD   T: 01728 602081

A good old-fashioned butcher's, selling local meats and a good range of local game – even the more unusual game birds such as teal and snipe.

Wild Meat Company

Low Road, Sweffling, Saxmundham, Suffolk IP17 2BU   T: 01728 663211
w: www.wildmeat.co.uk

farmers' markets   **mail order**

The quality control process at the Wild Meat Company is so stringent that they estimate they reject around a third of the game that they receive from local shoots. All of the game offered is from Suffolk and includes the harder to find varieties, such as woodpigeon, wild duck and woodcock. Wild venison is also available. Call to find out which farmers' markets the Wild Meat Company attends or buy mail order. Wholesale supply available.

C E Brown

Southlawns, Main Street, Shudy Camps, Cambridgeshire CB1 6RA   T: 01799 584461
farm gate sales

Colin Brown knows which gamekeepers look after the game well before and after local shoots and they are the keepers he buys from. His stock is always very fresh because he collects the game either on the day of the shoot or the day after and prepares it all himself. Wild venison, hare, rabbit, pheasant, partridge and mallard are all local and he also has grouse from Yorkshire.

Clive Lancaster

1 Eaton Place, Market Square, Bingham, Notts NG13 8BD   T: 01949 875010

Alongside quality meat from local farms, Clive Lancaster stocks game birds sourced from one local gamekeeper.

super hero

RACHEL GODWIN AND JEANETTE EDGAR, of Alternative Meats,
Weston-under-Redcastle (see below)

Quality control can often be an issue with wild game. How can you tell if a game bird will be young and tender? Just how old was that wild rabbit when it was shot? Rachel and Jeanette at Alternative Meats are fanatical about quality. Every item of game that they stock has been rigorously checked and anything that is questionable will be rejected. Buying from the same gamekeepers enables them to build a rapport – the keepers know what Rachel and Jeanette want and won't try to fob them off with something of dubious quality. Wild boar can also be tricky. Less scrupulous dealers will sometimes try to pass off old male pork as wild boar. Rachel and Jeanette can't be fooled – they insist on DNA testing the meat.

Though it is difficult to offer watertight guarantees with wild game – by its very nature there is a degree of the unknown about birds and animals shot in the wild – Alternative Meats really do put in the effort to offer as much reassurance as possible and the honesty and openness of their approach is a real treat in an industry that has often suffered from an unwelcome air of 'muck and magic'.

MIDLANDS   BURNTWOOD

Bradshaw Bros Ltd

76 High Street, Chase Terrace, Burntwood, Staffordshire WS7 8LR   T: 01543 279437

This traditional butcher is a licensed game dealer, including wholesale, and stocks wild game, predominantly game birds, from a local shoot. Richard Crisp, the manager, says the key to getting good-quality game is to always buy from a trusted source – he never sources game from dealers he does not know.

MIDLANDS   SHREWSBURY

Alternative Meats   super hero

Hough Farm, Weston-under-Redcastle, Shrewsbury, Shropshire SY4 5LR
T: 01948 840130   W: www.alternativemeats.co.uk
✉ **mail order**

A great range of wild game, including rabbit, hare, venison, and all the game birds, from trustworthy sources. Quality control is rigorous, down to DNA testing to ensure that the wild boar is just that and not regular pork! Free-range duck is also available, as is free-range goose at Christmas. See the Super Hero box, opposite, for more information.

Sillfield Farm

super hero

Endmoor, Kendal, Cumbria LA8 0HZ   T: 01539 567609
w: www.sillfield.co.uk

🏪 **farmers' markets**   ✉ **mail order**

Peter Gott of Sillfield Farm rears free-range, rare-breed pigs and wild boar and makes dry-cured bacon as well as pancetta and other interesting preserved meats. See the Super Hero box, page 261, for more information.

The Housekeeper's Store at Tatton Park

Tatton Park, Knutsford, Cheshire WA16 6QN   T: 01625 534424
w: www.tattonpark.org.uk

The Housekeeper's Store at Tatton Park recently won a Great Taste Award for their hot-smoked venison. Marinated in juniper berries, the venison haunch is smoked over oak and the meat is then ready to eat, needing no more cooking. The venison comes from Tatton Park's own deer, which are culled at 18 months to produce a mildly flavoured meat without the strong gamey taste often associated with venison.

The shop also sells a selection of home-cured hams, bacon and gammon, as well as cheeses and deli goods, all from British small-scale producers.

Lords of Middleton

18 Old Hall Street, Middleton, Manchester M24 1AN   T: 0161 643 4160
w: www.lordsofmiddleton.co.uk

✉ **mail order**

Wild Scottish venison is available at Lord's and in season there is a wide range of British game. Scotch beef hung for a minimum of four weeks, Highland lamb and free-range pork are all available.

Arley Wild Boar

Moss Cottage, New Road, Crowley, Northwich, Cheshire CW9 6NY   T: 01565 777326

farmers' markets

Free-range wild boar, slowly matured for a full-flavoured meat. The boar are given a GM-free feed to supplement the root crops they forage for. The meat is hung for ten days after slaughter at a local abattoir and is available from Eddisbury, Nantwich, Ashton-under-Lyme and Birkenhead farmers' markets. A member of the British Wild Boar Association.

The Teesdale Trencherman

Startforth Hall, Barnard Castle, Co. Durham DL12 9AG   T: 01833 638370
w: www.trencherman.co.uk

mail order

Fresh game from local shoots, including quail, venison, partridge and mallard, is available here, all plucked or skinned and hung on site. The venison and pheasant are available traditionally oak-smoked, too – the venison taking three days in the smokehouse before it is ready. The Teesdale Trencherman also has lots of interesting deli-style products on offer – local cheeses, including the hard to find blue Wensleydale, traditional air-dried Cumberland hams and rare imported goods, such as black rice from China, French red rice from the Camargue and pumpkin seed oil.

J B Cockburn & Sons

12 Market Place, Bedale, North Yorkshire DL8 1EQ   T: 01677 422126

The game here comes from one of nine local estates and the Cockburns collect straight from the shoots, ensuring only the best is on offer to their customers. Wild boar is also available, and organic Highland beef from the butcher's own farm, local organic Swaledale lamb and free-range Berkshire pork are all popular.

PETER GOTT, of Sillfield Farm, Kendal (see page 259)

Peter Gott rears pigs and wild boar free-range on his Cumbrian farm but he's not just content to keep one type of each. Middle White, Berkshire and Gloucester Old Spot pigs rub shoulders with Russian, German, French and Polish wild boar and from these animals he makes all manner of unusual meats – prosciutto, pancetta and air-dried fillets of boar, and Bath chaps, Cumberland Speck and brawn – alongside the more well-known dry-cured bacon. With old-fashioned husbandry and natural feeds, the animals produce old-fashioned meat – dense, firm and intensely flavoured. The secret, says Peter, lies in two factors. Firstly, the animals live almost exactly as they would in the wild – rooting around in woodland – and so are fit and healthy. Just as important is the age of the animals at slaughter – the wild boar are never less than 18 months, which gives a mature, rich flavour. Peter has tried many different breeds in the search for the tastiest. Some unscrupulous suppliers sell pork from ageing pigs as wild boar, passing off the pungent meat as its wild counterpart, but there really is no comparison – Peter Gott's is the real thing, reared with immense care and attention, and the flavour testifies to this. The meats are available by mail order, or find them at Liverpool, Manchester and Carlisle farmers' markets or Borough Market in London SE1.

NORTH EAST   **DURHAM**

Teesdale Game & Poultry

Durham Indoor Market, Market Square, Durham DH1 3NJ   T: 0191 375 0664 (MARKET) OR 01833 637153 (MAIL ORDER)   E: teesdalegame@aol.com

✉ **mail order**

Game birds, including the hard to find teal and woodcock, wild rabbit and hare, and venison are supplied by Teesdale. The owners, Stephen and Alison Morrell, know where everything comes from (estates around Northumberland and Cumbria) and can supply recipe sheets to help those unfamiliar with some of the more unusual produce.

NORTH EAST HARROGATE

Hutchinsons

Main Street, Ripley, Harrogate, North Yorkshire, HG3 3AX T: 01423 770110

The game at Hutchinsons is sourced directly from local gamekeepers and includes wild rabbits, venison, pigeon, pheasant and duck.

NORTH EAST LEEDS

C & G Starkey

8 Wolsey Parade, Sherburn-in-Elmet, Leeds LS25 6BQ T: 01977 682696
W: www.c-gstarkey.co.uk

delivery service **mail order**

Plenty of game sourced from Yorkshire, a really wide selection, including hard to find teal and snipe, is available from this shop.

NORTH EAST RICHMOND

Yorkshire Game

Station Road Industrial Park, Brompton-on-Swale, Richmond, North Yorkshire DL10 7SN
T: 01748 810212 W: www.yorkshiregame.co.uk

mail order

Yorkshire Game is the home of the National Game Dealers Association and the staff here are all passionate about sympathetic game management and high quality standards, so their sourcing of game is extremely careful. The range is extensive and game sausages are also available. Wholesale supply is available.

NORTH EAST RIPON

Wensleydale Wild Boar

Goose Park, Thornton Steward, Ripon, North Yorkshire HG4 4BB T: 01677 460239

farm gate sales **mail order**

European wild boar are reared free-range in paddocks. Slowly matured, the boar are not slaughtered until they are about 18 months old, for a dark and gamey meat, and there are many different cuts to choose from. Available direct from the farm or by mail order. A member of the British Wild Boar Association.

Thornbeck Farm

Calf Fallow Lane, Norton, Stockton-on-Tees, Cleveland TS20 1PF   T: 01642 365661 OR 07715 023102

✉ **farm gate sales**

Many people don't like to find lead shot in the pheasant they are eating and so Peter Wallis at Thornbeck Farm rears pheasants in exactly the same way as he rears his chickens – corn-fed on locally grown corn – and they are killed in the same way as chickens, not by shooting. This means that there are no nasty surprises when you cut into the meat and no damage caused by poor shooting and a hard landing! The corn-fed chickens and pheasants are available all year and there are turkeys available at Christmas, direct from the farm, but please call first.

Coffey's Butchers

380 Lisburn Road, Belfast BT9 6GL   T: 028 9066 6292   w: www.coffeysbutchers.co.uk

✉ **mail order**

Coffey's sell meat reared on their own and neighbouring farms but they are also game specialists. The game is collected direct from the estates where it is shot and has to pass a tough inspection before it is allowed on to the counter. It arrives at the shop in furred or feathered form and is processed on site. Wild venison, pheasant, woodpigeon, rabbit, hare and guineafowl are all available in season.

Finnebrogue Venison Company

20 Finnebrogue Road, Downpatrick BT30 9AB   T: 028 4461 7525

✉ **farm gate sales**

The focus of the Finnebrogue Venison Company is to produce venison that is as tender as possible and so the farmed red deer are all under 15 months old when slaughtered. This results in a much milder meat than wild venison, without the strong gamey flavour.

food facts

GAME: TIPS AND HINTS

Venison, like beef, benefits from hanging for up to two weeks; it can be cooked in the same ways as beef and is best eaten slightly rare. Unlike beef, venison is very low in fat. Red deer makes the strongest flavoured venison and is the type you will be most likely to find in butchers' shops.

Wild rabbit is generally considered to be tastier than its farmed counterpart but it is important to choose a young rabbit, aged between three and four months, or the meat may be tough with too strong a flavour. If you are planning to buy a whole unprepared rabbit, look for one with soft, easily torn ears, as this indicates a younger animal.

When buying wild pigeon, look for a good round, plump breast, which denotes a younger bird.

October and November is the time when partridges are considered to have the best flavour, although their shooting season lasts between September and February. Partridges fall into two types, the English Greyleg and French Redleg. Greylegs are generally wild and have a stronger and gamier flavour than the red, which are more often farmed. A simple roast is the best way to serve the Greylegs, while Redlegs are better served in casseroles and pot roasts.

A young pheasant will roast very well but if you have any doubt about the age of the bird it would be prudent to marinate it and/or use it in a casserole or similar dish. Hen birds are smaller, have less fat and are more tender than cocks.

If you'd like to learn more about buying and handling game, the Game Conservancy Trust is a mine of information, as is its publication, *The Game & Fish Cookbook*. See page 410 for contact details.

REPUBLIC OF IRELAND	BALLINALLEE

Drumeel Farm

Drumeel, Ballinallee, Co. Longford   T: 086 340 2824

🐄 **farmers' markets** ▨ **farm gate sales**

Although not certified organic, Pat Cremin's venison is organically reared, outdoor all year, mainly grass-fed. The deer are slaughtered at around two years old and hung for a week, giving a fine-grained meat with a less pronounced gamey flavour than you might expect from wild venison. Available from Temple Bar and Leopardstown markets, where home-reared lamb and free-range eggs are also on offer.

Molloys of Donnybrook

Donnybrook Road, Dublin 4   T: 01 269 1678

A classic game merchant/fishmonger's. The fish is from local waters, almost always day caught, and the game includes wild venison, pheasant, pigeon, duck and rabbit, all from local shoots.

SCOTLAND · ABERFELDY

Aberfeldy Butchers

12 Bank Street, Aberfeldy, Perthshire PH15 2BB   T: 01887 820310
✉ **mail order**

Venison from Balmoral is a cross between wild and farmed – the gamekeepers there intervene only in harsh weather, to supplement the deer's natural food. They also monitor the deer carefully, shooting only when it is the correct age for eating. Game birds are also available from local estates, including duck and all kinds of pigeon. All the meat is available mail order.

SCOTLAND · ALNESS

Highland Wild Boar

Millcraig Mill, Alness, Ross-shire IV17 0YA   T: 01349 883734
🛒 **farmers' markets**

The wild boar at Millcraig Mill have plenty of space in which to roam and eat additive-free feed. They do not go to the local abattoir until they are at least a year old, allowing the meat to develop flavour and texture. There are plenty of cuts available, and also sausages, burgers, bacon, ham and gammon, and the meat is dark and full-flavoured. Find the produce at Dingwall and Inverness farmers' markets, where you'll also be able to try the cooked sausages.

SCOTLAND · AUCHTERMUCHTY

Fletchers   super hero

Reediehill Farm, Auchtermuchty, Fife KY14 7HS   T: 01337 828369
w: www.fletchersscotland.co.uk
🛒 **farm shop** 🛒 **farmers' markets**

The Fletchers are fervant campaigners for venison and have been producing it successfully for the last 30 years. See the Super Hero box, page 267, for more information.

Fair and Square Game Butchery

The Larder, Auchessen Estate, Crianlarich, Perthshire FK20 8QS T: 01567 820975

🡇 **farm shop** 🡒 **farmers' markets**

Wild game from Auchessen Estate and other local sources, all from trusted gamekeepers, bought direct from the shoots. Wild venison is also available, and recipe sheets and advice on cooking are happily given. The butchery will supply to order.

D J MacDougall

Canal Side, Fort Augustus, Inverness-shire PH32 4AU T: 01320 366214

A full range of local game is offered here, including wild venison. MacDougall is also the only butcher in the UK to hold a Q Guild Diamond award for its haggis.

Robertson Jeen

34 New Kirk Road, Bearsden, Glasgow G61 3SL T: 0141 942 0154

Ian Jeen prides himself on his locally reared beef but he also offers a great selection of wild game. Fresh local grouse, woodcock and pheasant are on offer, alongside quail and quails' eggs, wild hare and rabbit. The venison stocked is wild, which Ian believes has a cleaner flavour than its farmed counterpart.

Forbes Raeburn & Sons

7 Bogie Street, Huntly, Aberdeenshire AB54 8DX T: 01466 792818
w: www.fobbiethebutcher.com

The butchers at Forbes Raeburn feel that wild venison is preferable to farmed – they say it hangs better and is a firmer, more robust meat – and so they only stock the wild variety, from local red deer. Other local game is also available – pheasant, wild duck and partridge. Everything is prepared on site.

GAME

Hilton Wild Boar

Johnston's Butchers, 46 High Street, Newburgh, Fife KY14 6AQ   T: 01337 842867
w: www.hiltonwildboar.co.uk

🛒 **farmers' markets**   ✉ **mail order**

The wild boar at Hilton Farm are free-ranging, living in small family groups. Slowly reared to a year old or more, the meat is very different from commercial pork – dark and well marbled. Sausages – including some flavoured with prune and claret or honey and mustard – haunches, loin and dry-cured bacon are all available and the butchers at Hilton are experimenting with salami and air-dried hams. All this is available from the shop or from Perth, Edinburgh, Glasgow, Stirling, Cupar and Kirkaldy farmers' markets.

super hero

NICHOLA AND JOHN FLETCHER, of Fletchers, Auchtermuchty
(see page 265)

Nichola and John Fletcher have spent the last 30 years producing venison and understand that 'happy deer are healthy and unstressed, and will produce the best meat'. The deer never leave the farm – they are shot in the fields and so never have the stress of a trip to the abattoir; it's all over in an instant. This lack of stress is very important in venison production – a stressed deer will produce unpleasantly tainted meat. The carcasses are then hand-skinned, prepared by a skilled butcher and hung for up to three weeks. This, says Nichola Fletcher, 'gives superb flavour and tenderness, but without that bitter or musty taste which some people regard as a gamey taste, but which is in fact just poor handling.'

The Fletchers were nominated for a coveted Slow Food Award for their attention to detail, their long hanging of the meat and their insistence on the highest standards – practices that allow meat to develop good texture and flavour. Nichola is a fervent campaigner for venison as she believes it to be the perfect meat – low in fat and cholesterol, high in the healthy fatty acids found in oily fish – and she is a mine of information regarding handling and cooking venison.

FOOD HEROES OF BRITAIN

The Galloway Smokehouse

Carsluith, Newton Stewart, Wigtownshire DG8 7DN T: 01671 820354
w: www.gallowaysmokehouse.co.uk
shop mail order

The wild venison and other game arrive at the Galloway Smokehouse from local shoots still in their furred and feathered condition. This allows Allan Watson to check them over for age and quality – he never accepts anything that has already been plucked or skinned. The game and venison is available fresh, or there is smoked venison. This is brined in a secret mixture and then smoked for four days over oak chips from old port or whisky barrels.

Rannoch Smokery

Kinloch Rannoch, By Pitlochry, Perthshire PH16 5QD T: 01882 632344
w: www.rannochsmokery.co.uk
mail order

Oak chips from old whisky casks are used to smoke all kinds of Scottish meats at Rannoch Smokery. Wild local venison is tenderized by brine soaking first, allowing more mature, tastier animals to be used. Pheasant and grouse from local shoots and Scotch beef, lamb and pork are also given the smoking treatment. All available by mail order.

Old Knockelly Smokehouse

Scaur Water, Penpont, Thornhill, Dumfriesshire DG3 4NF T: 01848 600298
w: www.oksmoke.co.uk
shop mail order

The Old Knockelly Smokehouse uses the old-fashioned natural draft method to smoke the produce, which takes much longer than more modern techniques, but which results in more delicate flavours. The produce is sourced locally: pigeon, trout, salmon, duck, pheasant and venison. The venison is also transformed into salami and ham, each taking a month to be ready for eating – long curing, smoking and air-drying times are required to achieve the perfect texture and best flavour. The principle aim here is quality, not quantity.

Owen Roberts & Son

Corwas, Amlwch, Anglesey LL68 9ET   T: 01407 830277
w: www.owenrobertsandson.com

✉ **mail order**

Much of the game offered at this traditional butcher's shop is local
and wild boar is also available at Christmas. Meat from local farms
within a 15-mile radius of the shop is also available.

The Welsh Venison Centre

Middlewood Farm, Bwlch, nr Brecon, Powys LD3 7HQ   T: 01874 730929
w: www.welshvenison.com

⬦ **farm shop** ✉ **mail order**

The red deer at the Welsh Venison Centre are farmed as naturally as
possible, with an additive-free diet. Slaughtered locally, the deer are
hung and butchered on site. Visitors to the farm shop can see the
deer grazing in the hills.

Much of the food we eat is produced 'to a price'. This means that the price has been decided first and the produce reared or grown to meet this price. As a nation we demand cheap food and, inevitably, short cuts are taken in production to cut costs, in order to keep the price down. One of the casualties will be time, after all, time is money, and this is particularly true in meat production.

Often a modern intensive farm will choose hybrid breeds of animals that have been developed to carry more meat and to grow quickly. They are given concentrated feed to bulk them up more quickly so that they reach slaughtering age earlier. Often animals are transported around the country, from farm to farm, to abattoir, to packing centre. Hanging the meat to develop flavour and texture would be a costly delay and so often it is butchered and sold immediately. We are getting cheap meat but I wonder what the real price is? It is now widely agreed that the BSE crisis occurred because cattle were fed to cattle to save money. There were also suggestions that the recent outbreak of foot-and-mouth disease began and was made worse due to cost-saving activities taking precedence over sensible animal husbandry.

meat

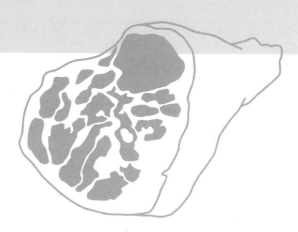

The meat producers I have listed here do things differently. Many rear their animals organically, offering assurances regarding the feed and welfare of the livestock. Many feed their animals on home-grown feed, with the lamb and beef being predominantly grass-fed. The animals won't be kept in cramped conditions, causing stress and disease; they'll range freely. The biggest difference of all, though, is how, when and where these farmers slaughter their livestock. Allowed to mature slowly, the animals go to slaughter much later than their intensively reared counterparts and they will be taken to a local abattoir to reduce the stress of travelling to a minimum (an animal stressed at the point of slaughter leads to inferior meat). Though most beef producers are forced to slaughter their animals before they are 30 months old (a rule imposed to try to control BSE), some of the farmers featured have government permission to slaughter at up to 42 months, as their farming methods make BSE so unlikely as to be virtually no risk. You'll almost certainly find that the meat these farmers produce will have a richness of flavour and a firmness and density of texture that will have people of a certain age crying delightedly 'this is how meat used to taste'.

FOOD HEROES OF BRITAIN

Moorland Farm Shop

Axbridge, Somerset BS26 2BA   T: 01934 733341   E: moorlandfarm@btinternet.com

⬆ **farm shop** ⬇ **farmers' markets**

Aberdeen Angus beef, from a closed herd, is grass-fed all year. Hung for three to four weeks, the beef is a rich ruby colour and is sold fresh, not frozen.

Norwood Farm

Bath Road, Norton St Philip, nr Bath, Somerset BA2 7LP   T: 01373 834356
(OFFICE HOURS) OR 01373 834856 (AFTER HOURS)   W: www.norwoodfarm.co.uk

⬆ **farm shop**

Among the organically reared, rare-breed meats available here are no fewer than 12 different breeds of lamb, alongside rare-breed beef and pork. The farm shop also stocks home-grown organic vegetables and local Somerset cheeses.

The Real Meat Company

7 Hayes Place, Bear Flat, Bath BA2 4QW   T: 01225 335139   W: www.realmeat.co.uk

A traditional butcher's selling drug-free, welfare-friendly meat that comes from breeds chosen for their flavour and slow-growing nature. This shop was the winner of the 2002 *BBC Good Food Magazine* Best Sausage in Britain award. See the Super Hero box, page 363, for more information about The Real Meat Company.

Adeys Farm Organic Meats

Adeys Farm, Breadstone, Berkeley, Gloucestershire GL13 9HF   T: 01453 511218
E: cwilson@adeysfarm.fsnet.co.uk

⬇ **farmers' markets** ⬌ **farm gate sales** ✉ **mail order**

Adeys is a treasure-trove of rare-breed meat, including Gloucester Old Spot pork, Suffolk lamb, Hereford and Aberdeen Angus beef, all reared outdoors, only being brought in during bad weather. Dry-cured bacon is also on offer. The meat is available from Cheltenham, Stroud and Thornbury farmers' markets as well as from the farm and by mail order.

Pomeroy Rare Breeds Farm Shop & Delicatessen

MEAT

8–11 Butchers Row, Pannier Market, Bideford, Devon EX39 2DX   T: 01237 473447
w: www.pomeroyrarebreeds.co.uk

✉ **mail order**

Pomeroy sells extensively reared meat from a wide range of rare breeds – Gloucester Old Spot and Tamworth pigs, Soay sheep, and occasionally Red Poll and Dexter beef. The pigs are free-range and all the animals have an additive-free diet. Beef is hung for three weeks, pork for at least one. Dry-cured bacon and ham, pastrami and gluten-free sausages are all available.

The Real Meat Company

10 Silver Street, Bradford-on-Avon, Wiltshire BA15 1JY   T: 01225 309385
w: www.realmeat.co.uk

The owners of this butcher's shop are chefs by trade and add a different element to the welfare-friendly, chemical-free meats available here. Combining both butchery and chefs' skills, they make salami and all manner of charcuterie and can provide all the ingredients for a dinner party meal, from the meat to the accompaniments. The staff are very enthusiastic and full of information about their products. See the Super Hero box, page 363, for more information about The Real Meat Company.

Becklands Farm

Whitchurch Canonicorum, Bridport, Dorset DT6 6RG   T: 01297 560298
E: becklandsorganicfarm@btopenworld.com

⬇ **farm shop** ✉ **mail order**

Francis and Hilary Joyce of Becklands Farm produce Red Devon beef, geese, free-range eggs, farm-made preserves and some seasonal fruit and vegetables, all accredited by the Soil Association. They have a small farm shop on the farm and also sell mail order. As well as stocking their own produce, Hilary also sells produce from her fellow members of the West Dorset Organic Foods co-operative, a group of 15 or so organic farmers. This means that the range of produce available from Hilary's farm shop is much wider than they alone could produce, with a great selection of rare-breed meats and a continuity of supply that they would not otherwise be able to provide. The co-operative is a great example of farmers pooling resources for maximum benefit. The phone number for the co-operative is 01297 561100

Denhay Farms Ltd

Broadoak, Bridport, Dorset DT6 5NP   T: 01308 458963   W: www.denhay.co.uk
✉ **mail order**

Great-Taste-Award-winning air-dried ham, dry-cured bacon and gammon and Cheddar cheeses, all hand-made at the farm.

Modbury Farm

Burton Bradstock, Bridport, Dorset DT6 4NE   T: 01308 897193
E: timgarry@btinternet.com
🥄 **farm shop**

Organically reared, rare-breed Saddleback pigs produce pork, sausages and bacon, which are sold in the Garry family's farm shop. Also available are organic Jersey milk and cream (unpasteurized), home-grown organic seasonal vegetables and other local produce. Open all day, every day.

---

super hero

SWADDLES GREEN ORGANIC FARM, Chard (see page 276)

Bill Reynolds from Swaddles Green Farm feels intense disappointment over the way the food industry has developed over the last few decades. Buying on price seems to be the key for both retailers and consumers. 'Unique in Europe, we spend as little as possible each year on food. As a result of these lamentable habits, farming is virtually finished in Britain.' Bill's mission is to promote organic produce grown or reared in this country, where the standards are amongst the highest in the world – at present, over 70% of the organic produce consumed in the UK is from abroad. If organic farming is to achieve its potential of 'that noble ideal of producing great food humanely and with minimal damage to wildlife and the environment', then we need to support the producers on our own doorstep and be prepared to pay fairly for good-quality food. Swaddles Green Farm makes this easy, with beef, lamb, pork and chicken, all reared with sympathetic husbandry and with great flavour as the key aim.

Wyld Meadow Lamb

Wyld Meadow Farm, Monkton Wyld, nr Bridport, Dorset DT6 6DD   T: 01297 678318

farmers' markets   **farm gate sales**   **mail order**

Slowly reared Poll Dorset lamb, grass-fed all year without concentrates, is butchered on site at Wyld Meadow Farm and hung for ten days for a mature flavour. Available from many Dorset, Devon and Somerset farmers' markets – call for details or to arrange an order by mail or to collect from the farm.

J C Burdge

Fenswood Farm, Says Lane, Langford, nr Bristol, North Somerset BS40 5DZ
T: 01934 852639

farm gate sales

Traditional British breeds form the basis of the meat produced on Fenswood Farm, all organically. The Burdges operate a customer list, which Mrs Burdge works her way through whenever one of their livestock is sent to the abattoir. Call to get on the list.

Bill the Butcher

RBST
Rare Breeds Survival Trust

11 High Street, Bruton, Somerset BA10 0AB   T: 01749 812388

Accredited by the Rare Breeds Survival Trust, Bill the Butcher stocks native and rare breeds of meat from local smallholdings. Breeds can include Gloucester beef, Norfolk Horn lamb and British Lop pork.

Brewhamfield Organic Dairy Farm

North Brewham, Bruton, Somerset BA10 0QQ   T: 01749 850108 OR 01749 850469

farm gate sales   **mail order**

Beef from an unusual Aberdeen Angus and Jersey cross, reared according to organic principles, although not certified. The animals go to a local abattoir to reduce stress and the meat is then hung for three weeks before being butchered to order. There is also delicious pork to order from rare-breed British Lop pigs: the old pig of the West Country. Limited stocks are available at any one time. A cheese – Brewhamfield blue made with the Jersey milk – is also in development.

The Real Meat Company

21 London Road, Calne, Wiltshire SN11 0AA   T: 01249 812362   w: www.realmeat.co.uk

The very enthusiastic husband and wife team at this butcher's sells only welfare-friendly, drug-free meat from the Real Meat Company, specializing in own-recipe faggots, parma ham and salamis, all made without artificial preservatives. See the Super Hero box, page 363, for more information about The Real Meat Company.

Wild Beef

Hillhead Farm, Chagford, Devon TQ13 8DY   T: 01647 433433
farmers' markets   delivery service

Rare- and native-breed cattle graze on traditional pasture (rather than commercially sown grasses) at Hillhead Farm. Welsh Blacks, North, South and Red Devons and Herefords come in all shapes and sizes but all are hung for four weeks to produce flavourful beef. Find them at farmers' markets and at Borough Market in London's SE1.

Old Castle Farm

Buckland St Mary, Chard, Somerset TA20 3JZ   T: 01460 234453
w: www.oldcastlefarm.co.uk
farmers' markets

Accredited by RSPCA Freedom Foods, the pork at Old Castle Farm comes from pedigree Saddleback pigs, reared in a straw-based yard system, with plenty of room to move around. GM-free feed is used, and homeopathy in cases of sickness. All the regular meat joints are available, along with home-made sausages. Find the produce at Crewkerne, Wincanton and Axbridge farmers' markets.

Swaddles Green Organic Farm

Chard, Somerset TA20 3JR   T: 0845 456 1768   w: www.swaddles.co.uk
mail order

Swaddles Green Farm produces great-flavoured beef, lamb, pork and chicken with sympathetic husbandry. See the Super Hero box, page 274, for more information.

Hill End Farm

Brinkworth, Chippenham, Wiltshire SN15 5AZ T: 01666 510261
🚚 **delivery service**

The Welfare-friendly veal here comes from Hereford/Friesian cross
cattle. Hill End Farm operates a closed herd, which means that all
the cattle are born on the farm, and the calves have plenty of space
to roam around their straw-bedded barn. With natural feed, milk and
silage, the meat is rose veal not the white veal associated with the
continental veal crate system. Call to find out about the delivery
round and availability.

Langley Chase Organic Farm

Kington Langley, Chippenham, Wilts SN15 5PW T: 01249 750095
w: www.langleychase.co.uk
📪 **farm gate sales** ✉ **mail order**

Buy Langley Chase organic lamb (from a breed native to the Isle of
Man) at the farm gate by appointment or mail order and see the
Super Hero box, page 284, for more information.

Sandridge Farmhouse Bacon

Sandridge Farm, Bromham, nr Chippenham, Wiltshire SN15 2JL T: 01380 850304
w: www.sandridgefarmhousebacon.co.uk
🥓 **farm shop** 🏪 **farmers' markets** ✉ **mail order**

Traditional bacon curers, Sandridge offers bacon and ham cured
using some interesting regional recipes. Sausages and charcuterie,
including prosciutto, are also available and all the meat used is
raised on the farm.

Owls Barn

Derritt Lane, Sopley, Christchurch, Dorset BH23 7AZ T: 01425 672239
w: www.owlsbarn.co.uk
🥓 **farm shop**

Poll Dorset and Llanwenog lamb and Hereford beef from a closed
herd are all organically certified and reared on the farm.

Chesterton Farm Shop

off Chesterton Lane, Cirencester, Gloucestershire GL7 6JP   T: 01285 642160

farm shop   ✉ **mail order**

There is a big range of traditional and rare-breed meat at this farm shop, all from local farms, and they also offer their own cured and smoked bacon.

The Cotswold Gourmet

The Butts Farm, South Cerney, Cirencester, Gloucestershire GL7 5QE   T: 01285 862224
w: www.cotswoldgourmet.com

✉ **mail order**

There is always a good choice of rare-breed meats from local farms at this shop, all reared extensively and slowly for old-fashioned flavour.

Smallicombe

Northleigh, Colyton, Devon EX24 6BU   T: 01404 831310   w: www.smallicombe.com

farmers' markets   **farm gate sales**

Beef from Ruby Devon and Dexter cattle, grass-fed all year and hung for three weeks, Dorset Down lamb and Berkshire and British Lop pigs (made into bacon and award-winning sausages) are all reared slowly for full flavour. Ian and Maggie Todd from Smallicombe Farm attend many local farmers' markets – call to find out where or to arrange an order to collect from the farm. Smallicombe Farm is a member of the British Pig Association.

Hazelbury Partners

Hazelbury Manor, Box, Corsham, Wiltshire SN13 8HX   T: 01225 812088

farmers' markets

Many rare breeds of all kinds of livestock are reared organically at Hazelbury Manor, including the native Wiltshire Horn lamb, Saddleback pork and Welsh Black beef. Free-range hens' and ducks' eggs are also available. Produce from Hazelbury Manor is available from farmers' markets in Bath.

Pipers Farm

Cullompton, Devon EX15 1SD   T: 01392 881380   w: www.pipersfarm.com

✉ **farm gate sales** ✉ **mail order**

Pipers Farm is the hub of a network of small Devon farms, all
producing high quality meats. Traditional breeds are reared,
including Devon Red Ruby beef, and the Grieg family at Pipers Farm
control every aspect of the rearing, from their own formulation feed
to the choice of one small local abattoir. The farm also has a shop in
Exeter, see below.

West Hembury Farm

Askerswell, Dorchester, Dorset DT2 9EN   T: 01308 485289   w: www.westhembury.com

🚚 **delivery service**

Buy organic rare-breed meat (from White Park beef and Southdown
lamb) here. The beef is hung for three weeks and the lamb is
available as year-old hogget for fuller flavour or even as mutton, for
still more flavour. The meat is available through a local delivery
round; call for details.

Pipers Farm

27 Magdalen Road, Exeter, Devon EX2 4TA   T: 01392 274504   w: www.pipersfarm.com

For details, see under the Cullompton entry, above.

Churchtown Farm

Lanteglos, Fowey, Cornwall PL23 1NH   T: 01726 870375

✉ **farm gate sales** ✉ **mail order**

Churchtown Farm is a coastal National Trust farm, rearing organic
lamb and beef from traditional breeds on herb- and clover-rich
pasture. They are previous winners of the prestigious Best Beef and
Best Lamb awards at the Soil Association Organic Food Awards.
Available direct from the farm (phone first) or by mail order.

Richard Kittow & Sons

1–3 South Street, Fowey, Cornwall PL23 1AR T: 01726 832639

Richard Kittow won't source much of his produce from outside
Cornwall, so most of the meat comes from local farms. There is a
good selection of extensively reared, rare-breed meat and he breeds
Hereford beef on his own farm and has his own slaughterhouse.
Also available is home-cured bacon and unusual items such as
brawn and Hog's Pudding, a Cornish version of black pudding.

Lagan Farm Meats

Park Farm, Shaftesbury Road, Gillingham, Dorset SP8 5JG T: 01747 822169
E: laganfarms@rarebreeds.freeserve.co.uk
⟶ **farm shop** ⊨ **farm gate sales**

Meat from slowly matured, rare-breed cattle and pigs, including the
unusual Irish moiled beef and British Lop pork. The animals have
traditional feed, free from additives, and the beef is hung for four
weeks. Wild venison, shot on the farm, is also available, as is mutton
ham and smoked mutton and free-range eggs from rare-breed hens.

Ham Street Farm Produce

Baltonsborough, nr Glastonbury, Somerset BA6 8QB T: 01458 850508
⊨ **farmers' markets**

Free-range pork, bacon, sausages, gammon and faggots from
Tamworth and Middle White pigs that are fed without artificial
additives are the speciality of Ham Street Farm. The pigs are slowly
matured to up to a year old, giving a fuller flavoured meat. Call to
find out which farmers' markets they attend.

Wallace's of Hemyock

Hill Farm, Hemyock, Devon EX15 3UZ T: 01823 680307 w: www.naturalmeats.co.uk
⊨ **farm gate sales** ✉ **mail order**

Grass-fed Aberdeen Angus beef and bison and also venison,
outdoor-reared pork and dry-cured bacon, are all reared slowly and
naturally by Wallace's.

MEAT

Gittisham Herd at Combe Estate

Beech Walk, Gittisham, Honiton, Devon EX14 3AB   T: 01404 45576
w: www.reddevonbeef.co.uk

🗺 **farmers' markets** ✉ **mail order**

Traditional Ruby Red Devon cattle are reared 'slowly and gently' at
Combe Estate, grass-fed all year on conservation grazing. The beef
is hung for three weeks and is well marbled, tender and mature in
flavour. Available from Ottery St Mary, Seaton, Exeter and Newton
Abbott farmers' markets.

The Country Butcher   ▽**RBST**
Rare Breeds Survival Trust

Main Road, Huntley, Gloucester GL19 3DZ   T: 01452 831023
w: www.countrybutcher.co.uk

The Country Butcher is RBST accredited, with all kinds of rare-
breed meat from local farmers whom the butcher personally knows.

super hero

JUDITH AND GILES BLATCHFORD, of Cranborne Farms Traditional Meats,
Wimborne (see page 292)

At the Cranborne Estate in Dorset, Judith and Giles Blatchford are determined
that native pig breeds, such as Tamworth, Gloucester Old Spot and British Lop,
will not be replaced entirely with intensively reared pigs that are a cross-breed
specifically designed to grow fast, lean and big. The pork they produce at
Cranborne Farms is from a range of rare-breed pigs and these animals are
reared in the woodlands around the farm (a pig's natural habitat), rooting around
for much of their diet, which is topped up with farm-grown produce. The
resulting rich, dark, densely flavoured meat is not the only benefit of this. The
Blatchfords are helping to sustain the rare breeds and they are also encouraging
the hobby of keeping rare-breed pigs by selling the best of the piglets to other
rare-breed pig enthusiasts – 'We aim to create a market and underpin it with
prices that make the hobby of rare-breed pig-keeping affordable.'
The pork products are available from the farm shop at Cranborne Estate.

Fowlescombe Farm

Ugborough, Ivybridge, Devon PL21 0HW   T: 01548 821000   w: www.fowlescombe.com

farm gate sales   ✉ **mail order**

The rare-breed pedigree Manx Loaghtan and Hebridean sheep at Fowlescombe are not slaughtered until they are at least a year old; the meat is lean, with a slightly more gamey flavour than conventional lamb. Pure Aberdeen Angus beef from a pedigree herd is also available. Barbara Barker runs a customer list and can also do mail order by arrangement.

Fountain Violet Farm

Mount Ridley Road, Kingswear, Devon TQ6 0DA   T: 01803 752363
E: ed@fvfarm.freeserve.co.uk

✉ **mail order**   **box scheme**

A box scheme with a difference – Fountain Violet Farm's boxes contain a variety of cuts of their pure-breed South Devon beef, born and reared on the farm, grass-fed with home-grown supplements. Each 8kg box will contain 'a bit of everything'.

Pitney Farm Shop

Glebe Farm, Pitney, Langport, Somerset TA10 9AP   T: 01458 253002
E: robwalrond@wagonhouse.freeserve.co.uk

farm shop

A great environmentally aware, community-minded farm shop, Pitney Farm does lots of organic goodies, such as vegetables, eggs, beef, lamb and pork, all home-produced, and foods from other very local producers – milk, ice cream and honey. Shoppers arriving by bike or on foot even get a discount.

Philip Warren & Son

1 Westgate Street, Launceston, Cornwall PL15 7AB   T: 01566 772089 OR
01566 777211   w: www.philipwarrenbutchers.co.uk

This butcher's shop has some really interesting produce, including a selection of rare-breed meat. They also stock local game in season.

Cornish Country Meats

Treverbyn Mill, St Neot, Liskeard, Cornwall PL14 6HG   T: 01579 320303
w: www.cornishcountrymeats.co.uk

farmers' markets   **delivery service**

Traditionally reared beef and lamb and free-range pork all graze on
unsprayed fields. Venison – from a closed herd of pure Hungarian
deer – and wild boar are also available. The Barrow family offer home-
made pies, including wild boar pasties! Call to find out which farmers'
markets they attend or to discuss their local delivery service.

Bill and Sue Osborne

2 Orchard Cottages, Lydney Park Estate, Lydney, Gloucestershire GL15 6BU
T: 01594 841970 OR 07958 920430   E: castlemears2@hotmail.com

farm gate sales

Dexter beef, Manx Loaghtan and Ryeland lamb and Berkshire pork,
and free-range Bronze turkeys at Christmas, are all reared with high
attention to welfare by the Osbornes. Although not registered
organic, the animals have an additive-free diet and are treated
homeopathically when ill. The Osbornes have a customer list and
they phone around when there is meat ready to be bought – quality,
not quantity, is the key here, so meat is not always available.

Heritage Prime

Shedbush Farm, Muddyford Lane, nr Lyme Regis, Dorset DT6 6DR   T: 01297 489304
w: www.HeritagePrime.co.uk

farm gate sales

Shedbush Farm is a mixed, biodynamic farm producing beef, lamb
and pork from the oldest British breeds. The animals graze fertilizer-
free pasture and are born, raised and finished according to
biodynamic principles and slaughtered locally and humanely. Ian and
Denise Bell, the farmers, run a 'larder list' of customers whom they
call when meat is available, so they can stock up their freezers –
phone Denise for details.

Temple Farming

Rockley, Marlborough, Wiltshire SN8 1RU   т: 01672 514428

farm gate sales   **mail order**

Organic, naturally reared, free-range veal is available only between September and December from Temple Farming.

SOUTH WEST   MINEHEAD

Hindon Organic Farm

Exmoor Organic Hill Farm Produce, nr Minehead, Exmoor, Somerset TA24 8SH
т: 01643 705244   w: www.hindonfarm.co.uk

farmers' markets   **farm gate sales**   **mail order**

Hindon Farm offers slowly reared organic meats from traditional breeds – Gloucester Old Spot pork, Aberdeen Angus beef and Exmoor lamb. Dry-cured bacon, gammon, ham and sausages, all accredited to Soil Association standards, are available by mail order and from West Somerset farmers' markets as well as at the farm gate.

super hero

JANE KALLAWAY, of Langley Chase Organic Farm, Chippenham (see page 277)

Jane Kallaway breeds organic Manx Loaghtan lamb, an ancient type of sheep native to the Isle of Man. This is a primitive breed, unlikely to be found on bigger commercial farms as they take far too long to reach maturity – in Jane's case, her lambs are 18 months old before they go to slaughter. Why does she wait so long for the Manx Loaghtans when other breeds are ready much sooner? Jane told me: 'I believe that good food should add to the quality of life. I care passionately about how livestock is reared, produced and processed. My aim is to produce the finest organic lamb and mutton. The flock are bred and reared on the farm to Soil Association organic standards with total traceability of each animal. They are also registered with the Rare Breeds Survival Trust. Our ewes are allowed to mature slowly, producing their first lambs when they are two years old. We should nurture all our old breeds to ensure their survival and to provide the public with variety and quality of taste. I totally believe in producing food which is the antithesis of fast food – pure, healthy – the natural way – with a natural breed.'

East Hill Pride

High Street, Newton Poppleford, Devon EX10 0ED   T: 01395 567848

⬥ **farm shop**

Home-produced beef, which is hung for a month, pork and Wiltshire-cure bacon are available from this traditional farm. The animals are fed only home-grown feed, giving complete traceability.

Dartmoor Happy Hogs

Moorland Farm Shop, Whiddon Down, Okehampton, Devon EX20 2QL   T: 01647 231666

⬥ **farm shop**

Tamworth, Saddleback and Gloucester Old Spot pigs are all reared at Moorland Farm, producing pork, ham, bacon and a range of around 20 different award-winning sausages. The pigs are free-range and slowly reared to maturity.

Eweleaze Farm

c/o The Cartshed, Church Lane, Osmington, Dorset DT3 6EW   T: 01305 833690
E: peter.broatch@virgin.net

📧 **farm gate sales**

The Aberdeen Angus beef, matured on the bone for three weeks before sale, and Poll Dorset lamb, matured for ten days, available from The Cartshed, have been slowly reared to Soil Association standards. Peter Broatch, the farmer, firmly believes that the flavour in meat comes from the fat and that the fat on organic meat, with its higher level of polyunsaturates, tastes better than its conventional counterpart. Also available are organic eggs from hens free to range amongst the trees and hedgerows of the farm. All the produce is available direct from the farm or through the West Dorset Organic Foods co-operative (see the entry for Becklands Farm, page 273).

Lenterns Butchers

1 Chapel Street, Penzance, Cornwall TR18 4AJ   T: 01736 363061
w: www.lenterns.com

✉ **mail order**

Recently named Retail Butcher of the Year, Simon Lentern is committed to stocking only local meat in his shop. The shop is filled with meat from farms where animal welfare is a high priority, and a local speciality is also featured – Hog's Pudding, the Cornish version of black pudding.

Well Hung Meat

Carswell Farm, Holbeton, Plymouth, Devon PL8 1HH   T: 01752 830494
w: www.wellhungmeat.com

✉ **mail order**

The organic lamb from Well Hung Meat is the 2001 and 2002 award winner for Best Lamb at the Soil Association Organic Food Awards. Hung for nine days after slaughter, the meat is tender and well flavoured. Organic beef is also available.

The Real Meat Company

14 Bournemouth Road, Lower Parkstone, Poole, Dorset BH14 0ES   T: 01202 747972
w: www.realmeat.co.uk

Humanely reared meat without growth promoters or antibiotics, from slow-growing, traditional breeds of animal. There are 23 different types of sausage available, including the South African boerewors. See the Super Hero box, page 363, for more information about The Real Meat Company.

Clive Downs Butchers

High Street, Porlock, Somerset TA24 8PT   T: 01643 862667   w: www.clivedowns.co.uk

Dry-cured bacon, free-range veal, wild Exmoor venison and Exmoor lamb are the specialities here, all locally sourced.

MEAT

Primrose Herd

Primrose Cottage, Busveal, Redruth, Cornwall TR16 5HF   T: 01209 821408

🍴 farmers' markets ✉ farm gate sales

Sally Lugg rears Gloucester Old Spot and Large Black rare-breed pigs, allowing them to grow slowly on GM-free feed, ranging freely outdoors. A Taste of the West award winner, her pork and bacon have a great old-fashioned flavour and can be found at many Cornish farmers' markets, including Truro, Lostwithiel and Falmouth, or call Sally to collect direct from the farm.

Crooked End Farm

Ruardean, Forest of Dean, Gloucestershire GL17 9XF   T: 01594 544482

🥄 farm shop

All the produce on display at Crooked End Farm shop is either produced on the farm itself or comes from neighbouring farms. This can include organic fruit and vegetables, free-range eggs, rare-breed beef and lamb and free-range pork – all the animals are fed on locally produced feed. All produce is accredited by the Soil Association.

John Thorner's Ltd

Bridge Farm Shop, Pyle, Shepton Mallet, Somerset BA4 6TA   T: 01749 830138
E: johnthorner@freeuk.com

🚚 delivery service

Local beef from the Mendips, free-range pork and venison from the Balmoral estate in the stalking season. John Thorner has three shops in central Somerset; call to find your nearest store. A delivery service is also available within a 20-mile radius.

Haymans Butchers

6 Church Street, Sidmouth, Devon EX10 8LY   T: 01395 512877
w: www.haymansbutchers.co.uk

The current Mr Hayman running this butcher's is the fourth
generation of his family to do so, and it was for the ox-tongue
prepared to his grandmother's recipe that he received a recent
Q Guild award. A real family affair, the beef stocked here comes
from the butcher's cousin and, for those concerned about food
miles, the meat has a round trip of only 16 miles from farm to
butcher's.

SOUTH WEST   STREET

Cedar Walk Farms

Slugg Hill, Somerton Road, Street, Somerset BA16 0SU   T: 01458 446609
w: www.cedarwalk.com

farm shop   **mail order**

Cedar Walk Farms are committed to very high standards of animal
welfare and eating quality. The meat offered is mainly from their own
land, with some occasionally from neighbouring farms, and much of
it is from rare breeds – their particular speciality is pork from
Gloucester Old Spot pigs. Preparation methods are traditional – their
free-range chickens are hung for a week before being dry-plucked.

SOUTH WEST   STROUD

Allen Hale Butchers

New House, Friday Street, Painswick, nr Stroud, Gloucestershire GL6 6QJ
T: 01452 813613

Allen Hale is a butcher who feels that food has been largely 'messed
around too much – especially meat'. Such is his concern about the
way conventional meat is produced, he stocks only welfare-friendly
meat from the Real Meat Company (see the Super Hero box, page
363, for more information). This meat comes from slow-growing
breeds of animals chosen for their flavour and reared traditionally
without growth promoters or antibiotics.

Star Farm

Hazelbury Bryan, nr Sturminster Newton, Dorset DT10 2EG   T: 01258 817285

⬣ farm shop

Organic home-reared, rare-breed meat is available at this newly opened farm shop – Aberdeen Angus beef, Oxford Sandy & Black pork, dry-cured bacon and sausages and Poll Dorset and Llanwenog lamb.

California Farm

Priests Way, Swanage, Dorset BH19 2RS   T: 01929 423829

▨ farm gate sales

Organic Dorset Down lamb, native to the area, is left to mature at California Farm until slightly older than commercial lamb; the meat ends up well marbled with a full flavour and is available as whole or half lambs.

Eastbrook Farms Organic Meat

Bishopstone, Swindon, Wiltshire SN6 8PL   T: 01793 790340

w: www.helenbrowningorganics.co.uk

✉ mail order

Eastbrook Farm was one of the pioneers of organic meat and is still revered for the high standards of animal welfare that are maintained there. A full range is available, including veal and poultry.

Beer Mill Farm

Beercrocombe, Taunton, Somerset TA3 6AQ   T: 01823 480249

w: www.portlandsheep.co.uk

▨ farm gate sales

Hilary and Brian Howell rear the rare Portland sheep, renowned for its leanness and flavour, due in part to the length of time the lambs take to mature – two or three times longer than most commercial breeds. Fed only on fertilizer-free pasture, the lamb is available direct from the farm but please call before visiting.

Lyng Court Organic Meat

West Lyng, Taunton, Somerset TA3 5AP   T: 01823 490510
✉ **farm gate sales**

Lyng Court Farm produces lamb and beef from Norman breeds on the Somerset levels. The breeds were chosen because the grazing here is so similar to that in the animals' native Normandy. Reared naturally on grass and home-grown barley, the meat is available direct from the farm but please call first.

Pampered Pigs Pantry

2 The Green, Tolpuddle, Dorchester, Dorset DT2 7EX   T: 01305 848107
w: www.pampered-pigs.co.uk
🖐 **farm shop** 🛒 **farmers' markets**

Kevin and Amanda Crocker are part of the Countryside Stewardship Scheme and farm with conservation as a priority. The farm produces organic Hereford cross beef and a variety of traditional breeds of pork that are allowed to range freely in family groups. There is a small shop on site and the Crockers also attend numerous local farmers' markets.

P G Mewton

Nancarrow Organic Farm, Marazanvose, Truro, Cornwall TR4 9DQ   T: 01872 540343
🛒 **farmers' markets** ✉ **farm gate sales** 🚚 **delivery service**

Grazing on clover-rich pasture, the South Devon cattle at Nancarrow Farm produce organic beef. The slaughterhouse and butcher are next door, so full traceability is offered. Find the beef at many Cornish farmers' markets – call for details.

Country Ways

High Bickington, Umberleigh, Devon EX17 9BJ   T: 01769 560503
w: www.country-ways.net
✉ **farm gate sales**

The rare-breed pork at Country Ways is usually a mixture of Gloucester Old Spot, Berkshire and Tamworth, from pigs reared

free-range on GM-free feed. Bacon, gammon and joints are
available and, occasionally, Dexter beef. This is a small farm, so
produce is not always available – phone to find out.

Higher Hacknell Farm

Burrington, Umberleigh, Devon EX37 9LX   T: 01769 560909   w: www.higherhacknell.co.uk
✉ **mail order**

Higher Hacknell Farm produces organic beef, lamb and pork and
they produce particularly good free-range chicken. Previously voted
Producer of the Year at the Soil Association Organic Food Awards,
the meat is available by mail order.

Boyton Farm

Boyton, Warminster, Wilts BA12 0SS   T: 01985 850208 OR 01985 850371
w: www.boytonfarm.co.uk
⬇ **farm shop** 🛒 **farmers' markets** ✉ **mail order**

Caroline at Boyton Farm breeds the rare Tamworth pig – not
surprising, given that her mother-in-law was a founder member of
the Rare Breeds Survival Trust. Caroline's is the largest and oldest
herd in the country. The pigs are all born and reared on the farm,
fed with home-grown feed and slowly matured.

food facts

PORK, BACON AND SAUSAGES

Nowhere does the battle between small-scale, thoughtful rearing of animals and
mass production rage more fiercely than with pigs. Few people can tolerate the
idea of such intelligent animals spending their lives in cramped conditions. It's a
sad fact that over 40% of the pork we eat is intensively reared, imported meat.
Why won't we pay a bit more and look after our own farmers? Maybe then we
could reverse the fact that 40% of farms sold in the last year went to non-
farmers. The producers listed here believe that pigs should be as free ranging as
possible and allowed to grow slowly, because this creates the tastiest meat. Often
they will be native-breed pigs, which produce better roasting joints because they
have a good fat covering which, in addition to tasting so good, leads to great
crackling. For the same reason they also make the best sausages and bacon.

Cranborne Farms Traditional Meats

Pound Farm, Cranborne, Wimborne, Dorset BH21 5RN T: 01725 517168
w: www.cranborne.co.uk/farm

farm shop ✉ mail order

Cranborne Farm rare-breed pigs are reared in the woodlands around the farm to produce rich-tasting dark meat. See the Super Hero box, page 281, for more information.

Burscombe Cliff Farm

Egerton, nr Ashford, Kent TN27 9BB T: 01233 756468

🛒 farmers' markets

Home-produced organic pork, beef and lamb, available at Wye, Lenham, Faversham and Dulwich farmers' markets. The beef is native Sussex beef, hung for at least two weeks, and there is cured, smoked bacon, ham and gammon available.

Little Omenden Sussex Beef

Little Omenden Farm, Smarden, Ashford, Kent TN27 8QP T: 01580 291272
w: www.easisites.co.uk/littleomendensussexbeef

🛒 farm gate sales

Sussex beef is a new venture for this Countryside Stewardship farm. Disillusioned with rearing beef for supermarkets, David Harrison has turned to a native breed and is slowly rearing the cattle on a natural diet of grass and rolled oats. His first beef should be available around the end of 2003; call him for more details about buying.

Wealden Farmers Network

Homestead Farm, Darwell Hill, Netherfield, nr Battle, East Sussex TN33 9QL
T: 01424 838252 E: joamos2000@hotmail.com

farm shop

Wealden Farmers Network is a co-operative of five farms, one of which is registered organic, while the others farm organically without being registered. The emphasis is on breeds of animal native to the area, so the rare Sussex beef is a speciality. Traditional-breed pork and lamb is also available. All the livestock is reared extensively, all are born on the farm, allowed to live in family groups, and go to a local abattoir to eliminate stress. The animals are fed entirely on grass or home-grown feed. The meat is available from the farm shop but call first.

Eastwoods of Berkhamsted

15 Gravel Path, Berkhamsted, Hertfordshire HP4 2EF   T: 01442 865012
w: www.eastwoodsofberkhamstead.co.uk

✉ **mail order**

Winner of the Q Guild's Top Shop award in 2001, and many times winner at the Soil Association Organic Food Awards, Eastwoods stock a great range of free-range and organic meats, with an emphasis on animal welfare.

food facts

TRACEABILITY

How much do you know about the sources of the food you eat? Who grew or reared it, and where has it been on the way to your plate? Food, and particularly meat and livestock, seem to be trucked endlessly around the country before reaching the shop shelves. The food industry has changed so much over the last half century or so, and we now have little sense of connection with the producers of our food. Buying meat direct from a good producer, or from a really good butcher, is different. They'll tell you as much as you want to know – where the animal was reared and slaughtered, what it was fed, its age, how long it was hung for. Many of the meat producers we feature run closed herds, so almost every animal they have was born on the farm. This old-fashioned style of husbandry means that you can feel confident that, yes, you do know where your food comes from, and this is welcome reassurance in this time of endless food scares.

Dennis of Bexley

1–2 Bourne Parade, Bourne Road, Bexley, Kent DA5 1LQ   T: 01322 522126
w: www.dennisofbexley.co.uk

Winner of Best Butcher's Shop in Britain in 1995, Dennis of Bexley also won the European Fresh Food Championship in Utrecht, Holland in 2000, and their turkey and ham pie won a Good Housekeeping Award in 2002. They offer locally produced meat and a good range of game – local pheasant, rabbit and wild venison are available in season.

J M Walman Family Butchers

1 Station Road, Launton, Bicester, Oxfordshire OX26 5DS   T: 01869 252619

John Walman stocks plenty of slowly and naturally reared rare-breed meats, including the unusual British Lop pork – the rarest breed of pig in this country. The meat is labelled with the breed and details of its provenance and John Walman finds people travel from neighbouring counties to buy the produce.

Pounsley Hill Produce

Pounsley Hill Cottage, Pounsley, Blackboys, East Sussex TN22 5HT   T: 01825 830377
w: www.pounsleyhillproduce.co.uk
 farm gate sales

David and Angela Lewis run a smallholding specializing in free-range pork and lamb. Although not certified as organic, the farm is free from chemicals; the lambs eat nothing but grass and hay and the pigs are fed on home-grown corn and grains. David and Angela sell direct to the public and have an open-door policy – they are happy for visitors to see how the smallholding is run.

Foxbury Farm

Burford Road, Brize Norton, Oxfordshire OX18 3NX   T: 01993 844141
w: www.foxburyfarm.co.uk
 farm shop

Home-reared, rare-breed meat (Hereford beef, lamb, and Gloucester Old Spot pork), all extensively reared, is supplemented at the farm shop with locally grown fruit and vegetables and locally made cakes.

SOUTH EAST BURFORD

W J Castle

11 High Street, Burford, Oxfordshire OX18 4RG T: 01993 822113

Free-range chicken, Cotswold lamb and Gloucester Old Spot pork are the main stars at Castle's but everything they stock is fully traceable meat from local farms.

SOUTH EAST CANTERBURY

Chandler & Dunn Ltd

The Laurels, Lower Goldstone, Ash, Canterbury, Kent CT3 2DY T: 01304 812262
W: www.chandleranddunn.co.uk

farm shop

Well-marbled beef from rare Sussex cattle, hung for three weeks, as well as home-reared lamb and locally produced pork is available from the farm shop.

SOUTH EAST CARSHALTON BEECHES

The Real Meat Company

9 Gordon Road, Carshalton Beeches, Surrey SM5 3RG T: 0208 395 8946
W: www.realmeat.co.uk

All the meat at Don Wenham's butcher's shop is welfare-friendly and extensively reared, supplied by farmers he knows he can trust – he has visited most of the farms. The beef stocked here is hung for around five weeks for a tender, traditional meat. See the Super Hero box, page 363, for more information about The Real Meat Company.

SOUTH EAST DOVER

Sladden Farm

Alkham Valley Road, Alkham, nr Dover, Kent CT15 7BX T: 01304 825188

farmers' markets **farm gate sales**

Dexter cattle are a breed believed never to have suffered a single case of BSE. The Dexter beef at Sladden farm is a close-grained, full-flavoured meat, raised traditionally on grass. The farm also produces Saddleback and Gloucester Old Spot pork, sausages, home-cured ham and bacon and Wiltshire Horn lamb.

food facts

LAMB

It's odd that we import so much lamb from New Zealand, transporting it halfway across the world, when Britain produces an impressive array of different types of tasty lamb, from the small, gamey-flavoured native breeds to the delicacy of the more modern types of lamb. I have nothing against New Zealand lamb but there is so much to choose from in the UK and Ireland. Welsh saltmarsh lamb is delicately flavoured by the salty Sparta grasses, washed by the tide twice a day, that the sheep graze on. Or try heather-fed lamb from Northumbria or lamb from upland farms, with its richer flavour and muscular texture. There are many different breeds of lamb to try – Castlemilk Moorit, Manx Loaghtan, Wensleydale and Soay will all have subtle differences in flavour and texture and you generally need to seek out small-scale producers to find these.

You can even choose the maturity of lamb. Many of the producers listed, instead of offering only spring lamb, which has the mildest of flavours, will offer the more flavoursome hogget, which is year-old lamb or older. Some even offer mutton, which can be from up to five-year-old sheep; however, this will not be the tough, rather pungent meat some people associate with the term, but a more robust, intensely flavoured version of the younger lamb.

SOUTH EAST   **EAST HORSLEY**

F Conisbee & Son

Park Corner, Ockham Road South, East Horsley, Surrey KT24 6RZ   T: 01483 282073

The Conisbee family are butchers who like to know exactly where all their meat has come from and how it has been reared. 'From conception to consumption,' they can tell their customers everything about the produce in their shop. The family rear their own beef and seasonal turkeys; almost everything else comes from local farms – Neil Conisbee goes to the farms himself to select the animals.

SOUTH EAST   **EPSOM**

Kenneth J Eve

9 Corner House Parade, Epsom Road, Ewell, Epsom, Surrey KT17 1NX   T: 020 8393 3043   W: www.kjeve.co.uk

One of the specialities at this butcher's shop is the free-range Cornish chicken, reared traditionally without antibiotics, hormones or growth promoters. Norfolk free-range pork is also popular and Eve's recently won a Guild of Q Butchers gold award for their 'Leeky Lamb' in 2003.

Tablehurst Farm

Forest Row, East Sussex RH18 5DP T: 01342 823173 E: tablehurst_farm@talk21.com
↳ **farm shop**

Biodynamic and organic meats from many different rare breeds, all from closed herds, are butchered on site. An amazing 25 different types of sausage are produced here and seasonal home-grown vegetables and organic eggs are also available.

C H Wakeling Ltd

41 Farncombe Street, Godalming, Surrey GU7 3LH T: 01483 417557
w: www.wakelings.co.uk
✉ **mail order**

A Q Guild member, Wakeling's source as much meat as possible from local farmers. Local Aberdeen Angus beef and free-range and rare-breed (Saddleback) pork, reared on chemical-free pasture without hormones or GM food. They also have Soil Association accredited organic veal and free-range chicken, and game in season. Wakeling's won a five-star Good Housekeeping Award in October 2002 for their home-cooked smoked ham on the bone.

Gabriel Machin

7 Market Place, Henley-on-Thames, Oxfordshire RG9 2AA T: 01491 574377
w: www.gabrielmachin.co.uk

Classified as a butcher, Gabriel Machin offers much more than the local Chiltern lamb, free-range pork from Norfolk and Scottish beef he stocks. There is a traditional smokehouse on the premises, used to smoke Scottish salmon and eel from Loch Neagh, and there is a vast cheese selection – some are local, most are from the UK, with a few continental varieties too.

Shiprods Farm

Bashurst Hill, Slinfold, West Sussex RH13 0PD   T: 01403 790485
w: www.shiprods.co.uk

🏪 **farmers' markets** 🖃 **farm gate sales**

Grass-fed Aberdeen Angus beef, hung for four weeks and butchered on site and also lamb and mutton are available from this farm. Buy it at eight local farmers' markets or direct from the farm, but call first.

The Swan Inn

Craven Road, Lower Green, Inkpen, Hungerford, Berkshire RG17 9DX T: 01488 668326 w: www.theswaninn-organics.co.uk

🥄 **farm shop**

The Swan Inn is a must for those with a passion for organics. The farm shop sells organic beef reared by the owner himself, and organic lamb and pork from nearby farms. Chickens, fruit and vegetables and dairy produce – again, all organic and all local. The restaurant and pub follow with this theme – all the wines and Champagnes served are organic, as are many of the beers.

The Isle of Wight Bacon Company

Moor Farm, Godshill, Isle of Wight PO38 3JG   T: 01983 840210
w: www.isleofwightbacon.co.uk

🏪 **farmers' markets** ✉ **mail order**

The free-range pigs at Moor Farm are reared on an additive-free diet, with humane husbandry. All cuts of pork, sausages and dry-cured bacon and ham are available.

Piggybank Farm

Hollybank, Lenham Heath Road, Sandway, Lenham, Kent ME17 2NB   T: 01622 859776
w: www.piggybank-farm.co.uk

🖃 **farm gate sales** 🚚 **delivery service**

The Tamworth and Middle White pigs at Piggybank Farm have three acres of woodland to forage and roam in. They don't have their teeth or tails clipped and are fed on locally produced nuts. Allowed to mature to six months old, the meat is richly flavoured. Available to order as fresh pork delivered to your door locally, or Piggybank Farm will do a rare-breed hog roast for your event.

SOUTH EAST — LONDON

Kingsland Edwardian Butchers

140 Portobello Road, London W11 2DZ T: 020 7727 6067

Everything at this butcher's is free-range or organic – lamb and pork from Dorset, Aberdeen Angus beef from Scotland, free-range chickens and free-range Bronze turkeys at Christmas.

SOUTH EAST — LONDON

C Lidgate

110 Holland Park Avenue, London W11 4UA T: 020 7727 8243

Organic and/or free-range meats, some from the prestigious Gatcombe and Highgrove royal estates.

SOUTH EAST — LONDON

A S Portwine & Sons

24 Earlham Street, London WC2H 9LN T: 020 7836 2353
w: www.portwinebutchers.co.uk

A good selection of free-range, rare-breed and organic meat is available from this traditional butcher's.

SOUTH EAST — LONDON

G G Sparkes

24 Old Dover Road, Blackheath, London SE3 7BT T: 020 8355 8597
w: www.ggsparkesorganicbutchers.com
🚚 delivery service

A traditional butcher's specializing in organic meats, including veal.

SOUTH EAST — LONDON

Stenton Family Butchers

55 Aldensley Road, Hammersmith, London W6 9PL T: 020 8748 6121

Mr Stenton is keen to buy the meat he stocks direct from the farms and most of the farms he buys from are organic. Believing that Britain produces the best food in the world, supporting small-scale farmers is a priority for him; none of the meat in the shop is imported.

SOUTH EAST MILTON KEYNES

Fullers Organic Farm Shop

Manor Farm, Beachampton, Milton Keynes, Buckinghamshire MK19 6DT
T: 01908 269868 E: fullersorganics@farmline.com
farm shop

The Fullers are passionate about rare and native breeds and their farm shop is filled with rare-breed pork, beef, lamb and poultry (including duck and quail), all reared and butchered on site.

SOUTH EAST NEW MALDEN

Head Fine Foods

135 Kingston Road, New Malden, Surrey KT3 3NX T: 020 8942 0582

Roland Head only stocks meat from the Real Meat Company (see the Super Hero box, page 363), because he believes it is 'the best meat on the market – it addresses all the concerns the public have about meat farming'. Dry-cured bacon and home-baked pies are his specialities.

SOUTH EAST NEWICK

Little Warren Farm

Fletching Common, Newick, East Sussex BN8 4JH T: 01825 722545
farm gate sales

Organic, humanely reared veal: the calves stay with their mothers and are free-range. The cows are Jersey, so the calves have a rich Jersey milk diet, contributing to the meat's flavour. Available direct or from C H Wakeling Ltd in Godalming (see page 297) and G G Sparkes in London (see page 299).

SOUTH EAST PEASE POTTAGE

Sussexway Meat

Home Farm, Tilgate Forest Lodge, Pease Pottage, West Sussex RH11 9AF T: 01342 834940 W: www.sussexwaymeat.com
mail order

Sussexway Meat is a co-operative of organic farmers, producing meat from native breeds such as Sussex and Hereford cattle, and

Dorset, Suffolk and Lleyn sheep. Grass-fed all year, the animals graze amongst river meadows, wetlands and heathlands. Tamworth pork, bacon and hams are also available.

Lower Thorne Farm

Smarden Road, Pluckley, Kent TN27 0RF   T: 01233 840493
farmers' markets

Organic British White beef, Soay lamb and pork from rare-breed Tamworth pigs are joined by free-range organic chickens and turkeys at Christmas and free-range eggs occasionally. Lower Thorne's produce is available from many farmers' markets – call for details.

Ranger Organics

Holmes Oak Farm, Collins End, Goring Heath, Reading, Berkshire RG8 7RJ   T: 01491 682568   w: www.ranger.organics@virgin.net
farmers' markets

The beef from Ranger Organics, which was commended at the 2002 Soil Association Organic Food Awards, can be from a variety of different breeds, including Aberdeen Angus, Hereford, Devon and Sussex. Theresa Whittle cuts the steaks to customers' requirements in front of them at her farmers' market stalls, ensuring they get exactly what they want. Salt beef and home-made sausages are also available – find Theresa at Notting Hill farmers' market on Saturdays, Chiswick on Sundays and closer to home at local farmers' markets – call to find out where she'll be.

Whitings Butchers

20 Coldicutt Street, Caversham, Reading RG4 8DU   T: 01189 472048

A butcher who cares passionately about animal welfare and good husbandry, Martin Howarth takes all the meat for his shop from the Real Meat Company (see the Super Hero box, page 363, for more information). Martin has visited most of the farms the meat comes from and is totally confident in his sources. A full range of drug-free, welfare-friendly meats is offered.

Wysipig

Ellis's Hill Farm, Sindlesham Road, Arborfield, Reading RG2 9JG   T: 0118 976 2221
w: www.wysipig.com

⭢ farm shop ✉ mail order

The rare-breed pigs at Ellis's Hill Farm are reared in family groups, with plenty of access to woodlands, a pig's natural habitat. Slowly matured, without routine antibiotics or growth promoters, the meat – from Saddlebacks, Large Blacks, Middle Whites, Gloucester Old Spots, Tamworths and Berkshires – is dark and intensely flavoured.

Rudgwick Organic Beef & Veal

Canfields Farm, Lynwick Street, Rudgwick, West Sussex RH12 3DL   T: 01403 822219
w: www.rudgwickorganic.co.uk

⭢ farm gate sales

Organic Aberdeen Angus/Blonde crossed beef from a closed herd and welfare-friendly, free-range veal, reared naturally with their mothers, are available direct from this farm.

Sunbeam Farm

Udimore Road, Broad Oak Brede, nr Rye, East Sussex TN31 6DG   T: 01424 883237

⭢ farmers' markets

Free-range and additive-free meat – Sussex beef, Romney lamb and Gloucester Old Spot cross pork, all fed on GM-free feed. Free-range chickens from a slow-growing French breed are available, and free-range turkeys at Christmas. Find the produce at Rye, Rolvenden, Brede, Battle and Lewes farmers' markets.

Ashgood Farm

Stanwell Road, Horton, Slough, Berkshire SL3 9PA   T: 01753 682063

⭢ farm shop

Ashgood Farm is a small farm shop selling home-produced Aberdeen Angus and Shorthorn cross beef, and rare-breed pork. Sausages are made on the premises and are all additive-free with a high meat content.

Fuglemere Rare Breeds

48 Northcroft, Slough, Berkshire SL2 1HR   T: 01753 642029

🛒 **farmers' markets** ✉ **mail order**

Rare-breed lamb from a variety of breeds, from the small, gamey-flavoured native types such as Castlemilk Moorit to the larger and milder White Faced Woodland, is offered alongside traditional Portland mutton in season. All the sheep are reared on grass and home-grown barley and are hung for around a week. Longhorn beef, well marbled and hung for three weeks, is also available. Find the produce at Beaconsfield and Henley farmers' markets.

Osney Lodge Farm

Byers Lane, South Godstone, Surrey RH9 8JH   T: 01342 892216
W: www.britmeat.com

🛒 **farm shop** 🛒 **farmers' markets** ✉ **mail order**

The farm shop at Osney Lodge Farm acts as a permanent farmers' market, with locally produced meat, dairy, vegetables and fruit from small-scale producers. The speciality is the pedigree Sussex beef, reared on the farm itself. Slowly reared, grass-fed and hung for three weeks, this is a mature, well-marbled meat.

Uptons of Bassett

351 Winchester Road, Bassett, Southampton, Hampshire SO16 7DJ   T: 023 8039 3959

Uptons won a clutch of 2002 Great Taste Awards – for dry-cured bacon (made to the present owner's great grandfather's 1901 recipe), for air-dried ham (which can take up to a year to be ready) and for pâtés. The pork used is free-range, from a Surrey farm, and other locally produced meat is available. Game is also a strong part of the business and comes from just two local estates, where it is collected personally by the butcher.

Dairy Barn Farm Shop

North Houghton, Stockbridge, Hampshire SO20 6LF T: 01264 811405
E: dairybarnshop@aol.com

↓ farm shop ✉ mail order

Rare-breed meat, including Dexter and Belted Galloway beef,
Saddleback pork and Manx Loaghtan and Portland lamb, is farmed
on unfertilized, herb-rich pasture and available from the farm shop
or mail order.

A G Millers

152 Waldegrave Road, Teddington, Middlesex TW11 8NA T: 020 8977 2753
W: www.agmillers.com

All the meat at Miller's comes from the Real Meat Company (see the
Super Hero box, page 363, for more information), so the butchers
here are confident that the beef comes from farms that have never
had a reported case of BSE, and from animals that have been
reared without routine antibiotics or growth promoters.

M Newitt & Sons

10 High Street, Thame, Oxfordshire OX9 2BZ T: 01844 212103 W: www.newitt.co.uk

Newitt's were named Britain's Best Butcher in 2002 and also
scooped 23 medals out of a possible 24 at the international meat
awards at Utrecht in 2003. The meat they sell is sourced direct from
farms personally visited by the Newitt family.

Evans & Paget

Stark House Farm, Goose Hill, Headley, Thatcham, Berkshire RG19 8AR
T: 01635 268205

🛒 farmers' markets ⊨ farm gate sales

Grazing on unsprayed fields, the Hereford cattle at Stark House
Farm mature slowly. The meat is matured well on the bone before
traditional butchering. Saddleback pork is also produced on the
farm, from a free-range herd. Find Evans & Paget at Andover,
Basingstoke, Newbury and Winchester farmers' markets.

MEAT

Taste of the Past ▽RBST
Rare Breeds Survival Trust

2b Bridge Street, Walton-on-Thames, Surrey KT12 1AA T: 01932 241084

Properly hung and traditionally butchered meat is the theme here, with some rare-breed meats, including Hereford and Longhorn beef and Gloucester Old Spot pork.

The Real Meat Company

4 Mill Walk, Wheathamstead, Hertfordshire AL4 8DT T: 01582 834656
w: www.realmeat.co.uk

Selling only welfare-friendly, drug-free meat from the Real Meat Company, this traditional butcher's will cut all the meat according to customers' requirements. A full range of meats is available here: free-range chicken, pork, beef and lamb are all produced without routine antibiotics or hormones. See the Super Hero box, page 363, for more information about The Real Meat Company.

J Wickens Family Butchers

Castle Street, Winchelsea Town, East Sussex TN36 4HU T: 01797 226287

The speciality at Wickens is Sussex beef, sourced from just one local farm – a fine-grained, well-marbled and sweet-tasting meat.

Hepburns of Mountnessing

269 Roman Road, Mountnessing, Brentwood, Essex CM15 0UH T: 01277 353289

A Q Guild award-winner, Hepburn's maple-cured bacon (a unique recipe) won at the 2002 Smithfield Awards. Some interesting meats are available here – beef reared on the butcher's own farm, organic meats from the Prince of Wales's Duchy Estate, and local pork.

Longwood Farm

Tuddenham, Bury St Edmunds, Suffolk IP28 6TB   T: 01638 717120
E: matthew@longwood127.fsworld.co.uk
🥄 **farm shop**

Longwood Farm has been organic for 12 years and produces
organic South Devon beef, Saddleback pork, lamb and free-range
chickens, all allowed to grow slowly at a natural pace. Open on
Fridays and Saturdays, the on-site farm shop also stocks local
organic vegetables, locally baked organic bread and a huge range of
organic groceries.

Better Beef

Fenton House, Conington, Cambridge CB3 8LN   T: 01954 267615
W: www.betterbeef.co.uk
📫 **farm gate sales**

The Burgesses rear the very rare Gloucester beef, hanging the
mature, marbled meat for a full four weeks before sale. Fed on grass
and home-produced hay, the cattle are allowed to mature at their
own pace before being taken to a local abattoir. Meat is not always
available – phone to check first. Better Beef is a member of the
Gloucester Cattle Association.

P & S Cruickshank

124 Wulfstan Way, Cherry Hinton, Cambridge CB1 8QJ and also at 10 South Street,
Comberton, Cambridge CB3 7DZ   T: 01223 566054 (WULFSTAN WAY); 01223 262212
(SOUTH STREET)

One of the largest selections of rare-breed meats in the country,
including some difficult to find breeds such as Castlemilk Moorit
lamb and Gloucester beef can be found at Cruickshank's.

Buntings Butchers

18 Church Street, Coggeshall, Essex CO6 1TU   T: 01376 561233

A traditional butcher's with a selection of rare-breed meat from
mainly local farms, including Jacob lamb, Gloucester beef and

Gloucester Old Spot pork. There is another branch in Maldon (see page 308).

(see page 308).

EAST ANGLIA   COLCHESTER

Weylands Farm

Stoke by Nayland, Colchester, Essex CO6 4SR   T: 01206 337283

🖃 **farm gate sales**

Pork from the rare Large Black Suffolk pigs, slow-reared for an intensely flavoured meat, is available from Weylands Farm; call for details.

EAST ANGLIA   DEREHAM

Ash Farm Organics

Ash Farm, Stone Lane, Bintree, Dereham, Norfolk NR20 5NA   T: 01362 683228
w: www.ashfarmorganics.co.uk

🛒 **farm shop**

Saddleback cross pork and bacon, beef, lamb and chicken are all organically reared on home-grown feed. The farm also holds occasional open days with trailer rides so that customers can see the animals and see how the farm works.

EAST ANGLIA   HUNTINGDON

Monach Farms

The Green, Hilton, Huntingdon, Cambridgeshire PE28 9NB   T: 01480 830426
w: www.monachfarm.co.uk

🖃 **farm gate sales**

Old-fashioned traditional husbandry and slow-growing rare breeds produce great eating qualities in the meat from Monach Farms. Dexter and Highland beef, Shetland lamb and mutton and even pure-bred goat meat are available direct from the farm.

EAST ANGLIA   IPSWICH

Baylham House Rare Breeds Farm

Mill Lane, Baylham, nr Ipswich, Suffolk IP6 8LG   T: 01473 830264
w: www.baylham-house-farm.co.uk

🖃 **farm gate sales**

Traditionally reared, rare-breed lamb from a variety of breeds – Castlemilk Moorit, Grey-Faced Dartmoor, Herdwick and Norfolk

Horn to mention just a few. The lambs are reared on additive-free feed and grass. Mutton and Large Black pork and bacon are also available. Call to get on to the customer list.

EAST ANGLIA   MALDON

Buntings Butchers

89 High Street, Maldon, Essex CM9 5EP   T: 01621 853271

This is the sister branch to Buntings in Coggleshall (see page 306), which specializes in organic meats. Beef, lamb and pork, along with free-range organic poultry, is available.

EAST ANGLIA   NORTH WALSHAM

Tavern Tasty Meats

The Farm Shop, The Street, Swafield, North Walsham, Norfolk NR28 0PG   T: 01692 405444 w: www.taverntasty.co.uk

farm shop   **farmers' markets**

A really wide range of rare-breed meats is all either home-reared or from small-scale local producers. All the meats are extensively and traditionally reared and you can find them at farmers' markets in Norfolk as well as at the farm shop.

EAST ANGLIA   NORWICH

Stonehouse Organic Farm

West Harling, Norwich, Norfolk NR16 2SD   T: 01953 717258
E: stonehouse-farm@farming.co.uk

delivery service

Organic, slowly reared beef, pork and lamb are offered here. The beef and lamb is grass-fed, grazing on clover-rich meadowlands. Richard Evans, the farmer, runs a home delivery service – call for details.

EAST ANGLIA   SAXMUNDHAM

Emmett's Store

Peasenhall, Saxmundham, Suffolk IP17 2HJ   T: 01728 660250
E: emmettsham@aol.com

This fine food store has an array of interesting produce, from olives through fresh vegetables to chocolates, but the real star is their sweet pickled ham and bacon. Locally produced pork is pickled in molasses and beer and then traditionally smoked; it has a Royal Warrant from the late Queen Mother as an endorsement.

Red Poll Beef

Botany Farm, Farnham, Saxmundham, Suffolk IP17 1QZ   T: 01728 688166
E: redpolls@btinternet.com

farmers' markets **farm gate sales**

Botany Farm is currently in conversion to organic status and specializes exclusively in indigenous Red Poll beef – a breed renowned for finely grained, moist meat. It is available direct from the farm or from Felixstowe and Woodbridge farmers' markets.

Steeple Wick Farming Company

Steeple Wick Farm, Stansgate Road, Steeple, Essex CM0 7LQ   T: 01621 773368
E: steeplewickfarm@aol.com

farm gate sales

A great selection of rare breeds is reared on this farm, grazing on conservation land. The farm has an open policy – visitors are welcome to see the animals. The meat is only available directly from the farm.

Five Winds Farm Smokehouse and Butchery

The Station, Melton, Woodbridge, Suffolk IP12 1LS   T: 01394 461481
W: www.fivewindsfarm.com

farm shop

Five Winds Farm has recently won an award for its bacon cured in Guinness and black treacle. The bacon comes from local free-range pork. Smoked Suffolk ham and black sweet pickled ham are also available, along with smoked free-range chicken and local fish.

Barkers

West Farm, Ruckley, nr Acton Burnell, Shropshire SY5 7HR   T: 01694 731318

farmers' markets **farm gate sales**

Sue Barker rears rare-breed Large Black pigs using old-fashioned husbandry – no teeth or nail clipping, no castration, a natural

organic diet and access to pasture all year. She then makes
sausages using traditional skins, and dry-cured bacon. Lamb comes
from the primitive North Ronaldsay breed, producing a gamey meat,
and beef is Dexter, a mature, well-marbled meat.

MIDLANDS	BARKBY THORPE

Picks Organic Farm Shop

The Cottage, Hamilton Grounds, King Street, Barkby Thorpe, Leicestershire LE7 3QF
T: 0116 269 3548

⮟ **farm shop**

Slowly matured Dexter beef, Gloucester Old Spot pork, lamb,
Aylesbury ducks, guineafowl and turkeys at Christmas are all
organic, all home-produced at Picks. The farm shop also stocks
local organic vegetables and dairy produce.

MIDLANDS	BIRMINGHAM

M Finn Butchers

17 Stanton Road, Great Barr, Birmingham B43 5QT   T: 0121 357 5780

✉ **mail order**

Vaughan Meers of M Finn is keen to stock extensively reared,
chemical-free meat and offers free-range chickens, wild boar and
properly hung beef and lamb, all from local farms. Staffordshire
Black dry-cured bacon is a speciality.

MIDLANDS	BOSTON

F C Phipps

Osborne House, Mareham-Le-Fen, Boston, Lincolnshire PE22 7RW   T: 01507 568235
W: www.britainsbestbutcher.co.uk

✉ **mail order**

F C Phipps offers a good choice of rare-breed meats and poultry,
including the famous Lincoln Red beef. Lincolnshire Chine (cured
shoulder ham stuffed with parsley) is also available.

MIDLANDS	BOURNVILLE

S & A Rossiter

247 Maryvale Road, Bournville, West Midlands B30 1PN   T: 0121 458 1598

A real find for anyone passionate about organics, Rossiter's stock
locally produced organic meat from farms personally known to the

butcher, and also cheese, eggs, bread, including locally made organic Italian specialities, fish, including organic trout and salmon, and home-made sausages and charcuterie.

A Johnson & Son

1 Hadley Street, Yoxall, Burton-on-Trent, Staffordshire DE13 8NB   T: 01543 472235
E: yoxallbutcher@aol.com

John Bailey is passionate about his work and stocks some really interesting meats, including great rare-breed beef, pork and lamb and even seaweed-fed lamb from Scotland. Because John uses mainly local farmers and his own slaughterhouse, the meat is fully traceable. John was voted Butcher of the Year in 2002 by the RBST. The shop also stocks around 40 different British farmhouse cheeses.

Lower Hurst Farm

Hartington, nr Buxton, Derbyshire SK17 0HJ   T: 01298 84900
W: www.lowerhurstfarm.co.uk
📬 **farm gate sales** ✉ **mail order**

Organic Hereford beef is allowed to grow slowly at Lower Hurst Farm and is hung for three weeks after slaughter. Every piece of meat is supplied to the customer with an ID pack, guaranteeing full traceability.

Berkswell Traditional Farmstead Meats

The Farm Shop, Larges Farm, Back Lane, Meriden, nr Coventry, Warwickshire CV7 7LD
T: 01676 522409
⚓ **farm shop**

All kinds of rare-breed meat are available here, butchered to order. The staff know where everything has come from and will happily explain all the details to customers. Dry-cured bacon, sausages and burgers are also available, all made on the premises.

D W Wall & Son

Corvedale Road, Craven Arms, Shropshire SY7 9NL T: 01588 672308

With over 90% of their meat being rare breed, Wall & Son really are specialists. They offer a fantastic selection of breeds, including the very difficult to find Irish Moiled beef, hung for a month for a mature flavour. Most of the meat is from nearby farms, including the free-range chicken. There is also a branch in Ludlow (see page 318).

Checketts of Ombersley

Ombersley, Droitwich, Worcestershire WR9 0EW T: 01905 620284
w: www.checketts.co.uk

The Checketts have been in the butchery business for over 100 years and have won many awards for their products. The emphasis here is on meat sourced from local farmers with whom they have built lasting relationships. Game is also available in season and can include pheasant, partridge, wild duck, hare and rabbit.

Detton Beef and Lamb

Detton Hall Farm, Little Detton, Cleobury Mortimer, Kidderminster, Worcestershire DY14 8LW T: 01299 270173 w: www.detton.co.uk
🛒 **farmers' markets** 🚜 **farm gate sales** ✉ **mail order**

Grass-fed beef from steers only (no bull beef, which is sometimes considered to have a tainted flavour), is reared extensively on this traditional family farm. Hung for three weeks, the beef is mature but lean. Lamb is also available, direct from the farm, by mail order or from Bewdley, Kidderminster, Bromsgrove and Stourbridge farmers' markets. Detton is a member of Heart of England Fine Foods.

Chantry Farm Shop

Kings Newton Lane, Kings Newton, Derbyshire DE73 1DD T: 01332 865698
🛒 **farm shop**

Although the farm shop is not certified organic, most of the rare-breed meat sold here is reared organically and sourced mainly from local farms. There is lots of variety and all the meat is properly hung and butchered.

Routledge's Butchers

182 Nuncargate Road, Kirkby-in-Ashfield, Nottinghamshire NG17 9EA
T: 01623 753267   W: www.routledges-butchers.co.uk

Beef from local farms at Routledge's is well marbled and from rare breeds such as Hereford. The butcher uses rare-breed pork (Gloucester Old Spot) for his home-made, dry-cured bacon.

Meynell Langley Farm Shop

Meynell Langley, Kirk Langley, Derbyshire DE6 4NT   T: 01332 824815
⏣ **farm shop**

Organic Welsh Black beef, Cheviot lamb and chickens are produced on the farm for sale in the farm shop. All the breeds are chosen specifically for their slow-growing nature and good flavour. Organic pork from a neighbouring farm is also available.

John Miles Traditional Breeds Butcher

21 The Homend, Ledbury, Herefordshire HR8 1BN   T: 01531 632744
W: www.johnmiles.co.uk

John Miles is happy to tell you exactly where each cut of meat in his shop came from – the meat is almost all from local farms, most no more than ten miles away. A huge range of traditional-breed meat is available.

Heards of Wigston

69 Long Street, Wigston, Leicester LE18 2AJ   T: 0116 288 0444

Heards source their meat direct from local farms and will happily arrange for customers to visit the farms to see the animals in situ. The meat is free-range and drug-free, some certified organic and some from rare or traditional breeds, such as the Gloucester Old Spot pigs.

super hero

ROB AND FIONA CUNNINGHAM, of Maynards Farm Bacon, Shrewsbury
(see page 320)

Rob Cunningham has a fascination with bacon; to him, it is not just the ubiquitous essential for a cooked breakfast – it is the expression of a 17th-century craft and an evocation of a region. Dry-curing the local free-range pork into bacon is not a simple task at Maynards. There are any number of cures to choose from, from the Welsh Black recipe, strong and hearty, to the local Shropshire Mild, with spices and coriander. The current range stands at around 20 regional curing recipes but Rob and his wife, Fiona, are searching for more and have added a variety of smoked bacons and hams to their selection. Starting with good local pork and continuing with such attention to detail (it takes about a month to transform pork into bacon using the traditional cures) results in bacon that is a far cry from the floppy, watery specimens we are more likely to come across from factory farming. Maynards' bacon does not sizzle with excess moisture in the pan. 'The sound it makes is more like a contented murmur,' states Rob.

MIDLANDS   **LEICESTER**

Quenby Hall Organic Foods

nr Hungarton, Leicester LE7 9JF T: 0116 259 5224 w: www.quenbyfoods.co.uk
🚩 **farm gate sales**

English Longhorn cattle are a rare breed associated with the East Midlands since the 18th century. Freddie de Lisle rears them outside on grass all year round and the beef is then hung on the bone for three weeks. A variety of vacuum-packed cuts, from a minimum quantity of 10kg upwards, is available direct from the farm, but phone first.

MIDLANDS   **LEICESTER**

The Real Meat Company

8 Allandale Road, Stoneygate, Leicester LE2 2DA T: 0116 270 3396
w: www.realmeat.co.uk

The butcher here has been in the business for 40 years and made the decision to stock only Real Meat Company meat because he was so concerned about standards in the majority of meat production. He firmly believes that good husbandry and attention to welfare issues makes for better meat and is proud of the meat he sells. See the Super Hero box, page 363, for more information about The Real Meat Company.

MIDLANDS   **LEICESTER**

Michael F Wood

51 Hartopp Road, Leicester LE2 1WG   T: 0116 270 5194   W: www.mfwood.co.uk

There is plenty of organic meat to choose from here, from small local producers whom the butcher has personally visited to inspect. Beef traditionally hung for three weeks and dry-cured bacon are a couple of the specialities.

MIDLANDS   **LINCOLN**

Curtis of Lincoln

Long Leys Road, Lincoln LN1 1DX   T: 01522 527212
✉ **mail order**

A long-established Lincolnshire butcher, Curtis is famous for the regional speciality, Lincolnshire Chine, a cured shoulder ham stuffed with parsley.

MIDLANDS   **LINCOLN**

Elite Meats

89 Bailgate, Lincoln LN1 3AR   T: 01522 523500

Plenty of locally produced meats are available here, including the native Lincoln Red beef. Hung for three weeks, this beef is slowly reared on grass all year. Organic pork, free-range, corn-fed chicken and lamb all come from nearby farms.

MIDLANDS   **LITTLE DEWCHURCH**

Henclose Farm Organic Produce

Henclose Farm, Little Dewchurch, Hereford HR2 6PP   T: 01432 840826
✉ **farm gate sales**

Jacob cross lamb, Gloucester Old Spot/Berkshire cross pork, bacon and sausages, kid meat, and goats' milk, and free-range eggs, all organic. This is a very small farm, and produce is not always available, so phone first to check.

food facts

ORGANIC MEAT

It is relevant to mention the organic movement in relation to meat production. Respect for animal welfare is a crucial factor in the production of safe, good-quality meat and in the prevention of the spread of disastrous diseases such as BSE and foot-and-mouth disease. Compassion in World Farming, a UK-based operation campaigning to end factory farming, say that the Soil Association's regulations in meat production are the most stringent, and the highest in terms of animal welfare in the UK. Feed must be free from animal byproducts, antibiotics and growth promoters. The animals must have access to fields (themselves unsprayed with chemicals) and be able to express their natural behaviour. Travelling to abattoirs is kept to a minimum. Farms are encouraged to be diverse, with mixed species, which is better for the environment, and organically raised animals must be kept separate from those reared conventionally.

Equally, biodynamic farms are producing great meat. A biodynamic farm is an organic one taken a little further and run entirely holistically – it will be a mixed farm, where balance and harmony with nature is strived for. Closed herds are a key feature of biodynamics and this means every animal is totally traceable, often back through several generations. On a biodynamic farm planting and harvesting are conducted according to a strict calendar and the farm is treated as a self-contained organism with any inputs kept to an absolute minimum. Many of the producers we list are Soil Association or Demeter (biodynamic) accredited and many more, though not accredited, farm to the Soil Association's standards.

MIDLANDS   **LOUGHBOROUGH**

Home Farm Organics

Home Farm, Woodhouse Lane, Nanpantan, Loughborough, Leicestershire LE11 3YG
T: 01509 237064   w: www.growingconcern.co.uk

⚓ **farm shop**

A family-run farm shop, selling meat only from their own land. Lots of rare-breed meat here, all fully traceable, properly hung and matured. The on-site café/restaurant, Beth's Kitchen, serves food from the farm.

Manor Farm

MEAT

77 Main Street, Long Whatton, Loughborough, Leicestershire LE12 5DF
T: 01509 646413   w: www.manororganicfarm.co.uk

farm shop **box scheme**

Organic vegetables are cut freshly every morning for the farm shop
at Manor Farm; home-reared Longhorn beef, Lleyn lamb (both
entirely grass-fed), alongside pork from a neighbouring farm are all
on offer. Manor Farm operates a box scheme in Loughborough.
Everything is organic.

Stephen Morris Butchers

26–27 High Street, Loughborough, Leicestershire LE11 2PZ   T: 01509 215260

Stephen Morris specializes in organic and biodynamic meats, mainly
sourced from one local biodynamic farm, where the meat is hand-
picked by the butcher. The meat is all traditionally reared for an old-
fashioned flavour.

Lakings of Louth

33 Eastgate, Louth, Lincolnshire LN11 9NB   T: 01507 603186

Lakings is a traditional butcher's that specializes in local meat; signs
tell the customer exactly where each piece of meat has come from.
They also stock a full range of local game in season.

Orleton Farm Shop

Overton Farm, Orleton, nr Ludlow, Shropshire SY8 4HZ   T: 01568 780750
w: www.orletonfarmshop.co.uk

farm shop

Winner of the National Farmer's Union Great British Food Award,
Orleton Farm Shop sells its own Aberdeen Angus beef, lamb and
poultry, all of which is in conversion to organic status. Also available
are vegetables and fruit from nearby farms.

G & R Tudge

The Bury, Richards Castle, Ludlow, Shropshire SY8 4EL   T: 01584 831227
w: www.tudge-meats.co.uk

farmers' markets

The Tudge family rear rare-breed Tamworth and Berkshire pigs,
freely ranging in small family groups. The pigs are reared on GM-,
antibiotic- and growth-promoter-free feed. Dry-cured bacon and
ham are available as well as joints. Free-range chicken from
slowly growing breeds is also on offer; all the produce can be
found at Hereford, Ludlow, Leominster, Malvern and Abergavenny
farmers' markets.

D W Wall & Son

14 High Street, Ludlow, Shropshire SY8 1BS   T: 01584 872060

For details, see under the Craven Arms branch on page 312.

Malvern Country Meats

37 Church Street, Malvern, Worcestershire WR14 2AA   T: 01684 568498

mail order

Rare-breed and free-range meats from local farms and award-
winning sausages are on offer at the shop or by mail order.

Corvedale Organic Lamb

Corve House, Rowe Lane, Stanton Long, Much Wenlock, Shropshire TF13 6LR   T: 01746
712539   w: www.corvedale.com

delivery service

Paul Mantle rears the large Suffolk sheep, a breed you are unlikely
to find in supermarkets as they do not fit within the size restrictions
supermarkets impose. The lambs graze parkland rich in herbs, wild
garlic and wild grasses and Paul feels this benefits the flavour of the
meat. Available through a delivery round in Ludlow – call for details.

Wenlock Edge Farm

Longville-in-the-Dale, Much Wenlock, Shropshire TF13 6DU　T: 01694 771203
W: www.wenlockedgefarm.com

⬇ farm shop

Customers at Wenlock Edge can watch the home-reared pork being transformed into dry-cured bacon or sausages while they shop at the farm. Home-reared lamb and beef from a neighbouring farm are also available.

Northfield Farm　　　　　　　　⟨☆⟩ **RBST**
Rare Breeds Survival Trust

Whissendine Lane, Cold Overton, nr Oakham, Rutland LE15 7QF　T: 01664 474271
W: www.northfieldfarm.com

⬇ farm shop ✉ mail order

Fantastic rare- and traditional-breed meats, including home-reared Dexter beef. The staff will happily tell you the breed, age and diet of any of the meat they have on offer. As well as the shop and mail order Northfield Farm sells at Borough Market, London SE1 and the Food Market at Festival Square, Basingstoke.

Huntsham Farm – Pedigree Meats

Goodrich, Ross-on-Wye, Herefordshire HR9 6JN　T: 01600 890296
W: www.huntsham.com

✉ mail order

Properly hung meat from Middle White pigs, Ryeland lamb and Longhorn beef, all chosen for their taste and texture.

G N F & G A Browning　　　　　

Feldon Forest Farm, Frankton, Rugby, Warwickshire CV23 9PD,　T: 01926 632246
E: georgebrowning@farmersweekly.net

✉ farm gate sales

All kinds of organic goodies are available here, the speciality being rare-breed meats from Shetland cattle and Castlemilk Moorit sheep. Organic strawberries, other fruit and various vegetables are also available in season, along with eggs, wool and sheepskins.

Ted's Traditional Taste of Shropshire

Hungerhill Farm, Sherrifhales, nr Shifnal, Shropshire TF11 8SA   T: 01952 461146

Rare-breed and native meats – from Aberdeen Angus and Hereford cattle, Large Black pigs and local lamb – are all reared for an old-fashioned flavour and texture and sausages and dry-cured bacon are also available.

Curradine Angus

Church Farm, Shrawley, Worcestershire WR6 6TS   T: 01905 620283
w: www.farmhouseflora.com

👇 **farm shop**

Pure-bred Aberdeen Angus beef from cattle born on the farm and grass-fed all year is hung for at least two weeks and so has a traditional, well-marbled texture.

Maynards Farm Bacon   super hero

Hough Farm, Weston-under-Redcastle, Shrewsbury, Shropshire SY4 5LR
T: 01948 840252   w: www.maynardsfarm.co.uk

✉ **mail order**

An ever-increasing range of at least 20 varieties of bacon cured to traditional regional recipes is available here. See the Super Hero box, page 314, for more information.

Hockerton Grange Farm Shop

Hockerton Grange, Hockerton, nr Southwell, Nottinghamshire NG25 0PJ
T: 01636 816472   w: www.farmshopfoods.co.uk

👇 **farm shop** ✉ **mail order**

Locally produced rare-breed meats, such as native Lincoln Red beef, Gloucester Old Spot, Large Black and Tamworth pork, and South Down, Ryeland, Soay and Hebridean lamb are all sourced from nearby farms that pay particular attention to animal welfare.

Happy Meats

MEAT

Bank House Farm, Stanford Bridge, Worcestershire WR6 6RU   T: 01886 812485
w: www.happymeats.co.uk

⬇ **farm shop**   ▦ **farmers' markets**   ✉ **mail order**

Traditional tasty meat as it used to be is reared on this farm where
animal welfare comes first. Rare-breed pork, lamb and beef from
this small, sustainable Teme Valley farm is all free-range, fed on
locally produced food with no additives, growth promoters,
antibiotics or GM ingredients. The animals are old, traditional rare
breeds, so they take longer to mature but the taste is well worth
the wait. Most of the pork is Gloucester Old Spot and the beef
Long Horn and Dexter. There is also grass-fed hogget and mutton,
home-dry-cured bacon and sausages with none of the usual
preservatives or colouring. In season there is wild venison, pheasant
and partridge and non-farmed fish, which is smoked in a traditional
oak smokehouse.

Steve Brooks Butcher

13 Lawton Road, Alsager, Stoke-on-Trent, Staffordshire ST7 2AA   T: 01270 882248
w: www.qualitycuts.co.uk

✉ **mail order**

Most of the produce at Steve Brooks comes from local farms and
there is plenty of local game to choose from in season, including
wild rabbit, partridge, quail, guineafowl, hare, pigeon and wild
Scottish hill venison. There is also a branch in Sandbach (see
page 328).

Michael Kirk

56 Woolpack Street, Wolverhampton, West Midlands WV1 3NA   T: 01902 425064
w: www.porkiepies.com

A traditional butcher's offering locally reared meats, including free-
range goose, and beef hung for four weeks. The shop has won
many awards, particularly for its sausages and pork pies, including
from the Q Guild.

food facts

BEEF AND VEAL

The beef we often see is bright red, wet-looking meat with little evidence of fat. When you buy from some of our listed producers, you might be surprised by the dark colour of the meat, the marbling of fat running through the cut and the closely grained texture. This is meat that has been properly hung for three or four weeks, vital for the development of flavour and for a tender cooked meat, from breeds chosen specifically for their eating qualities and decent fat cover. It is fat that keeps all meat moist in cooking and adds immeasurably to the flavour; even if you choose not to eat it, it is so important that it is allowed to remain on the meat for cooking. Breeds such as the Lincoln Red, White Park, Hereford and Red Poll can all provide fantastic-quality beef.

Many of our producers insist that their beef is entirely grass-fed, so the animals graze on rich, fresh pasture for most of the year, with hay or silage for the winter months, not concentrated feed. Grass-fed beef will not only taste better, but it is better for you, with higher levels of the healthier polyunsaturated fatty acids than the unhealthier, saturated kind. It also contains a substance called conjugated linoleic acid, which enables our bodies to break down fatty acids more efficiently.

We also feature a couple of producers who rear veal in a welfare-friendly fashion, allowing us to enjoy this delicacy with a clearer conscience. The method known as *veaux de lait élevé sous la mère*, allows the calf to stay with its mother, free-range, suckling her rich milk until it's weaned. The producers are adamant that this results in a far higher quality of meat. As with all the meat producers in this book, beef farmers rearing with great respect for their livestock, and an unhurried attitude, are producing great results.

NORTH WEST   APPLEBY-IN-WESTMORLAND

Barwise Aberdeen Angus

Barwise Hall, Hoff, Appleby-in-Westmorland, Cumbria CA16 6TD   T: 01768 353430
E: barwise@btinternet.com

delivery service   **mail order**

Pedigree Aberdeen Angus beef, grass-fed and traditionally reared and hung for three weeks to mature on the bone. Available in boxes of mixed cuts or as single joints – phone for details.

Bromley Green Farm

Ormside, Appleby-in-Westmorland, Cumbria CA16 6EJ   T: 01768 353327

🛒 **farmers' markets**   🛒 **farm gate sales**

Norma Thompson rears Aberdeen Angus cattle, which are grass-fed in summer and have hay and silage grown on the farm in winter. A local slaughterhouse and butcher are used and, after hanging, the meat is available direct from the farm or at any one of the seven local farmers' markets Norma attends – call for details.

Border County Foods

The Old Vicarage, Crosby-on-Eden, Carlisle, Cumbria CA6 4QZ   T: 01228 573500
w: www.cumberland-sausage.net

🛒 **farmers' markets**   ✉ **mail order**

Traditional Cumberland sausage, made with home-reared, rare-breed pork – Gloucester Old Spot, Tamworth, Saddleback ... the list goes on! The pigs are reared extensively, outside whenever weather allows. Dry-cured bacon is available and 'real' black pudding. Austen, the sausage-maker, is a vigorous campaigner for a relaxation in the laws governing the making of black pudding. Currently, makers are forced to use dried blood, usually from abroad. Austen uses fresh and told me that it makes a huge difference to the quality of the pudding. All the products are available at many farmers' markets in the north of England or by mail order.

Castletown Farmshop

Floriston Rigg, Rockcliffe, Carlisle, Cumbria CA6 4HG   T: 01228 674400
w: www.castletownfarmshop.co.uk

🍃 **farm shop**

A farm shop with a dedication to stocking very local produce, with organic, home-grown vegetables, meat and game from surrounding farms and a good selection of cheeses, including some from Cumbria.

Hallsford Farm

Hethersgill, Carlisle, Cumbria CA6 6JD T: 01288 577329 w: www.hallsford.co.uk
🛒 **farmers' markets** ✉ **mail order**

Well-marbled and mature Shorthorn beef and rare-breed Llanwenog lamb from this hillside Cumbrian farm (currently in conversion to organic status), slowly reared for flavour. Hardy breeds, the animals are fed largely on grass and organic barley. Available by mail order or from many local farmers' markets.

Whiteholme Farm

Roweltown, Carlisle, Cumbria CA6 6LJ T: 01697 748058 w: www.whiteholmefarm.co.uk
🛒 **farm gate sales** 🚚 **delivery service**

Black Faced lamb, Saddleback pork, free-range poultry and Shorthorn cross beef are all reared slowly and organically at Whiteholme. All the butchery is carried out on the farm, which has Countryside Stewardship status and belongs to Cumbria Organics – the Perkin family are dedicated to sustainable farming and conservation. All the meat, as well as local organic vegetables, is available direct from the farm or through the local delivery round.

Keer Falls Forest Farm

Arkholme, Carnforth, Lancashire LA6 1AP T: 01524 221019 w: www.keerfalls.co.uk
🛒 **farm gate sales** 🚚 **delivery service**

Keer Falls Farm is an organic farm where attention to the welfare of the livestock is paramount. White Faced Woodland lamb, Aberdeen Angus beef, free-range mallard ducks and a choice of organic herbs are all available through farm gate sales, or a local delivery round.

The Manx Loaghtan Marketing Co-operative Ltd

Ballaloaghtan, Kerrowkeil Road, Grenaby, Isle of Man IM9 3BB T: 07624 492850
w: www.manxloaghtan.com
✉ **mail order**

Slow-maturing, primitive breed Manx Loaghtan lamb is slow-growing (slaughtered at around 18 months, compared to around four to six for other breeds) and the finely grained meat has a gamey flavour, with less fat and cholesterol than conventional lamb.

Farmer Sharp

Dalton-in-Furness, Cumbria LA15 8XQ   T: 01229 588299   W: www.farmersharp.co.uk
farmers' markets ✉ **mail order**

Farmer Sharp is a co-operative of Cumbrian farmers producing the native Herdwick lamb. The sheep are reared on the fells and have an unusual gamey flavour and a closely textured meat. In addition to mail order, meat can be bought at Borough Market, London SE1.

Aireys Farm Shop

Snowdrop Villa, Ayside, Grange-over-Sands, Cumbria LA11 6JE   T: 01539 531237
farm shop

Although conventional meat is sold here, the specialities are home-reared, rare-breed meats – Angus and Hereford beef, reared by the owner, and Gloucester Old Spot, Middle White and Saddleback pork, reared on a nearby farm.

Savin Hill Farm

Savin Hill, Lyth Valley, Kendal, Cumbria LA8 8DJ   T: 01539 568410
W: www.eatbestbeef.co.uk AND www.eatprimepork.co.uk
farmers' markets

Beef from pure-bred British White cattle and pork from pure Middle White pigs, ranging free at the farm throughout the summer months and bedded on straw, housed in purpose-built buildings during the wetter, colder season. The animals are fed a GM-free diet and no artificial fertilizers are used on the land. Find the produce at specialist food events nationally and farmers' markets throughout the north, including Orton, Manchester, Liverpool, Houghton Towers, Kendal, Wirral and Rochdale.

Yew Tree Farm

Rosthwaite, Borrowdale, Keswick, Cumbria CA12 5XB T: 01768 777675
W: www.yew-tree-farm.co.uk

farm shop

Slowly growing Herdwick lamb is the speciality of Yew Tree Farm. This
is a breed native to Cumbria, not ready for eating until it is at least a
year old (conventional lamb is often eaten at three months). Reared all
year on the fells, it has a gamey flavour, and looks like venison.

Kitridding Farm Shop

Luckton, nr Kirkby Lonsdale, Cumbria LA6 2QA T: 01539 567484
E: christine@kitridding.co.uk

farm shop

Really local produce is available at this farm shop; most of the foods
stocked are from within a five-mile radius. The ethos of the Lambert
family is to encourage customers to rediscover traditional, local
foods, and Kitridding Farm produces its own beef, and Swaledale
lamb, home-made sausages and home-cured bacon. The farm is
accredited by RSPCA Freedom Foods.

Lune Valley

Nether Hall, Kirkby Lonsdale, Cumbria LA6 2EW T: 01524 273193
W: www.rearednaturally.co.uk

mail order

A wide choice of meat cuts from extensively reared livestock – beef
and free-range pork. The Kelly family use a local abattoir and all the
meat is traceable. The farm is accredited by RSPCA Freedom Foods.

Mansergh Hall Farm

Mansergh Hall, Kirkby Lonsdale, Lancashire LA6 2EN T: 01524 271397
W: www.manserghhall.co.uk

farm shop **mail order**

This farm shop sells home-reared lamb and Aberdeen Angus beef,
grass-fed on clover-rich pasture all year and hung properly after

slaughter. Gloucester Old Spot sausages and dry-cured bacon are also available. Jim Hadwin, the farmer, bases his business on honesty with his customers – he'll tell you exactly how the animals have been reared.

NORTH WEST   MILLOM

Richard Woodall

Lane End, Waberthwaite, nr Millom, Cumbria LA19 5YJ T: 01229 717237 OR
01229 717386 W: www.richardwoodall.co.uk
✉ **mail order**

Legendary air-dried Cumbrian ham, Cumberland sausages, pancetta and bacon, all made from pigs reared on the farm, which focusses particularly on animal welfare.

NORTH WEST   NANTWICH

Brookshaws of Nantwich

8–10 Hospital Street, Nantwich, Cheshire CW5 5RJ T: 01270 625302
W: www.brookshaws.com

Aberdeen Angus beef, hung for three weeks, Gloucester Old Spot pork and saltmarsh lamb from Wales are some of the treats available at Brookshaws, as well as a good choice of local game.

NORTH WEST   PENRITH

Greystone House

Stainton, Penrith, Cumbria CA11 0EF T: 01768 866952
⬎ **farm shop**

Marjorie Dawson enthusiastically runs this farm shop, stocking home-reared Galloway beef and lamb, organic vegetables from Lancashire and home-made bread and cakes, including a very popular red onion bread. There is also a café upstairs. Open every day.

NORTH WEST   PENRITH

The Old Smokehouse & Truffles Chocolates

Brougham Hall, Brougham, Penrith, Cumbria CA10 2DE T: 01768 867772
W: www.the-old-smokehouse.co.uk
🗺 **farmers' markets** 🛒 **shop**

Georgina and Jo at The Old Smokehouse won five Great Taste awards in 2002 for their produce. Particularly highly praised was the smoked lamb – they get the lamb from Mansergh Hall Farm (see the entry on page 326) and then traditionally smoke it over oak. Smoked wild Windermere char, venison, pheasant, quail, duck, sausage and cheeses are also available. When they're not smoking local produce, Jo and Georgina are busy making their own chocolate truffles, with fresh fruit and local cream. Their produce is available from the shop on site or at Kendal, Carlisle, Penrith, Orton, Brough and Barnard Castle farmers' markets.

NORTH WEST	PENRITH

Slacks of Cumbria

Newlands Farm, Raisbeck, Orton, Penrith, Cumbria CA10 3SG   т: 01539 624667
E: slacks@fsbdial.co.uk
✉ mail order

Slacks produce very old-fashioned dry-cured bacon, produced from locally sourced pigs, which are fed on whey to enhance the flavour. The pigs are antibiotic and growth promoter free. The bacon is cured and then air-dried in a four-week process, giving an intense flavour and no nasty white residue in the pan.

NORTH WEST	PENRITH

Stoneyhead Pork

Stoneyhead Hall Farm, Sunbiggin, Orton, Penrith, Cumbria CA10 3SQ   т: 01539 624456
🛒 farmers' markets

Pork from a wide selection of breeds – Gloucester Old Spot, Large Black and Saddleback – all reared in deep-bedded straw yards, slowly, for a mature-flavoured meat. Find the pork at lots of Cumbrian farmers' markets – call for details.

NORTH WEST	SANDBACH

Steve Brooks Butcher

25 High Street, Sandbach, Cheshire CW11 1AH   т: 01270 766657
w: www.qualitycuts.co.uk
✉ mail order

For details, see under the Stoke-on-Trent branch on page 321.

Steadman's

2 Finkle Street, Sedbergh, Cumbria LA10 5BZ T: 01539 620431
w: www.steadmans-butchers.co.uk

Almost everything on sale at Steadman's has originated within
Cumbria, including the local whey-fed pork, Aberdeen Angus beef
and Kendal Rough Fell lamb. There is also a good range of locally
shot game in season. Steadman's are holders of an award for Best
Dry-cured Bacon in the North West.

Broughs of Birkdale

20 Liverpool Road, Birkdale, Southport, Merseyside PR8 4AY T: 01704 567073
w: www.broughs.com

A traditional butcher, offering Scotch beef, local pork and chicken.
Dry-cured bacon is produced using traditional salt beds and finished
with honey and brown sugar, and this product is not only a Q Guild
of Butchers award winner but also won a Good Housekeeping
award.

R F Burrows & Sons

Old Post Office, Bunbury, nr Tarporely, Cheshire CW6 9QR T: 01829 260342
w: www.burrowsandsons.co.uk

Local pheasant, wild duck and Scottish wild venison are available at
Burrows, alongside traditional meats.

Rock Midstead Organic Farm Shop

Alnwick, Northumberland NE66 2TH T: 01665 579225 w: www.rockmidstead.co.uk
⬇ **farm shop**

Organic meat from animals reared in small family groups and fed on
home-grown feed. Rare and native breeds (Dorset lamb, Aberdeen
Angus beef and Tamworth pork) have been chosen here, producing
meat with an old-fashioned flavour.

R Carter & Son Butcher

Front Street, Bamburgh, Northumberland NE69 7BW   T: 01668 214344

This butcher's shop is famous for its traditional Scotch pies and sausage rolls, all made the old-fashioned way.

Westholme Farm Meats

Westholme Farm, Marwood, Barnard Castle, Co. Durham DL12 8QP   T: 01833 638443

🥩 **farmers' markets**   🚚 **delivery service**

Lesley and Martin Bell specialize in beef, which is fed on home-grown cereals and grass and then hung traditionally after slaughter. The beef is reared for a lean meat, with light fat cover. The Bells attend many north east farmers' markets and run a delivery round – call for details.

super hero

LISHMANS OF ILKLEY (see page 332)

An award-winning Q-Guild butcher, Lishman's have won the Champion of Champions award from the *Meat Trades Journal* for their sausages. The secret, says David Lishman, lies in the pork used – 'We produce our own rare-breed pigs (Saddlebacks and British Lops), the pigs which were common 40 years ago. They mature slower, and put down more fat than their modern-day counterparts, overall producing a far higher quality.' The same attention to detail is given to all the meat stocked – David has strong views on modern conventional farming techniques: 'In recent years the pursuit of healthy, lean meat, coupled with the farmers' commercial interest in producing livestock more quickly and economically, has reduced the eating quality of modern farmed animals to the tasteless, often dry texture that is common today.' David sources meat farmed the old-fashioned way; it is this, he states, that produces the three factors that give meat good eating qualities – 'succulence, tenderness and flavour, enhanced by the presence of fat, both on the surface and marbled throughout the flesh itself'.

R G Foreman & Son

13 Woolmarket, Berwick-upon-Tweed, Northumberland TD15 1DH   T: 01289 304442
w: www.borderbutcher.co.uk

For details, see under the Eyemouth branch on page 347. There are also branches in Coldstream and Norham-on-Tweed (see pages 346 and 334).

Piperfield Pork

The Dovecote, Lowick, Berwick-upon-Tweed, Northumberland TD15 2QE
T: 01289 388543   E: grahampeterhead@yahoo.com

farmers' markets   **mail order**

Pork, sausages, dry-cured bacon, gammon, chorizo and traditional air-dried ham from Middle White and Saddleback pigs can be found at this farm. The pigs are reared free-range in small family groups in grassy paddocks, without growth promoters or antibiotics – Piperfield has increased the national herds of Middle White and Saddleback pigs by 10% in the last year and has become an important factor in the conservation of these rare-breed pigs. Piperfield won the Champion Traditional Breed Sausage award at the 2001 National Festival of Meat for their Middle White sausages. All their products are available by mail order or from Berwick, Edinburgh and Newcastle farmers' markets.

Well Hung and Tender

Baldersbury Hill Farm, Berwick-upon-Tweed, Northumberland TD15 1UY
T: 01289 386216   w: www.wellhungandtender.com

farmers' markets   **farm gate sales**

Pure-bred Aberdeen Angus beef is available fresh or frozen from Baldersbury Hill Farm. All the cattle are born and reared on the farm, so total traceability is guaranteed. The meat is matured on the bone for a minimum of three weeks to allow the flavour to develop fully. The meat is available from the farm direct or from many local farmers' markets – call for details.

F Simpson & Son

The Croft, Cockfield, Bishop Auckland, Co. Durham DL13 5AA   T: 01388 718264

Third-generation traditional butchers, Simpson's sell a range of beef from native breeds and lamb from their own farm. Traditional-breed pork from local farms is available, with home-made black pudding and home-baked breads and pies.

Rose Cottage Foods

Rose Cottage, Garton-on-the-Wolds, Driffield, East Yorkshire YO25 3ET
T: 01377 253743

🛒 **farmers' markets** 📦 **farm gate sales**

Aberdeen Angus beef and Gloucester Old Spot pork provide the basis for the meats offered at Rose Cottage. Dry-cured bacon, sausages and pies are all traditionally made without the fillers and additives commonly found in these products and the steaks and pork cuts have the mature flavour of slowly reared animals, free from hormones and antibiotics. Local game is often available, direct from local shoots.

Northumbrian Quality Meats

Monkridge Hill Farm, West Woodburn, Hexham, Northumberland NE48 2TU
T: 01434 270184   W: www.northumbrian-organic-meat.co.uk

🛒 **farmers' markets** ✉ **mail order**

Locally produced organic and rare-breed meats, including heather- and clover-fed Black Faced lamb, hill-bred Aberdeen Angus beef, organic chicken and free-range pork, can all be bought from Northumbrian Quality Meats at farmers' markets or by mail order.

Lishmans of Ilkley

25 Leeds Road, Ilkley, West Yorkshire LS29 8DP   T: 01943 609436

Award-winning sausages are one of the attractions at Lishmans, made with the pork from the Saddleback pigs reared by the butcher himself. Other rare-breed meats are available. See the Super Hero box, page 330, for more information.

Jack Scaife

Mill Lane, Oakworth, Keighly, West Yorkshire BD22 7QH   T: 01535 647772
W: www.jackscaife.co.uk

✉ **mail order**

Traditional, dry-cured bacon, ham and black pudding made using free-range pork from traditional British breeds, have made Jack Scaife a winner at previous Great Taste Awards.

Lartington Lamb

Low Crag Farm, Lartington, Co. Durham DL12 9DJ   T: 01833 628427
W: www.lartingtonlamb.com

🛒 **farm gate sales** ✉ **mail order**

Seasonal lamb, outside all year, grazing on unsprayed pasture. The lambs are allowed to grow at their own pace and the ewes are not forced to lamb early to give spring lamb. This means the first of the season's lamb is not available until August at the earliest but it is worth the wait. Visitors to the farm, which is part of the Countryside Stewardship Scheme, are welcome.

Happy Piggy Pork

Manor Grange Farm, Low Lane, Carperby, Leyburn, North Yorkshire DL8 4DP
T: 01969 663399

🚚 **delivery service**

Rare-breed pork, including Tamworth and Gloucester Old Spot, slowly matured, and reared free-range on a healthy diet of fruit and vegetables, is available locally by home delivery from Happy Piggy Pork – call for details.

Capri Lodge

Morpeth, Northumberland NE61 3BX   T: 01670 511467
E: caprilodge2003@yahoo.co.uk

🛒 **farmers' markets** 🚚 **delivery service**

Believe it or not, goat is actually the meat that is eaten more than any other in the world – but we Western Europeans have yet to become familiar with it. Muriel Brown rears both dairy and meat goats and says that the meat is leaner than lamb, doesn't shrink as much when cooked, is lower in cholesterol – but is just as tasty. Joints and sausages are available and she also makes unpasteurized cheese from the milk. Find Muriel at Newcastle, Hexham, Tynemouth, Alnwick and Blythe farmers' markets or phone to see if she can deliver.

NORTH EAST   NEWCASTLE-UPON-TYNE

George Payne Butchers

27 Princes Road, Brunton Park, Gosforth, Newcastle-upon-Tyne NE3 5TT
T: 0191 236 2992

Lots of rare-breed meats from Northumberland farms are on offer here, all reared without additives, non-intensively. White Park and Dexter beef, Wensleydale lamb and Middle White pork are all popular.

NORTH EAST   NORHAM-ON-TWEED

R G Foreman & Son

8 Castle Street, Norham, Norham-on-Tweed, Northumberland TD15 2LQ
T: 01289 382260   w: www.borderbutcher.co.uk

For details, see under the Eyemouth branch on page 347. There are also branches in Berwick-upon-Tweed and Coldstream (see pages 331 and 346).

NORTH EAST   NORTHALLERTON

Langthornes Buffalo Produce

Crawford Grange, Brompton, Northallerton, North Yorkshire DL6 2PD   T: 01609 776937

🛒 farmers' markets ▱ farm gate sales

The water buffalo at Crawford Grange are grass-fed all year, producing tasty, low-cholesterol meat. Their milk is used to make a range of cheeses, including the classic buffalo mozzarella (the cheeses are made by local dairies). Farmed venison, goats' meat (free-range) and rose veal (with a much higher attention to welfare than white veal) are all available, too. Find the meat at local farmers' markets (call for details) or direct from the farm on Wednesdays and Thursdays.

Highside Butchers

Main Street, Kirkby Malzeard, Ripon, North Yorkshire HG4 3RS   T: 01765 658423
E: highsidebutcherskm@hotmail.com

Highside Butchers recently won a Q Guild award for their Beef Arran
– their own recipe, this is silverside of beef, brine-cured for a week
and then roasted with cloves. It is then toasted with breadcrumbs
and Arran mustard. This traditional butcher's also offers good,
locally produced meat – when I contacted them there was rump
steak available that had been hung for six weeks. Free-range Bronze
turkeys are available at Christmas.

Oxford Sandy & Black Pigs

Burgate Farm, Harwood Dale, Scarborough, North Yorkshire YO13 0DS
T: 01723 870333

✉ **farm gate sales**

Katrina Cook started rearing her own pigs because she was
disappointed with the pork she was able to buy from supermarkets.
The Oxford Sandy & Blacks she rears are free-range and matured
for longer than most commercial pigs. She has a customer list,
ringing people when meat is available – phone her to get on the list.

The Real Meat Company

950 Ecclesall Road, Sheffield S11 8TR   T: 0114 266 1197   W: www.realmeat.co.uk

Specializing in butchery to order – customers bring their recipes in
and the staff cut the meat to specific requirements – all the meat
here is from the Real Meat Company, guaranteed drug-free and
welfare-friendly. Dry-cured bacon and ham are specialities. See the
Super Hero box, page 363, for more information about The Real
Meat Company.

Larberry Pastures

Longnewton, Stockton-on-Tees, Cleveland TS21 1BN   T: 01642 583823
E: larberry@farmersweekly.net

🍴 **farmers' markets**   ✉ **farm gate sales**

Home-produced organic beef and free-range eggs, locally reared
organic pork, dry-cured bacon, ham and sausages and lamb can be
bought at Larberry, and also available are organic fruit and
vegetables, local baking, chutneys and preserves.

Bowlees Farm Shop

Wolsingham, Weardale, Co. Durham DL13 3JF   T: 01388 528305
W: www.bowleesorganicfarm.com

🥄 **farm shop**

Bowlees Farm was the first Soil Association accredited farm in
County Durham and is now a haven for all kinds of wildlife, due to
the sensitive methods of farming employed. Rare-breed pork is
produced, truly free-range – Large Blacks, Tamworths and
Saddlebacks. Grey Blue Galloway beef is also available, along with
Suffolk-Lleyn cross lamb. The next project for the farm shop is an
organic café, which they aim to open in the autumn of 2003.

A Flanigan & Son

1 Scotch Street, Armagh BT61 7BY   T: 028 3752 2805

Much of the meat sold here comes from the Flanigans' own farm,
where they specialize in beef and lamb. Other meats are sourced
from local farms and dry-cured bacon and ham is available.

Wysner Meats and Restaurant

16–18 Anne Street, Ballycastle, Co Antrim   T: 028 2076 2372

A key product at Wysner's is their own-recipe black pudding – a
distinctive flavour and something of a legend in Ballycastle.

MEAT

Ballylagan Organic Farm

12 Ballylagan Road, Straid, Ballyclare, Co. Antrim BT39 9NF   T: 028 9332 2867
w: www.ballylagan.com
farm shop

Ballylagan produces beef, lamb, pork and poultry, reared almost
exclusively on grass and grain grown on the farm. A wide range of
fruit and vegetables is available throughout the year, with as much
as possible being home-grown. A comprehensive selection of
organic groceries is also sold by the shop.

E R Jenkins Butchers

41 Main Street, Ballyclare, Co. Antrim BT39 9AA   T: 028 9334 1822

Another good, traditional butcher from the Elite Guild of Butchers,
selling locally sourced meat including beef that has been hung for
up to four weeks.

David Burns Butchers

112 Abbey Street, Bangor BT20 4JB   T: 028 9127 0073

Plenty of traditionally reared, locally sourced meat, including some
organic, and beef from the butcher's own herd, can be bought at
David Burns.

Owen McMahon

3 Atlantic Avenue, Belfast BT15 2HN   T: 028 9074 3535   w: www.owenmcmahon.com

McMahon's have won the accolade of producing the best pork
sausage in Belfast and, come the summer, they offer all manner of
imaginative barbecue meats – everything is produced in Ireland,
nothing is imported. Part of the shop is given over to a fish section,
where you can find locally caught fresh fish.

O'Kane Meats

69 Main Street, Claudy, Co. Londonderry BT47 4HR   т: 028 7133 8944
w: www.okanemeats.com

This multi-award-winning butcher's shop specializes in sausages, having won the Champion Beef Sausage award from the Northern Ireland Master Butcher's Association in 2002. Local beef is available, hung for a minimum of three weeks for a mature flavour.

Pheasants' Hill Farm Shop

3 Bridge Street, Link, Comber, Co. Down BT23 5AT   т: 028 9187 8470
w: www.pheasantshill.com
farm shop

Pheasants' Hill Farm produces rare-breed pork, including dry-cured bacon and ham, and stocks locally produced Dexter beef, Soay lamb, organic Aberdeen Angus beef and organic chickens and turkeys. Local dairy produce and organic fruit and vegetables are also on offer. At Christmas, free-range geese are available. There is also a shop in Downpatrick (see below).

Pheasants' Hill Farm Shop

37 Killyleagh Road, Downpatrick, Co. Down BT30 9BL   т: 028 4483 8707 OR
028 4461 7246   w: www.pheasantshill.com
farm shop

For details, see under the Comber branch, above.

Turley's

57 St Patrick's Avenue, Downpatrick, Co. Down BT30 6DN   т: 028 4461 5333

All meat served at Turley's is from local farms, with complete traceability. The main attraction at this butcher's is the home-baked pies – traditionally made and filled with top-quality ingredients.

MEAT

Arkhill Farm

25 Drumcroone Road, Garvagh, Co. Londonderry T: 028 2955 7920
E: arkfarmministry@aol.com

📮 **farm gate sales** 📦 **box scheme**

Organic lamb and rare-breed chicken, Saddleback pork and free-range hens' and ducks' eggs are all available, all organic, either direct from the farm or through the local box scheme – call for details.

Thompson's Butchers

7 Ballyclare Road, Glengormley, Co. Antrim BT36 5EU T: 028 9083 2507

Good-quality meat from local farms, traditionally butchered – the beef is hung for three weeks – is available from Thompson's.

Norman Hunter & Son

53–55 Main Street, Limavady, Londonderry BT49 0EP T: 028 7776 2665

A traditional butcher's shop, selling only Northern Irish produce, mainly from local farms. The emphasis is on 'chemical-free' produce and specialities include home-cooked meats, including roast beef and hams, dry-cured bacon and, in the deli section, Irish cheeses. Norman Hunter was Deli of the Year for Northern Ireland in 2002.

John R Dowey & Son

20 High Street, Lurgan, Co. Armagh BT66 8AW T: 028 3832 2547 E: jrdowey@aol.com

Local meats, Irish cheeses, salads and deli goods and home-made pies can be obtained from this Elite Guild of Butchers member.

McKees Butchers

26 & 78 Main Street, Maghera, Co. Londonderry BT46 5AY T: 028 7964 2559

McKees are famous not just for their great quality, properly butchered local meats but also for their home-baked pies – the two shops also boast deli and bakery sections.

Moss Brook Farm

6 Durnascallon Lane, Magherafelt, Londonderry BT45 5LZ   T: 028 7963 3454
E: mossbrookbaconboys@utvinternet.com

🛒 **farmers' markets**   ⛩ **farm gate sales**

Dry-cured bacon is a speciality that has become hard to find in
Ireland but Moss Brook farm is happily restoring the tradition, curing
the bacon to its own sweet recipe. Ten different varieties of sausage
and cured gammon on the bone are also made from the meat of the
farm's own pigs. Available from St Georges Market in Belfast,
Dungannon farmers' market, or direct from the farm, but call first.

McCartney's of Moira

56–58 High Street, Moira, Co. Down BT67 0LQ   T: 028 9261 1422

Award-winning sausages, of which over 30 varieties are made on
the premises from local meats.

super hero

FRANK KRAWCZYK, of Krawczyk's West Cork Salamis, Schull (see page 344)

Frank Krawczyk takes the finest free-range or organic Irish pork and creates a
range of six salamis and a pancetta, all made by hand. He is also working on
the recipe for a dry-cured smoked ham but the attention to detail this
demands means that it is taking, quite literally, years because Frank is not yet
satisfied that he has got the recipe perfect. Having won two Great Taste
Awards and an award for 'pioneering work and constant innovation in the area
of salamis', and having been named as Artisan Producer of the Year by the
legendary food writers John and Sally McKenna, he is still determined to
remain a small-scale producer, in control of everything. Find Frank's
charcuterie at Clonakilty, Bantry, Leopardtown and Cork City farmers' markets
and Temple Bar Market in Dublin.

MEAT

Mr Eatwells

16 Campsie Road, Omagh, Co. Tyrone BT79 0AG   T: 028 8224 1104

Sausages and home-made pies are the speciality for Mr Eatwells and the roast beef is very popular. Traditional butchery skills are an important part of the Elite Guild of Butchers, and they are well demonstrated here.

T Knox & Sons

38b West Street, Portadown, Co. Armagh BT62 3JQ   T: 028 3835 3713

This is a butcher's and deli combined, with lots of locally produced, traditionally prepared meat (the beef is hung for three weeks). There are also home-cooked pies and 'dishes to go'; Knox is a previous winner of Deli of the Year.

J E Toms & Sons

46 The Promenade, Portstewart, Co. Londonderry BT55 7AE   T: 028 7083 2869

Another butcher from the Elite Guild of Butchers, with a commitment to locally sourced meats and traditional butchery skills; the speciality here is imaginative barbecue meat.

Michael Hickey

Gortrua, New Inn, Cashel, Co. Tipperary   T: 062 72223

✉ **farm gate sales**

Tipperary is legendary for beef production and Michael Hickey produces benchmark organic grass-fed Aberdeen Angus beef, as he has for the last 22 years. Buy direct from the farm.

On The Pigs Back

The English Market, Cork   T: 021 427 0232   W: www.onthepigsback.ie

Home-made terrines, such as pork and plum, and pâtés, like the legendary chicken liver pâté with garlic and brandy, are what On The

Pigs Back are famous for, all made with local free-range pork, free-range eggs and organic venison. Their market stall also has artisan Irish and continental cheeses, locally cured meats, continental specialities like foie gras and dried mushrooms and breads from Arbutus breads (see page 45).

REPUBLIC OF IRELAND	DUBLIN

O'Toole's Butchers

138 Terenure Road North, Dublin 6W   T: 01 490 5457   E: otoolebutchers@eircom.net

Danny O'Toole is renowned for his selection of Irish-reared organic meats; the beef is from a local farm and hung for three weeks and there is also organic free-range chicken and pork. A second shop can be found in Dun Loaghaire (see below).

REPUBLIC OF IRELAND	DUN LOAGHAIRE

O'Toole's Butchers

1b Glasthule Road, Sandycove, Dun Loaghaire   T: 01 284 1125

For details, see under the Dublin branch, above.

REPUBLIC OF IRELAND	DUNGARVAN

John David Power

57 Main Street, Dungarvan, Co. Waterford   T: 058 42339

A traditional butcher's widely believed to make some of the best dry-cured bacon in Ireland, Power's is a member of the Associated Craft Butchers of Ireland.

REPUBLIC OF IRELAND	GALWAY

Tormey's Butchers

Galway Shopping Centre, Galway   T: 091 564067

These three butcher's shops (the others are in Mullingar and Tullamore, see opposite and page 344) are run by the Tormey brothers and the beef they sell is slowly reared on the family's own farm. Pork, lamb and poultry come from other local producers.

Continental Sausages

Fossa, Killarney, Co. Kerry   T: 064 33069

✉ **mail order**

An interesting range of sausages and charcuterie, all made with high-quality Irish meats.

McGrath's Butchers

Main Street, Lismore, Co. Waterford   T: 058 54350

The key to the quality of the meat at McGrath's is the fact that the majority of it is home-reared and slaughtered in the shop's own abattoir – giving McGrath's control of the whole process and guaranteeing traceability. McGrath's is a member of the Associated Craft Butchers of Southern Ireland.

Tormey's Butchers

Harbour Place, Mullingar, West Meath   T: 044 45433

For details, see under the Galway branch, opposite. There is also a branch in Tullamore (see page 344).

McGeogh's Butchers

Lake Road, Oughterard, Co. Galway   T: 091 552351

Find a good choice of locally sourced, traditionally reared meat, with the main attraction being the old-fashioned air-dried lamb, for which McGeogh's won a gold medal at the 2003 awards at Utrecht. McGeogh's is a member of the Associated Craft Butchers of Ireland.

Caherbeg Free Range Pork

Caherbeg, Rosscarbery, Co. Cork   T: 023 48474   W: www.caherbegfreerangepork.ie

🛒 **farmers' markets**   ✉ **farm gate sales**

The Saddleback pigs at Caherbeg are reared slowly and with great regard for animal welfare. A full choice of pork cuts, bacon, ham and sausages is available and also Aberdeen Angus beef. Buy the produce direct from the farm or at Clonakilty market every week.

REPUBLIC OF IRELAND   SCHULL

Gubbeen Smokehouse

Schull, Co. Cork   T: 028 27824   w: www.gubbeen.com
📧 **farmers' markets**

Fingal Ferguson takes the meat of the pigs his father rears (fed on organic grain and whey for a sweet-tasting meat) and creates all kinds of charcuterie. Salami, bacon and ham are all available but it is perhaps for the bacon that he is best known – produced with no artificial preservatives, a long, slow process of hanging, curing, smoking and air-drying creates a really tasty product, a million miles from the commercial bacon you'll find in supermarkets. Find the produce at Cork English Market, and Midleton, Bantry, Skibbereen and Clonakilty farmers' markets and delicatessens.

REPUBLIC OF IRELAND   SCHULL

Krawczyk's West Cork Salamis   `super hero`

Derreenatra, Schull, Co. Cork   T: 028 28 579
📧 **farmers' markets**

An award-winning producer of salamis, Frank Krawczyk, a member of Slow Food International, believes in attention to detail. See the Super Hero box, page 340, for more information.

REPUBLIC OF IRELAND   TULLAMORE

Tormey's Butchers

Bridge Street, Tullamore, Co. Offaly   T: 0506 21426

For details, see under the Galway branch on page 342. There is also a branch in Mullingar (see page 343).

SCOTLAND   ABERFELDY

Lurgan Farm Shop

Dull, by Aberfeldy, Perthshire PH15 2JQ   T: 01887 829303   w: www.lurganfarmshop.co.uk
🚜 **farm shop** 📧 **farmers' markets**

Classic Scottish meats – Aberdeen Angus beef, Highland beef and heather-fed Black Faced lamb and wild venison – are available direct from the farm shop or from Perth farmers' market.

ORKNEY ORGANIC MEAT, Holm (see page 347)

The farm at Orkney Organic Meat was one of the first commercial farms to go into organic conversion on Orkney and Tony and Elizabeth Brown are proud that their farming system 'works with nature and is sustainable 21st-century farming'. Not content just to follow Soil Association guidelines, they have researched the effect of the balance of minerals in the soil on the eating qualities of the meat reared on it and have come up with some pretty interesting results – 'We have learned that a correct balance of minerals in the soil is vital for adequate nutrition of the animal, and how the animal is fed relates directly to how the meat tastes.' The Browns constantly monitor their soil, sending it off to labs for analysis to achieve this perfect balance. The meat produced is Aberdeen Angus beef and heather-fed lamb, both organic. The taste is only one benefit of this kind of farming, says Elizabeth: 'In the summer our animals graze our organic pastures and in the winter we feed home-grown organic grass silage, grass juice and seaweed meal. This diet promotes good health in the animal and produces meat which is beneficial to human health also – our way of farming produces meat that is higher in beneficial essential nutrients such as omega-3 polyunsaturated fatty acids, vitamin E and beta-carotene.'

SCOTLAND   ABERLOUR

Speyside Organics

Knockanrioch, Knockando, Aberlour, Moray AB38 7SG   T: 01340 810484
E: jandcfraser@aol.com

🍽 **farmers' markets**   🚚 **delivery service**   ✉ **mail order**

Traceability can be guaranteed as every piece of meat sold at Speyside Organics comes from animals born, reared and finished on the farm. Limousin, Shorthorn, Hereford and Highland beef are all grass-fed and allowed to mature fully before slaughter. Carcasses are then hung for a minimum of three weeks. Cheviot lamb is also available, as is mutton. Speyside Organics sell at Elgin and Inverness farmers' markets and also at the farm and by mail order.

FOOD HEROES OF BRITAIN

Jamesfield Organic Farm

Abernethy, Perthshire KY14 6EW   T: 01738 850498   w: www.jamesfieldfarm.co.uk

⟿ **farm shop** ✉ **mail order**

Organic Aberdeen Angus beef, Black Faced lamb and organic pork from the farm's own land, and organic chickens from a neighbouring farm, can be bought from Jamesfield Farm.

Ardalanish Farm

Bunessen, Isle of Mull PA67 6DR   T: 01681 700265

▨ **farm gate sales** 🛒 **delivery service**

Highland beef and Hebridean lamb and mutton are all fed on home-grown feed and accredited by the Soil Association. The animals are slowly reared at their own pace. The meat is available direct from the farm or through local delivery.

Ramsay of Carluke Ltd

Wellriggs, 22 Mountstewart Street, Carluke, South Lanarkshire ML8 5ED
T: 01555 772277   w: www.ramsayofcarluke.co.uk

✉ **mail order**

Ramsay's award-winning traditional Ayrshire bacon, dry-cured to an 1857 recipe, was named as 'the best bacon in Scotland' by the *BBC Good Food Magazine*.

R G Foreman & Son

68 High Street, Coldstream, Berwickshire TD12 4DG   T: 01890 883881
w: www.borderbutcher.co.uk

For details, see under the Eyemouth branch, opposite. There are also branches in Berwick-upon-Tweed and Norham-on-Tweed (see pages 331 and 334).

MEAT

Findlays of Portobello

116 Portobello High Street, Edinburgh EH15 1AL   T: 0131 669 2783
w: www.findlaysthebutchers.co.uk
✉ **mail order**

Among the Scottish meat and poultry at Findlays are the home-
made haggis, made to a traditional recipe using local ingredients.
So good are they that they have been voted winners of the Scottish
Haggis Championship by the Scottish Federation of Master
Butchers.

R G Foreman & Son

4 Chapel Street, Eyemouth, Berwickshire TD14 5HF T: 01890 750209
w: www.borderbutcher.co.uk

Lots of rare-breed meats, all from farms within a 30-mile radius.
David Foreman, the owner, personally visits the farms, choosing
each individual animal. Welfare standards are always high. Breeds
include Dexter, Longhorn and Belted Galloway beef, Oxford Sandy &
Black, and Middle White pork. Free-range, organic, corn-fed
chicken is also available. There are branches of Foreman's in
Coldstream (see opposite), Berwick-upon-Tweed (see page 331)
and Norham-on-Tweed (see page 334).

Macbeths

11 Tollbooth Street, Forres, Moray IV36 1PH   T: 01309 672254   w: www.macbeths.com
✉ **mail order**

A variety of properly hung and butchered beef is available at
Macbeths, from Aberdeen Angus, Highland and Shorthorn cattle.

Orkney Organic Meat

New Holland, Holm, Orkney KW17 2SA   T: 01856 781345
w: www.orkneyorganicmeat.co.uk
⊟ **farm gate sales** ✉ **mail order**

Organic Aberdeen Angus beef and heather-fed lamb are produced
at Orkney Organic, one of the first farms on the Orkney Islands to

go into organic conversion. See the Super Hero box, page 345, for more information.

See the Super Hero box, page 345

SCOTLAND   KIRKNEWTON

Mrs Hamilton's Organic Beef & Lamb

Cairns Farm, Kirknewton, West Lothian EH27 8DH   T: 01506 881510
w: www.cairnsfarm.co.uk

farmers' markets   farm gate sales

Farm Assured, organic Aberdeen Angus beef and Black Faced lamb. Slaughtered locally and butchered on site, the lamb is hung for ten days, and the beef for around three weeks. Both are available from Edinburgh and Stirling farmers' markets.

SCOTLAND   LERWICK

Globe Butchers

49–53 Commercial Road, Lerwick, Shetland ZE1 0NJ   T: 01595 692819
w: www.globebutchers.co.uk

mail order

A traditional family butcher's selling uniquely flavoured Shetland lamb, Orkney beef and Shetland specialities including 'Reestit Mutton' – cured and air-dried Shetland lamb, very specific to these islands.

SCOTLAND   LOCHGILPHEAD

Ormsary Farm

by Lochgilphead, Argyll PA31 8PE   T: 01880 770700

farm gate sales   mail order

Slowly reared, properly matured Highland and Shorthorn beef, from the Ormsary prize-winning fold of Highland cattle, plus venison from the island of Jura and lamb from the hills of Ormsary Farm, are all butchered and packed ready to use or freeze.

SCOTLAND   OBAN

The Cured Pig

Corachie Farm, Taynuilt, Oban, Argyll PA35 1HY   T: 01866 822564

farm gate sales   mail order

Tamworth free-range pork, sausages and bacon from slowly reared pigs can be bought from The Cured Pig direct or by mail order.

Saulmore Farm Shop

Connel, by Oban, Argyll PA37 1PU T: 01631 710247 W: www.saulmore.com

⬇ farm shop ✉ mail order

Highland cattle and Black Faced lambs graze coastal pasture at
Saulmore Farm and the resulting meat has a unique salty flavour,
similar to that of Welsh saltmarsh lamb. Also available are wild boar
and venison.

Eastside Lamb

Eastside Farm, Penicuik, Midlothian EH26 9LN, T: 01968 677842
W: www.pentland-hills-produce.co.uk

🛒 farmers' markets ✉ mail order

A member of Pentland Hills Produce, a co-operative of producers
rearing meat on the Pentland Hills. Eastside Lamb specializes in
heather-fed Black Faced lamb, which graze the heather-rich hills all
year. The lambs are not ready until September, as they are not
forced along but grow at their own pace. The lamb is hung for a
week after slaughtering to develop flavour and is available by mail
order or from local farmers' markets; call for details.

Brig Highland Beef

Farm Office, Dunkirk Park, Bridge of Earn, Perth PH2 9DY T: 01738 812456
E: hamish@dunkirkpark.freeserve.co.uk

⬇ farm shop 🛒 farmers' markets

Beef from Highland cattle, slowly matured and slaughtered just
before reaching 30 months. The cattle are grass-fed, with their diet
supplemented with home-grown forage in winter. The farm is
accredited by RSPCA Freedom Foods.

J & M Stewart

Langraw Farm, St Andrews, Fife KY16 8NR T: 01334 473061

🛒 farmers' markets

Highland beef is the speciality at Langraw Farm and John Stewart,
who is a member of Scottish Quality Meats Farm Assurance, feeds

his cattle on home-grown feed, sends them to a local slaughter house and hangs the meat on the bone for up to three weeks for a traditional flavour. John's farm is accredited by RSPCA Freedom Foods. Find him at Kirkcaldy and Cupar farmers' markets.

WALES **ABERGAVENNY**

Daren Farm

Cym Yoy, Monmouthshire NP7 7NR   T: 01873 890712
🥩 **farmers' markets**

Biodynamic Welsh Black beef, slowly matured and hung for at least two weeks, White Faced Woodland, Tor Wenn and Tor Ddu rare-breed lamb and British Lop pork are all available from Usk, Abergavenny, Monmouth and Chepstow farmers' markets.

WALES **BUILTH WELLS**

New House Farm

Bryngwyn, Rhosgoch, Builth Wells, Powys LD2 3JT   T: 01497 851671
w: www.new-house-farm.co.uk
🏠 **farm gate sales**

New House Farm is a hill farm and the lamb that Sue and John levers produce here is lean and tasty. They also rear Highland cattle and all the animals are fed nothing but grass, silage and grains. The meat is available direct from the farm but call first. The levers also do B&B and evening meals, all with their own produce.

WALES **BUILTH WELLS**

Penmincae Welsh Black Beef & Lamb

Gellynen Lodge, Penmincae Farm, Cwmbach, Builth Wells, Powys LD2 3RP
T: 01982 551242   E: welshblackbeef@fsmail.net
🥩 **farmers' markets** 🏠 **farm gate sales**

Organic, grass-fed Welsh Black cattle grow slowly and produce a uniquely flavoured, well-marbled beef. Total traceability is ensured – every animal is born on the farm, none is bought in and a small local abattoir is used. The meat is available at Brecon farmers' market or you can call to make an arrangement to buy directly from the farm.

Pigs Folly

Irfon Valley Mill, Garth, Builth Wells, Powys LD4 4AS   T: 01591 620572
w: www.pigsfolly.co.uk
➼ **farm shop**

A good selection of rare-breed meats, including Dexter and
Aberdeen Angus beef, Tamworth pork and native Beulah
Speckleface lamb. All the meat is extensively reared and Dave Lang,
the owner, is happy to state that only his own meat is used in the
on-site restaurant.

Gorno's Speciality Foods

Unit 3, Fairfield Industrial Estate, Main Road, Gwaelod-y-Garth, Cardiff CF15 8LA
T: 02920 811225

Franco Gorno has been making traditional Italian charcuterie for
over 25 years and makes a wide range of meats, from the familiar to
the types that you seldom see outside Italy. When asked what
makes his meats so good, he says it is the lack of artificial additives,
the quality of the ingredients, the balance of spices and the
maturation he allows the produce. Gorno's mainly sell to other
retailers but you can buy the charcuterie from their factory shop.

J T Morgan

44–46 Central Market, Cardiff CF10 2AU   T: 02920 388434 OR 02920 341247
✉ **mail order**

A fantastic selection of Welsh produce – Black beef and saltmarsh
lamb heading the list. Free-range poultry and pork is available, along
with a range of rare-breed meats.

John James

Fferm Tyllwyd, Felingwm-Uchaf, Carmarthen SA32 7QE   T: 01267 290537
▨ **farm gate sales**

Organic Welsh Black beef, hung for three weeks after slaughter, is
available in a 'farmhouse box' – a mixed box containing a good
variety of cuts.

FOOD HEROES OF BRITAIN

Edwards of Conwy

18 High Street, Conwy, North Wales LL32 8DE   T: 01492 592443
w: www.edwardsofconwy.co.uk

✉ **mail order**

The famous Harlech saltmarsh lamb is available here, along with plenty of meat from local farms, all traditionally reared and butchered. Edwards have won awards at European level and were voted the best shop in the Wales True Taste 2002 Awards.

Bumpylane Rare Breeds

Shortlands, Druidston, Haverfordwest, Pembrokeshire SA62 3NE   T: 01437 781234
w: www.bumpylane.co.uk

🛒 **farmers' markets** 🚚 **delivery service** ✉ **mail order**

Organic lamb and beef from the rare breeds of sheep and cattle born and reared on this coastal farm. These traditional breeds, bred for their flavour, include White Faced Woodland, Grey-Faced Dartmoor, Llanwenog and Kerry Hill sheep, together with Longhorn and White Park cattle. Pam and David sell their organic meat at Haverfordwest and Fishguard farmers' markets. Freezer-ready packs of lamb and beef are also available by mail order, with free delivery in Pembrokeshire.

Knock Farm Organics

Knock Farm, Clarbeston Road, Haverfordwest, Pembrokeshire SA63 4SL
T: 01437 731342

🚚 **delivery service**

Knock Farm produces organic beef, pork and Llanwenog lamb, and organic free-range eggs. The pork is also made into dry-cured bacon and ham. All the produce is available through a delivery round that encompasses Cardiff, Bristol and Cheltenham – phone for more details.

CAMBRIAN ORGANICS, Llandysul (see page 355)

Cambrian Organics is a co-operative of small-scale Welsh farmers, selling organic meat, often from native Welsh breeds, such as Black beef and Welsh Mountain lamb. All the farmers share the same ethics of conservation and environmental awareness and all the meat is fully traceable back to the farm it was reared on. Customers can visit the farms and find out about organic farming and the mail order phone line is always staffed by one of the farmers. Lamb is a speciality of the group and the farmers all have strong views on the rearing of lambs – the fashion for early spring lamb is viewed with deep suspicion by these farmers because they feel it is distorting the life cycle of the sheep. Mick Shaw, one of the leaders of Cambrian Organics, told me: 'Nature has provided our sheep with a way of timing the birth of their lambs. Ovulation in ewes is triggered by the shortening days in autumn so that the lambs are born to coincide with the growth of spring grass. Here in Wales our mountain lambs are being born at Easter, not being eaten at Easter! When conventional farms want to produce spring lamb, the ewe has to be brought into ovulation in mid summer, and this is done by hormone impregnation. The lambs are born in late December/early January and are then encouraged to eat as much concentrates as they can. They are slaughtered for the Easter trade at about 16 weeks of age and, frequently, they will have eaten no grass at all in their short lives. As you might expect, although young and tender, such lambs tend to have very little flavour. For us at Cambrian Organics, spring lamb for Easter is anathema. We believe in natural feeding and raising our stock on grass. The wilder and more varied the grasses, and the higher up the mountain, the better. Our lambs are born in spring, and are ready for the table from late summer onwards.' I'm sure the flavour is worth the wait! The lamb, beef, pork and chicken from the co-operative are available mail order or from local farmers' markets.

WALES   HAVERFORDWEST

Llain Farm Fresh Meats

Llain Farm, Mathry, Haverfordwest, Pembrokeshire SA62 5JA T: 01348 831210
E: gl.waters@llainfarm.sfnet.co.uk
⬐ **farm shop** ✉ **mail order**

Welsh Black beef, Oxford Sandy & Black pork and dry-cured bacon and sausages and Jacob lamb (a primitive, gamey lamb), are all reared organically on home-produced feed at Llain Farm.

Welsh Hook Meat Centre

Woodfield, Withybush Road, Haverfordwest, Pembrokeshire SA62 4BW
T: 01437 768876   W: www.welsh-organic-meat.co.uk

🢂 **farm shop** ✉ **mail order**

The Welsh Hook Meat Centre has won awards many times at the
Soil Association Organic Food Awards. The farm shop sells home-
reared beef and lamb and other meat from local organic farms.
Rare-breed and native meats are well represented, including Welsh
Black and Dexter beef. The centre is a member of the Humane
Slaughter Association.

Julia Coviello

Gelli Gwenyn, Silian, Lampeter, Ceredigion SA48 8AU   T: 01570 423545
E: Julia@coviello.co.uk

🚚 **delivery service**

A rare opportunity to experience the taste of very young, pure-bred
Vendéen lamb, reared on their dams' milk, grazing the wild
herb/grass and clover pastures of west Wales. The Vendéen breed
has been chosen for its exceptional flavour and early maturity. As a
pure meat breed, it is ready for slaughter from the age of ten weeks.
All lambs are from a scrapie-tested flock, providing the fullest
traceability. The lambs go to a small local abattoir, where carcasses
are hung for two weeks and butchered to individual requirements.
Julia has delivery rounds in London and Hampshire; call to see if
she can deliver to you.

The May Organic Farms

Panteg, Cellan, Lampeter, Carmarthenshire SA48 8HN   T: 01570 423080
E: anniemay@mayfold.freeserve.co.uk

📧 **farm gate sales** ✉ **mail order**

The Mays have a commitment to indigenous breeds of animal and
rear Highland beef, Welsh Mountain lamb and Carmarthen Buff free-
range chickens, all organically. Members of the Beef Assurance
Scheme, the Mays are allowed to take their cattle past the
30-month slaughter rule, which can produce a much more
traditionally flavoured, mature meat. The Mays are also members of
the Humane Slaughter Association and Slow Food International and
their meat is available direct from the farm or by mail order.

Graig Farm Organics

Dolau, Llandrindod Wells, Powys LD1 5TL   T: 01597 851655   W: www.graigfarm.co.uk
⬇ farm shop ✉ mail order

A previous winner of the Organic Retailer of the Year award from the Soil Association, Graig Farm has a good range of organic meats, most of which are reared on the farm itself, supplemented by meat from the Graig Farm Producer Group of organic farms in Wales and the borders. Organic fish, baby food, dairy, fruit and vegetables, bakery and dry goods are available.

Cambrian Organics

super hero

Horeb, Llandysul, Ceredigion SA44 3JG   T: 01559 363151
W: www.cambrianorganics.com
✉ mail order

Cambrian Organics is a co-operative of small-scale Welsh farmers, committed to environmental awareness, producing organic, native-Welsh-breed lamb. See the Super Hero box, page 353, for more information.

Beef Direct and Lamb Direct

Plas Coedana, Llanerch y Medd, Anglesey LL71 8AA   T: 01248 470387
🛒 farmers' markets ✉ farm gate sales

This is the outlet for two neighbouring farms in Anglesey, one registered organic, the other not, although neither farm uses any artificial fertilizers or pesticides. The cattle (Welsh Black) and sheep thrive outside all year, fed on home-grown feed.

Edward Hamer

Plynlimon House, Llanidloes, Powys SY18 6EF   T: 01686 412209
W: www.edwardhamer.co.uk
✉ mail order

This traditional Welsh butcher offers a full selection of Welsh meat, including Welsh Black beef.

Rose Park Organic Farm

Llanteg, Pembrokeshire SA67 8QJ   T: 01834 831111

⬇ **farm shop** ✉ **mail order**

Rose Park Farm operates an open policy, with farm walks available, so that visitors can see how the lambs are reared. A mixture of breeds, the lambs are reared organically with animal welfare as a priority. Hung for a week after slaughter, the lambs are butchered on site at the farm shop.

Maestroyddyn Organics

Maestroyddyn Fach, Harford, Llanwrda, Carmarthenshire SA19 8DU   T: 01558 650774
E: sjwallis@lineone.net

✉ **farm gate sales**

Beef from Hereford cattle and lamb from Portland and Llanwenog sheep is available direct from the farm. The beef has been slowly reared and properly hung for full flavour and the animals go to a local slaughterhouse, minimizing stress and food miles.

N S James & Son

Crown Square, Raglan, Monmouthshire NP15 2EB   T: 01291 690675

Much of the meat sold here is extensively reared rare breeds from one local farm. The butcher has his own abattoir and so everything is traceable.

Eynon's of St Clears Ltd

Deganwy, Pentre Road, St Clears, Carmarthenshire SA33 4LR   T: 0800 731 5816
W: www.eynons.co.uk

✉ **mail order**

Three times winner of the *Meat Trades Journal* 'Wales No.1 Butcher' award, Eynon's specialize in Welsh Black beef and saltmarsh lamb from local farms. Phone for a price list and mail order details.

Penrhiw Farm Organic Meats

Trelewis, Treharris, Mid Glamorgan CF46 6TA T: 01443 412949
E: penrhiw.farm@virgin.net

 farmers' markets   farm gate sales

From their dedicated cold room, Celia and John Thomas sell their organic Aberdeen Angus beef and South Welsh Mountain lamb to a growing band of loyal customers. All the cuts are available and it is Celia's mission to educate her customers regarding cooking the less popular cuts; the properly hung meat is so tasty, her customers even clamour for the brisket. Home-made burgers and sausages, traditionally made with all meat, with no rusk added, are also popular. Buy direct from the farm or find Celia at Usk or Cardiff farmers' markets.

Pentre Pigs

Pentre House, Leighton, Welshpool, Powys SY21 8HL T: 01938 553430
W: www.pentrepigs.co.uk

 farm gate sales   delivery service   mail order

Slowly reared, traditional and rare-breed pigs – Tamworth, Berkshire and even the unusual Kune Kune breed – enjoy GM-free feed and plenty of fruit and veg and range totally freely at Pentre Pigs. Most pork cuts are available as well as dry-cured bacon, gammon, sausages and offal. New customers buying half a pig even get a free cookery book.

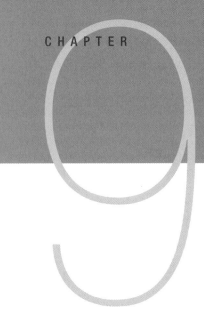

CHAPTER

9

Many of the producers and suppliers in this chapter also offer other types of meat and, equally, many of those listed in the meat chapter sell poultry. I have chosen producers for this section for whom poultry is a speciality, who have won awards for their poultry or who simply excel at rearing poultry. Individual entries describe the complete range offered by the supplier or producer.

Chicken is our favourite meat and we consume, quite literally, millions of chickens every year. This hasn't always been the case – not so long ago, chicken was very much a luxury food and goose, guineafowl, duck and game birds would have been eaten as frequently. Most of the chicken we buy now will have been reared in factory, or battery, conditions but there are plenty of alternatives to this – farms slowly rearing plump and active free-range birds, often corn-fed to produce a rich colour and flavour. I've listed producers who offer a range of poultry, all of which will be very different from intensively reared birds. Reared without antibiotics, which force the pace of growth, these birds will have no added water, which renders the meat soft and flabby, and will in many cases have been dry-plucked, allowing for a properly crisp skin

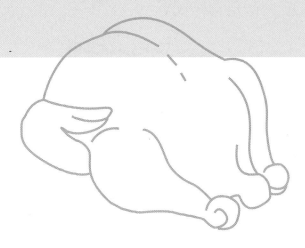

when cooked. Properly free range birds will be fit and healthy, having had an active life and so the meat will be dense and firm.

As with every other kind of meat, the eating qualities of poultry are enhanced by good husbandry, and there really is no substitute for time. The producers we feature allow their chickens to grow for much longer than factory broiler birds, in many cases for over twice the length of time, and the flavour reflects this. This goes for all the different types of poultry reared on the farms listed in these pages – the goose, duck and turkey producers featured here don't rush their birds along, but wait until they have slowly developed a full flavour and good texture. Many of them are also using old fashioned breeds like the Norfolk Black turkey, or the Cornish Red chicken. These breeds may not yield the greatest quantity of the breast meat so slavishly sought by large scale commercial producers, but they often offer a more intensely flavoured meat. There is, of course a price to pay for these labour-intensive rearing practices, a good free range bird will cost more than a factory reared one, but it really is worth it.

The Meat Joint

Hillsborough House, Loxhore, Barnstaple, Devon EX31 4SU   T: 01271 850335
E: themeat.joint@care4free.net

farmers' markets   farm gate sales

All kinds of rare-breed meats are reared at The Meat Joint –
Aberdeen Angus beef, hung for up to four weeks for a mature
flavour, Saddleback pork and Poll Dorset lamb – and all are reared
slowly to allow the flavour to develop. But it is with the chicken
reared here that the differences between extensively reared organic
meat and its conventional counterpart are most marked. The free-
range chickens are allowed to grow for twice as long as
conventional birds and they are partly grass-fed, giving their
flesh a lovely golden yellow hue, and the flavour is of an intensity
that factory farming can never achieve. Available direct from the
farm (phone first) or from Barnstaple and Combe Martin farmers'
markets.

Bath Organic Farms

6 Brookside House, High Street, Weston, Bath BA1 4BY   T: 01225 421507
W: www.bathorganicfarms.com

farm shop   farmers' markets   mail order

All kinds of locally produced organic meat is available here,
including lamb and mutton from the farm's own flock. A speciality is
the free-range organic chicken, slowly reared for flavour, and there
is also organic turkey and, unusually, organic guineafowl.

Home Farm Shop

Tarrant Gunville, Blandford Forum, Dorset DT11 8JW   T: 01258 830208
E: rod@rbelbin.fsnet.co.uk

farm shop

Free-range Aylesbury ducks, free-range chickens, quails' eggs
and free-range hens' eggs, all home-produced. Also available are
beef and pork from the farm and local lamb and cheeses from
nearby suppliers.

Wixon Farm

Chulmleigh, Devon EX18 7DS T: 01769 580438

💺 **farmers' markets** 📩 **farm gate sales**

The organic chickens at Wixon Farm are reared entirely free-range. Their diet does not encourage unrealistic growth, so the birds develop great texture and flavour and the grass in their diet gives the flesh a lovely yellow colour. Organic Aberdeen Angus beef is also available, direct from the farm (phone first), or from Devon farmers' markets.

Ark Chicken

Roosters of Babylon, Babylon Lane, Silverton, nr Exeter, Devon EX5 4DT
T: 01392 860430   w: www.arkchicken.co.uk

💺 **farmers' markets** 📩 **mail order**

Free-range chickens, guineafowl and quail are reared in small flocks, housed in moveable arks, giving the birds access to continually fresh pasture. The birds are slow-growing breeds, allowed to mature fully, and are processed and hand-finished on site. Available from many Devon farmers' markets, including Totnes, Tavistock, Exmouth and Honiton, Taunton farmers' market in Somerset, and by mail order.

South Torfrey Farm

Golant, Fowey, Cornwall PL23 1LA T: 01726 833126 E: southtorfreyfarm@macace.co.uk

📩 **farm gate sales**

Small flocks of chickens are reared in mobile houses at South Torfrey Farm. A slow-growing French breed is used and the birds are allowed to mature. Processed on site, they are dry-plucked and hung for a few days, resulting in a traditional texture and flavour.

Providence Farm

Crosspark Cross, Holsworthy, Devon EX22 6JW T: 01409 254421
w: www.providencefarm.co.uk

👉 **farm shop** 💺 **farmers' markets** 📩 **mail order**

Free-range organic pigs are slowly reared at Providence Farm, with the resulting meat winning a Soil Association Organic Food Award for

Best Pork several years running. Free-range and organic chicken, duck, goose and guineafowl and traditional-breed lamb and beef are also available and you can find all this at the Tavistock Pannier Market every Friday, as well as at the farm, or buy mail order.

SOUTH WEST   LANGPORT

Cracknells Farm

Aylesbury Rise, Union Drove, Picts Hill, Langport, Somerset TA10 9EY   T: 01458 252659
farm gate sales

All kinds of free-range poultry – chickens, ducks and geese (at Christmas) – are fed without antibiotics, on GM-free feed and are traditionally dry-plucked. The poultry is available direct from the farm but call first to place your order.

SOUTH WEST   MINEHEAD

Exmoor Organic

Higher Riscombe Farm, nr Minehead, Somerset TA24 7JY   T: 01643 831184
W: www.exmoor-organic.co.uk
farm gate sales   mail order

Exmoor Organic are specialist producers of organic free-range ducks and organic Christmas geese. In 2002 the ducks won Best Poultry in the Organic Food Awards and a bronze Taste of the West award. As exclusive supplier to Duchy Originals of Christmas geese, Exmoor Organic ensures traceability and the highest standards, with all produce being reared and processed at Higher Riscombe Farm, high in the hills of Exmoor National Park.

SOUTH WEST   WARMINSTER

The Real Meat Company   super hero

Warminster, Wiltshire BA12 0HR   T: 01985 840562   W: www.realmeat.co.uk

---

The headquarters of The Real Meat Company, which has franchises and approved stockists throughout the country. Richard Guy, one of the founders of the company, believes that 'eating meat is a privilege, not a right' and farms supplying the company are trusted sources, adhering to strict regulations. See the Super Hero box, opposite, for more information.

POULTRY

.Somerset Farm Direct

Bittescombe Manor, Upton, Wiveliscombe, Taunton, Somerset TA4 2DA
T: 01398 371387   W: www.somersetfarmdirect.co.uk
✉ **mail order**

Free-range chickens and Aylesbury ducks are reared naturally here,
without additives or antibiotics. Local Exmoor lamb and mutton are
also available, hung on the bone for three weeks.

super hero

RICHARD GUY, of The Real Meat Company, Warminster (see opposite)

Of the millions of chickens eaten every year in the UK and Ireland, most will be
breeds specifically selected to produce as much breast meat as possible. These
breeds have been manipulated with this in mind, and one little-known effect of
this causes immeasurable distress to the birds – their legs are not strong enough
to support their unnaturally large breasts and, as a result, they suffer from
deformities and broken legs and often cannot stand up for more than
15 minutes. Richard Guy wants no part of this cruelty and feels that such birds
cannot be part of a good, healthy diet. Instead, he rears breeds of bird that have
not been modified for such mercenary reasons and they can be seen on the
farm, ranging freely and happily, growing fit and healthy. Their diet is free from
antibiotics and growth promoters; they are fed by hand and they are killed by
hand. Of course, this breed does not grow and fatten quickly like the intensively
reared birds; the benefit of this is, when slaughtered at twice the age of factory-
reared counterparts, Richard's chickens will have developed a flavour and texture
almost certainly lacking in those from the battery hen house.

The attention to detail doesn't stop there – after slaughter, the birds are
allowed to mature before being sold, allowing the flavour to develop further.
Richard Guy believes that 'eating meat is a privilege, not a right' and he
extends his welfare-based farming practices to the production of pork, beef
and lamb, too. The farms used to supply meat to the Real Meat Company are
trusted sources, monitored constantly – animals are reared to extremely tight
regulations and the farmers who produce the beef have never had a case of
BSE. See the meat chapter for addresses of Real Meat Company shops
around the country, many of which buy their meat exclusively from Richard.

Dunning Quality Geese

Goose Slade Farm, East Coker, Yeovil, Somerset BA22 9JY   T: 01935 863735
E: dunning@gooseslade.fsnet.co.uk

⬇ **farm shop**   🛒 **farmers' markets**

Free-range seasonal (Christmas and Easter) geese, bred on the farm.
The geese are grass-fed, supplemented with home-grown grain.
Traditionally dry-plucked and hung for a week, the geese are available
from the farm shop, which is also stocked with local produce.

Homewood Partners

Peach Croft Farm, Radley, Abingdon, Oxfordshire OX14 2HP   T: 01235 520094
W: www.peachcroft.co.uk

⬇ **farm shop**   🚚 **delivery service**

Seasonally available free-range geese, reared on grassy paddocks
from slow-growing breeds. The birds are fed a natural diet of grass
and some home-grown wheat and are reared without antibiotics or
additives for growth promotion. The poultry are hand-plucked and
then allowed to mature for up to ten days prior to Christmas.
Available fresh from the farm, via the delivery service or from local
butchers during the month of December. Homewood is a member of
the British Goose Producers Association and accredited by the
Traditional Farmfresh Turkey Association.

Cranleigh Organic Farm Shop

Lower Barrihurst Farm, Dunsford Road, Cranleigh, Surrey GU6 8LG   T: 01483 272896
E: organicfarmshop@btopenworld.com

⬇ **farm shop**

Open every day except for Tuesdays, Cranleigh Organic Farm
Shop sells home-reared, free-range, organic, traditional-breed
chickens. Fed on organic corn and home-produced vegetables, the
chickens are reared in small flocks. Processed on site, they are dry-
plucked. Geese are available at Christmas and there are also home-
grown vegetables in season and a full range of groceries.
Everything is organic.

POULTRY

The Weald Smokery

Mount Farm, Flimwell, East Sussex TN5 7QL   T: 01580 879601
w: www.wealdsmokery.co.uk

✉ **mail order**

Hand-prepared, traditionally smoked meat and fish are all prepared
without dyes, additives or artificial preservatives at The Weald
Smokery, who have won numerous Great Taste awards, notably for
their smoked duck breast and smoked salmon.

super hero

PETER AND JULIET KINDERSLEY, of Sheepdrove Farm, Lambourn
(see overleaf)

Sheepdrove Farm is part of the Organic Farm Network run by the Soil
Association (an 'open farm' scheme whereby the public can see how organic
farming works) and Peter and Juliet Kindersley are happy to let people visit and
see the farm as it functions. And what a glowing recommendation of the Soil
Association it is – the Kindersleys' mission is 'a farm that is self-sustaining,
protects the environment, and is able to invest in its people and future,
producing great food'. The farm teems with wildlife and is home to the Barn Owl
Conservation Network. The livestock breeds are all carefully chosen to suit the
extensive farming and to produce the tastiest meat. While all types of meat are
available (beef, lamb and pork), it is with the chickens that the effects of high-
welfare farming are the most obvious. The free-range chickens are a cross
between the native Cornish White and the Rhode Island Red, producing a bird
that is well muscled, growing slowly on a diet of home-produced grain. The
birds are well looked after – an animal behaviourist is consulted to make sure
the birds are all happy and healthy; when it is time (at over twice the age of
factory-farmed birds), they are slaughtered on site to minimize stress. For the
farmers at Sheepdrove, the level of care their livestock receives is well worth
the effort – 'We are inspired by support from our customers, who enjoy a direct
link to the source of their meat and poultry and can visit the farm at any time.
They can see our aim is to have the highest animal welfare standard, a diverse
habitat, and a sustainable production system.'

Sheepdrove Organic Farm

Warren Farm, Lambourn, Berkshire RG17 7UU   T: 01488 71659
W: www.sheepdrove.com

Sheepdrove Farm produces all types of extensively reared meat,
especially free-range chickens, and they welcome visitors. See the
Super Hero box, page 365, for more information.

Wyndham House Poultry

2–3 Stoney Street, (near Borough Market), London SE1 9AA   T: 020 7403 4788

Wyndham House is a poultry specialist, with a fantastic choice of
mainly free-range duck, chicken, game birds, goose and turkey,
with all kinds of related products. The birds are usually selected
direct from the producers.

M Feller Son & Daughter, Organic Butchers

54–55 The Covered Market, Oxford OX1 3DY   T: 01865 251164   W: www.mfeller.co.uk

Plenty of Soil Association accredited organic meat is on offer here,
with good-quality, free-range chicken.

Harvest Moon Organic Farm

Dawes Lane, Sarratt, Hertfordshire WD3 6BQ   T: 01923 285688
➥ **farm shop** ➢ **farmers' markets**

Organic free-range chickens from the slow-growing Master Gris
breed range freely over organic, herb-rich pasture at Harvest Moon
Farm. Free-range eggs are also available.

Great Grove Poultry

Whews Farm, Caston, Attleborough, Norfolk NR17 1BS   T: 01953 483216
➦ **farm gate sales**

Free-range chickens are available all year from Great Grove Poultry
and free-range Bronze turkeys are offered at Christmas.

POULTRY

Munson's Poultry

Emdon, Straight Road, Boxted, Colchester, Essex CO4 5QX   T: 01206 272637
w: www.munsonspoultry.demon.co.uk

farmers' markets

Free-range Norfolk Black turkeys, pork, beef and lamb, home-made
sausages and eggs (duck, hen, goose, guineafowl and pheasant)
are all available from Munson's stall at the Billericay farmers' market.

Kelly Turkey Farms

Springate Farm, Bicknacre Road, Danbury, Essex CM3 4EP   T: 01245 223581
w: www.kelly-turkeys.com

mail order

The free-range organic turkeys and chickens at Springate Farm are
slow-growing breeds, reared for flavour. They are dry-plucked by
hand and the turkeys are hung for around ten days.

Rumburgh Farm

Rumburgh, Halesworth, Suffolk IP19 0RU   T: 01986 781351
w: www.rumburghfarm.freeserve.co.uk

farm gate sales

Free-range Bronze and Norfolk Black turkeys for the Christmas
season. Slowly matured, for a closely grained, moist texture, the
turkeys are dry-plucked by hand and hung for 14 days. Turkeys are
available to collect from the farm but must be ordered in advance.

Farmyard Chicken Company
(S J Frederick & Sons)

Farm Office, Temple Farm, Roydon, Harlow, Essex CM19 5LW   T: 01279 792460
w: www.labelanglais.co.uk

mail order

Slow-growing, free-range chickens from breeds specifically selected
for flavour are the speciality here, maize-fed for flavour. The birds are
reared in some cases up to 100 days, which is a great deal longer

than conventionally reared chickens, and it is this increased lifespan which yields a flavour that broiler chickens can never achieve.

Morton's Traditional Taste

Grove Farm, Aylsham Road, Swanton Abbott, Norwich, Norfolk NR10 5DL
T: 01692 538067   w: www.mortonstraditionaltaste.co.uk
farm gate sales

Extensively reared free-range chickens, fed without GM products or antibiotics. The birds are kept in small flocks for a stress-free lifestyle. Available direct from the farm.

Peele's

Peele & Partners, Rookery Farm, Thuxton, Norwich, Norfolk NR9 4QJ   T: 01362 850237
farm gate sales   **mail order**

Free-range, rare-breed Norfolk Black turkeys, slowly reared on home-grown wheat, barley and beans, and free-range geese in season are available from Peele's.

super hero

SELDOM SEEN FARM, Billesdon (see opposite)

The free-range geese and Bronze turkeys at Seldom Seen Farm are allowed to grow at their own pace, unforced, raised on grass and home-grown corn. They are processed by hand on the farm, dry-plucked and hung for 12–14 days and are available direct from the farm between October and Christmas. Around Christmas, the farm has a Christmas shop, with every kind of food you could possibly need for the season, including their famous Three Bird Roast – a goose, stuffed with a chicken, stuffed with a pheasant, layered with pork and orange – enough to feed 15–20 people. Absolutely everything is done by hand at Seldom Seen Farm and the level of attention to detail really does make the produce stand out from the crowd.

Great Clerkes Farm

Little Sampford, Saffron Walden, Essex CB10 2QJ T: 01799 586248
w: www.clerkesgeese.co.uk

⊯ farm gate sales ✉ mail order

Free-range, grass-fed geese, reared slowly and dry-plucked in the traditional manner. The geese have a home-grown cereal supplement to their diet, which gives their flesh a golden hue. They are available from late November.

Seldom Seen Farm

super hero

Billesdon, Leicestershire LE7 9FA T: 0116 259 6742

⊯ farm gate sales ✉ mail order

Seldom Seen Farm raises free-range geese and Bronze turkeys. See the Super Hero box, opposite, for more information.

Woodlands Organic Farm

Kirton House, Kirton, Boston, Lincolnshire PE20 1JD T: 01205 722491
w: www.woodlandsfarm.co.uk

⊞ farmers' markets ✉ mail order ⊠ box scheme

Woodlands Farm specializes in free-range, organic Bronze turkeys, which have access to grassy paddocks at all times. They are reared in small groups and slaughtered on the farm to reduce stress. Organic vegetables and organic Lincoln Red beef are also available through the box scheme the farm operates, and at many farmers' markets throughout Lincolnshire.

W E Botterill & Son

Lings View Farm, 10 Middle Street, Croxton Kerrial, Grantham NG32 1QP
T: 01476 870394

⊯ farm gate sales

Free-range geese and Bronze turkeys, along with some local game, are all available seasonally.

POULTRY

Springfield Poultry

Steen's Bridge, Leominster, Herefordshire HR6 0LU   T: 01568 760270

🖾 **farm gate sales**

Using a slowly growing breed from Ireland, the Mee family rear chickens in small groups. The birds are killed at twice the age of conventional broilers, producing well-developed flavour in the meat. Turkeys are available at Christmas and Easter.

Goodman's Geese

Goodman's Brothers, Walsgrove Farm, Great Witley, Worcester WR6 6JJ
T: 01299 896272   W: www.goodmansgeese.co.uk

🖾 **farm gate sales** ✉ **mail order**

The geese at Walsgrove Farm are all reared free-range, with a natural diet of grass, corn and straw. Bronze turkeys are also available in season (September to Christmas).

Holly Tree Farm Shop

Chester Road, Tabley, Knutsford, Cheshire WA16 0EU   T: 01565 651835
W: www.hollytreefarmshop.co.uk

🖖 **farm shop**

Holly Tree Farm Shop is a cornucopia of traditional local produce but the main draws are the free-range geese and ducks, reared by the shop owner, Karol Bailey. The farm is run with great emphasis on animal welfare and environmental concern and land is rested properly between batches of poultry to maintain natural fertility.

The Ellel Free Range Poultry Company

The Stables, Ellel Grange, Galgate, nr Lancaster LA2 0HN   T: 01524 751200
W: www.ellelfreerangepoultry.co.uk

🖾 **farm gate sales** ✉ **mail order**

Free-range chickens and guineafowl throughout the year, and turkeys and geese at Christmas are available here, all reared with great attention to animal welfare.

POULTRY

Burtree House Farm

Burtree Lane, Darlington, Co. Durham DL3 0UY T: 01325 463521
w: www.burtreehousefarm.co.uk

⌣ **farm shop** ⌂ **farmers' markets**

Robert and Lea Darling rear free-range chickens very slowly, which
are not killed until 12–16 weeks old, compared to the short 42 days
of conventional broiler chickens, producing a much fuller flavour.
Lea also makes an amazing selection of cakes, including 11
different varieties of tea loaf, all made using the free-range eggs
from her own hens. Other local produce is available, including
award-winning dry-cured bacon. Kelly Bronze free-range turkeys are
available in season. Burtree House Farm produce is available direct
from the farm (call first if you want a chicken) or from local farmers'
markets.

Piercebridge Farm Organics

Piercebridge, Darlington, Co. Durham DL2 3SE T: 01325 374251
E: piercebridgefarm@zoom.co.uk

⌣ **farm shop**

Commended for their free-range eggs in the 2002 Soil Association
awards, Piercebridge Farm also offers traditional, dry-plucked,
organic chickens, which are slowly matured and hung. The farm
shop also has home-reared organic lamb and potatoes, organic
beef, sausages and pork, an excellent range of organic vegetables
and fruit, and even an organic coffee shop and is a member of
Northumbria Organic Producers.

Highlands Farm

Lindhead Road, Burniston, Scarborough, North Yorkshire YO13 0DL T: 01723 870048

⌂ **farmers' markets**

All kinds of free-range poultry are reared at Highlands Farm – geese
and Norfolk Kelly Bronze turkeys are available at Christmas and
ducks and chickens are available all year. The geese and ducks are
particularly lucky – access to a river means they live as nature
intended. The chickens are killed at 14–15 weeks old, around twice
the age of commercial broilers. Suffolk cross lamb, hung for two
weeks for flavour and tenderness, is also on offer, available from
Driffield, York and Malton farmers' markets.

food facts

WHAT SHOULD I ASK WHEN CHOOSING POULTRY?

What makes good poultry on the plate is very simple. It comes down to breed, feed, welfare and age at slaughter. Good producers will choose the breed of bird that they rear specifically for good eating qualities; it may not be the fastest growing, but it will taste good. They won't fill their birds with the cheapest high-protein ration from an unknown source, containing all sorts of additives – they'll give them home-produced feed, or a good-quality ration, often organic. The flock will also have access to fresh pasture and will be fit and healthy – meat is muscle, so a fit bird will produce better quality meat. Finally, they'll be allowed to mature at their own pace, and will be slaughtered considerably later than factory-farmed birds, which means that the taste of the meat is allowed time to develop.

NORTHERN IRELAND   BALLYMENA

'O' Kane Poultry Ltd

170 Larne Road, Ballymena, Co. Antrim BT42 3HA T: 028 2564 1111
w: www.okanepoultry.com

Look out for 'O' Kane free-range chickens in Marks & Spencer's stores across Northern Ireland, sold under the Irish Free Range label. They are sourced from small NI farms and are specifically chosen, slower growing breeds. With access to open fields, reared in smaller flocks and fed a GM-free diet that does not force their growth, the chickens develop an old-fashioned flavour and texture. An organic free-range Bronze turkey is seasonally available, too.

NORTHERN IRELAND   COLERAINE

Culdrum Organic Farm

Aghadowey, Coleraine, Co. Londonderry BT51 3SP T: 028 7086 8991
w: www.culdrum.co.uk

🛒 farmers' markets ▨ farm gate sales ▨ box scheme

A mixed organic farm, with inspiring principles – the farming is as environmentally sensitive as possible. Free-range chickens are reared in small groups, fed an entirely natural diet of crushed oats, barley and vegetables and allowed to grow at their own pace. There are also plenty of organic vegetables and pork and sausages from the rare Saddleback breed. The vegetables can be obtained through the weekly box scheme the farm runs or at St Georges Market in Belfast, where the chicken and pork are also available.

Ulster Wildlife Trust

John McSparran Memorial Hill Farm, Glendun, Cushendun, Co. Antrim BT44 0PZ
T: 028 2176 1403   w: www.ulsterwildlifetrust.org
farm gate sales

Organic free-range turkeys, a Norfolk Black cross breed, available from the farm gate at Christmas time. The rare Irish Moiled beef, Scottish Black Faced lamb and Galway lamb are also occasionally available – call to find out when.

food facts

ANTIBIOTICS AND THE POULTRY INDUSTRY

There is real fear these days among a good number of scientists that the routine use of antibiotics in livestock feed, which is particularly prevalent in intensive poultry rearing, is partly to blame for the failure of antibiotics in human medical use and the rise of 'superbugs' that are resistant to antibiotics. It is interesting to note that instances of salmonella in chickens has increased, not decreased, as the routine use of antibiotics has increased. It is not just chickens that are intensively reared and subject to antibiotic use either, turkeys and ducks are also sometimes reared in these conditions. In Sweden, the routine use of antibiotics in the chicken industry was banned in 1984 and, since then, salmonella has decreased significantly. Farming authorities are at pains to point out that antibiotics are not used as growth promoters but simply as a defence against disease, but the reality is that antibiotics do promote growth and yet don't seem to do much to prevent the spread of disease. If the birds were not kept in such cramped conditions, and if the market hadn't pushed the price of poultry so unrealistically low, then antibiotics would not be needed at all. A well-reared, free-range bird goes a long way towards avoiding these problems and its price represents its real value.

FOOD HEROES OF BRITAIN

Mullan Farm

84 Ringsend Road, Limavady, Co. Londonderry BT49 0QJ   T: 028 7776 4157

🛒 **farmers' markets** 🏠 **farm gate sales**

Organic poultry in many different varieties – Black turkeys at Christmas, chickens, ducks and geese – are all reared organically in small flocks at Mullan Farm. The poultry houses are moved regularly, so the birds always have fresh pasture and plenty of space to range. Available from the farm itself or every Saturday at St Georges Market in Belfast.

Maughanasilly

 super hero

Kealkil, Bantry, Co. Cork   T: 027 66111

🛒 **farm shop**

A mixed farm producing organic, free-range poultry, Maughanasilly encourages visitors to get involved; see the Super Hero box, opposite, for more information.

Ballysimon Organic Farm

Midleton, Co. Cork   T: 021 463 1058

🛒 **farmers' markets**

Organic, free-range chickens – a slow-growing French breed, reared to 12 weeks old for a full flavour – and Aberdeen Angus slowly matured organic beef are available at Midleton farmers' market every week.

Gartmorn Farm

Alloa, Clackmannanshire FK10 3AU   T: 01259 750549   w: www.gartmornfarm.co.uk

🛒 **farmers' markets** 🏠 **farm gate sales** ✉ **mail order**

Gartmorn Farm free-range turkeys, chickens, ducks and geese are reared in open barns and have access to fields and the orchard; the ducks also have their own pond. Produce can be bought directly from the farm, by mail order or from Perth, Stirling, Cupar, Glasgow, Paisley, Kirkcaldy, Loch Lomond and Clarkston farmers' markets.

super hero

YVONNE O'FLYNN, of Maughanasilly Farm, Bantry (see opposite)

Maughanasilly is a mixed farm where attention to animal welfare is a priority. When any of the animals become ill, they are treated with homeopathy, although in such an extensive system of rearing, sickness is very rare – Yvonne couldn't remember the last time she had to call the vet out. Organic free-range ducks, geese and chickens are available and also pork and vegetables in season, cut to order. When children from cities visit her farm when they are on holiday in the area Yvonne is often shocked that they know so very little about where food comes from. The O'Flynns happily let these kids collect eggs from the hen house, feed the animals and generally get a sense of what goes on at a farm, hoping in this way to help bridge the gap between town and country.

SCOTLAND   HUNTLY

The Chicken Lady

North Horntowie Free Range Poultry, North Horntowie, Cairnie, Huntly, Aberdeenshire AB54 4TA T: 01542 870329
🚚 delivery service

Liz Jones rears her own free-range chickens, slowly grown for maximum flavour, and delivers them locally to customers. She has got together with a group of other local producers and now offers a range of great local foods – her own chicken, quail, lamb and Aberdeen Angus beef, and from other producers, free-range eggs, free-range pork, organic venison, fresh garlic and dry-cured bacon.

SCOTLAND   LOCHGILPHEAD

Highland Geese

Corranmor Farm, Ardfern, by Lochgilphead, Argyll PA31 8QN T: 01852 500609
w: www.highlandgeese.co.uk
✉ farm gate sales ✉ mail order

Free-range geese from the farm's own laying stock and day-olds brought in from trusted breeders, fed only on grain and grass. The geese are available fresh at Christmas and frozen for Easter.

FOOD HEROES OF BRITAIN

Caithness Goose Company

Oliclett Farm, Thrumster, Caithness KW1 5TX   T: 01955 651387
w: www.caithness-goose.co.uk
✉ **farm gate sales** ✉ **mail order (Scotland only)**

Free-range geese are reared traditionally on grass and oats here –
the oats impart a robust flavour to the meat. Dry-plucked and hung
for two weeks, the geese are available direct from the farm. Islay
MacLeod and Guy Wallace, the farmers, are in the early stages of
resurrecting an old Caithness speciality – smoked goose – from
references to this dish found in an 1824 cookbook. Caithness Goose
Company is a member of the British Goose Producers Association.

Coedwynog Free Range Geese

Felindre Farchog, Crymych, Pembrokeshire SA41 3XW   T: 01239 820306
w: www.coedwynog-geese.co.uk
✉ **farm gate sales**

The Careys rear geese from day-old chicks, ranging free on
18 acres of pasture, with the grass they eat supplemented with
home-grown wheat. Dry-plucked by hand, the flesh of the geese is a
rich honey colour, due to their natural lifestyle. Geese are available
direct from the farm in December and from butchers' shops
throughout the south west. Goose fat is available all year round.

Wern Poultry Products

Wern Villa, Rhydcymerau, Llandeilo, Carmarthenshire SA19 7RP   T: 01558 685591
w: www.wernorganics.co.uk
✉ **farmers' markets** ✉ **farm gate sales**

The chickens reared at Wern Poultry Products are bred to be slow
growing and strong, a breed called the Carmarthen Buff, based on
the Cornish Red chicken. They mature slowly without suffering the
problems conventional broiler chickens suffer, such as broken legs,
due to their skeletons being unable to support their fast, forced
growth. The birds here are grown to over 100 days old, well over the
minimum stipulated by the Soil Association, and this results in meat
with well-developed flavour and texture. Fed on corn, beans and
peas, the flesh of the birds has a rich yellow colour. Free-range
organic eggs are also available. Buy direct from the farm (visitors
are encouraged) or from Cardiff Riverside farmers' market.

Cefn Goleu

Pont Robert, Meifod, Powys SY22 6JN   T: 01938 500128

farm gate sales

Anne and Michael Moorhouse rear unusual-breed turkeys – Norfolk Black, Bronze, Bourbon Red, Buff and Nebraskan. They are reared organically, processed on the farm and hung properly before dressing. Free-range organic table chickens and organic turkey eggs – very unusual! – are also available. Call to arrange an order to collect from the farm.

Cefn Maen Farm

Usk Road, Raglan, Monmouthshire NP15 2HR   T: 01291 690428

farm gate sales

Free-range seasonal Bronze turkeys, dry-plucked and hung for two weeks for an old-fashioned flavour. Customers can visit the farm to see how the turkeys are reared. Call to arrange this or to place an order for collection. Order by mid November to be sure of getting the size you want.

Penucha'r plwyf Farm

Llantrisant, nr Usk, Monmouthshire NP15 1LS   T: 01291 620093

farmers' markets

These organic, slowly reared chickens, which are traditionally hung before sale, are available from Usk farmers' market on the first and third Saturdays of the month.

using the maps

The key opposite shows which areas of the UK and Ireland are included in each of the maps in this section. Select the area of interest to you, note the number and turn to the relevant map.

key to map symbols

Producers are marked on the map with one of the following symbols, which relate to the different chapters of the book.

✖	bread	◆	fish
✖	dairy and eggs	◼	fruit and vegetables
✚	delicatessens and specialist food shops	▽	game
		◆	meat
O	drinks	✳	poultry

maps

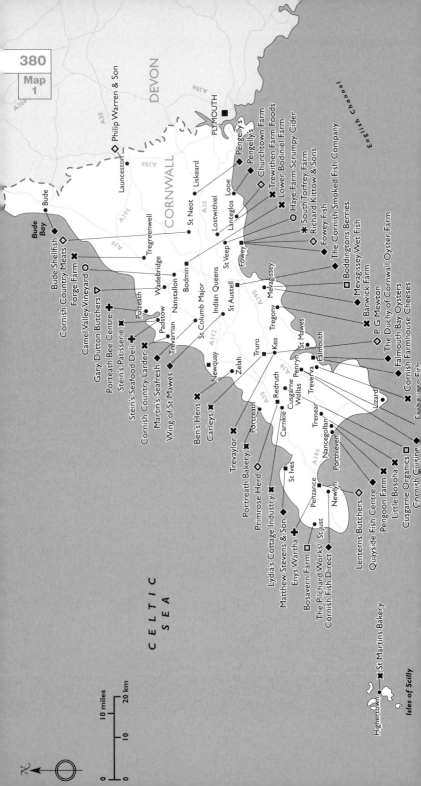

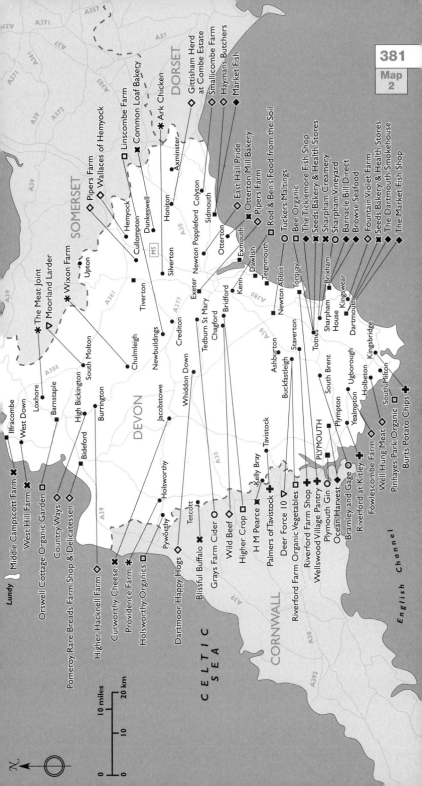

DORSET

Gittisham Herd at Combe Estate
Smallicombe Farm
Haymans Butchers
Market Fish

SOMERSET

Linscombe Farm
Common Loaf Bakery
Ark Chicken
Pipers Farm
Wallaces of Hemyock

Hemyock
Cullompton
Dunkeswell
Upton

The Meat Joint
Moorland Larder
Wixon Farm

Loxhore
Barnstaple

Axminster
Honiton
Silverton
Tiverton
Chulmleigh
South Molton
High Bickington

East Hall Pride
Otterton Mill Bakery
Pipers Farm
Rod & Ben's Food from the Soil

Newton Poppleford Colyton
Sidmouth
Otterton
Exmouth

Tuckers Maltings
Bee Organic
The Ticklemore Fish Shop
Seeds Bakery & Health Stores
Sharpham Creamery
Sharpham Vineyard
Barnacle Bill Direct
Browse Seafood
Fountain Violet Farm
Seeds Bakery & Health Stores
The Dartmouth Smokehouse
The Market Fish Shop

Dawlish
Teignmouth
Kenn
Newton Abbot
Torquay
Brixham
Kingswear
Dartmouth
Sharpham House

DEVON

Crediton
Tedburn St Mary
Chagford
Bridford
Newbuildings
Whiddon Down
Jacobstowe
Burrington

Exeter

Ashburton
Staverton
Buckfastleigh
Totnes

Orswell Cottage Organic Garden
Country Ways
Pomeroy Rare Breads Farm Shop & Delicatessen
Higher Hacknell Farm

Middle Campscott Farm
West Hill Farm
Ilfracombe
West Down

Bideford
Holsworthy

Pyworthy
Tetcott

Curworthy Cheese
Providence Farm
Holsworthy Organics
Dartmoor Happy Hogs

Blissful Buffalo
Grays Farm Cider
Wild Beef
Higher Crop
H M Pearce
Palmers of Tavistock
Deer Force 10
Riverford Farm Organic Vegetables
Riverford Farm Shop
Wellswood Village Pantry
Plymouth Gin
Ocean Harvest
Bramley and Gage
Riverford at Kitley

Kelly Bray
Tavistock

PLYMOUTH

Plympton
Yealmpton
South Brent
Ugborough
Holbeton
Kingsbridge
South Milton

Well Hung Meat
Fowlescombe Farm
Pinhayes Park Organic
Burts Potato Chips

CORNWALL

Lundy

CELTIC SEA

English Channel

10 miles
20 km

10

0

N

0   0

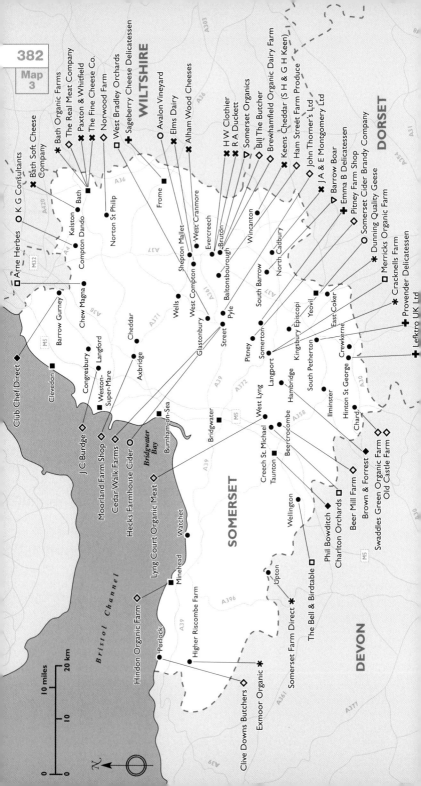

WILTSHIRE

DORSET

SOMERSET

DEVON

Bristol Channel

K G Consultants

Arne Herbes

Bath Soft Cheese Company

Bath Organic Farms

The Real Meat Company

Paxton & Whitfield

The Fine Cheese Co.

Norwood Farm

West Bradley Orchards

Sageberry Cheese Delicatessen

Avalon Vineyard

Elms Dairy

Alham Wood Cheeses

H W Clothier

R A Duckett

Somerset Organics

Bill The Butcher

Brewhamfield Organic Dairy Farm

Keens Cheddar (S H & G H Keen)

Ham Street Farm Produce

John Thorner's Ltd

J A & E Montgomery Ltd

Barrow Boar

Emma B Delicatessen

Pitney Farm Shop

Somerset Cider Brandy Company

Dunning Quality Geese

Merricks Organic Farm

Cracknells Farm

Provender Delicatessen

Lefkro UK Ltd

Club Chef Direct

J C Burdge

Moorland Farm Shop

Cedar Walk Farms

Hecks Farmhouse Cider

Bridgwater Bay

Lyng Court Organic Meat

Hindon Organic Farm

Clive Downs Butchers

Exmoor Organic

Somerset Farm Direct

The Bell & Birdtable

Higher Riscombe Farm

Phil Bowditch

Charlton Orchards

Beer Mill Farm

Brown & Forrest

Swaddles Green Organic Farm

Old Castle Farm

Kelston

Bath

Compton Dando

Norton St Philip

Frome

West Cranmore

Shepton Mallet

West Compton

Evercreech

Bruton

Wincanton

Barrow Gurney

Chew Magna

Congresbury

Langford

Weston-Super-Mare

Cheddar

Axbridge

Wells

Glastonbury

Street

Baltonsborough

Pyle

South Barrow

North Cadbury

Clevedon

Burnham-on-Sea

Bridgwater

West Lyng

Langport

Pitney

Somerton

Kingsbury Episcopi

South Petherton

Yeovil

East Coker

Crewkerne

Hambridge

Ilminster

Hinton St George

Chard

Watchet

Minehead

Porlock

Upton

Creech St. Michael

Taunton

Beercrocombe

Wellington

N

10 miles   20 km

10   0

0

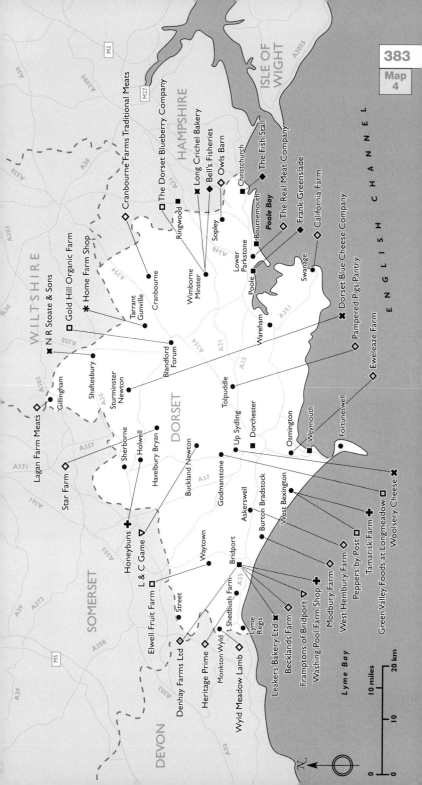

ISLE OF WIGHT

HAMPSHIRE

WILTSHIRE

DORSET

SOMERSET

DEVON

ENGLISH CHANNEL

Poole Bay

Lyme Bay

Cranbourne Farms Traditional Meats
The Dorset Blueberry Company
Long Crichel Bakery
Bell's Fisheries
Owls Barn
The Fish Stall
The Real Meat Company
Frank Greenslade
California Farm
Dorset Blue Cheese Company
Gold Hill Organic Farm
Home Farm Shop
N R Stoate & Sons
Pampered Pigs Pantry
Eweleaze Farm
Lagan Farm Meats
Star Farm
Honeybuns
L & C Game
Elwell Fruit Farm
Denhay Farms Ltd
Heritage Prime
Monkton Wyld
Wyld Meadow Lamb
Leakers Bakery Ltd
Becklands Farm
Framptons of Bridport
Washing Pool Farm Shop
Shedbush Farm
West Hembury Farm
Modbury Farm
Peppers by Post
Tamarisk Farm
Green Valley Foods at Longmeadow
Woolsery Cheese

Ringwood
Cranbourne
Tarrant Gunville
Wimborne Minster
Sopley
Christchurch
Bournemouth
Lower Parkstone
Poole
Swanage
Wareham
Tolpuddle
Up Sydling
Dorchester
Osmington
Weymouth
Fortuneswell
Blandford Forum
Sturminster Newton
Shaftesbury
Gillingham
Sherborne
Holwell
Havelbury Bryan
Buckland Newton
Godmanstone
Askerswell
Burton Bradstock
West Bexington
Waytown
Bridport
Street
Lyme Regis

Isle of Wight

10 miles
20 km

N

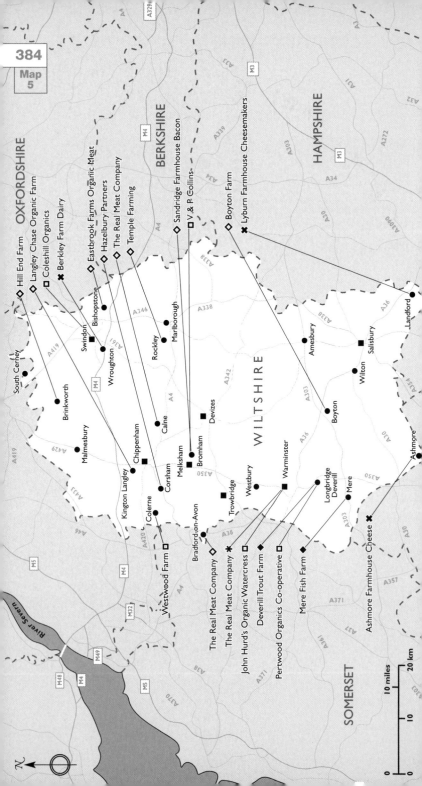

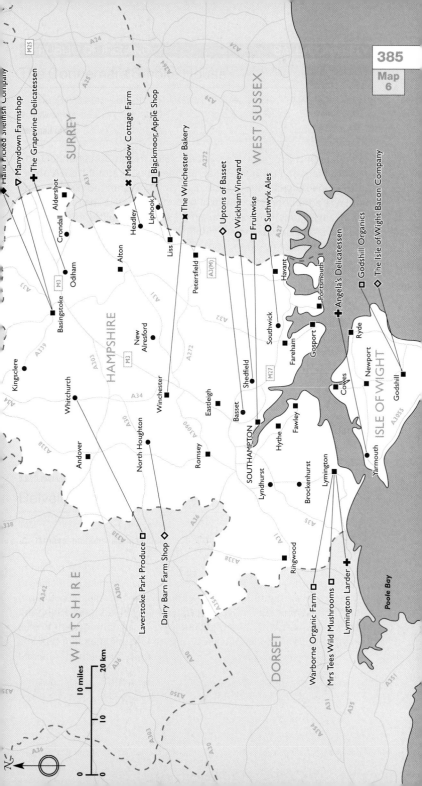

Hand Picked Shellfish Company
Manydown Farmshop
The Grapevine Delicatessen
Aldershot
Crondall
Odiham
Basingstoke
Kingsclere
Whitchurch
Andover
North Houghton
Laverstoke Park Produce
Dairy Barn Farm Shop
Meadow Cottage Farm
Blackmoor Apple Shop
Headley
Liphook
The Winchester Bakery
Liss
Alton
New Alresford
HAMPSHIRE
Winchester
Eastleigh
Romsey
Petersfield
Uptons of Basset
Wickham Vineyard
Fruitwise
Suthwyk Ales
Basset
Shedfield
WEST SUSSEX
Havant
Southwick
Portsmouth
Fareham
Gosport
Angela's Delicatessen
Godshill Organics
The Isle of Wight Bacon Company
Ryde
Cowes
Newport
Godshill
ISLE OF WIGHT
Yarmouth
Fawley
Hythe
SOUTHAMPTON
Lyndhurst
Brockenhurst
Lymington
Warborne Organic Farm
Mrs Tees Wild Mushrooms
Lymington Larder
Ringwood
Poole Bay
DORSET
WILTSHIRE
SURREY

M25
M3

N

10 miles
20 km

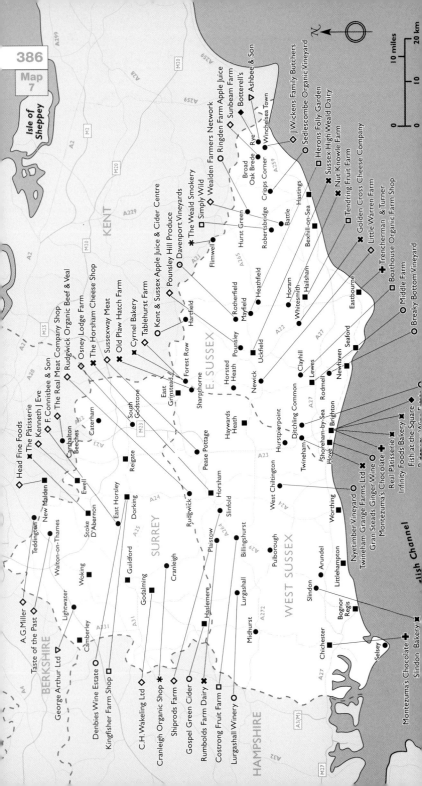

Isle of
Sheppey

Botterell's

J Wickens Family Butchers

Ashbee & Son

Ringden Farm Apple Juice

Winchelsea Town

Sunbeam Farm

Sedlescombe Organic Vineyard

Rye

Herons Folly Garden

Sussex High Weald Dairy

Wealden Farmers Network

Broad
Oak Brede

Nut Knowle Farm

The Weald Smokery

Simply Wild

Cripps Corner

Hastings

Tending Fruit Farm

Golden Cross Cheese Company

Davenport Vineyards

Hurst Green

Battle

Bexhill-on-Sea

Little Warren Farm

KENT

Pounsley Hill Produce

Robertsbridge

Kent & Sussex Apple Juice & Cider Centre

Flimwell

Trencherman & Turner

Boathouse Organic Farm Shop

Tablehurst Farm

Hartfield

Rotherfield

Heathfield

Horam

Hailsham

Middle Farm

The Horsham Cheese Shop

Mayfield

Whitesmith

Eastbourne

Osney Lodge Farm

Old Plaw Hatch Farm

Cyrnel Bakery

Breaky Bottom Vineyard

Rudgwick Organic Beef & Veal

Sussexway Meat

Forest Row

Pounsley

The Real Meat Company Shop

Sharpthorne

Horsted
Keynes

Uckfield

F.Connisbee & Son

Kenneth J Eve

East
Grinstead

Newick

Seaford

The Pâtisserie

Caterham

South
Godstone

Newhaven

Head Fine Foods

Carshalton
Beeches

Haywards
Heath

Clayhill

Lewes

Rodmell

Reigate

Pease
Pottage

Ditchling Common

A.G.Miller

New Malden

Ewell

Stoke
D'Abernon

East Horsley

Dorking

Horsham

Hurstpierpoint

Twineham

Brighton

Taste of the Past

Teddington

Walton-on-Thames

Slinfold

West Chiltington

Shoreham-by-Sea

Hove

Fish at the Square

George Arthur Ltd

Lightwater

Woking

Guildford

Godalming

Cranleigh

Rudgwick

Plaistow

Billingshurst

SURREY

WEST SUSSEX

Twineham Grange Farms Ltd

Gran Steads Ginger Wine

Infinity Foods Bakery

Real Pâtisserie

Denbies Wine Estate

Camberley

Nyetimber Vineyard

Montezuma's Chocolate

Kingfisher Farm Shop

Lurgashall

Midhurst

Pulborough

Worthing

C.H.Wakeling Ltd

Cranleigh Organic Shop

Shiprods Farm

Gospel Green Cider

Rumbolds Farm Dairy

Costrong Fruit Farm

Lurgashall Winery

Haslemere

Arundel

Littlehampton

HAMPSHIRE

Slindon

Bognor
Regis

Chichester

Montezuma's Chocolate

Selsey

Slindon Bakery

E. SUSSEX

BERKSHIRE

English Channel

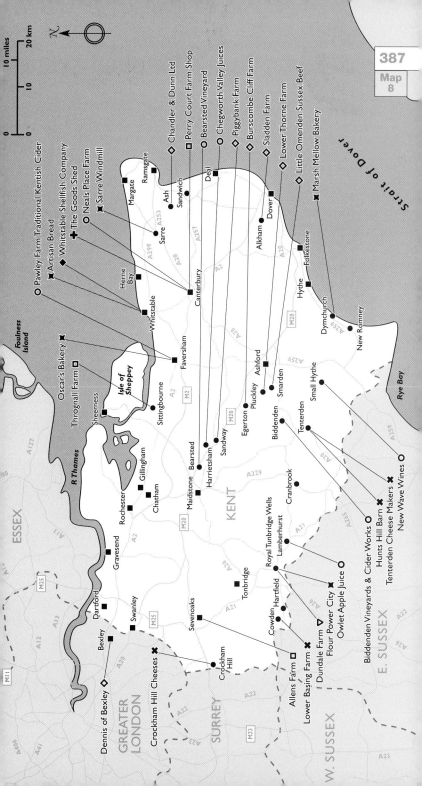

GREATER LONDON

ESSEX

SURREY

E. SUSSEX

W. SUSSEX

KENT

Strait of Dover

Foulness Island

Isle of Sheppey

R Thames

Rye Bay

10 miles
20 km

N

Pawley Farm Traditional Kentish Cider
Artisan Bread
Whitstable Shellfish Company
The Goods Shed
Neals Place Farm
Sarre Windmill
Chandler & Dunn Ltd
Perry Court Farm Shop
Bearsted Vineyard
Chegworth Valley Juices
Piggybank Farm
Burscombe Cliff Farm
Sladden Farm
Lower Thorne Farm
Little Omenden Sussex Beef
Marsh Mellow Bakery

Oscar's Bakery
Thrognall Farm

Dennis of Bexley
Crockham Hill Cheeses
Allens Farm
Lower Basing Farm
Dundale Farm
Flour Power City
Owlet Apple Juice
Biddenden Vineyards & Cider Works
Hunts Hill Barn
Tenterden Cheese Makers
New Wave Wines

Ramsgate
Margate
Ash
Sandwich
Deal
Dover
Sarre
Herne Bay
Whitstable
Canterbury
Alkham
Folkestone
Hythe
Dymchurch
New Romney
Faversham
Sheerness
Sittingbourne
Gillingham
Chatham
Rochester
Maidstone
Bearsted
Harrietsham
Sandway
Egerton
Pluckley
Ashford
Smarden
Small Hythe
Tenterden
Biddenden
Cranbrook
Royal Tunbridge Wells
Lamberhurst
Tonbridge
Sevenoaks
Swanley
Gravesend
Dartford
Bexley
Cowden
Hartfield
Crockham Hill

Straits of Dover

A253
A257
A28
A299
A2
A251
A2
A20
A259
A259
A28
A229
M20
M2
M25
M20
A21
A26
A263
A262
A21
A22
A23
M23
M11
M25
A12
A127
A13
A2
A20
A228
A405
A61
A41
A249

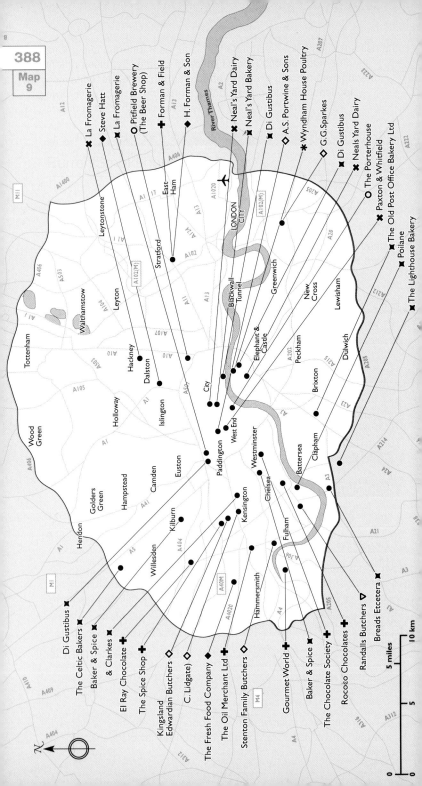

✕ La Fromagerie
◆ Steve Hatt
▰ La Fromagerie
○ Pitfield Brewery (The Beer Shop)
✚ Forman & Field
▰ H. Forman & Son
River Thames
✕ Neal's Yard Dairy
▰ Neal's Yard Bakery
▰ Di Gustibus
◇ A.S. Portwine & Sons
✳ Wyndham House Poultry
▰ G.G.Sparkes
◇ Di Gustibus
✕ Neals Yard Dairy
○ The Porterhouse
✕ Paxton & Whitfield
▰ The Old Post Office Bakery Ltd
▰ Poilane
▰ The Lighthouse Bakery

East Ham
Leytonstone
Stratford
LONDON CITY
Blackwall Tunnel
Greenwich
New Cross
Lewisham
Walthamstow
Leyton
Dalston
Hackney
City
West End
Elephant & Castle
Peckham
Brixton
Dulwich
Tottenham
Holloway
Islington
Paddington
Westminster
Battersea
Clapham
Wood Green
Golders Green
Hampstead
Camden
Euston
Kilburn
Kensington
Chelsea
Fulham
Hendon
Willesden
Hammersmith

▰ Di Gustibus
▰ The Celtic Bakers
▰ Baker & Spice & Clarkes
✚ El Ray Chocolate
✚ The Spice Shop
◇ Kingsland Edwardian Butchers
◇ C. Lidgate)
◆ The Fresh Food Company
✚ The Oil Merchant Ltd
◇ Stenton Family Butchers
✚ Gourmet World
✚ Baker & Spice
✚ The Chocolate Society
✚ Rococo Chocolates
▽ Randalls Butchers
▰ Breads Etcetera

10 km
5 miles
5
0

N

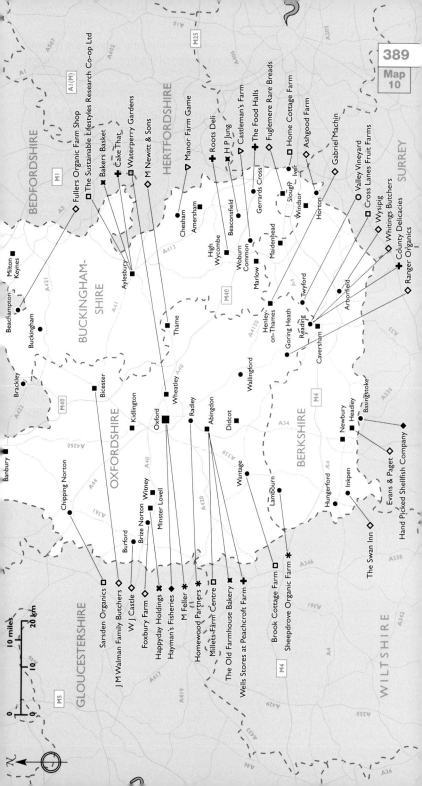

BEDFORDSHIRE

HERTFORDSHIRE

SURREY

BUCKINGHAM-
SHIRE

OXFORDSHIRE

BERKSHIRE

GLOUCESTERSHIRE

WILTSHIRE

Milton
Keynes

Beachampton

Buckingham

Brackley

Banbury

Bicester

Kidlington

Chipping Norton

Burford

Brize Norton

Witney

Minster Lovell

Oxford

Wheatley

Thame

Radley

Abingdon

Didcot

Wallingford

Wantage

Lambourn

Hungerford

Inkpen

Newbury

Headley

Basingstoke

Chesham

Amersham

High
Wycombe

Beaconsfield

Woburn
Common

Marlow

Maidenhead

Gerrards Cross

Slough

Windsor

Iver

Horton

Arborfield

Twyford

Reading

Caversham

Henley-
on-Thames

Goring Heath

Aylesbury

Fullers Organic Farm Shop

The Sustainable Lifestyles Research Co-op Ltd

Bakers Basket

Cake That

Waterperry Gardens

M Newitt & Sons

Manor Farm Game

Roots Deli

H P Jung

Castleman's Farm

The Food Halls

Fuglemere Rare Breeds

Home Cottage Farm

Ashgood Farm

Gabriel Machin

Valley Vineyard

Cross Lanes Fruit Farms

Wysipig

Whitings Butchers

County Delicacies

Ranger Organics

Evans & Paget

Hand Picked Shellfish Company

The Swan Inn

Sarsden Organics

J M Walman Family Butchers

W J Castle

Foxbury Farm

Happyday Holdings

Hayman's Fisheries

M Feller

Homewood Partners

Millets Farm Centre

The Old Farmhouse Bakery

Wells Stores at Peachcroft Farm

Brook Cottage Farm

Sheepdrove Organic Farm

10 miles

20 km

N

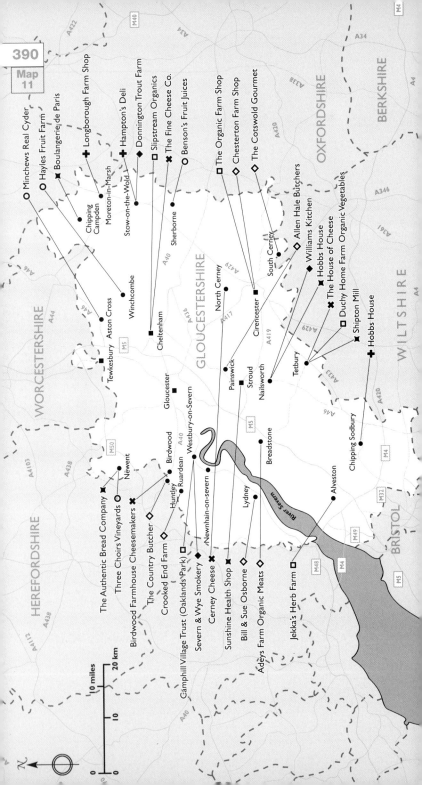

BERKSHIRE

OXFORDSHIRE

WORCESTERSHIRE

GLOUCESTERSHIRE

HEREFORDSHIRE

WILTSHIRE

BRISTOL

Minchews Real Cyder

Hayles Fruit Farm

Boulangerie de Paris

Longborough Farm Shop

Hampton's Deli

Donnington Trout Farm

Slipstream Organics

The Fine Cheese Co.

Benson's Fruit Juices

The Organic Farm Shop

Chesterton Farm Shop

The Cotswold Gourmet

Allen Hale Butchers

Williams Kitchen

Hobbs House

The House of Cheese

Duchy Home Farm Organic Vegetables

Shipton Mill

Hobbs House

Chipping Campden

Moreton-in-Marsh

Stow-on-the-Wold

Sherborne

Winchcombe

Aston Cross

Tewkesbury

Cheltenham

South Cerney

North Cerney

Cirencester

Painswick

Stroud

Nailsworth

Tetbury

Chipping Sodbury

Gloucester

Westbury-on-Severn

Birdwood

Ruardean

Huntley

Newent

Newnham-on-severn

Lydney

Breadstone

Alveston

The Authentic Bread Company

Three Choirs Vineyards

Birdwood Farmhouse Cheesemakers

The Country Butcher

Crooked End Farm

Camphill Village Trust (Oaklands Park)

Severn & Wye Smokery

Cerney Cheese

Sunshine Health Shop

Bill & Sue Osborne

Adeys Farm Organic Meats

Jekka's Herb Farm

River Severn

M5

M50

M4

M32

M48

M49

M4

M40

A44

A46

A38

A422

A417

A419

A429

A436

A40

A34

A346

A361

A338

A4

A420

A433

A46

10 miles

0

10

20 km

N

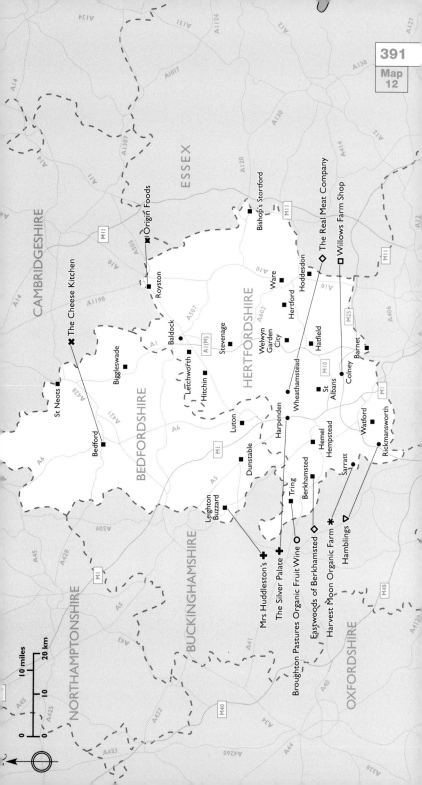

CAMBRIDGESHIRE

ESSEX

HERTFORDSHIRE

BEDFORDSHIRE

BUCKINGHAMSHIRE

NORTHAMPTONSHIRE

OXFORDSHIRE

Origin Foods

The Cheese Kitchen

The Real Meat Company

Willows Farm Shop

Royston

Bishop's Stortford

Ware

Hoddesdon

Hertford

Baldock

Welwyn Garden City

Hatfield

Biggleswade

Stevenage

Colney

Barnet

St Neots

Letchworth

Hitchin

Wheathampstead

St Albans

Bedford

Luton

Harpenden

Watford

Rickmansworth

Dunstable

Hemel Hempstead

Sarratt

Leighton Buzzard

Tring

Berkhamsted

Mrs Huddleston's

The Silver Palate

Broughton Pastures Organic Fruit Wine

Eastwoods of Berkhamsted

Harvest Moon Organic Farm

Hamblings

10 miles

20 km

10

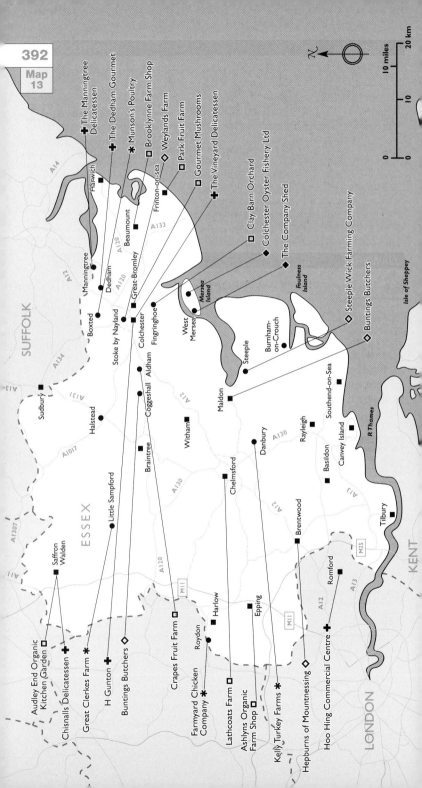

The Manningtree Delicatessen
The Dedham Gourmet
Munson's Poultry
Brooklynne Farm Shop
Weylands Farm
Park Fruit Farm
Gourmet Mushrooms
The Vineyard Delicatessen
Clay Barn Orchard
Colchester Oyster Fishery Ltd
The Company Shed
Steeple Wick Farming Company
Buntings Butchers

Harwich
Frinton-on-sea
Beaumount
A133
Manningtree
Dedham
A120
Great-Bromley
Boxted
Stoke by Nayland
Colchester
Fingringhoe
West Mersea
Mersea Island
Foulness Island
Isle of Sheppey
Burnham-on-Crouch
Steeple
SUFFOLK
A134
A12
A131
Sudbury
Halstead
Aldham
A12
A130
Coggeshall
Braintree
Witham
Maldon
Rayleigh
Southend-on-sea
Basildon
Canvey Island
A13
ESSEX
Little Sampford
A1017
A120
Chelmsford
Danbury
A130
Brentwood
A12
A13
Tilbury
KENT
R Thames
M25
Saffron Walden
A11
A1307
Harlow
Epping
M11
Romford
A13
A12
LONDON

Audley End Organic Kitchen Garden
Chisnalls Delicatessen
Great Clerkes Farm
H Gunton
Buntings Butchers
Crapes Fruit Farm
Roydon
Farmyard Chicken Company
Lathcoats Farm
Ashlyns Organic Farm Shop
Kelly Turkey Farms
Hepburns of Mountnessing
Hoo Hing Commercial Centre

20 km
10 miles
0   10

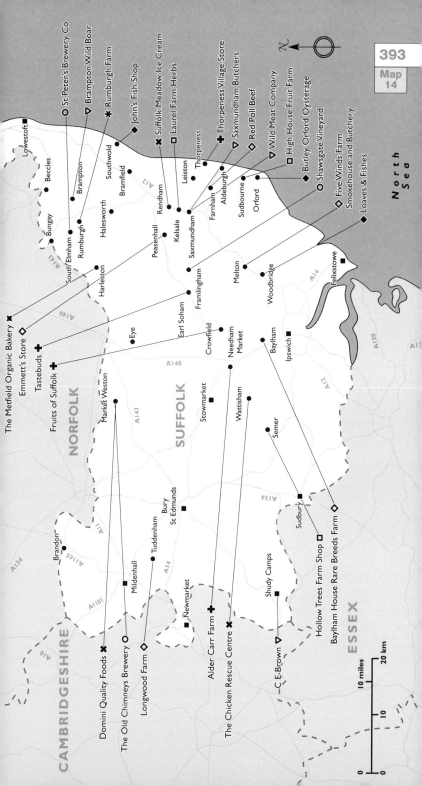

North
Sea

St Peter's Brewery Co
Brampton Wild Boar
Rumburgh Farm
John's Fish Shop
Suffolk Meadow Ice Cream
Laurel Farm Herbs
Thorpeness Village Store
Saxmundham Butchers
Red Poll Beef
Wild Meat Company
High House Fruit Farm
Butley Orford Oysterage
Shawsgate Vineyard
Five Winds Farm
Smokehouse and Butchery
Loaves & Fishes

Lowestoft
Beccles
Brampton
Bungay
South Elmham
Rumburgh
Halesworth
Harleston
Southwold
Bramfield
Rendham
Peasenhall
Kelsale
Saxmundham
Thorpeness
Leiston
Aldeburgh
Farnham
Sudbourne
Orford
Framlingham
Melton
Woodbridge
Felixstowe

The Metfield Organic Bakery
Emmett's Store
Tastebuds
Fruits of Suffolk

NORFOLK
SUFFOLK
CAMBRIDGESHIRE
ESSEX

Eye
Earl Soham
Crowfield
Needham Market
Baylham
Ipswich
Market Weston
Stowmarket
Wattisham
Semer
Brandon
Bury St Edmunds
Tuddenham
Mildenhall
Newmarket
Shudy Camps
Sudbury

Domini Quality Foods
The Old Chimneys Brewery
Longwood Farm
Alder Carr Farm
The Chicken Rescue Centre
C E Brown
Hollow Trees Farm Shop
Baylham House Rare Breeds Farm

A12
A14
A140
A143
A11
A1101
A134
A1065
A10

10 miles
20 km
0
10
0

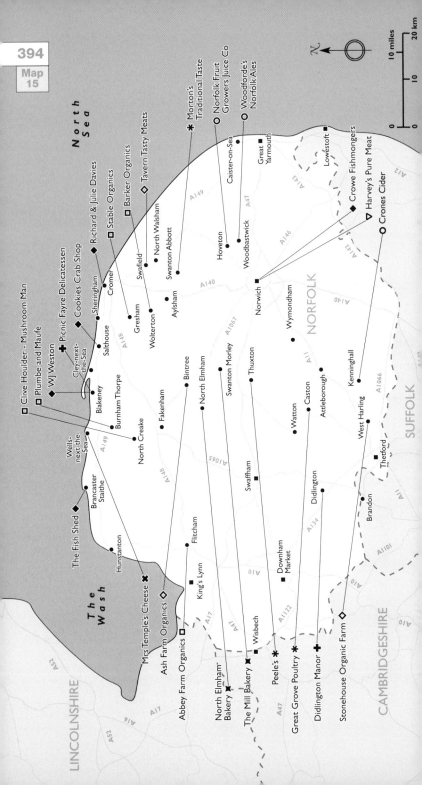

North Sea

The Wash

LINCOLNSHIRE

NORFOLK

SUFFOLK

CAMBRIDGESHIRE

N

10 miles
20 km

Clive Houlder – Mushroom Man
Plumbe and Maufe
W J Weston
Picnic Fayre Delicatessen
Cookies Crab Shop
Richard & Julie Davies
Stable Organics
Barker Organics
Tavern Tasty Meats
Morton's Traditional Taste
Norfolk Fruit Growers Juice Co
Woodforde's Norfolk Ales

Sheringham
Cromer
Cley-next-the-Sea
Blakeney
Salthouse
Gresham
Wolterton
Swafield
North Walsham
Swanton Abbott
Aylsham
Hoveton
Woodbastwick
Caister-on-Sea
Great Yarmouth
Lowestoft

Crowe Fishmongers
Harvey's Pure Meat
Crones Cider

The Fish Shed
Brancaster Staithe
Wells-next-the-Sea
Burnham Thorpe
North Creake
Hunstanton
Fakenham
Bintree
North Elmham
Swanton Morley
Thuxton
Norwich
Wymondham
Kenninghall
West Harling
Thetford
Brandon

Mrs Temple's Cheese
Ash Farm Organics
Flitcham
King's Lynn
Swaffham
Downham Market
Watton
Caston
Attleborough
Didlington

North Elmham Bakery
The Mill Bakery
Peele's
Great Grove Poultry
Didlington Manor
Stonehouse Organic Farm

Wisbech

A149
A148
A148
A140
A1065
A47
A149
A146
A140
A143
A12
A143
A11
A1067
A1066
A134
A1122
A1101
A10
A10
A17
A47
A17
A16
A52
A52
A51

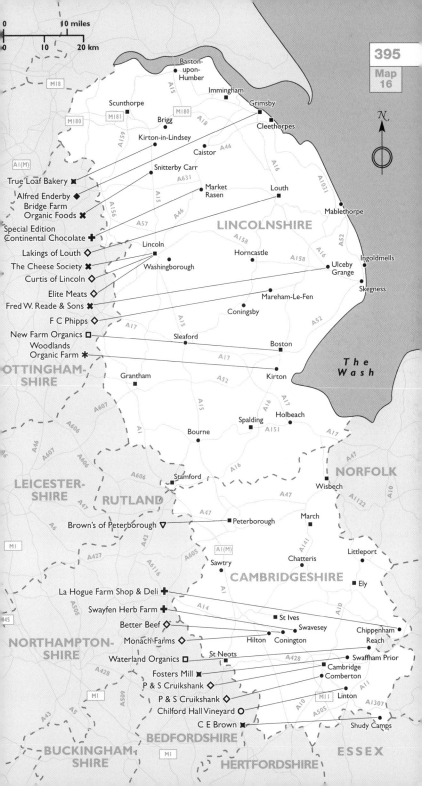

10 miles

0   10   20 km

N

Barton-upon-Humber

Immingham

Scunthorpe

Grimsby

Brigg

Cleethorpes

Kirton-in-Lindsey

Caistor

Snitterby Carr

True Loaf Bakery

Market Rasen

Louth

Mablethorpe

Alfred Enderby

Bridge Farm Organic Foods

Special Edition Continental Chocolate

LINCOLNSHIRE

Lakings of Louth

Lincoln

Horncastle

Ingoldmells

The Cheese Society

Washingborough

Ulceby Grange

Curtis of Lincoln

Skegness

Elite Meats

Fred W. Reade & Sons

Mareham-Le-Fen

F C Phipps

Coningsby

New Farm Organics

Sleaford

Boston

Woodlands Organic Farm

OTTINGHAM-SHIRE

Grantham

Kirton

The Wash

Spalding

Holbeach

Bourne

LEICESTER-SHIRE

Stamford

NORFOLK

Wisbech

RUTLAND

Brown's of Peterborough

Peterborough

March

Sawtry

Chatteris

Littleport

CAMBRIDGESHIRE

Ely

La Hogue Farm Shop & Deli

Swayfen Herb Farm

St Ives

Chippenham

Better Beef

Swavesey

Reach

Monach Farms

Hilton

Conington

NORTHAMPTON-SHIRE

Waterland Organics

St Neots

Swaffham Prior

Fosters Mill

Cambridge

P & S Cruikshank

Comberton

P & S Cruikshank

Linton

Chilford Hall Vineyard

BEDFORDSHIRE

C E Brown

Shudy Camps

BUCKINGHAM-SHIRE

HERTFORDSHIRE

ESSEX

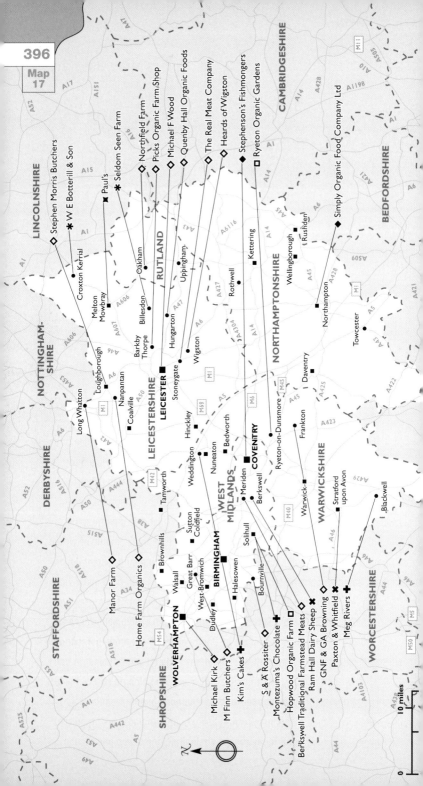

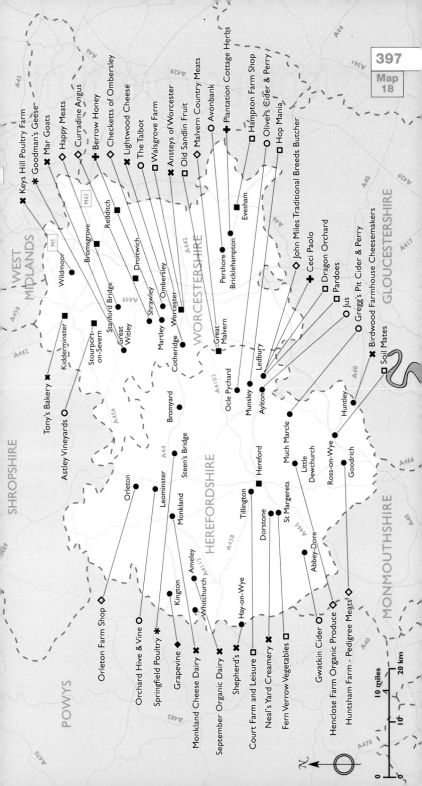

SHROPSHIRE

WEST
MIDLANDS

WORCESTERSHIRE

HEREFORDSHIRE

GLOUCESTERSHIRE

MONMOUTHSHIRE

POWYS

Keys Hill Poultry Farm
Goodman's Geese
Mar Goats
Happy Meats
Curradine Angus
Berrow Honey
Checketts of Ombersley
Lightwood Cheese
The Talbot
Walsgrove Farm
Ansteys of Worcester
Old Sandlin Fruit
Malvern Country Meats
Avonbank
Plantation Cottage Herbs
Hampton Farm Shop
Oliver's Cider & Perry
Hop Mania

John Miles Traditional Breeds Butcher
Ceci Paolo
Dragon Orchard
Pardoes
Jus
Gregg's Pit Cider & Perry
Birdwood Farmhouse Cheesemakers
Soil Mates

Tony's Bakery
Astley Vineyards

Orleton Farm Shop
Orchard Hive & Vine
Springfield Poultry
Grapevine
Monkland Cheese Dairy
September Organic Dairy
Shepherd's
Court Farm and Leisure
Neal's Yard Creamery
Fern Verrow Vegetables
Gwatkin Cider
Henclose Farm Organic Produce
Huntsham Farm - Pedigree Meats¹

Kidderminster
Stourport-on-Severn
Bromsgrove
Redditch
Stanford Bridge
Great Witley
Droitwich
Shrawley
Ombersley
Martley
Worcester
Cotheridge
Great Malvern
Evesham
Pershore
Bricklehampton
Munsley
Ledbury
Aylton
Ocle Pychard
Bromyard
Leominster
Steen's Bridge
Monkland
Orleton
Kington
Ameley
Whitchurch
Hay-on-Wye
Tillington
Dorstone
St Margarets
Abbey-Dore
Hereford
Much Marcle
Little Dewchurch
Ross-on-Wye
Huntley
Goodrich

Wildmoor

A44
A46
A45
A449
A441
A442
A417
A40
A466
A470
A465
A438
A4103
A456
A458
A442
A489
A4112
A483
A429
A361

N

10 miles
20 km

0   10   20

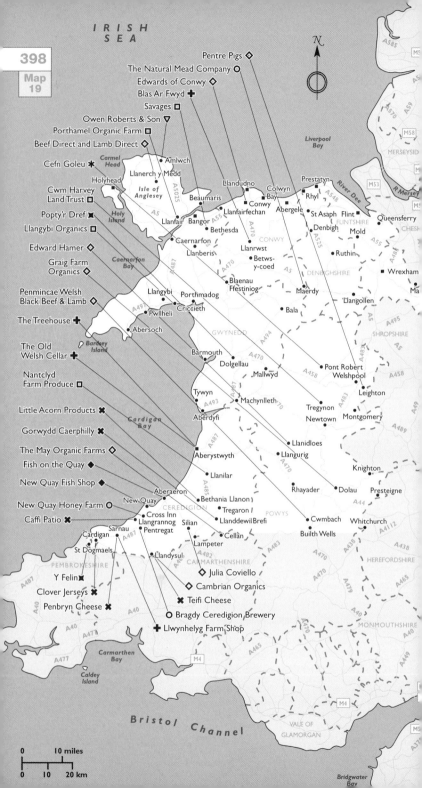

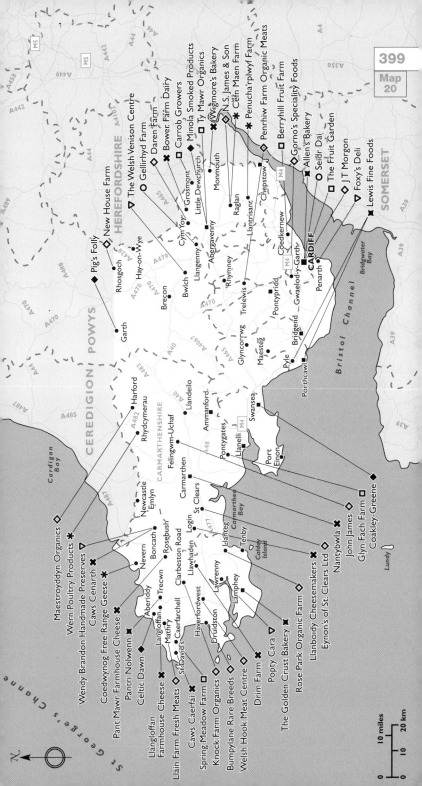

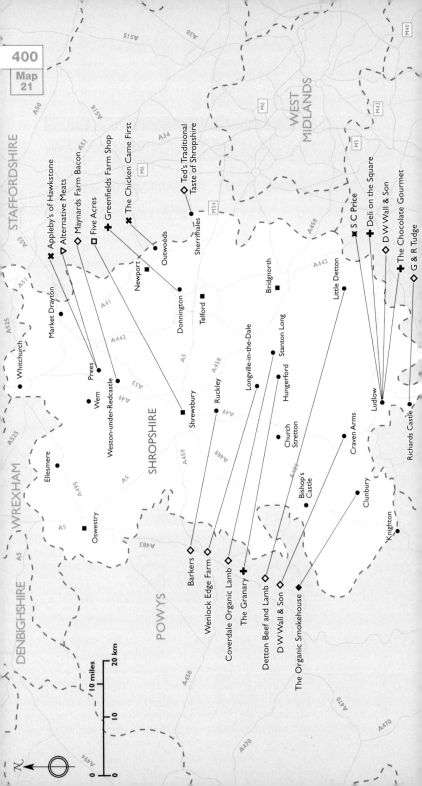

STAFFORDSHIRE

WEST
MIDLANDS

M40

A50

A518

A38

A51

A519

A525

A41

A34

M6

M54

M42

M5

M6

A442

A458

A49

A53

A442

A41

A5

A458

A49

A488

A458

A5

A495

A525

A483

A5

A494

A470

A458

A470

A470

WREXHAM

SHROPSHIRE

DENBIGHSHIRE

POWYS

Whitchurch

Market Drayton

Ellesmere

Wem

Prees

Weston-under-Redcastle

Oswestry

Shrewsbury

Ruckley

Longville-in-the-Dale

Stanton Long

Hungerford

Church Stretton

Bishop's Castle

Craven Arms

Clunbury

Knighton

Richards Castle

Ludlow

Little Detton

Bridgnorth

Telford

Donnington

Newport

Outwoods

Sherriffhales

✕ Appleby's of Hawkstone
▽ Alternative Meats
◇ Maynards Farm Bacon
☐ Five Acres
✚ Greenfields Farm Shop
✕ The Chicken Came First
◇ Ted's Traditional Taste of Shropshire

✕ S C Price
✚ Deli on the Square
◇ D W Wall & Son
✚ The Chocolate Gourmet
◇ G & R Tudge

◇ Barkers
◇ Wenlock Edge Farm
◇ Coverdale Organic Lamb
✚ The Granary
◇ Detton Beef and Lamb
◇ D W Wall & Son
◆ The Organic Smokehouse

20 km
10 miles
10

N

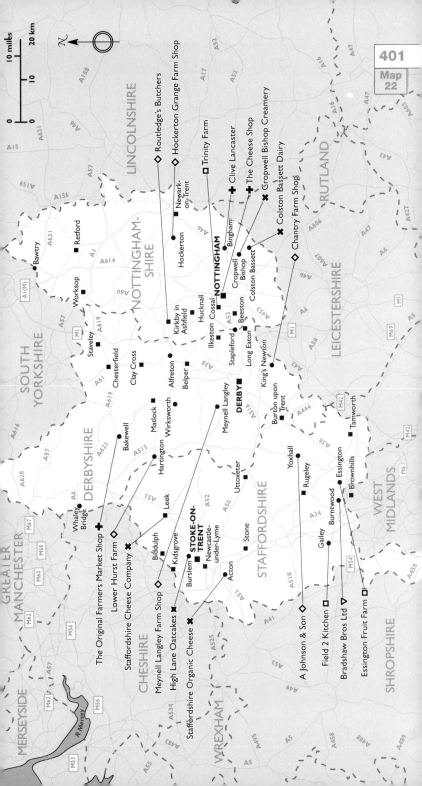

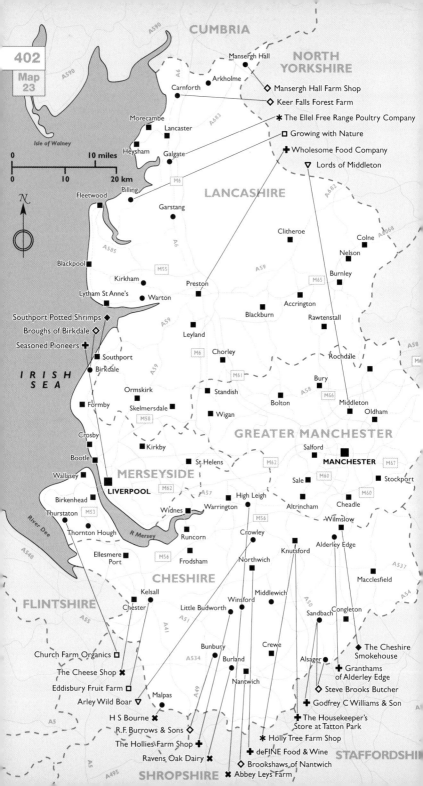

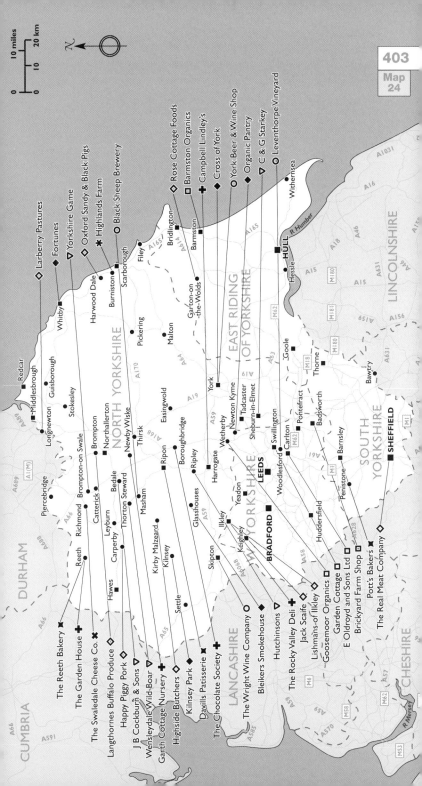

NORTH SEA

10 miles

20 km

NORTH YORKSHIRE

NORTHUMBERLAND

DURHAM

CUMBRIA

SCOTLAND

ISLE OF MAN

IRISH SEA

Lindisfarne Oysters
R. Carter & Son Butcher
Swallow Fish
Northumbrian Hamper
Robertson's Prime
Rock Midstead Organic Farm Shop
Jo's Home Baked Bread
Ridley's Fish & Game
Capri Lodge
North East Organic Growers Ltd
Northumberland Cheese Co.
Bywell Fish and Game Smokery
Wheelbirks Farm
George Payne Butchers
Thomson's Bakery
The Herb Patch
Lanchester Fruit
Bowlees Farm Shop
Teesdale Game & Poultry
Eggleston Hall
F Simpson & Son
Lartington Lamb
Thornbeck Farm
Burtree House Farm
Piercebridge Farm Organics
Westholme Farm Meats
Bluebell Organics
Cotherstone Cheese Company
The Teesdale Trencherman
Barwise Aberdeen Angus
Bromley Green Farm
Country Fare
Slacks of Cumbria
Stoneyhead Pork
Bessy Beck Trout Farm
Think Drink
Staff of Life
Kitridding Farm Shop
Lune Valley
Silfield Farm
Aireys Farm Shop

R G Foreman & Son
Well Hung & Tender
R G Foreman & Son
Piperfield Pork
Doddington Dairy
Northumbrian Quality Meats
Whiteholme Farm
Hallsford Farm
Border County Foods
Cream of Cumbria
Castletown Farmshop
The Village Bakery
Thornby Moor Dairy
The Watermill
Greystone House
The Old Smokehouse & Truffles Chocolates
Yew Tree Farm
Steadman's
1657 Chocolate House
Low Sizergh Barn Farm Shop
The Cheese Shop
Strawberry Bank Liqueurs
Whitebeck Farm
Savin Hill Farm
Richard Woodall
Hawkshead Trout Farm
Cowmire Hall Damson Gin
The Broughton Village Bakery
Flodder Hall
Demel's Sri Lankan Chutneys
Cartmel Sticky Toffee Pudding Co
Farmer Sharp
Howbarrow Organic Farm
Hazelmere Cafe and Bakery
The Organic Pudding Co Ltd

The Manx Loaghtan Marketing Cooperative Ltd
Moore's Traditional Curers

Berwick-upon-Tweed
Norham
Lowick
Ross Farm
Doddington
Bamburgh
Seahouses
Alnwick
Bedlington
Morpeth
Seaton Burn
Gosforth
NEWCASTLE UPON TYNE
Durham
Ebchester
Lanchester
Wolsingham
Cockfield
Norton
Darlington
Barnard Castle
Lartington
Eggleston
Hoff
Kirkby Stephen
Newbiggin-on-Lune
Sedbergh
Kendal
Crosthwaite
Endmoor
Kirkby Lonsdale
Rowtown
Herthersgill
Blackford
Crosby-on-Eden
Melmerby
Penrith
Brougham
Raisbeck
Ormside
Corbridge
Bywell
Hexham
West Woodham
Stocksfield
Alston
Little Salkeld
Carlisle
Rockcliffe
Thursby
Keswick
Borrowdale
Lane End
Hawkshead
Flodder Hall
Ayside
Ulverston
Dalton-in-Furness
Cartmel
Grange-over-Sands
Barrow-in-Furness
Broughton-in-Furness
Peel
Grenaby

A1
A697
A696
A68
A69
A66
A686
A6
A591
A595
A75
A74(M)
M6
A1(M)
A19
A59
A61
A165
A166
A64
A171
A170
A703
A701
A721
A713
A712
A76
A75
A3

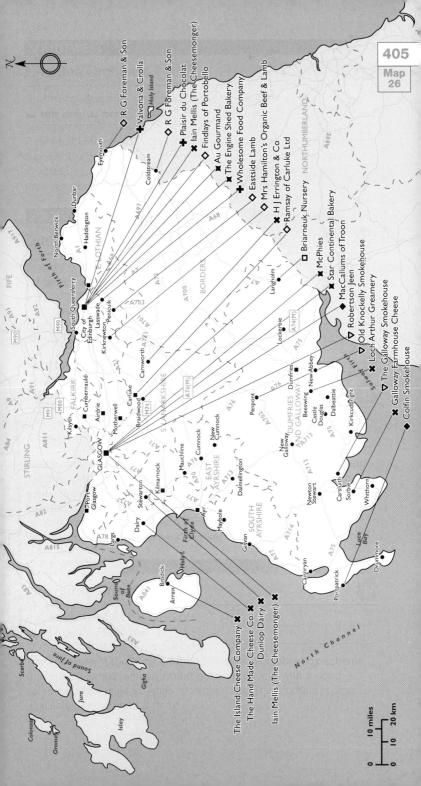

R G Foreman & Son
Valvona & Crolla
Holy Island
R G Foreman & Son
Plaisir du Chocolat
Iain Mellis (The Cheesemonger)
Findlays of Portobello
Au Gourmand
The Engine Shed Bakery
Wholesome Food Company
Eastside Lamb
Mrs Hamilton's Organic Beef & Lamb
H J Errington & Co
Ramsay of Carluke
Briarneuk Nursery
Star Continental Bakery
McPhies
MacCallums of Troon
Robertson Jeen
Old Knockelly Smokehouse
Loch Arthur Greamery
The Galloway Smokehouse
Galloway Farmhouse Cheese
Colfin Smokehouse

The Island Cheese Company
The Hand Made Cheese Co.
Dunlop Dairy
Iain Mellis (The Cheesemonger)

NORTHUMBERLAND

Eyemouth
Coldstream
Dunbar
North Berwick
Haddington
LOTHIAN
South Queensferry
City of Edinburgh
Lasswade
Kirknewton
Penicuik
Carnwath
BORDERS
Langholm
Lockerbie
Dumfries
New Abbey
Beeswing
Castle
Douglas
Dalbeattie
Kirkcudbright
Pennont
DUMFRIES
AND GALLOWAY
New
Galloway
Newton
Stewart
Carsluith
Sorbie
Whithorn
Drummore
Portpatrick

FIFE
Firth of Forth
STIRLING
FALKIRK
Kilsyth
Cumbernauld
Airdrie
Motherwell
Carluke
Braidwood
GLASGOW
Port
Glasgow
Dalry
Stewarton
Kilmarnock
Mauchline
Cumnock
New
Cumnock
EAST
AYRSHIRE
Dalmellington
SOUTH
AYRSHIRE
Ayr
Maybole
Girvan
Cairnryan

S. LANARKSHIRE

Solway Firth

Luce
Bay

North Channel

Colonsay
Oronsay
Scarba
Jura
Islay
Gigha
Sound of Jura
Colonsay
Sound
of Bute
Brodick
Arran
Holy I.
Largs
Firth of Clyde

0   10 miles
0   10   20 km

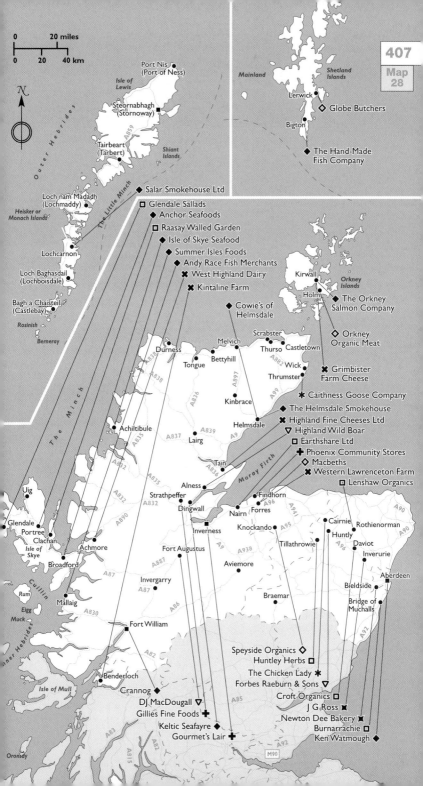

Map labels

Scale:
0 — 20 miles
0 — 20 — 40 km

N

Outer Hebrides:
- Isle of Lewis
- Port Nis (Port of Ness)
- Steornabhagh (Stornoway)
- Tairbeart (Tarbert)
- Shiant Islands
- Loch nam Madadh (Lochmaddy)
- Heisker or Monach Islands
- Lochcarnon
- Loch Baghasdail (Lochboisdale)
- Bagh a Chaisteil (Castlebay)
- Rosinish
- Berneray

The Little Minch
The Minch

Shetland Islands:
- Mainland
- Lerwick
- Globe Butchers
- Bigton
- The Hand-Made Fish Company

Producers:
- Salar Smokehouse Ltd
- Glendale Sallads
- Anchor Seafoods
- Raasay Walled Garden
- Isle of Skye Seafood
- Summer Isles Foods
- Andy Race Fish Merchants
- West Highland Dairy
- Kintaline Farm
- Cowie's of Helmsdale
- Scrabster
- Melvich
- Thurso
- Castletown
- Orkney Islands
- Kirwall
- Holm
- The Orkney Salmon Company
- Orkney Organic Meat
- Grimbister Farm Cheese
- Caithness Goose Company
- The Helmsdale Smokehouse
- Highland Fine Cheeses Ltd
- Highland Wild Boar
- Earthshare Ltd
- Phoenix Community Stores
- Macbeths
- Western Lawrenceton Farm
- Lenshaw Organics
- Durness
- Tongue
- Bettyhill
- Wick
- Thrumster
- Kinbrace
- Helmsdale
- Lairg
- Tain
- Achiltibule
- Alness
- Strathpeffer
- Dingwall
- Inverness
- Findhorn
- Forres
- Nairn
- Knockando
- Cairnie
- Rothienorman
- Huntly
- Tillathrowie
- Daviot
- Inverurie
- Aberdeen
- Bieldside
- Bridge of Muchalls
- Uig
- Glendale
- Portree
- Clachan
- Isle of Skye
- Broadford
- Achmore
- Fort Augustus
- Invergarry
- Aviemore
- Braemar
- Rum
- Eigg
- Muck
- Mallaig
- Fort William
- Benderloch
- Isle of Mull
- Crannog
- DJ MacDougall
- Gillies Fine Foods
- Keltic Seafayre
- Gourmet's Lair
- Speyside Organics
- Huntley Herbs
- The Chicken Lady
- Forbes Raeburn & Sons
- Croft Organics
- J G Ross
- Newton Dee Bakery
- Burnarrachie
- Ken Watmough
- Cuillin
- Oronsay
- Inner Hebrides
- Moray Firth

BELFAST

- ◇ The Vineyard Belfast Ltd
- ○ Four Seasons
- □ Coffey's Butchers
- ▽ Thompson's Butchers
- ◇ Walter Ewing
- ◆ Café Paul Rankin (Roscoff Bakery)
- ✖ Kirk's Home Bakery
- ✖ The Upper Crumb
- ✚ Feasts
- ✚ The Chocolate Room
- ◇ Owen McMahon
- ◇ Michel's Fresh Fruit & Veg
- □ The Olive Tree Comapany
- ✚

ATLANTIC
OCEAN

✖ Cheese Etc.

GALWAY

- ◇ Tormey's Butchers
- ✖ Sheridans Cheesemongers
- ✖ Goya's
- ✚ McCambridges of Galway Ltd
- ◆ McDonagh's Seafood House

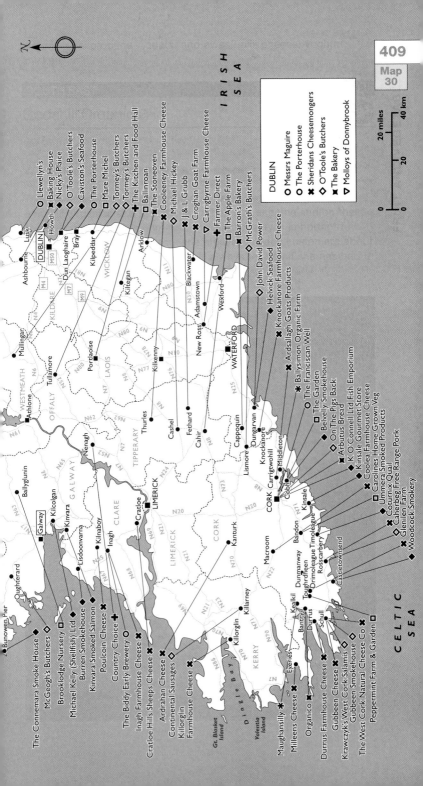

409

Map 30

IRISH SEA

CELTIC SEA

DUBLIN
○ Messrs Maguire
○ The Porterhouse
✕ Sheridans Cheesemongers
◇ O'Toole's Butchers
■ The Bakery
▽ Molloys of Donnybrook

○ Llewellyn's
■ Baking House
◆ Nicky's Place
◇ O'Toole's Butchers
● Caviston's Seafood
○ The Porterhouse
□ Mare Michel
◇ Tormey's Butchers
◇ Tormey's Butchers
✚ The Kitchen and Food Hall
■ Ballinroan
◆ The Stoneoven
✕ Cooleeney Farmhouse Cheese
◇ Michael Hickey
✕ & L Grubb
▽ Croghan Goat Farm
✕ Carrigbyrne Farmhouse Cheese
✚ Farmer Direct
□ The Apple Farm
◆ Barron's Bakery
■ McGrath's Butchers

● John David Power
✕ Helvick Seafood
✕ Knockanore Farmhouse Cheese
✕ Ardsallagh Goats Products
○ Ballysimon Organic Farm
✱ The Franciscan Well
○ The Garden
◆ Belvely Smokehouse
◆ On The Pigs Back
◆ Arbutus Bread
◇ K O'Connell Ltd Fish Emporium
□ Kinsale Gourmet Store
◆ Coolea Farmhouse Cheese
✕ Carolines Home Grown Veg
□ Ummera Smoked Products
◆ Coturnix Quail
✕ Caherbeg Free Range Pork
✕ Glenilen Cheese
✕ Woodcock Smokery

The Connemara Smoke House ◆
McGeogh's Butchers ◇
Brooklodge Nursery ●
Michael Kelly (Shellfish) Ltd ◆
Kinvara Smoked Salmon ✕
Poulcoin Cheese ✚
Inagh Farmhouse Cheese ◇
The Biddy Early Brewery ○
Cratloe Hills Sheeps Cheese ✕
Ardrahan Cheese ◇
Continental Sausages
Killorglin
Killorglin
Farmhouse Cheese ✕

Maughansilly ✱
Milleens Cheese ✕
Organico ✕
Durrus Farmhouse Cheese ✕
Gubbeen Cheese ◆
Krawczyk's West Cork Salamis ◇
Gubbeen Smokehouse ✕
The West Cork Natural Cheese Co □
Peppermint Farm & Garden □

acknowledgements

In compiling this guide I have been offered invaluable help by the institutions, publications and individuals listed below. Many of the organisations have extremely useful websites and I have included the addresses here in case you feel inspired to find out more about them and what they stand for.

organisations

Biodynamic Agricultural Association of Great Britain
TEL: 01453 759501   w: www.anth.org.uk/biodynamic

CAIS (Irish Farmhouse Cheesemakers Association)

The Campaign for Real Ale (CAMRA)   TEL: 01727 867201
w: www.camra.org.uk

The Campaign for Real Food   TEL: 0800 328 3750
w: www.thecarf.co.uk

Common Ground   TEL: 01747 850820
w: www.commonground.org.uk

Compassion in World Farming   TEL: 01730 264208
w: www.ciwf.co.uk

English Wine Producers   TEL: 01536 772264
w: www.englishwineproducers.com
(with special thanks to Julia Trustram Eve)

The Food Commission   TEL: 020 7837 2250
w: www.foodcomm.org.uk

The Game Conservancy Trust   TEL: 01425 652381
w: www.gct.org.uk

Guild of Fine Food Retailers   TEL: 01747 822290
w: www.finefoodworld.co.uk

Guild of Q Butchers   TEL: 01383 432622
w: www.guildofqbutchers.co.uk

Marine Stewardship Council   w: www.msc.org

The National Federation of Fishmongers

National Game Dealers Association   TEL: 01325 316320
w: www.yorkshiregame.co.uk

Northern Ireland Seafood   TEL: 028 9045 2829
w: www.niseafood.co.uk

The Organic Trust   TEL: +353 1 853 0271
w: www.iol.ie/~organic/trust.html

Rare Breeds Survival Trust   TEL: 02476 696551
w: www.rare-breeds.com

Soil Association   TEL: 0117 929 0661   w: www.soilassociation.org

The Specialist Cheesemakers Association   TEL: 020 7253 2114
w: www.specialistcheesemakers.co.uk

Sustain – The Alliance for Better Food and Farming   TEL: 020 7837
1228   w: www.sustainweb.org (with special thanks to Dan Keech)

Welsh Development Agency   TEL: 01443 845500
w: www.wda.co.uk (with special thanks to Mike Caplan-Hill)

Wholesome Food Association   TEL: 01803 866877
w: www.wholesomefood.org

publications

The Bridgestone Guides www.bestofbridgestone.com –
The Bridgestone Food Lover's Guide to Northern Ireland and
The *Bridgestone Food Lover's Guide to Ireland* (both Estragon Press).
With special thanks to Caroline Workman

British Baker magazine www.britishbaker.net

Thanks also to Avril Allshire from Caherbeg Free-range Pork, Clodagh
McKenna from West Cork Slow Food, Giana Ferguson from Gubbeen
Farmhouse and Jenny Davies from Llwynhelyg Farm Shop.

notes

notes

notes